ASSHOLE

A MEMOIR

ASSHOLE

A MEMOIR

WILD STORIES OF TRAUMA, TRUTHS, AND TRANSFORMATION

ROB TONKIN

ASSHOLE

By Rob Tonkin

First Edition Copyright © 2025 by Rob Tonkin

Published by

Munn Avenue Press

300 Main Street, Ste 21

Madison, NJ 07940

MunnAvenuePress.com

Hardcover: 978-1-960299-70-3

Paperback: 978-1-960299-71-0

Ebook: 978-1-960299-72-7

Printed in the United States of America

"Make it quick, there's a game to see." – **Jack Nicholson**

"I'm not doing it that way." – **Gene Simmons, KISS**

"Who are you?" – **Lou Reed**

"I'm not going on stage until you pay me my bonus." – **Hunter S. Thompson**

"Your original offer is shameful and insulting." – **Don Henley, Eagles**

"It's okay mate, they're leather." – **Billy Idol**

"Would you mind giving me a lift to the bike shop?" – **Kenny Loggins**

"Oh, hey, thanks, Rob." – **Travis Barker, blink-182**

"Thanks, I'll have a Pepsi." – **Dennis Hopper**

ADVANCE PRAISE FOR *ASSHOLE*, A MEMOIR

"Not only are the stories incredibly entertaining, but they're also poignant insights into trauma."

– Kathryn O'Brasky, LCSW

"Unflinchingly honest: a memoir from depravity to redemption."

– Kevin Lyman, Founder of Vans Warped Tour

"A harrowing yet ultimately inspiring journey from trauma to triumph. This book is a powerful testament to bravery. Highly recommended for anyone affected by sexual abuse or childhood trauma, and for those who support them."

– Ashley Turner, Licensed Psychotherapist, Yoga-Meditation Teacher

"Rob is a master storyteller, and the stories he tells are simply amazing. You'll laugh with him, cry with him, love him, hate him, and at times be utterly stunned by the events that unfold."

– Thomas K. Arnold, Publisher of Media Play News, Veteran Journalist

"I witnessed the author grow through a lifetime of chrysalis experiences into a badass butterfly."

– Andrea Brook, International Performing Artist—Sonic Butterfly, Yoga Teacher/Life Catalyst

AUTHOR'S NOTE

To protect the privacy of certain individuals, and to allow myself the creative freedom necessary to tell this story authentically, some names and identifying details have been changed. I trust you'll understand the need for this delicate balance between truth and discretion as you embark on this journey with me.

Warning: Please be advised that this book contains mature themes, including detailed descriptions of trauma and sexual abuse. This content may be triggering for some readers. Please proceed with caution.

*"Then there's the question
of whether the pain comes from writing
or the writing comes from pain."*

—Elisa Gabbert, *The Paris Review*

TABLE OF CONTENTS

PROLOGUE

Has anyone ever called you an asshole?

The boy on the cover? Cute kid, right? He became an asshole.

Now, he wasn't *always* an asshole.

Feeling unwanted and unloved as a child, betrayed in the most horrific way imaginable when he was just fourteen, he built up defenses and vowed to get even with the world. Somewhere on the path to adulthood, navigating the turbulent waters of youth, he lost his way. He made mistakes, screwed people over, and, ultimately, earned that unsettling "asshole" label.

That boy was me.

But please, don't judge a book by its cover—or a person by their worst moments. My story shows there's always hope for redemption. That there's a way for that innocent, smiling little guy inside to find his way out of the asshole he became.

■ ■ ■

My father always stressed the importance of a college education, particularly a liberal arts degree. He attended UC Berkeley but enlisted in the military during World War II. Dad spoke of it with humor: "I'd requested to serve in the European theater, but I got sent to Okinawa, Japan. I guess *someone* in the Army needed a better map."

Dad had this idea of a better life for me, rooted in classic American values: hard work, education, and a good, solid, nine-to-five job. But these values felt rigid and outdated in the face of the cultural revolution swirling around me. I turned five just before the Summer of Love, after all, and while for the next decade, I was stuck in Sacramento, the epicenter of change was in nearby San Francisco—a city that pulsed with a vibrant counterculture, beckoning with its promise of freedom. My father's vision clashed with my own burgeoning sense of self, and I felt this strong pull to rebel, to carve out my path, to learn on my terms.

> "Dear Grandma Kay, I don't mind it here in Bakersfield, although a year is my limit.... Recently, I spent a weekend in Los Angeles, which I **really** enjoyed. That's my city, eventually. First, I want to live in San Diego or San Francisco. I see life as a short time on earth, and if one can enjoy every minute and remain consistently happy with everything—most of the time—what else is there? That's a hard question to answer, but I've set goals for myself, and with the help of a positive mental attitude, I hope to reach every single one of them and keep on setting them higher and higher. Life should be a challenge!"

As I wrote those words to my step-grandmother shortly after turning nineteen and moving from Sacramento to the cow town of Bakersfield for my first real away-from-home job, I didn't realize how prophetic they would become. Unlike many people who spend years searching for their place in the world, at the age of fourteen, I'd already locked onto my goals with ferocious determination. And so, like a preordained path unfolding, after my stay in Bakersfield, I subsequently found myself in San Diego for a decade and then in Los Angeles.

Yet honing my skills in the chaotic world of entertainment while living with thorny secrets was stressful. It required huge amounts of self-control and false confidence. Almost everything throughout my life fell apart and became messy—in stark contrast to that still-innocent, pre-asshole teenager penning articulate letters to his grandma. Life happened: unfiltered, exciting, and at times painfully raw.

PART ONE

US

1

JUMPIN' JACK FLASH

It was New Year's Eve, 1992, in Aspen, Colorado. While snow and icy cold reigned outside, inside Mezzaluna, a sister to the famed LA dining establishment, the air was warm with holiday cheer. The windows were blacked out, covered with rolls of brown craft paper to shield this elite gathering of the rich and famous from Los Angeles, New York, and other hot spots around the globe from the outside world.

A friend, whose father was a wealthy Wall Street trader, had secured a coveted table at the exclusive restaurant for their annual family gathering. I, a mere guest for the week between Christmas and New Year's, was fortunate enough to be included. Fresh off landing a dream gig with the prestigious Westwood One radio network—and with a new house in Laurel Canyon to my name—I was flush with cash and confidence, about as full of myself as any not-yet-thirty-year-old showbiz wannabe could be. As I strutted back from the restroom through the dimly lit hallway, a hush fell over the room. That's when I heard it.

"Listen, puss, you know where to find me. If you need me, I'll be at my post."

That voice. I recognized it instantly. I half turned, and there was Jack Nicholson, looking every bit as charming and yet menacing as he did in his acting roles in *Chinatown* and *The Shining*. Nicholson's cadence and delivery are both obscure and iconic. To my young, brash, and immature self, hearing him utter such a cheesy line in my left ear while scooching past him and the lovely woman who had captured his attention was like understanding the afterlife. The loud music and chatter in my right ear suddenly came to a screeching halt for one surreal moment. I had suspended myself above the room, the building, and all of snowy white Aspen. The pickup line was one that only an old-school Jack could and would dare to deliver.

This was Jack-fucking-Nicholson! The cockiest of the cocky. The man, I at the time, in my crass, youthful naivete, aspired to be and pictured myself as one day becoming even though I sensed deep down this was an unattainable goal, an impossible dream. Even among this small crowd of aristocrats, I felt like an outsider, accepted into their circles but still not one of them. I couldn't stop gawking, but I had to discreetly keep moving.

Jack Nicholson, after all, was the coolest of the cool—and all my life, I had strived to run with the cool kids, *to be* one of the cool kids. On-screen and off, Jack Nicholson was known for his masculinity, his wit, his rebelliousness, and his overly confident, devil-may-care attitude. He was the pinnacle of Hollywood, the leader of the pack. He represented sex, danger, and good times, all rolled into one person.

During my twenties, I was still a boy in search of love and acceptance, and I saw Jack as someone who could provide that. I bought into the whole Hollywood dream—that if you're somebody, people will love you. And I believed with all my heart that if I could have just a little bit of what Jack Nicholson had—the fame, the access—then people would love me, too.

I also saw a lot of myself in Jack. Like me, he had had a turbulent childhood. He grew up believing that his grandmother was his mother and that his young mother was his sister. He only learned the truth at age thirty-seven. His early years were challenged by a persistent question mark about who he was, as he struggled with an unhealed wound. A passion for acting during his high school years became Jack's escape and creative outlet.

My childhood, too, was marked by confusion, complexity, and

emotional upheaval. But, like Jack, I had turned this childhood trauma into the foundation for a career in show business. Little did I know I would go on to see this pattern in many successful people. It would seem to be an escape and form of survival to pursue something with such fervor that it helps soothe inner emotional pain—and sometimes leads to astonishing career success.

But the pain, the trauma—is not able to heal that way.

2

BORN TO RUN

May 1, 1962, my innocent entry into the world. Oblivious to what lay ahead, I slept peacefully, tiny fingers curled, unaware of the extraordinary scene in Aspen that awaited me years later.

John F. Kennedy was our president, and the space race was heating up as the first American orbited Earth, a major victory in the Cold War against the Soviet Union. It was the dawn of a fresh technological age punctuated by the first commercial communications satellite, *Telstar 1*, enabling live television broadcasts across the Atlantic, ushering in a new era of global communication. All the while, civil rights were gaining force with a fight for racial equality. It was also a dynamic period in American music, characterized by groundbreaking female artists like The Supremes, emerging trends like Bob Dylan's unique brand of folk, and a foreshadowing of a British invasion as the Beatles gained momentum in the UK.

But these global events seemed a world away from my quiet nursery. I was given the name "Robert," resonant with Germanic origins meaning "bright fame." It also had the same first letter as the name of my maternal grandmother who had a biblical tag, Ruth. She died around the time I was born, so I'd never have the chance to know her. My middle name, John—also with religious significance, evoking qualities of strength, kindness, and faith—was selected to honor my mother's younger brother. I was the fourth child in my family. My three siblings—brother James and sisters Susan and Anna—had been born eleven, ten, and nine years before me. To maintain a consistent pattern, our names were abbreviated to three-letter words: Rob, Ann, Sue, and Jim.

To the outside world, we were the archetypical upper-middle-class family, reaching for the American Dream. Our home in Sacramento was in the charming William Land Park neighborhood. It was a stately two-story manor with a generous 4,300 square feet of living space. As guests entered, they were greeted by a large foyer, adorned with a wide curved stairway and a thin steel banister. The house had an appealing exterior, with white wooden siding and painted brick walls. There was also a spacious basement with a large wet bar stocked with collectible bottles filled with spirits. Outside there was a sizable front lawn and a small backyard with a detached garage. To many, we might have been considered wealthy.

Our neighborhood was characterized by wide streets and sidewalks, facing a 235-acre park with picturesque duck ponds, a golf course, open spaces packed with trees and grass, the city zoo, and a charming children's amusement park known as Fairy Tale Town. My mother, Carole, drove a forest green Ford station wagon with faux wood paneling on the sides. My father, Millard, opted for a beige Cadillac Sedan de Ville, which antisemites referred to as the "Jew canoe."

We were part of a tiny community of about 3,800 Jews in Sacramento, united by our shared identity. At the time the state of Israel was still young, and Jewish refugees, mostly from Europe, were transforming themselves into a nation while here in the United States, Jews were integrating through intermarriage and the embrace of democratic values. And yet Jews were still not fully accepted by the white-bread, Cold War society as there were covenants and restrictions against Jews living in specific neighborhoods and joining certain clubs.

My mother was not religious. Her family had emigrated from Germany to New York City and then moved to New Haven, Connecticut. She was born in Portland, Oregon, and raised in San Francisco. She and her mother and younger brother would spend their summers on the East Coast, where her grandfather had a sizable three-family house in a small beach community near Milford, Connecticut, called Woodmont. Woodmont was a bustling summer destination and retreat for wealthy families and celebrities from New Haven, New York, and worldwide. Mom's family was what's known as "assimilated Reform Jews," with few Jewish friends. They all had Christmas trees, a big Christmas dinner, and Easter celebrations with baskets of candy and toys. As a kid, I couldn't understand why Mom eschewed Judaism and Jewish holidays in favor of Christian ones. Now I see it was perhaps what she'd seen the grown-ups around her do to be accepted in America. I think as a child my mom developed an awareness of fitting in, of wealth, and the advantages it provided her during her Woodmont trips. The daily exposure to people living more affluent lives impressed her.

My dad's family had emigrated to the United States in 1906 from what is now Ukraine. He, too, was born in Portland and raised in San Francisco. Unlike my mother's family, my father's family kept many Jewish traditions and continued to belong to a synagogue and celebrate Jewish holidays. I was forced, primarily by my father, to endure Sunday school—yes, even us Jewish kids have it—so I could receive my Jewish confirmation. Bar Mitzvah would be a mandate that I'd have a tough time following.

My father once told me about an incident with a neighbor kid on his street in San Francisco. It took place around the late 1920s, just before the Holocaust. Dad was playing ball with neighborhood kids outside after school when he felt pelts striking him. He suddenly realized that one of the kids was shooting a BB gun at him. Some of the other kids began shouting, "Hey Jew-boy!" and "You're a Christ-killer!" He felt the stinging pain of the BBs and reached to find little divots they made in his neck and arm, which made his heart skip a few beats. He wasn't seriously injured, but this was his first exposure and realization that he was considered different from others.

The father of the BB gun kid was a firefighter, and my grandmother took my dad to their front door after he told her the story. A force of nature in a floral dress, Grandma Fanny didn't bother with a polite knock. She pounded on the door and when it flew open, her voice boomed, "I'm Fanny Tonkin, my son is Millard, and your son fired a gun at him while calling him terrible names. I demand an apology from your boy!" And she got it, too. Fanny Tonkin wasn't a woman who left a battlefield empty-handed.

My first exceedingly painful experience with overt antisemitism, beyond the occasional veiled joke, happened in fourth grade, almost three decades after the Holocaust ended. We were playing soccer in PE, and I probably said something stupid to one of the guys. The next thing I knew, he was screaming "You're a kike!" and kicking me right in the balls. The pain was unreal. I hit the ground, doubled over in agony.

The slur alone felt deeply offensive, and my parents weren't the type I could easily open up to about personal stuff, so I was too embarrassed to tell them about the assault at the time. For weeks, I noticed some initial swelling, and then I sort of got used to it. However, my groin, precisely one of my testicles, would feel sensitive now and then, causing mild discomfort. Finally, several years after the kick, finding a rare quiet instant with my mom, I got the courage to mention it. She made sure the doctor checked it during my physicals, and that's when I learned what it was: a hydrocele, a fluid-filled swelling caused by injury. The doc said, "If it grows to the size of an orange and bothers you, we'll remove it; otherwise everything should be fine." The school, though? They dismissed the assault as "boys being boys."

3

STAY TOGETHER FOR THE KIDS

I rarely spent time with my classmates outside of school, but I had several friends in my neighborhood. We would construct forts in the trees at the park across the street or engage in Viking-themed pretend games in one of the kids' backyards. We played board games, hopscotch, hide-and-seek, and all sorts of ball games, and we also spent lots of time just biking around.

On the surface, I enjoyed a rather typical suburban upbringing. But the truth was far darker—rooted in the fact that I was neither wanted by my parents nor really loved by them. When I was a teenager, my mother Carole explained to me, "I regretted marrying your father. People had warned me against it. I knew from the start that it wasn't a good choice."

I imagine Carole felt stressed, burned out, and trapped by the time I was conceived. She'd already been married to my father and raising their children for over a decade. However, she must have felt she had no choice. It was 1961, and the concept of abortion was still considered radical partly due to highly restrictive laws against it.

Carole probably sighed, cigarette smoke curling around her perfectly coiffed hair, quietly muttering, "*Another* one?"

Millard, ever the optimist, would have beamed. "A new baby! It's a blessing!" while thinking, *Another tie that binds you to me.*

Carole, however, likely rolled her eyes internally. "Oh, Millard," she might have said with a forced smile, "you always know just what to say." But inside, she was already planning her next escape—a shopping spree, a luncheon with friends, anything to avoid confronting the reality of a fourth pregnancy at the age of thirty-six. She was a chain smoker, a heavy drinker, and most likely sick of kids.

These feelings of resentment were compounded by the fact that I was the only one of her four children to be delivered via C-section, leaving her with a huge scar. I believe her resentment toward me began during pregnancy, was amplified by childbirth, and then continued in full force every time my behavior took on characteristics of my father or when I had one of my many tantrums. She would scream, "Millard, you deal with him!"

As a child, I learned a great deal by accompanying my dad to work. He was a partner in a bottling plant, a five-county franchise for 7-Up, and, later, A&W Root Beer and other soft drinks.

"See that, Robbie?" he'd say, gesturing toward the whirring machinery. "That's the filler. It can fill hundreds of bottles a minute!"

My eyes would widen. "Wow! How does it work?"

He'd patiently explain the process, the intricate dance of bottles, liquid, and machinery. Dad was 5'10 with a slender fit frame and a thin face that accentuated his pronounced nose. His dark hair, always combed straight back, was thinning a bit and he had a warm, wide smile. I peppered him with questions, absorbing every detail about the organization, production, systems, quality control, and even the merchandising side of things.

Dad carried himself with an air of quiet authority. At fifty, he was a picture of classic 1960s and '70s business style, with a neatly tailored gray or dark blue suit. Although he sometimes opted for the more relaxed combination of a sportscoat, tie, and slacks. He always topped his "fit" off with a white lab coat embroidered with "Millard" on the chest pocket. Dad had keen dark eyes, magnified by strong bifocal glasses with black rims. He favored classic leather wingtip shoes and had a couple of pairs in different colors.

I think one of Mom's primary life goals was to gain wealth, and she pushed Dad to earn more so he could help achieve that goal. They both measured success by money. But what Dad, like my mother, failed to provide was the necessary parental love and nurturing.

"Maybe next weekend, buddy," he'd say, his voice apologetic, as he rushed out the door. And "I've got this important board meeting with the Sacramento Safety Council." Or perhaps he was off to accompany a Rotary Club sing-along on the piano. Dad was the most helpful of men, president of the Rotary Club, a dapper people-pleaser who relished the chance to shine in his own circles. But while he was a pillar of the community, his absence at home left a void in our lives.

One day Dad commanded, "Robbie, I'm signing you up for Little League baseball." To some kids, this might have sounded great, but I hadn't really played much baseball prior to that and he wasn't the type to play catch with me. Dad made sure the team was sponsored by 7-Up and provided soft drinks. But he only attended a grand total of one of my many games, which was still better than Mom, who never attended any.

During one game I stood at the plate, gasping, stunned as I realized that my twenty-seven-inch Louisville Slugger bat was broken, with a piece flung somewhere, before I dropped the handle and ran around the bases, propelled by equal parts adrenaline and determination. "HOME!" *I'd hit a home run!* Flush with excitement, I looked around and wished, *If only Mom and Dad were here to see this.*

Any time I was honored for something, anything, I felt emptiness as I watched other families celebrate together, while mine were MIA. *Why did Dad push me so hard to participate if he didn't care enough to show up?* Each rejection, each disappointment, was another brick in the wall I was building around my heart. Trusting Dad became a fragile thing, easily shattered.

At home, our living room stood apart, not by a closed door, but by an invisible barrier of silence and disuse. Plush sofas and armchairs sat untouched, their surfaces reflecting the unused grandeur of the dark wood upright piano against one wall. Above the piano, four separate wooden frames held our portraits. Each of us kids had been immortalized in pastels, our likenesses captured in soft, colorful strokes.

The room was out of reach, symbolizing something we had but didn't *need*. As a young boy, I'd wander in, drawn to its forbidden allure and the quiet. I'd trace the piano keys, hoping the discordant notes would attract attention, even if it meant getting in trouble. Yet, more than anything, that room filled me with a sense of unease. A nagging feeling of being different, of having more than others, grew within me.

Nevertheless, our home was never fully calm. Chaos seemed to rule within its four walls.

"You always get to pick the music!" my sister Anna would shriek from her shared bedroom with Susan.

"It's not my fault you have terrible taste!" Susan would retort. Their bickering was a constant soundtrack to our lives.

My brother Jim, ever the rebel, would saunter past, completely ignoring our parents' pleas to "Clean your room!" or "Get a haircut!"

And then there were the explosive fights between our parents. The tension would build, simmering beneath the surface until it erupted in a torrent of shouting, crashing objects, and vile obscenities.

"Where were you?!" Dad would accuse, his voice sharp as splintered glass.

"It's none of your damn business!" Mom would roar back. "I don't have to answer to you!"

I once witnessed my father break their bedroom door down, screaming at the top of his lungs, "Sweetie, let me in, you bitch!" And my mother crying loudly while screaming back, "Leave me alone, you, you *asshole*, I'm not your sweetie!"

These scenes played out with terrifying regularity, my parents' anxiety seeping into my pores. To compensate for their emotional absence, which left me feeling empty and desperate for connection, I constantly sought the approval of others, craving the spotlight. This pattern began early, and by kindergarten, I had cemented my role as the class clown, using humor and antics to mask my underlying insecurities and yearning to belong.

Whenever my parents were away, my nearly adult sisters or their friends would take turns babysitting me. But even with people around, there were still times when loneliness would creep in as I, the only small child in the home, wandered through the house, a shadow among the grown-up laughter and chatter, feeling strangely invisible. A longing would tug at me for a connection that went deeper, for someone to talk to, for someone to just be *with*. Someone to make me feel safe. I often felt like I was on the outside looking in, watching life happen from a distance.

We typically employed a live-in housekeeper who had a room conveniently located near the laundry area, kitchen, and back door. One evening, seeking answers to a question and finding no one else available, I ventured into Doris Unthank's room. She mumbled a reply, and I caught sight of her toothless gums. I flinched and ran out of the room, fear gripping me. Apparently, she wore removable dentures. To me though, she'd transformed into a horror figure. Later, as I slept, that unsettling encounter bled into my dreams, conjuring images as monstrous as the green-skinned witch from *The Wizard of Oz*.

4

SAN FRANCISCO

When I was about six years old, my parents thought I was old enough to travel alone. They stuck me on a Greyhound bus from downtown Sacramento to San Francisco. The Greyhound's engine growled, a metal beast about to devour me, as my stomach knotted with fear at the miles of highway stretched ahead. Grandma and Grandpa Tonkin waited at the other end—silent figures I barely knew. Knowing I'd be alone with them filled me with a sense of dread.

Joe Tonkin, my grandfather, had this gangster look that scared me. He was short and squat, a dead ringer for Edward G. Robinson, a Hollywood icon who always played the hard-boiled tough guy. Maybe it was his past that contributed to that aura. He'd been a man of the world, starting his career in the early 1900s with a stake in a liquor distributorship. But then Prohibition hit, throwing a wrench into the gears of his budding empire. Dad spoke of "filling bottles at the office" as a kid. I never knew for sure if Grandpa had skirted the law, keeping the liquor flowing during those dry years, but there was a glint in his eye that suggested a man who knew how to bend the rules. Ironically, Dad eventually found his own path in the beverage industry, though his world was one of fizzy drinks and sugary smiles, a far cry from the shadowy world of bootlegging that as I got older I'd imagine Grandpa inhabiting.

Grandpa also had a playful spirit and quiet eccentricity. I felt a jumble of emotions around him. Besides his elaborate practical jokes, he'd throw tough questions at me that made me think. It was confusing, to say the least. Sometimes he would quiz me: "What's your telephone number?" I would blurt out, "That's easy, Grandpa, 4-4-7-8-6-7-5!" And then he'd ask for my address, and I'd proudly say, "1731 13th Avenue!" He'd applaud and do it again. Successive correct answers made me feel accomplished because I knew these were important details in his eyes. The information burned into my mental hard drive and is easy to recall fifty-five years later.

My grandmother, Fanny, was taller than Grandpa Joe, with a more pointed and pronounced nose and her gray hair pulled back, often wearing a floral pattern apron. She kept busy in the kitchen listening to a Giants ballgame on her transistor radio or tending to her garden plants on the rooftop of their parking garage. She had a deep love of baseball, whereas my grandfather preferred comedy and music. He enjoyed TV, particularly the courtroom crime drama *Perry Mason* and the champagne music variety show *Lawrence Welk*. He adored comedic legends Jack Benny and Jackie Gleason. His home office, which I never saw him use, was filled with a spacious desk and a giant wall of books. I eyed a gold metal star-shaped badge on his desk that read, "San Francisco Grand Jury, Foreman."

When Grandpa Joe told me, "Robbie, you can have one book from the wall; just pick one!" what I really wanted was that badge, but I selected a poetry book titled, *It Can Be Done, Poems of Inspiration*. I hoped that reading it would positively impact me, that it would be easier to read than a whole book, and perhaps even help me approach girls.

My grandparents lived at 2121 Broadway, on the first floor of a row-style apartment building in the heart of the city. I always felt excitement in the Broadway tunnel we had to drive through before reaching their place. I'd yell, "Honk the horn!" no matter who was driving.

A highlight of visiting my grandparents was hearing them speak Yiddish. I learned many popular words and phrases. They also would call out to each other, "*Dearie*, where are the car keys?" But I didn't understand the nickname "dearie." The keys I knew—that meant we were going to Miz Brown's Feed Bag, a burger-and-shake joint on California Street. The place had orange vinyl booths, each with a jukebox, along with a counter with metal-backed swivel chairs facing a gas grill. I would eagerly order a burger, fries, and vanilla shake on every visit. But the most thrilling part was the little translucent plastic monkeys they would hang on the shake glasses. These monkeys came in an array of different colors: red, blue, orange, and green. To me, they were even more exciting than the prizes in a box of Cracker Jack. I collected and saved all of the colors.

Once, when we were leaving the restaurant, Grandma Fanny was closing the door of their Ford Thunderbird sedan and my fingers got caught in it. This car had "suicide" doors that opened backward, like a Lincoln Continental. I wasn't used to it. I screamed in agony, "My fingers! My fingers! The door, my fingers!" for what seemed like an eternity, although it was probably only five seconds until Grandma Fanny realized what had happened. I felt as though it was my fault. These were the same fingers I used to comfort myself by sucking on as a toddler and still did, even though I was six. After that incident, I stopped.

In addition to my grandparents, I regularly visited my cousins on my father's side, who lived in Presidio Terrace, an incredibly exclusive, gated community in San Francisco. It was a secluded oval lined with grand mansions, lush gardens, and an air of Old-World elegance. It's so private that many San Franciscans don't even know it exists. Mayor Joseph Alioto lived just down the block, while the Magnins, of department store fame, lived right next door.

My cousins lived in a mansion that resembled a five-star Old-World hotel. The grand entrance, the sweeping staircase, the chandeliers that glittered like diamonds—it was all breathtaking. Yet my cousins remained remarkably grounded. Looking back, I realize that their kindness and genuine warmth made a far greater impression on me than the opulence of their surroundings.

I have fond memories of playing with their son, Johnny, who was a bit older than me, around eight years old. We'd have a blast exploring the grand houses and hidden corners of this upscale neighborhood. From the depths of their basements to the dusty reaches of their attics, it was a world of discovery where a young boy's imagination could run wild.

One of my most remarkable adventures involved an unexpected find in the attic of a friend's house. It was a stash of magazines hidden away like a secret treasure. The glossy pages, filled with images of women we'd never seen before, were both intriguing and a little bit frightening. *Playboy, Penthouse,* and *Oui,* with its European sophistication, particularly captivated me—a flash of awakening, a glimpse into the complexities of adult life and the mysteries of sexuality.

5

VACATION, HAD TO GET AWAY

As a kid, I had a knack for weaseling my way into other families' adventures. I would soak up their warmth and connections like a thirsty plant. Who could resist a tag-along, eager to join their tribe, share in their laughter, and bask in the glow of a happy family? It was a stark contrast to the awkwardness at home, and I knew how fortunate I was to get a glimpse of something different, something many kids never got to experience.

There was one particularly wonderful family on our street, the Christians, that I got to know quite well. The parents were Maynard and Beverly, while the children, my schoolmates, were Lisa, Leif, who was nicknamed "Gruff," and Amy. Maynard was an incredibly skilled anesthesiologist, and their family always seemed to radiate love and happiness. They had a noticeably more rugged lifestyle than ours. They were accustomed to chopping wood, wore minimal makeup, didn't prioritize money, and seemed to possess an overall carefree attitude.

Around third grade, Gruff and I were inseparable. We were always cooking up some grand adventure, transforming ourselves into anything our imaginations could conjure. One minute we were fearless Vikings, plundering the backyard in search of buried treasure. The next, we were the resourceful Swiss Family Robinson, constructing an elaborate treehouse hideaway from salvaged branches and blankets. Our days were spent lost in a world of our own making. We built intricate tunnels, fortresses that towered toward the sky, and entire civilizations hidden in ordinary trees and bushes or their trimmings. It was like living inside a video game, but way before computers and virtual reality were common-place. We were limited only by the boundaries of our imaginations.

The Christian family owned a sturdy four-wheel-drive International Harvester family wagon, which we would take on trips to an extraordinary place in nature called Salmon Lake. Located northeast of Sacramento, this hidden gem lies between the breathtaking Plumas National Forest to the north and the stunning Tahoe National Forest to the south. Salmon Lake was a charming body of water nestled within a striking granite bowl. It was surrounded by polished slopes, granite terraces, and an expansive conifer forest. The lake was privately owned by the Christian family, with a lodge resting on its shoreline and a few abandoned cabins hiding on the mountainsides.

Our arrival involved parking the truck on one side of the lake, and then embarking on a small barge to transport ourselves and our supplies to the lodge. Gruff and I would spend our days exploring the mountainside, channeling the spirit of old gold miners as we ventured through hillside cabins, an abandoned mill, and the rugged lodge itself—all remnants of the area's mining history. The mill had once been employed to crush the quartz containing precious flakes of gold. We'd also heard stories about forbidden locations, which only heightened the sense of adventure this place sparked within us. It was, indeed, an exhilarating and activity-filled oasis.

Eventually, the Christians moved to Reno, Nevada, to the east of Salmon Lake, closer to Lake Tahoe. There, they acquired a vast property with a grand residence that seemed like a mansion to me. I jokingly referred to it as the Beverly Hillbilly mansion, acknowledging Beverly, Gruff's mom, as well as the TV show, which was one of my favorites.

My childhood was defined by television. I was a TV baby, devouring every show I could, from *Hogan's Heroes* to *The Beverly Hillbillies*. The TV screen was a portal to a world so much more appealing than my own. I didn't just watch these shows; I inhabited them, dreaming of a life like theirs. I longed for the warmth of *The Brady Bunch* home, the adventures of *Lost in Space*, and the excitement of *Mod Squad*. The sheer volume of shows I *watched is almost comical now: I Love Lucy, The Banana Splits, Room 222, All in the Family, The Jeffersons, Good Times, Welcome Back, Kotter, Love American Style, Gunsmoke, Bonanza, The Odd Couple, Get Smart, The Partridge Family*, and so many more—it was a constant stream of other lives, other possibilities. Looking back, I wonder if the isolation of *Gilligan's Island*, the idea of being stranded and building a community, resonated with me in some way, though I certainly didn't understand it then.

Once, when Mrs. Christian was clad in a parka and hiking boots, my mom and dad arrived to pick me up. Mom was dressed in a mink fur coat and stylish boots, to me, clearly conveying a preference for wealth over warmth. Her extravagant fashion choices and the ostentatious display of her wealth left me embarrassed. I considered the Christians the least pretentious people I knew, and their genuine nature greatly appealed to me. Sadly after a few visits to their new home, I would lose touch with Gruff and his family. Yet I knew, they were who I wanted to be like.

Lake Tahoe also held a great allure for me. It was an alpine wonderland conveniently situated near Sacramento, only a couple of hours away by car. My family went there on vacation several times. I also visited Tahoe on a few other occasions with different families. The sense of freedom and natural beauty that the lake and surrounding area exuded was palpable. I found myself beguiled by the Truckee River, the various parts of the lake, the pleasure of catching crawdads, boating, swimming, river rafting, and, of course, skiing in multiple ski areas every winter. Tahoe also offered incredible miniature golf courses. I loved mini-golf, although I cannot count a single instance when the game included my father, mother, or siblings.

I accompanied my Uncle John and his family to Hawaii. He was my mother's brother, with kids around my age. They lived in a large upscale modern home in Marin County. Around them, I felt uneasy, however, due to my aunt's disciplinary approach. She tended to shame my cousins and boss my uncle around. It bewildered me how everyone accepted her strict and curt remarks without protest. Sometimes, the kids would cry in response to her harsh words. Fortunately, I was somewhat shielded from her wrath. We'd visit Maui on a couple of occasions in my late preteens. These trips were filled with exciting activities, visits to upscale restaurants, and stays at deluxe hotels. Most importantly, I cherished the company of my cousins, who made the entire journey even more enjoyable. As I grew older, I'd learn to tolerate my aunt and even appreciate her company, too. At least she was there.

6

RING OF FIRE

Summer camp was another escape. No forced photos, no awkward family dinners, no pressure to be anyone other than myself.

Looking back, I realize how lucky I was to spend summers at a place where I could just be a kid, a privilege not everyone had. Being the child who froze and bailed on his cousin's wedding as the ring bearer in a tux (yes, that's the cover photo) and cringed in apprehension at every family gathering didn't exactly win me any popularity contests back home. But at camp? None of that mattered. It was pure freedom.

I felt alive and stable, and it showed. In the summer of 1969, I earned my greatest adolescent honor, the Skylake Yosemite Camp's Camper of the Week citation. This was awarded to one boy and one girl from lower division camp, and one boy and one girl from upper division camp. On Sunday nights, after dinner, the camp's head counselor would preside over a ceremony to honor each of these four campers for essentially being a good person. Hearing the weekly reveal was always exciting, since the selection process was highly secretive.

One Sunday evening in August, when I was seven, I joined the other campers and counselors in the lodge. About 200 of us, our bellies full from a hearty spaghetti dinner, stood listening expectantly. Then, I heard these words:

> "Here is a camper who, though small in structure, is great in stature. He gives his counselor no guff, discharges all

his responsibilities cheerfully and promptly, gets along well with all his tentmates, and displays an enthusiasm for camp life that won't quit.... This camper also possesses a remarkable versatility that allows him to be a 'dirty old man' one night and turn around the next morning to make a remark like this concerning the Chapel songs: 'I like those soft songs that let God know we love him.' This week's Camper of the Week from the Lower Division Boys' Camp is ROBBIE TONKIN."

I had no idea this was coming. I sat with my mouth open in disbelief, my heart pounding out a primal rhythm: *I won! I won! I won!* A surge of warmth flooded my entire body, and my palms grew slick with sweat. It felt like I had been etched into Mount Rushmore. A giddy sense of disbelief mixed with a powerful urge to climb to the tallest treetop and shout my victory to the world— was the most significant moment of my young life. I still get emotional when I think about it today, more than fifty years later. I was being recognized for *being me.*

There's a lot to unpack in what had been written about me. Even when my counselor began to speak, which could have been a tip, I had no idea he was talking about me until I heard my name. I didn't remember saying that quote about the "soft songs," and at seven years old had little idea what was meant by "dirty old man." I presume he was alluding to my reputation as the camp flirt, always teasing the girls I liked and pulling pranks on them, like sneaking into their tent cabins at night, to get their attention.

Skylake Yosemite Camp was hours away from my Sacramento home, but it felt like it was on another planet. Skylake was on Bass Lake in the Sierra National Forest, just east of Yosemite National Park. The camp borrowed its name from the country's very first national park, established in October 1890 at the behest of famed naturalist John Muir. And while it was just outside the national park boundaries, "Yosemite" gave the camp a marketing edge.

Skylake was a breath of fresh air. I met kids from all over and learned a ton of new skills—riflery, archery, horsemanship, athletics, sailing, you name it. It was what I lacked in school—we had the whole outdoors as our classroom. We hiked, we camped, we explored. It felt like a privilege to be there, immersed in nature. And the best part? No parents fighting. No one telling me to disappear. Just the freedom to be myself, surrounded by friends and the sounds of the forest. That experience instilled in me a love for nature that I still carry today.

Skylake's Gold Rush Day was a day-long event that everyone looked forward to, even though we had no idea when it would occur. One morning, as we ate breakfast in the mess hall, a counselor would ride into the room on a horse and declare the gold rush. Once word was given to release the campers, the goal was for each camper to collect as many "gold" rocks as possible, bring them to the assay office for weighing, and receive "gold rush dollars" for the bounty. This was a small simulation of the California Gold Rush of 1849. The effects of "gold fever" in California, which occurred when the sparkly precious metal was discovered near my hometown, had brought many new people into the area and led to the creation of the state a year later—along with the nickname, The Golden State.

I attended Skylake for six summers through 1975. One of those years I became a simulated Skylake gold baron—a 49'er, as they were referred to during the *actual* Gold Rush. I commandeered a wheelbarrow from the horse paddock. I was first to climb a steep path up a hill with the wheelbarrow empty and then began filling it with the biggest painted rocks I could lift. Once full, I aimed it downhill straight to the assay office and became wealthy on the first run.

But that didn't satisfy me. I started renting out the wheelbarrow to friends for a percentage of their payouts. Later, I was the camper assistant assigned to the assay office, a job I took most seriously. This wasn't just about weighing gold-painted rocks anymore; it was about touching all that cash, and controlling the flow of wealth. I meticulously recorded each deposit, handing out the corresponding gold rush dollars with an air of authority.

At camp, I thrived on challenges and the camaraderie. I was small for my age but determined to go on aggressive hikes outside the camp. In backpacking, it is customary to carry 25 percent of your weight on your back. My gear probably weighed at least 50 percent or 60 percent of my weight. I signed up for the Yosemite Half Dome hike, yet because I had such difficulty with the heavy pack on a previous hike, I wasn't allowed to go, so sadly I never made the ascent up the cables to the top of the dome. It is still on my bucket list to complete.

The Sierra National Forest offered many options outside of Yosemite for camping and hiking. I always signed up for the Angel Falls-Willow Creek hike, where we would swim in natural pools and use the water's current and slick granite rocks as slides. I had more outdoor fun than imaginable, except for the time I drifted beyond the designated area to discover a better slide. I was putting my feet in the current to see what was below the water, and then, *bam*, I slipped, got sucked down a small waterfall, and saw my life flash before my eyes. Fortunately, I recovered quickly and made my way back to the rocky shore. Only one other camper saw my embarrassingly dangerous maneuver.

The Mammoth Lakes hike, a longer and better version of Willow Creek with tall cliffs to jump from into chilly pools of water, made for carefree exhilaration. Chain Lakes was a long hike through a series of lakes, an introduction to mosquitos, gorgeous views, wildlife, birdwatching, rivers, little lakefront beaches, and plenty of excitement.

Bass Lake was another playground of adventure. Canoeing was fun, but water skiing was the real draw. It was a challenge, with only two campers allowed in the speedboat at a time, but it quickly became my favorite activity. After wiping out countless times, conquering the single slalom ski was a huge victory. It wasn't just about staying upright or ripping rooster tails; it was about proving to myself that I could overcome obstacles. That newfound sense of self-trust, that feeling of control, was exhilarating.

Scavenger hunts were also perfect diversions, with mindfulness and fun in a game where I collected items for a payout. Rewards caught and held my attention.

One of my fellow campers was a kid named Dewey Wohl, my rabbi's son and a good friend. Like me, he made sure he stood out from the other campers. But while my talent was surprising people with problem-solving skills, Dewey's was comedy and music, so much so that he was given his own night to entertain the crowd, "Dewey Wohl Night." This was highly unusual; the evening's entertainment was customarily handled by counselors or staff.

Dewey and I had lived down the street from one another and discovered Cheech & Chong and Neil Young together. Cheech & Chong's record was outrageously funny, controversial, and raw. We'd sneak a record player into an attic at a friend's house to hear vinyl recordings we had collected of the musical sketch comedy routines they performed. Burns and Schreiber were another comedy duo more accepted by parents, but we also found them entertaining and listened to their albums. When "Harvest" was released by Neil Young, "Heart of Gold" became (and remains) one of my favorite songs of all time. Dewey and I created skits involving music and comedy routines ripping off some of the best themes. This became the basis for Dewey's starring role at camp, with me as emcee and supporting cast member. Even if it was shared, I was in the spotlight. It felt great.

7

EVERY PICTURE TELLS A STORY

I found ways to express myself creatively, just as my mother had done throughout her life. At heart, Mom was an artist. She was exceptional at flower arranging, interior design, fashion, and visual arts. Music was one of her escapes. Our record player spun a mix of Frank Sinatra's classics, Perry Como's croons, and Neil Diamond's anthems. Mom's everyday handwriting style was highly original. Her penmanship was a blend of Old English calligraphy and stylized cursive. Frequently, she was asked to address weddings and other invitations. People would sometimes have her create an original and copy her work.

My father played music, which he interpreted by ear, often resorting to simple tunes like *Jingle Bells* or other Christmas classics—a touch ironic, considering his Jewish heritage. Bing Crosby's comforting voice and classical symphony filled my father with a quiet joy. Dad signed letters using a sophisticated gold Cross brand fountain pen, filled with green ink as an ode to 7-Up, complete with a dramatic flourish, a signature I admired and tried to emulate. Yet in my eyes, my father's artistic abilities were overshadowed by my mother's immense creativity. Nonetheless, he exuded the qualities of a dedicated and methodical businessman, which I found impressive.

Rock 'n' roll filled our house, thanks to my siblings. Jim's room pulsed with Santana's guitar riffs, then shifted to the soulful harmonies of The Chambers Brothers and The Temptations. His conga drums, probably a rhythmic rebellion against years of classical piano lessons, added another layer to the mix. Sue was lost in the poetic lyrics of Van Morrison and the brooding rock of The Doors, while Ann grooved to the smooth soul of Curtis Mayfield and Isaac Hayes. It was a musical melting pot that shaped my young ears.

I craved awe-inspiring experiences, and one afternoon, I found it in the most unexpected place. My Irish classmate Sean Duffy's mom, a Beatles fan, took us to see the animated film *Yellow Submarine*. Mom and Dad thought it was a typical cartoon and gave permission, but imagine being six and a half and suddenly plunged into a kaleidoscope of colors, music, and nonsensical fun. The Beatles' iconic tunes, woven seamlessly into the psychedelic visuals, resonated with me in a way I'd never experienced before. The Blue Meanies, the underwater world, and the characters from Pepperland, all mesmerized me, but it was the music that truly struck a chord. I was completely absorbed for ninety minutes. It was an animated adventure, my first taste of something akin to virtual reality, long before VR headsets existed. My parents wouldn't have dreamed of taking me to such an unconventional film. It taught me that sometimes, the most memorable experiences come from the most unexpected sources.

We subscribed to the *San Francisco Chronicle* newspaper, which arrived early every morning on our porch. Once I was a budding reader, Mom and Dad strongly encouraged me to keep up with current events. I had zero interest in their recommendation until, sitting around the breakfast table one day, a headline drew me in: "Congress Passes Gulf of Tonkin Resolution." I questioned why we, the Tonkins, were in the paper until Mom explained, "It's related to the war with Vietnam. It's not about us, but an actual body of water with the same name." I felt relief, realizing I wasn't suddenly the center of some international incident. Then, a flicker of curiosity ignited. What was this Vietnam place, and why was it causing such a stir? The world, it seemed, was a much bigger and more complicated place than I'd imagined.

Flipping through the lightweight paper that smelled of ink, I stumbled upon the comics section and then an ad for an art competition. It sparked an idea. I started entering art contests, and to my surprise, I actually won some! The thrill of seeing my name in the big city *Chronicle*, along with an honorable mention, was off the charts. I even won a lifetime entry pass to the San Francisco Fleishhacker Zoo, a fancy certificate with a symbolic key printed on it. Yet to my parents, caught up in the whirlwind of raising four kids and their own crap, it probably seemed like a trivial prize. We lived a couple of hours away from the zoo, and yet we never made it there. My lifetime pass got lost somewhere; our dog probably ate it, like so many other things lost back then.

I attended a small non-denominational private school managed by a husband and wife, with fewer than 100 students. Their daughter had studied in France and the UK and brought back sophisticated additions to the school's curriculum. She had studied calligraphy, italic handwriting in particular. When she joined the faculty, our French classes improved because of her French immersion, and we began to study italic handwriting as an extension of the school's penmanship classes.

I found italic dynamically stylish, like a model alphabet wearing a cool outfit. We were taught how to form individual italic letters, did practice exercises, and learned about nibs, fountain pens, nib widths, ink, and writing surfaces. A nib is the tip of the pen, comes in different sizes, and is screwed onto the pen body, which stores the dark ink. By depressing the nib onto paper, usually at a forty-five-degree angle, and controlling the distribution flow of ink with hand pressure, one could create art simply by forming the shape of each letter. My school didn't offer other art classes because our studies were intended to prepare us for top testing and university entrance requirements, so this appealed to me.

The graceful loops and flourishes of italic script melted away hours, as I practiced, my hand mimicking the strokes until they flowed effortlessly from my pen. Soon, I excelled and became the undisputed calligraphy champion of my class. My work even earned recognition from the National Italic Handwriting Association. With newfound confidence,

I began offering my services for a fee. Wedding invitations, awards, hand-lettered signs—suddenly, my calligraphy was in high demand.

Though I often felt like an artist on the inside, my appearance was that of an academic. Since the age of five, I'd been incessantly groomed for Stanford, Berkeley, or Harvard as the youngest and, perhaps, the last hope for my parents' academic aspirations. My friends' parents teased me, referring to me as "The Little Professor." I wore black-rimmed glasses, and my school uniform consisted of a white button-down shirt, black speckled corduroy pants, black Oxford shoes, and a belt. I carried an old-style briefcase and asked many precocious questions.

Mom dreamed I'd become a man of the establishment. "A lawyer, a doctor, maybe even a politician!" she'd declare, her eyes sparkling with ambition. "Someone who wears fine suits, commands a boardroom, has his name on a corner office, flies first class...." It was her idea of the picture-perfect life of success and prestige. I, however, without knowing it at the time, had other plans.

"Dad," I said several weeks before my birthday, mustering up the courage to voice my unusual birthday wish, "for my tenth birthday, I want to go to Folsom Prison, the one Johnny Cash sings about." It was in Folsom, a suburb of Sacramento. I loved the haunting sound of the train whistle in that song.

His eyebrows shot up. "Folsom Prison?"

I nodded, the image of that imposing fortress already taking shape in my mind.

To my surprise, he agreed. He actually listened to me. On the day of my birthday, instead of just cake and games, I found myself standing before the imposing gates of the prison with a group of my wide-eyed friends in tow. Inside, the air crackled with a strange mix of tension and creative energy. We wandered through the makeshift gallery, the walls lined with paintings, sculptures, and intricate crafts, all created by the men incarcerated within those walls. The music, the laughter, the shared joy—it was as if, in that very instant, we were able to "let that lonesome whistle blow our blues away," just as Johnny sang. The experience left an indelible mark on me, a stark reminder that even in the darkest of places, the human spirit can find a way to create and express itself.

At the end of our tour, Dad surprised me with an unexpected gift: I could choose any piece of art from the show. My eyes scanned the paintings, drawn to a darkly colored, oil-painted canvas: a majestic clipper ship battling a white-capped stormy sea. Waves crashed, sails strained, but the ship pressed on. Perhaps it was a subconscious choice, that ship mirroring the turbulent journey I sensed lay ahead. The image of that ship, a symbol of resilience, would remain in my mind and heart.

At the age of twelve, my father dropped me off at the University of California at Berkeley to visit my sister, who was attending the prestigious school. Susan, studying for a bachelor of arts degree in art, wanted to ensure that I had a memorable time during my stay. We went to see a film called *The Groove Tube*, a low-budget comedy satirizing current-day 1970s television and counterculture. Starring comedians Richard Belzer and Chevy Chase, it was the second R-rated movie I had ever seen. The first was *Deliverance*, which my dad unintentionally took me to see. He was always so preoccupied that he probably didn't even read the movie poster.

The aspect of *The Groove Tube* that resonated with me the most was the commercials inserted into the film. These commercials were sponsored by "Uranus," and they humorously showcased a unique polyester called "Brown 25," discovered by a group of scientists working at Uranus. The commercials acted as clever metaphors, subtly using different ways to indicate feces. I couldn't contain my laughter; it was one of the funniest things I had ever seen. Twelve-year-old me deeply appreciated the obvious undertones of the whole gag.

Later in the visit, with my camera in hand, I wandered the sunlit paths of the Berkeley campus, savoring some rare solitude. Susan was off somewhere, leaving me to explore this haven of knowledge and activism—a world I was only beginning to grasp. Each click of the shutter captured a piece of that vibrant energy: the soaring Campanile, echoing its Venetian counterpart; the bustling Sproul Plaza, a stage for countless protests and debates. It was as if the camera opened my eyes to a hidden language, transforming the familiar into something extraordinary. Later, my quirky high school photo teacher would tell me there was a word for this act of seeing and capturing the world through a lens: photopharcal. But right then, I was just living it.

The vibrant colors, the swelling music, the graceful curves—art jolted me awake. It was a grounding sensation in an unstable world around me.

8

COMFORTABLY NUMB

One morning in February 1972, when I was nine years old, my mom began frantically gathering my belongings into a suitcase for a surprise trip we were about to take together. It was the beginning of spring vacation, which at my private school was referred to as "ski week" because of the proximity to Lake Tahoe. It seemed strange to me that after we had breakfast and Dad left for work, Mom was suddenly scurrying around to collect my clothes and toothbrush for an adventure I hadn't heard of previously. "Robbie, focus, help me get us ready. We're going to Uncle John's in Marin. I'm sure you'll have fun with Aunt Bobbie and your cousins!" Uncle John was a chill type of guy. I began to get excited.

Then came the next surprise. "We're taking an airplane ride, not a car trip," she said. This was unusual because Uncle John's house was less than two hours away and we had never taken a flight for such a short distance. In fact, I had only been on an airplane once in my life. It was when we flew PanAm to Hawaii for my grandparents' fiftieth wedding anniversary celebration when I was four.

The thought of boarding a Boeing jet to San Francisco from the sleepy Sacramento metropolitan airport overjoyed me. The next mind-blowing surprise came after we landed in San Francisco when I asked, "Why isn't Uncle John here to meet us?" Mom replied, "Here's something you're gonna like, Robbie—we're about to jump onto another flight and it's a brand-new 747!" The Boeing 747, the "Queen of the Skies," had recently taken introductory flights. I'd learned from watching the news and reading the paper that it had wings like a basketball court with a tail towering six stories high. My heart pounded, not just at the sight, but at the *idea* of it. We were about to step onto one of those giant toys, and the world felt impossibly big.

Boarding this beast felt like the most exciting thing that had ever happened to me. I felt such exhilaration that the fact that Dad was missing in action didn't even cross my mind. After take-off, I couldn't wait to explore more of the cavernous American Airlines airplane I was in.

Mid-flight, Carole brought me up the circular stairway to the upper deck luxury lounge. A bar in the center was surrounded by a semi-circle of red sofas and dark wood side tables with attached chrome lamps. Billows of cigarette smoke came from the passengers engaged in chic cocktailing while flying coast-to-coast. The slogan for the lounge was, "You won't believe you're on an airplane." No seat belts, smoke everywhere, a child in a bar, no shit! Carole was having drinks and chatting people up just as I was nudged by a stewardess, a politically correct term at the time. "Sweetie, let me walk you back to your assigned seat," she said, putting her hand on my shoulder. Mom seemed oblivious to the fact that I had been unceremoniously ousted.

The excitement of the lounge quickly faded, replaced by a quiet disappointment as I found myself back in my seat. I pulled out a notepad and began to doodle, the rhythmic motion a comfort in the unfamiliar environment. My pencil sketched out fantastical shapes and scenes, transforming the blank page into a world of my own creation. I imagined myself in the cockpit of the 747, hands gripping the controls, soaring through the clouds with a sense of freedom and adventure. Frequently, I'd crane my neck, peering down the aisle, hoping to catch a glimpse of Mom returning. But the minutes stretched on, and on.

Imagine a different child in that situation. One who had been held and soothed during their moments of emotional pain, eventually learning to comfort themselves. That *wasn't* me. In my life that had *not* happened. Every hurt settled deep into my bones. Even if pushed away, those memories became etched into my symptoms, into my relationships, into my being.

The trip east to New Haven, Connecticut, was a haze, a few snapshots in a fog. Mom's voice: "Robbie, Dad's not coming. Too busy." He always was, so I believed her. "Have fun!" she chirped, but I was in a strange house that was definitely not Uncle John's, and was flown across the country. Fun? More like a heavy weight of boredom and unease in my gut. I had been deceived.

The strange house belonged to Ruthie, Mom's lifelong bestie. It was huge, a mansion hidden in the trees. Ruthie and her husband Bob, rich and important, tried to be nice, but all I saw were fake smiles, and all I heard were empty words. Their voices echoed in my head a hollow, dishonest sound. They seemed to be players in Mom's intricate web of deception, complicit with their silence and knowing smiles.

Then, they left me. Just me and the maid in that echoing house, while they went off to the blueblood Yale Club in New York City for a few nights. Mom loved that life. It made her feel special. But for me? Darkness. I swung between anger and hiding, my head spinning. "Mom's the worst. Where's Dad? This is all wrong!" I had been taken from my home, my family, and my friends under false pretenses and tossed into an unfamiliar environment with no one I could trust. I was shutting down.

The second week, the schoolwork arrived because ski week was over and out. Mom was on the phone, getting my assignments. They piled up, impossible to do; I felt so lost. I fought back: "I won't sleep, I won't eat, I won't do it!" I felt trapped.

Mom couldn't handle me.

"If only...." The words echoed in my head, a constant refrain. If only Dad was here. If only things were fair. If only someone would just tell me the truth. I'd bargain, promise to be good, just to get a scrap of what I wanted. But it never worked. Guilt twisted in my stomach, frustration burned hot, and shame crept in, cold and heavy.

When the anger faded, there was just emptiness. A hollow ache where my heart should have been. I curled in on myself, replaying the losses. Home? Gone. Friends? Gone. Every kid had a spring break. But my spring break was stolen. Did anyone even care? I just wanted to sleep, to disappear. To not feel the grief for the life I'd lost—the Dad, the friends, the normal days that were suddenly so far away.

Two weeks stretched out forever. With my schoolwork untouched, Mom finally took me home. My siblings had all moved out, and our house now felt more empty. Then, Mom's words, sharp as a knife: "Dad's not coming back. We're getting a divorce." The air left my lungs. The whole trip, the lies, it all crashed down. They'd tricked me, just to keep me quiet—to make *themselves* feel better. Betrayal cut deeper than any sadness. How could I ever trust anyone again?

Dad was no longer at home, and I now felt even emptier. He took me out one day on a visit, broke down in tears, and said, "Your mother doesn't love you, she never *wanted* you, and I *need* you, and if you don't choose to live with me, I just might *kill* myself."

Upon hearing this, my body froze because it stung so badly. I gulped a few breaths and swallowed hard, trying to hold back the tears. I wondered how this could be true. I retreated into myself, avoiding eye contact with him as tears began to fall. Unresponsive, I tried to process the information he told me. All I wanted was comfort and physical closeness, but he wasn't good at that. I knew not to try, but inside, I desperately needed reassurance and love.

9

LIVING IN THE U.S.A.

After school one day, Mom needed to run to the grocery store and I went with her. There was a parking lot in front of the store as well as a curb alternately painted red for no stopping and yellow for loading and unloading. Licensed drivers were required to know the color legend and adhere to it. Yet Mom had an innate ability to ignore the rules as if they were trivial details that didn't apply to her.

We rolled up in our Ford station wagon, and she parked it directly in front of Lucky's Supermarket in the red zone. Mortified? Yes! If I had been an adult it might not have bothered me as much. As a pre-teen who wanted to fit in, I was hyper-embarrassed, knowing everyone would be staring at *me*. I turned as bright red as the curb and begged her to move the car to a regular parking space. "Robbie, just sit tight, and I'll run in and grab only a few items," she said sharply.

I sank low in the passenger seat of the wagon and hoped like hell nobody I knew would see me or that the law wouldn't tow me away with the car. Mom returned with a whole bag of groceries and tossed it into the car. Then, before I could muster a sigh of relief, she said, "Robbie, come with me because there's this outfit I need to try on at Susie's." The grocery store was next to a women's fashion boutique.

She spent three times as long in that store as she had in the supermarket, chatting about all kinds of things with the store salespeople. I tried hard to ignore their conversations, which revolved around such critically important topics like whether "taking in the waist and adding a belt would work for her," or if "wearing a thicker, shinier belt would make her look thinner," or if "they had it in another color," or if "they could order it in another size." If this type of incident had been rare, my mother and I could have had a better relationship. Unfortunately, thousands of hours spent together were similar versions of this one with everything always about her, which made me feel small, like I was invisible. I also felt guilty because anytime we bought something, I knew Dad was going to come unglued and question if we needed it. The good news: the station wagon was still there, not ticketed or towed, when we returned.

Mom had an excessive need for admiration, a disregard for my feelings, an inability to handle any criticism, and a major sense of entitlement. A therapist would one day explain all of this to me as narcissism. Simmering inside, I'd think, "Yup, both Mom *and* Dad have those symptoms."

My parents seemed on a quest to outdo each other in the propaganda department. "He's cheap—he's always working or helping someone else, and he never paid any attention to me," Mom would say, nursing a couple of shots of straight vodka on the rocks in a wine glass. She had made the switch from Canadian whiskey around this time. Dad, in turn, would constantly repeat that Mom never wanted me, invariably adding, "She's an alcoholic and bleeding me dry of money." I was unsure what to say, think, or feel. At ten years old, I was too young to understand the intricacies of my parents' feelings and had no one I could trust to talk to about the situation.

Despite it all, I clung to any shred of hope, any promise of connection with Dad. Then one day, Dad announced, "We're going to finally spend some time together, a road trip in the station wagon, just the two of us."

He'd been talking about this for a year or more, even before the divorce had been announced, this epic father-son adventure across the country in Mom's Ford station wagon. And, now, it was finally happening. He handed me a roadmap of the USA, but this wasn't just any map. It was his guide to the soul of America, marked with handwritten notes. Dad's map pointed the way to many cool spots I'd heard about, like

Yellowstone's Old Faithful, the Statue of Liberty, and Mt. Rushmore.

"Study this," he said, a twinkle in his eye. "This is your future."

My heart soared. We were to hit the road together and I'd have that close love from Dad I so desperately wanted. But my hopes for a solitary journey with him evaporated as, one by one, Jim, Sue, and Ann joined us in the station wagon. Dad was reeling from the divorce proceedings, and they were determined to lift his spirits, even though each had their own complicated history with Dad. Instead of a father-son adventure, it turned into a Griswold-style family vacation, but in a rented thirty-foot Apollo motorhome with shag carpeting and questionable plumbing.

Day after day, as we drove on, Millard wallowed. My siblings and I were a captive audience to his endless "poor me" act playing on repeat. He wasn't doing it on purpose, but his pain was still dragging us down with him. What a vacation it was! There were five of us, crammed into a beige behemoth hurtling down the highway. Picture epic sibling squabbles erupting in the cramped confines, Dad trying to navigate with a map the size of a small tablecloth, and Jim's daily protesting that he take over the driving. This wasn't just a road trip; it was slammed cabinet doors, bickering siblings, and a constant cloud of Jim's cigarette smoke mingling with the aroma of my sisters' angst. We were a traveling circus of dysfunction, a sitcom episode on wheels, complete with a laugh track provided by Dad's increasingly strained chuckle.

Thankfully there would come a respite for me during our pitstop in Atlanta. My sisters stumbled upon this gem called Underground Atlanta. It was like stepping back in time, with buildings dating back to the post–Civil War Reconstruction era. Hidden beneath these buildings was an underground street full of juke joints and speakeasies. My age didn't stop my adventurous sisters from taking me out that night. We ended up in a small club where a larger-than-life performer named Abner Jay was belting out tunes. He played every instrument you can think of—drums, harmonica, guitar, banjo—and his folksy blues vocals were something else. That he could do it all at once—a one-man band—was genuinely mind-blowing.

Although I didn't fully understand the meaning behind his lyrics, I was captivated by his voice and the unique sounds he produced. It wasn't until many years later that I decided to research him on the internet, only to discover that he had independently recorded his music on his own label—an innovative move at a time when record companies were still the only way to go. When I found his songs on Spotify, I was astounded by their content. He would begin his songs with introspective commentaries like, "Most so-called folk singers don't even look like folk. Folk songs tell true stories, terrible stories. Terrible songs make big songs. Why do you think kids like rock 'n' roll?" One of his most popular tracks was called "I'm So Depressed," in which he sang, "At the end of the year we had nothing but grasshoppers... Looking back at my life, oh Lord, I'm so depressed." However, it was another song, "Cocaine," that truly left me shocked as I listened to it through the lens of adulthood. The lyrics included lines like "Cocaine, cocaine, oh, it's running around my heart, and oh Lord, it's running, it's running around my brain."

Clearly, this music was not suited for a younger audience, but it introduced me to the concept of authenticity—a series of monologues encompassing subjects such as politics, relationships, drugs, war, and even the Bible. Abner, a Black man whose grandfather had been a slave, fearlessly expressed himself through his music, directly and prolifically communicating from his heart. I consider myself incredibly fortunate to have been exposed to him and his music at such a young age, with its clear deviation from societal standards of the day. He opened my eyes and ears to the power of music, and I found solace in it through all the confusion surrounding me.

10

FAMILY AFFAIR

Ronald Reagan, who loomed larger than life in Sacramento as California's governor, had signed the nation's first no-fault divorce law about three years before Carole had filed. This meant that couples no longer needed to prove grounds for divorce, such as adultery or cruelty. They could simply cite "irreconcilable differences." While this had simplified the legal process, it didn't erase the emotional turmoil my family continued to endure. The divorce proceedings between Millard and Carole were long and painful—for my parents, for my brother and sisters, and for me.

Dad played the manipulative victim to us kids while Mom used me as a pawn in her quest for freedom and financial gain. She was determined to acquire as much as possible, believing she was legally entitled to half of my father's earnings throughout their marriage, and she had found the best attorney in town. Meanwhile, Dad saw Mom's desire for separation as sadistically ripping apart his very identity—one of an upstanding family man and successful business owner. He was enraged. His was an image he'd carefully curated in his Rotary Club, his temple, and his community.

Mom leveraged custody of me, allowing me to go to Dad, to secure a more substantial financial settlement, giving him the house too, and eliminating the need for alimony, which he was reluctant to pay. It took two long years for my parents' drawn-out and bitter divorce to end, with the court granting Mom cash, half the business, and community property, including artwork and furniture accumulated over twenty-three years. In the end, I felt like a mere casualty, my well-being sacrificed in their power battle for assets.

Once they parted ways, Dad completely erased Mom from his life, refusing any further communication or acknowledgment. Mom would try to be cordial with Dad while he steadfastly avoided being in the same room as her, creating an atmosphere of constant tension and unease during weddings or other significant occasions.

Looking back, though, I can almost see the divorce approaching, hearing the distant rumble inside my parents. It's like seeing the faint outline of cracks in a wall long after the earthquake has passed. The screws were loose, and I, a child, was oblivious.

I can't forgive their neglect, but maybe, just maybe, I can understand it. Mom, gathering her courage, making her escape plan, taking me, *kidnapping* me, 3,000 miles away—a shield against the fallout. Dad, volatile and unpredictable, was left reeling in disbelief. "Sweetie," he'd call her. That word, dripping with irony, echoed for years.

And Mom? Did she already have someone waiting in the wings? That mysterious "injured arm" from an elevator door smashing it on her trip to New York City (where I didn't join), needing a bone doctor back home. A convenient excuse or a seed of a new life already planted? I'll never know if my mistrust was warranted or not. The truth, like so much else from that time, remains shrouded in mystery.

Dr. Harold H. Robinson, Jr., who went by *Hal* or *Rob* or *Pop* or *Papa Doc*, depending on which group of friends or family he was with, stood tall at 6 feet 3, his presence commanding, sometimes accompanied by the sweet waft of pipe tobacco. Mom was quite impressed by his distinguished name, with its formal title and air of legacy. His voice, deep with a touch of gravel, emanated authority and trustworthiness. His classically handsome features exuded an air of quiet confidence; his physique, not overly muscular, and his attire, conservatively tailored, spoke of understated wealth. His dark hair, though thinning slightly with a touch of gray, was slicked back. When he smiled, his face lit up and instilled an immediate sense of ease in those around him. Every aspect of Dr. Robinson conveyed the image of a distinguished man, a respected orthopedist. He and Carole began dating almost immediately after her office visit.

While it took me years to timidly trust him, he would turn out to be the one human who would know how to listen and be unconditionally supportive. Some months later, Mom and Dr. Robinson married in Lake Tahoe, and "Rob" became my stepfather.

When I was around ten or eleven years old, he'd plop me on his lap while driving, his voice reverberating, "Steer the car, help me drive." The wheel felt huge in my hands, the road stretching ahead. No grown-up had ever trusted me like that. He'd laugh at my jokes, buy me ice cream, and out of the blue, these words would warm me like sunshine after a storm: "You're good at that, Robbie!"

Dad was hit hard by the divorce, as it toppled his entire identity. Many people outside his inner circle had been unaware he was a minority owner of the company he touted as his own. Mom had given him half the money to invest, which she had inherited from her parents. Ironically, his business success never quite lived up to her grand aspirations for him. He obtained the other half of his investment from his father through what was probably a complicated conditional agreement. His father's youngest brother, his Uncle Harry, became his business partner for the other ownership share. Combined, Mom and my great-uncle owned 80 percent of my "father's company," and Dad's 20 percent came from his father.

Yet Dad remained deeply involved in the soft-drink industry, which made me popular by association. However, beneath the surface, I struggled with shyness, and like Dad, I, too, developed a tendency to please people, almost as if I felt a need to buy their love and attention. As a result, I gave away soft drinks to friends as a means of survival. I felt uncertain about my true identity, so I clung to the role of being *the provider of soda pop*, the undisputed king of beverages, a sweet and bubbly symbol of an era in American life. Back then, nobody batted an eye at cracking open a can of pop. It was the go-to drink for kids and adults

alike, a staple in everyday life, and ubiquitous at birthday parties, pic-
nics, and family dinners. The health risks associated with excessive sugar
consumption weren't as widely known or understood. Soda was simply
a delicious treat, a refreshing escape from the ordinary. Ironically, if this
was today, I might be considered *the purveyor of poison.*

I became quite skilled in making soft drinks and spent much of my
time at Dad's bottling plant. It was my escape, a place where I mattered,
a part of something bigger than myself. The constant hum of activity,
each worker with their own part to play, fascinated me. I'd wander the
plant, more engrossed than I ever was in school. There was even a special
corner where I'd tackle my homework, surrounded by the sweet smell of
7-Up and the rhythmic clank of machinery. Over time, I absorbed every
detail of the business—from the carbonated drinks poured at restaurants
to vending machines to the rows of colorful cans and bottles ready to be
shipped out.

I knew the family business inside and out. I could practically taste
the "UnCola" syrup extract, and feel the rhythm of the bottling line in
my body. But no one ever said, "Hey, Robbie, want to run this place
someday?" It was like this unspoken thing, a path laid out for some, but
not for me. Jim, my brother, stepped right into it, following in Dad's
footsteps, just like Dad had done with *his* dad. My sisters? Well, back
then, it was a man's world, so they weren't really in the running. Me?
I was on the outside looking in, a constant whisper of "You're on your
own" in the back of my mind. It didn't stop me from soaking up everything I could about the business, though.

There were times when the operation encountered obstacles that
couldn't be quickly resolved. It was during these instances that my father
became tense. Dad's brow furrowed as he barked orders at the line supervisor with contagious urgency in his voice. I'd feel my pulse quicken and
my stomach tighten. The stalled conveyor belt, the growing backup of
unfilled bottles—every minute of downtime was money down the drain,
a silent counter ticking away the profits. It was like the tension in the air

was choking us all.

Running a manufacturing plant involves dealing with plenty of labor concerns. Dad believed he was fair in his dealings. Opinions on Dad were a mixed bag. Some of the workers at the plant practically spit when they said his name, grumbling about long hours and lousy pay. Others swore he was the best boss they ever had, a fair man who looked out for his people. But one thing was for sure: whether they loved him or hated him, their opinion *mattered*. Dad, for all his bluster and tough talk, cared deeply about what his employees thought. Their approval was like fuel to his fire, a validation he craved. A validation that mattered more to him than his own family.

One night, I woke with a jolt to Dad's panicked voice.

"Robbie! Get dressed! We have to go, *now!*"

My heart hammered. What was happening? I scrambled into my clothes, fear running through my entire trembling body. In the car, my questions were met with a tense silence, his evasive answers only fueling my anxiety.

We arrived at the plant bathed in flashing blue and red. Police cars and firetrucks cast long, eerie shadows that danced across the front of the main office building. The air was thick with a suffocating stench, a mix of burned rubber, skunk, and rotten eggs. My stomach churned. Dad ordered me to stay in the car, his voice strained. I huddled in the backseat, every nerve on higher alert, the putrid smell making me gag.

Finally, he returned, his face grim. "Stink bomb," he growled as we drove away. "Union thugs trying to scare us. Teamsters." The words sounded dangerous, laced with his disgust. Even I, a kid who barely understood unions, knew this was serious.

The next day, the tension at home was a living thing. Dad paced, phone pressed to his ear, his voice tight with worry. "They want to shut us down," he confessed that night, his usual bravado gone. "After all I've done for those people...." I saw the fear in his eyes, the vulnerability beneath the tough exterior. It scared me more than any stink bomb ever could.

Though it was a commercial establishment, I found moments of genuine human connection. There was Jim Elder, for instance, a man who could've wrestled a grizzly bear and won. He'd been with Dad forever, it seemed, and his son, Duke, drove a forklift like a stuntman. But what I remember most about Jim wasn't his size, but his heart—and maybe that ever-present cigar butt he chomped on, leaving a trail of saliva in its wake. He always had a smile for me, a kind word, and a surprise tucked away—a cool sticker, a funny placard, some little treasure to brighten my day. And then there were the hot dogs. Jim loved 'em raw, straight from the package. "Same as bologna, Robbie!" he'd declare, munching a whole pack like it was candy. He even offered me one once, chuckling, "It's bologna, kid!" I politely declined, but his good-natured weirdness always made me smile.

I had never encountered someone of such immense size before. His colossal stature filled me with a tinge of intimidation, leaving me wonderstruck at how he managed to navigate and fit into everyday tasks, like sitting behind the wheel or using a toilet. I recall observing this gentle giant drive his logoed company-issued Ford Ranchero, which he had modified by adding air to the tires on the driver's side to account for his extra weight and to keep the vehicle balanced. Jim occasionally took me along his delivery route to restaurants and vending machines. Being his passenger and sidekick was an absolute blast. We would listen to the radio and sing along while he drove, and I vividly remember the first time I discovered Hank Williams, thanks to Jim's love for the song "Hey, Good Lookin'." He would yodel, sing, crack jokes, and even whistle when the radio was silent. His humor never failed to make me burst into laughter.

I would try to get Jim to speak with Dad on my behalf, acting as my confidant and persuading Dad to grant me permission for activities he had previously forbidden. One such activity was earning money, which Jim proposed I could achieve by painting the long white fence bordering the road in front of the plant. This didn't require the use of any power tools, which Dad forbade, so, fortunately, Dad approved the idea. Jim provided me with the sandpaper, scraper, paint cans, and brushes and patiently taught me the technique. I vividly recall applying coat after coat of paint to that fence in lieu of more sanding, dedicating days to completing the task. Even though it made my arms ache, I truly cherished every moment of it, as it gave me a strong sense of accomplishment and belonging. That summer odd job, however, was only a prelude to a significant shift in my life. A turning point was just around the corner.

11

TEENAGE WASTELAND

Mom had no interest in anything to do with me. Eager to start building a new life for herself, she began an interior design business, spent time with Rob's family, started art painting classes, cultivated old and new social circles, and sailed with Rob on weekends in the San Francisco Bay Area. I felt abandoned, and that was a pretty bitter pill for me to swallow.

"Robbie, I'll find you a new mother," Dad said.

The fact that he had written Carole off as if she were dead only intensified the dissociation with my mother. As I entered my teen years, it felt like I was wandering through a crowded room, yet utterly alone. My eldest stepbrother, Rob—or rather, Rob3, as I called him because my stepdad was also Rob, and *his* son was also Rob—had three children, who, in a slightly confusing turn of events, were all basically my peers. Though I had some reservations, I cunningly managed to snag a ride with them on their family vacation from San Francisco to Disneyland, the land of manufactured dreams. My mother was desperate for her new family to work, so she obsessed over me getting along with Rob3, his wife, and their kids. Her pressure made me suspicious and anxious, killing any chance of actually relaxing on this so-called vacation. It was the same old story: perform, please, and maybe, just maybe, you'll get a scrap of approval.

I found myself in the company of relative strangers, feeling out of sorts, a misplaced cog in the perpetually turning wheel of their traditions. They had a peculiar custom in which an unsuspecting group member possessing a pair of Levi's jeans would be tackled and wrestled by an onslaught of relatives who tore off the red tab on the rear pocket. The rationale behind this curious move eluded me, yet I, too, played along. They seemed to like physical interactions as in our hotel room, feather pillows took the brunt of our wild swings, rupturing upon impact and scattering across the space. I thought we kids were doomed for this act, but to my surprise, the parents received it with laughter, which was all very new to me. Then there were the misadventures of Rob3, the father and navigator, who, with unwavering conviction, insisted on his knowledge of direction. He drove blindly along a maze of errant freeways, misleading us for hours on end, lost in Los Angeles.

A maze I was being flung around in—that's how my life felt. Still trying to find me a *new* mom, Dad had reached out to the temple rabbi, and he'd introduced Dad to this lady, Janine, a widow with two sons. At that age, I lacked the maturity to process that; all I knew was that while Janine had a similar hairstyle to my mom, she was a world apart from her in every way. She *wasn't* my mom. Compared to Mom, who at least in public knew how to be charming, this lady seemed cold, reserved, and disinterested. She dressed more conservatively, was shorter, and had a thick French accent. I had seen how Mom took pride in how she dressed and carried herself with a certain dignity and class. My siblings and I had even nicknamed Mom, "The Queen." That was *not* Janine.

She had a bland home, similar to her personality, in a tract development on the opposite end of town. Dad married her quickly. I think he was lonely and the rabbi's blessing held a lot of weight. The physical intimacy they shared may have comforted Dad, too. He thought Janine and her two sons could live with us in the spacious, elegant William Land Park house I had grown up in, which Dad had moved back into after being granted the house in the divorce. Janine had other plans. She wanted to stay in her dull home located in a small suburb called Fair Oaks. While our home was much bigger and nicer and would have been a decided step up for her and her two sons, she did not want to disrupt their lives by moving them to a new neighborhood and a new school. So, Dad took the initiative to sell the family home and move into her house.

I was devastated by this decision because Janine's home was forty-five minutes away from my K-8 school, which had previously been within easy biking distance. Not to mention my childhood friends were all on this end of the city, and I would be living in significantly smaller quarters with three people I didn't know.

Living in the tract house in Fair Oaks, I rode a public city bus to school. It was dark out when I boarded at Sunrise Mall, and the trip took at least an hour because of the many stops—including a transfer in downtown Sacramento where I had to walk several blocks in a sketchy neighborhood that was no place for a kid. The school had its own bus that made stops to gather kids from various points of town outside of biking or walking distance, but I lived far beyond the radius of school bus stops.

Much of my day was spent riding the bus. Exhaustion was my constant companion. Miles from home, I'd have to rely on my dad, stepmom, or stepbrothers to come get me. Sometimes they showed up quickly, other times I waited for what felt like forever. And a few times, no one was available to come at all, leaving me with no choice but to walk those last miles alone. The worst was when I'd drift off to sleep and miss my stop entirely. Suddenly, I'd awaken, heart pounding, realizing I was stranded miles from home with no way to reach anyone. There were no cell phones back then, just the hope of finding a payphone at the next stop and a prayer that someone would answer. I'd wait, anxiety gnawing at me, each minute stretching into an eternity.

And the tiny house felt suffocating. Five people crammed into a dwarf house, making the tension thick.

"Has anyone seen my basketball?" one of the stepbrothers would ask, his voice tight.

"Well, I haven't touched it," the other would retort, a hint of accusation in his tone.

Every sigh, every footstep, every slammed door echoed through the thin walls, amplifying the feeling of being constantly on edge.

"Shhh!" Janine would hiss whenever I accidentally dropped something. "Do you have to make so much noise?" Sometimes she would say, "Pwee!" referring to my smell, even *after* I showered.

The stepbrothers likely felt invaded by two extra people, and all our dynamics were stretched. Evenings were the worst. We'd sit crammed together on the uncomfortable sofa, the television blaring a show none of us really wanted to watch, each of us retreating into our own thoughts. "Can we please change the channel?" I'd ask tentatively, only to be met with a chorus of groans and complaints. It felt like we were all holding our breath, waiting for the window of opportunity when we could escape to the privacy of our own rooms, where closed doors were common.

Dad's relationship with Janine was rocky, so to give Janine a break, he moved us out and suggested I go to a public school instead of completing my final eighth-grade year at my private school, Brookfield. I was relieved as we moved from Janine's house to an apartment in Carmichael, and I went to nearby Winston Churchill Middle School. When that school year was over, unfortunately, we moved again, *back* to Janine's.

Janine and I never clicked. She'd often taunt me in French, lacing her words with profanity she assumed I didn't understand. "The truth hurts, doesn't it, Robbie?" she'd sneer, tearing me down after any sensitivity I dared to show. But what pricked me the most wasn't the "truth" itself, but the cruel twist in her voice, the way she seemed to relish in my discomfort. It was sadistic.

Living in that cramped house, the tension was a constant weight on my chest. Every little disagreement felt like a seismic event, sending tremors of anxiety through me. My face would flush crimson, my head would pound, and my whole body would thrum with a desperate need to escape.

Early one evening, still during daylight, the pressure finally reached its breaking point. An argument with Janine escalated, and with a flick of her wrist, she hurled her vodka screwdriver at me. Her pungent alcohol splashed violently onto my face and into my eyes. Something inside me snapped. For the first time, I unleashed the anger I'd kept bottled up, yelling back at her, "Go fuck yourself, Janine!"

Humiliation and rage propelled me forward. I tore out of the house, the echo of yelling fading behind me. My hands trembled, and my heart pounded in my ears. I'd crossed a line, spoken words I couldn't take back. Each breath was a struggle, my chest constricted with a mix of fear and madness. The smell of alcohol and orange juice, a sickening reminder of the drink she'd forcefully hurled at me, clung to me as I ran. I had no plan, no destination, just a desperate need to escape. I arrived at a schoolyard about a half mile away, tucked myself into a corner of the campus where no one was, and curled up into a ball. I could *not* stop crying. It was hard to catch my breath. Waves of heat from the pressure in my head erupted throughout my veins, pounding me with a discharge of energy. This was likely a panic attack. I was about thirteen years old.

Time ticked by as darkness fell. Dad was to arrive home from work with me gone. Nothing would have made me happier than knowing that Dad and Janine were worrying and wondering where I went and what I was doing, feeling guilty for pushing me into this state of being. I was exhausted as I mentally visualized Dad and Janine becoming aware that they were driving me crazy, which gave me a trace of relief. I then wondered if Dad would be upset with Janine for making me unable to function as a human. I hoped and prayed my absence would influence him. The relationship between my father and my stepmom had deteriorated, and I dreamed of peace beyond that horrible house in Fair Oaks.

When I finally mustered up the courage to walk back home, the intense confrontation and my subsequent mental health crisis vividly replayed in my mind. Although seeing my father at home brought a slight sense of relief, it was quickly overshadowed by the overwhelming dread of what was to come. I was emotionally drained. My stomach churned. *How would Dad react? What would Janine say?* I desperately wanted my father to scoop me up in a hug, to ask if I was okay, to side with me, but fear choked the hope in my throat. *What if he was furious? Disappointed?*

"Where the hell were you?" My father's voice was sharp. "We were worried sick. You can't do that to us! Did you really sling foul language at Janine?"

Shame washed over me. "I ... I couldn't handle it," I mumbled, avoiding his gaze. "And then I just snapped."

Janine's voice, dripping with accusation, cut in. "You know you can't *ever* speak to adults like that, Robbie. I won't have it in this house, *my* house!"

"I know ... sorry," I whispered, the guilt twisting in my gut. Even though Janine had thrown a drink in my face, even though she'd made the house feel like a war zone, I still felt responsible for the whole mess. Maybe if I'd just kept quiet. Maybe if I hadn't yelled back.

"Millard," Janine continued, her voice taking on a fabricated sweetness, "He needs to understand this isn't acceptable. We can't have him losing his marbles and running off like this. What will the neighbors think?"

My stepbrothers, their faces a mixture of annoyance and indifference, shifted uncomfortably. I braced myself for the lecture, the inevitable siding with their mother.

In the end, it unfolded exactly as I feared. Janine, with her practiced innocence, twisted the narrative. My father, caught in the middle, chose to believe her. I was alone, unsupported, and betrayed, with a knot of unease growing in my chest and no one to turn to.

Another incident that continues to haunt me involved my stepbrothers. It took place at Dad's bottling plant. They were tasked with washing the massive trucks on weekends. These trucks would carry pallets laden with cans and bottles and were adorned with masterfully painted logos and slogans of the company's various brands, including 7-Up, Orange Crush, and A&W Root Beer. I was fascinated by how these trucks looked and by my father's insistence that they always be kept in pristine condition, and I secretly dreamed of driving one someday.

One morning after Sunday school, my stepbrothers took me to the plant where they would wash the trucks. A vast weed-filled field was between the road in front of the plant and the railroad tracks on the other side. The stepbrothers commandeered a giant tractor tire they had found, and we were going to play with it, curling up inside it and having the others roll us down the road. They told me I was first.

They blindfolded me. They tied my hands together and pushed me down into the hard thick rubber edges of the tire's interior. Suddenly, my legs were thrown above my head as they spun the tire. My world was reduced to sounds: the rushing wind past my ears, the thud of the tire rolling and bouncing over the uneven ground, my heartbeat pounding like a drum in my chest. I shouted for them to get me out, but it felt like they were no longer there.

Disoriented with every spin, cold fear pulsed through me. This spinning prison held me captive, my fate unknown. Cries for help were useless, swallowed by the whirling tire. My body, flung against the rubber walls, was helpless to move. Then, an abrupt stop. A smack. The smell of hot asphalt. Trapped, my ears rang with the sudden silence.

Then came a sound that brought *more* panic. A car was approaching. What if the driver couldn't see me inside? I heard a screech of tires. *But would they get out and hear me screaming for help?* The metallic groan of the car door opening was the most beautiful clank I'd ever heard, and in an instant, I was rescued. But the relief was short-lived.

Returning to the plant, finding it locked, and realizing my stepbrothers had left me to this fate, ignited a hatred unlike anything I'd ever known. It was a white-hot fury that pulsed through my veins, eclipsing the fear, demanding retribution. I was going to hurt them—make them pay for what they did. This was rage! Armed with a broken glass bottle, I embarked on a revenge mission. Somehow, I made my way inside the grounds, pacing along a catwalk above the bottling line, which happened to be inactive at the time. I intended to wait until the stepbrothers arrived in that area and then hurl the sharp bottle at them.

I don't remember what happened next. I do recall my father and step-mother arriving at some point. I never did throw the bottle. Upon seeing Dad and Janine—the people who were *supposed* to be my parents—I ran toward them, crying and screaming about what had happened. And then, the ultimate betrayal. My father, my protector, the man I craved approval from, didn't understand. He superficially soothed, but he didn't *hear* me. He didn't see the terror, the violation, the rage. My stepmother, cold and dismissive, offered no comfort, only judgment. Even my stepbroth-ers, the perpetrators of this cruel joke, seemed to have more support than I did. I was alone, drowning in a sea of injustice, abandoned by the very people who should have been my refuge.

That day, something broke inside me. The world, once a place of safety and trust, became a battleground where those closest to me could become my tormentors. The tire incident became a symbol of that betrayal, a scar on my soul that time can never fully erase.

12

WAKE ME UP WHEN SEPTEMBER ENDS

I'm convinced my father, too, suffered trauma in his childhood and didn't have anyone help *him* develop healthy coping mechanisms or ways to self-soothe. He had frustrated outbursts and snarled asides, the message invariably the same: "Why does this always happen to *me*? What did *I* do to deserve this?" Dad would lash out instead of taking personal inventory for wrongs like his divorce. Over time, a creeping cynicism began to dull his worldview, obscuring any glimmer of hope.

I remember him telling me a story about his childhood that had erupted into a messy scenario. He said, "I can't remember what I had done that set my parents off, but I was so fearful of their retaliation that I had to leave town." Dad felt that his life was in such jeopardy that he needed to flee his home in order to survive. He was a young boy in the early 1930s when he escaped. He took Northern Pacific trains 635 miles from San Francisco to Portland, and showed up unannounced on his grandmother's porch. While he did eventually return home after evading the feared punishment, I believe this traumatic experience remained ingrained in his subconscious and was triggered throughout his life.

Dad wasn't the only one who endured turmoil during his adolescence. When it was time for me to go to high school, Mom pointed me to a private preparatory school for boys called Jesuit High School.

"It's got a great academic program," she said, "and it'll be a good fit for you. It's the perfect steppingstone."

She had been the one to insist I get a private K-8 education. Founded when I was a toddler and administered by the USA West Province of the Society of Jesus, Jesuit High School was a strange place for a Jew, but the school offered an incomparably better academic program than a public school. This seemed to fulfill Mom's long-held dreams for my future, the ones she'd often voiced about me becoming a lawyer or doctor. But deep down, I knew I wasn't cut out for that life. While I'd entertained the idea of becoming an architect, drawn to the creative aspects of design and construction, even that path felt too confined. The world of academia, with its rigid structures and expectations, felt suffocating. I yearned for something more expressive, more ... *me*.

Dad wasn't wild about the choice, likely due to the cost he would have to pay. After acceptance, I met with the school as part of the initiation. The campus was extremely well-manicured, and I noticed many crosses and crucifixes throughout. I had little knowledge of theology beyond the teachings of Judaism crammed into me through Sunday school, having a bar mitzvah, going to Grandma and Grandpa's, and growing up around the temple grounds.

I felt immediate intimidation and some physical discomfort. Then I went into an office, and a gentleman in a full-collar shirt and jet-black outfit, which I later learned was called a cassock, sat me in front of his desk and began describing how the school functioned and what classes I would be taking as a freshman. He showed me a list of five or six subjects, one of which was theology. I froze in fear, and my eyes probably popped out of my head.

"Theology?" I stammered; my voice barely above a whisper. "But ... I'm Jewish."

The man, whose name I later learned was Father O'Malley, smiled kindly. "That's perfectly all right," he reassured me. "Theology here is about exploring different faiths and beliefs, not converting anyone."

Yet the only thing I could think of was that kick in the balls that had left me injured when I was small and I was in fight-or-flight mode.

"But... there are no girls here," I blurted out, "and it's a long commute, and I'll have to wear a uniform again! I just want to be normal and go to a public school!"

Father O'Malley nodded understandingly. "I appreciate your honesty," he said. "It's important to find the right environment where you can thrive."

In a panic, I informed Dad that I was not comfortable going to a school where antisemitism could be prevalent. He didn't put up a fight. A few days later I was enrolled in a public high school, Del Campo High, close to Janine's house.

At school, I befriended a confident, shoulder-length, brown-haired, cool guy who was a senior. A group of us would ditch the school campus at lunchtime, head to his house in his black muscle car, and smoke weed laced with honey and hash oils. It wasn't my first time lighting up, though. My sister, Anna, and one of her high school boyfriends, a Black student nicknamed "Steamboat" (who, unfortunately, my parents disapproved of due to their prejudices), had introduced me to the joys of marijuana at the tender age of nine or ten. Back then, it was more about the thrill of the forbidden than the actual high, but it certainly made those lunchtime sessions feel a bit more familiar. There were always pretty girls who came along because my friend was popular, and I would ogle them.

A girl who was seemingly obsessed with me was Lolita Galinda. She'd pop up in the hallways alongside me multiple times daily. In any classes we shared, she sat near me and even called me at home out of the blue. She was much taller than I was, very thin, model-like, Latina, and charming. Yet I was busy stalking a quiet, popular hippie girl named Haven Biddle. I loved her first name, hairstyle, and how sweet and shy she looked.

One day, some weed gave me a surge of confidence, and I blurted out to Haven, "Can I walk you home?" The afternoon sun cast long shadows, as she walked, and I slowly rode my bike in circles. We awkwardly got near her house, and I lingered when we reached her doorstep. I waited for the invitation, the "Come on in." It never came. My stomach did a slow flip when she politely said, "Thanks, I've got it from here." Back then, a guy walking a girl home from school meant something more than just being friendly. I was sure she felt it, too, that unspoken spark. Maybe I was wrong. Had I misread everything?

Disappointment pricked at me, then the heat of embarrassment. I'd built it all up in my head, this perfect scene. Now, I just felt foolish. What would my friends say? I cringed, replaying every moment, searching for clues I'd missed. Maybe, though, we were just on different pages, two awkward teenagers stumbling through unspoken expectations.

To distract myself, I decided to give sports a try, and track seemed like a decent option. But instead of sprints or long distances, I went for the most outlandish event I could find: pole vaulting. Picture this: a skinny, uncoordinated kid flinging himself into the air with a flimsy pole, hoping to somehow clear a bar that seemed miles above the ground. Yeah, pure entertainment. Maybe it was Dad's fault. He'd been a runner in his day, and his enthusiasm for track felt a bit like pressure. Though maybe it was his way of subtly steering me away from the radio, from the world of music that had begun to consume me. Picking the most outlandish event was my way of rebelling, of choosing something so impossibly difficult that I could practically guarantee failure.

As for my home life, Dad and Janine announced we were moving to a larger house. "It'll give us all space to breathe," Dad said, his voice strained. The option of living with Mom never crossed my mind. Dad's words that should have never been uttered to a ten-year-old still echoed in my head: *Your mother never really wanted you. She wouldn't know what to do with you.* In reality, he was thinking solely of himself. To him, I was merely a possession, an object he twisted into a weapon against Mom, used to inflict pain and suffering. After all, he'd still say things like, "If you leave me, I'll have nothing left to live for." The threat of me being responsible for his suicide always hung in the air.

Unfortunately, the larger La Honda Court home didn't improve the relationships between Dad, his new wife, her sons, and me. It was a constant war of words that led to us being thrown out a few times to motels for shelter. After my freshman year would come a final separation, a divorce between the two warring family units, with Dad and I moving *again*. This time into a two-bedroom townhouse close enough to get myself to and from high school on my own.

13

EVERYBODY HURTS

As a young kid, I was fascinated by our hi-fi and later our upgraded home stereo system. Fiddling with the components became a hobby when I wasn't playing capture the flag or hide-and-seek with friends. I loved to entertain and be the center of attention, both at home and in school. So, spinning records at parties and dances seemed like a natural fit. I was resourceful when it came to acquiring the equipment I needed, whether it was "borrowing" components from our stereo, snagging the portable loudspeakers from the temple, or figuring out how to rent what I needed. Radio Shack, *the* retail chain store to go for all things electronic at the time, became a frequent stop for things like a Realistic microphone. I'd scour a local electronics supply house for other accessories.

I was now an officially minted teenager at fourteen years old, and I longed for acceptance and love. There was also an angry and scared part of me that wanted to push my parents away. An ambition to gain independence was raging within me. This caused confusion and vulnerability and would make me susceptible to anyone showing care, love, and the feeling of safety that I desperately needed.

I began playing phone-in radio contests because I was excited to hear my name, or sometimes even my voice, on the radio, announcing me as a winner. The attention made me feel acknowledged and heard; it validated my human existence. The afternoon deejay would solicit listeners to call the station: "Hi, this is The Spear Chucker, Chuck Hale, and you're listening to 14-70 K-N-D-E ... be the fourteenth caller now to *win*!"

Most of the time, when I tried calling, I'd hear a busy signal. But sometimes, I cracked the cadence of the promotional announcements and stood by my phone ready to punch in the numbers. You had to have a push-button phone, as opposed to a rotary dial, and fast fingers to be competitive. I made sure that my dad had push-button phones at our house. "Hi, you're caller five, try again," then a click. I tried again and again. And one day I nailed a prize from KROI FM I-97, an FM station I thought was new and cool at a time when AM radio still dominated the airwaves.

Mom would pick me up for a visit about once a week. She would say, "I've cried and cried since our last visit, I've missed you terribly." But I'd been conditioned to despise her and questioned her sincerity. I also couldn't shake the sense that when I was with her, she seemed to be simply going through the motions.

When she pulled up to my father's house a few days after I'd won the I-97 call-in-to-win contest, I begged her to drive me to the radio station. She begrudgingly agreed to do it and waited in the car outside while I went inside to claim my prize, which the deejay had only described as a "living thing" in honor of the new Electric Light Orchestra (ELO) song, "Was it an animal?"

Upon entering, there was a reception desk with nobody there. Being unsure what healthy boundaries were, I boldly wandered down a long hallway, thinking I might get a glimpse of the studio where the deejay was broadcasting. I spotted a guy in a room with a wall of reel-to-reel tape machines.

"Where are the turntables and the deejay?" I asked.

He motioned me to follow him. As we walked back toward the reception desk, he explained, "Don't tell any of your friends, but we're an automated station that tapes everything in advance." Just then, the receptionist emerged from the restroom. I wondered if she sensed how important I felt, having learned such a huge secret!

My new friend introduced himself as Robert John, which of course made an impression because that was also my first and middle name. I shared the coincidence with him while he laughed, and the receptionist gave me a gift certificate for a house plant that was revealed as the "living thing."

Back in the car, even my disconnected mom noticed how excited I was. I told her of my thrill at meeting a deejay and receiving my prize. "Oh, that's wonderful, Robbie," she said, without even looking at me. She glanced in the mirror while reapplying her lipstick. I kept the secret Robert John had told me to myself.

Back at school, I signed up to help with the yearbook, thinking I could submit photographs, do some graphics, maybe even write some captions, and learn how a book was created. Instead, I was assigned the unglamorous job of selling ads in the back of the book, either to parents congratulating their new high school graduates or to local pizza parlors or ice cream shops for a coupon ad offering discounts to students.

One day not long after visiting the radio station, I had an idea: If I call that guy at the station with the same name as me, maybe the station will buy an ad? It was worth a try. Unbelievably, the receptionist remembered me and put me through to Robert John. School let out, and I was off. My sturdy red, white, and blue ten-speed carried me toward the radio station as my heart pounded with anticipation. He'd invited me back, and I had a shot at selling an ad for the yearbook. The thought of returning to that world of microphones and music, of impressing him *and* my yearbook team, sent a thrill through me.

When I got to the station, I waited in the reception area and a moment later Robert John appeared. It turned out he was both the station's program director and a deejay who recorded his show using what they called automated "voice tracks." He had that classic 1970s deejay look: shoulder-length straight hair, shiny and dark; matching mustache and beard; black-rimmed aviator glasses; button-down, short-sleeve, swirling patterned shirt, untucked; and flared mahogany brown polyester pants. He was short and slim, with the beginnings of a beer belly. With a cigarette dangling from his mouth, he invited me to sit in his tiny office next to the reception area.

I went into my pitch: "Mr. John ...."

He interrupted, "Just call me Robert John."

I barked, "Remember, that's my name too!"

We both chuckled.

I continued: "I'm here because I want I-97 to buy an ad in the Del Campo yearbook."

He listened intently to my persuasive pitch and said, "I'd like to do it, but I can't make that decision, and even if I could, it wouldn't be fair for us to be in one high school yearbook and not in others."

I was disappointed because I had my hopes up that this would be a sale, and I felt as though I had accomplished something just by getting the meeting with such a big shot. Then a thought suddenly came to me.

"Robert John, listen, if there's anything you guys need here at the station, I'm really interested in working here. I love music, and I'm reliable and willing to sweep, clean, or do whatever you need. Maybe I can get school credits? My dream is to be a deejay on the radio."

He politely replied that there was no budget for a paid intern, but he'd consider hiring me to answer song request phone lines on the condition that a parent sign a document acknowledging that I would get no pay and that I was working as a minor with their permission.

I took the piece of paper home and swiftly found Dad. "I got an internship that will give me great experience, but you have to sign this, please," I told him, so excited the words all seemed to run together. After the usual barrage of questions and conditions such as, "Will you still have time to do your schoolwork ... because otherwise, I'll pull the plug on it," he signed the document.

I was fourteen years old, and most of my friends didn't even have jobs. The ones who did mowed lawns or washed cars. Me? I was a freshman in high school working at a real radio station. It was exhilarating being around the deejays, the music, the energy of it all. Robert John, especially, made me feel like I was part of something special. As program director, he decided what music we played and what contests we ran. He knew everything about radio, and he was teaching me the ropes. He treated me like an equal, like a younger brother, and I soaked up his attention like a sponge. While other kids my age were doing chores or hanging out at the mall, I was learning about music programming and promotions, feeling the thrill of being the youngest one in the room, and being treated like an adult by someone I admired.

Several months into my job, Dad was as distant as ever, lost in his own world of work and worry. Stress seemed to weigh heavily on him, his mind miles away. I was riding my bike to and from the studio after school, getting home late, and falling behind in my schoolwork, despite my promise to him, but he was so consumed by his own troubles that he didn't even notice.

One evening, Dad announced, "Robbie, I have to go out of town this weekend for a bottling convention. Your mother, well, as usual, she won't be around. Hey, didn't you mention your boss, Robert John, lives nearby?"

"Yeah," I replied, surprised he even remembered.

"Well," Dad continued, "do you think he might be able to keep an eye on you while I'm gone?"

My heart leaped. "Sure, Dad! I can ask him."

"That's a relief," Dad said with a distracted pat on my shoulder. He was already halfway out the door, his briefcase in hand, his thoughts clearly elsewhere.

By then, Robert John had met Dad and gained his trust. And when Robert John offered to let me crash on his couch, Dad readily agreed to leave me in the care of this so-called adult.

I remember sitting on a lima bean-colored sofa with him in his small living room. He brought out a yellow box of Triscuit crackers, a foil package of Philadelphia cream cheese, a bottle of barbecue sauce, and several cans of cheap beer, and set everything up on the worn wood-grain coffee table. He told me we could watch some TV and explained that he was working with a young actor named Philip McKeon, who was on the sitcom *Alice* and was also interested in being a radio deejay. I was awestruck that he knew people in Hollywood. He spread some cream cheese on a cracker and added a dollop of barbecue sauce, followed by a few swigs of beer. I was impressed with this tasty treat, too young and wide-eyed to see it as a hillbilly concoction.

Then he lit up some weed flowers and we shared a joint. *He is da man*, I thought. He'd shown me how radio stations operate, the technical aspects, and what each job required. *Maybe he'll give me a deejay gig one day!* He was also taking more of an interest in me than in any of the other employees. I felt like I was his little buddy. I trusted him, as much as I could trust anyone, and our friendship was like this secret we kept from everyone else. We would talk about all sorts of subjects, including girls and sex, stuff I didn't feel comfortable discussing with anyone in my family. Sometimes Robert John would touch me in ways that felt brotherly, like a hug, tickles, and even a little massage.

That evening, he placed his hand around my shoulder and began to rub my belly with his other hand. "Doesn't that feel good?" he asked. I didn't know what to say. I merely nodded in agreement. Inside, though, something felt off. I got a gut feeling my space was being violated. *What is he doing to me?* I thought.

He rubbed my belly some more. I closed my eyes and clenched my jaw as my body froze and I tried to wish myself somewhere else. Suddenly I found my zipper being undone. He reached his hand through the opening, rustled around in my underwear until he felt my penis, and then began stroking, pulling, stroking, pulling.... I felt weak, dizzy, and couldn't move. I didn't understand how what I had interpreted as a caring friendship was now a horrendous nightmare. My heart was racing. My mouth was dry. I felt tremors in my body. Then, things got even worse. I got an erection, giving me a semblance of complicity. There was something hideous and monstrously awful about this and I wanted to throw up. The entire episode was over in a few minutes, but the wound would last a lifetime.

After that, I was more withdrawn around Robert John and he could tell. "Hey," he'd said, his voice soft, "I know you enjoyed it. It'll be our little secret. I won't tell anyone, as long as you don't." He, the predator, the perpetrator of this crime, tried to enlist me as an accomplice. As a boy, I bought his disgusting tricks, but as an adult survivor, I realize the child I was didn't deserve, or desire, any aspect of what he did to cripple my spirit and further erode any ability to trust.

14

MAD WORLD

I tried to block out what had happened from my mind and continued to work for the station, partly out of desperation to belong to something, and also because I kept hearing that by "paying my dues" I would succeed. "Just keep at it," one of the deejays had said, "and you'll get your shot."

Fortunately, Robert John kept his distance and moved on a few months later. His exit came when the station changed owners, commercialized its format, and moved its studio to a trendier part of town to join its AM sister station 1240 KROY.

The new studio was no longer a bike ride away, so I took the bus to continue my work in the hope of eventually getting on the air as a bona fide radio deejay. I spent every free moment at the station, mastering the radio equipment, poring over albums, and losing myself in the world of music. It felt as though I could practically run the station myself. Driven by this passion, I even studied for and earned my FCC deejay license, officially known as a "restricted radiotelephone operator permit." That meant a trip to San Francisco to take a test I had judiciously studied for. I was a teenage kid, navigating the big city by myself for the very first time, all for the chance to chase my dream. I had made friends with other deejays and employees and felt like part of the station's family. But I also knew I didn't want to trust the wrong person again.

The new program director granted me a Saturday night spot on the air and I became what the station proudly billed as "Sacramento's

Youngest Deejay." With Robert John gone, it was like a new start. This wasn't just a job. *It was a dream come true.*

I had also begun playing records at my Jewish temple. Uncle John owned a retail outdoor recreation store called Marin Surplus. In the future, when I'd get my driver's license, he'd take a chance on me and hire me to spin at the store's Christmas parties in San Rafael, about an hour-and-a-half-long drive away.

School bookings were great, too. For my gigs, I used a set list similar to a live band, with pre-selected songs I would spin to get everybody on the dance floor at one time or another. The more people drank, the more they would get into it. Curating a good playlist and discovering which songs got people dancing gave me insight into popular music. And unlike radio deejays, who couldn't see who was listening, I could see exactly what type of people liked what type of music.

At my job at I-97, the phone was always ringing. People would call the shared switchboard with the AM station, looking to hire a deejay for their events. The receptionist had no one to refer them to, so I saw an opportunity.

"Hey," I said to her one day, "if anyone calls looking for a deejay, give them my name and number."

She looked surprised. "Really? You want to deejay all those gigs?"

"Not exactly," I explained. "I'll handle all the details—the contracts, the equipment, the bookings. Then I'll get one of our on-air deejays to actually spin the tunes." It was a world I was comfortable and familiar with. I either owned or knew where to get the necessary equipment, and I had a good grasp of how to book gigs.

She smiled. "Smart! You're like a deejay agent."

And that's how it started. My weekends soon included organizing parties, weddings, and school dances. I was the behind-the-scenes guy, making sure the music played and the good times rolled. Deejays liked having me as a resource, leading to a growing business.

One unforgettable memory happened in a shopping center. There was a newer mall called Country Club Plaza, which was a short distance from an older mall called Country Club Centre. The newer mall had trendy marquee stores, while the old one had discount stores and other less posh offerings. The newer mall was neat, clean, and buzzing with foot traffic. The old one was dated, shabby, and half-empty.

The old mall's management, desperate for business, was willing to try almost anything to attract more people. So, I was asked to provide the setup for a nostalgic 1950s-style sock hop at the Country Club Centre. I would spin the records and provide a sound system, while a radio station deejay would host dances and contests.

The pair of speakers I was using were thin columnar stacked loud-speakers built into an encasement about four feet tall. Each column stood independently, spaced about twelve feet apart, but their top-heavy design made them somewhat unstable. The deejay system for spinning the records was on a center table, slightly behind the speakers.

The event was coordinated by a sales representative from the radio station named Dick Fleming. He was an older man, probably in his early to middle 50s, experienced, kind, and calmer than most of the younger salespeople. I was happy to help him and took pride in my job that evening. Seeing the sparse crowd, I realized the several people who'd started dancing weren't attracting much attention. If we wanted the promotion to be a success, we needed to draw a bigger audience. My instinct was to get more people involved and I nudged the deejay to make more announcements on the mic. Luckily, a few of my radio station colleagues were also there, and when they joined the dancers, passersby stopped to watch, and the crowd began to grow. Even Dick joined in.

I was feeling good about the growing crowd when, out of the corner of my eye, I saw Dick stumble and grab a speaker for support. Then, in a horrifying instant, his face turned ashen, his eyes rolled back, his veins turned dark blue and he collapsed with a thump. The speaker toppled onto his forehead, blood gushing from the impact. He lay motionless, the music suddenly jarring against the stunned silence. My heart pounded in my chest as panic surged through the crowd. Someone yelled for help, but it was clear this was beyond first aid.

I felt a wave of nausea wash over me as I frantically shut off the music. We couldn't continue; it felt obscene. As people gathered around Dick's lifeless body, I numbly began packing up the equipment, my hands shaking. Paramedics arrived what felt like an eternity later, but it was too late. They pronounced Mr. Fleming dead.

The image of his fall, the sickening thud of the speaker, the stark whiteness of his eyes against his ashen skin—it haunted me for weeks. Sleep offered no escape from the gruesome replay. This was my first encounter with death, a sudden and brutal one, and it shook me to my core. Watching Dick, a kind and gentle soul, die before my eyes before he hit the ground made me realize how quickly one can go from life to death—and how good people tend to be the ones to pass on first. The fragility of life, the abrupt transition from vibrant energy to lifeless stillness, was terrifyingly real.

15

GIVE A LITTLE BIT

The station's new Program Director, Richard Irwin, was slender, button-nosed, balding, and mustachioed. He listened to me, encouraged me, took my suggestions seriously, and even implemented some of my ideas. Outwardly, I was friendly and willing to learn, work hard, and listen. Inside, I weighed the value of being on the air against my reluctance to be his friend when deep down something felt *off*.

"You've got a good ear, kid," he'd said with a wink, "a real knack for this." Richard wasn't shy about wanting to spend time with me. "Come on," he'd say, "let me show you how to sequence songs through system codes." He explained the why behind every action, the subtle art of connecting with an audience, building a mood, and crafting an unforgettable listening experience. He was busy converting the station from taped automation to live deejays around the clock, and I was fascinated and felt special as he unlocked the secrets of the radio universe I would need to succeed in broadcasting. He wasn't just teaching me the nuts and bolts of running a radio station, he was sharing accumulated wisdom, insights, and strategies he'd honed over many years in the industry. Sometimes his encouragement gave me a rush of adrenaline and made me believe in him and even gain some trust, like he cared about me. Yet he had a creepy vibe that bordered on obsessive, and he began to make me feel uncomfortable.

I was not too familiar with homosexuality before meeting Richard Irwin. Robert John was a seemingly straight guy with some closeted predilection for young boys. Richard Irwin, on the other hand, was rumored to be gay but conflicted about it. He also seemed weird and socially awk-ward. I sensed a sinister vibe beneath his surface-level courtesy. I didn't trust him the way I did Robert John, but I did look up to him and sensed his attraction to me through long stares. At about fifteen years of age, I was a late bloomer to puberty, and that might have explained part of Robert John's and Richard's curiosity with me, as I appeared to be more innocent and docile, exactly what predators are looking for—victims whom they can groom to become dependent on them in some manner.

For some reason that I can't remember, I ended up in his dingy apartment. And that's where he struck. It still makes my stomach hurt to talk about this, but Richard went further in his sexual acts with me than Robert John. I remember, "Give a Little Bit" from Supertramp playing in the background, the smell of his Brut aftershave, and how impressed he was with his bicep muscles.

First, he tried to make me loosen up by sharing lame impersonations and bad jokes. His witticisms contained racist and misogynistic under-tones. I wasn't sure if he was trying to impress me or test my boundaries, but it left me feeling uneasy. It was a strange mix of attempted hospi-tality and awkward tension, and I couldn't quite shake the feeling that something wasn't right. He laughed out loud at his own punchlines, seemingly oblivious to my discomfort, and I forced a smile, unsure how to respond. And somehow, after he plied me with weed and alcohol—rum and Cokes, heavy on the rum—he convinced me to take my shirt off.

Then he deviously glared, raping me with his wanting little beady eyes. I wanted to vomit from disgust. He must have felt my trepidation as he then made promises—followed by direct threats. Painfully, I remem-ber disassociating from my being, my inhibitions being lowered, and succumbing to him fondling me while being so drunk and stoned that I could hardly stand up. As I crept in and out of consciousness, his aggres-sion continued.

"No!" I yelled in moments of lucidity. Or "Stop!" But he disregarded my words. My efforts to avoid further physical contact failed and he began orally copulating me and rubbing his body against mine with an erection on at least two occasions. I was able to push him further away from me those times. In my hazy state, I tried to put it all out of my mind, thinking, *If I can put up with this, it'll all be okay and I'll get to do what matters to me—radio, music.* I felt like I'd forsaken myself.

Then if all that had already taken place wasn't enough, Richard snapped a few Polaroids with me half-naked and quickly stashed them in a locked military-style trunk the size of a small coffee table.

"*I* have these, and you're getting what *you* wanted. Remember who put you on the air!" he warned as he gestured toward his trunk, showing me he had the upper hand if I ever told anyone about what happened.

Overwhelmed with degradation, I went to the bathroom and threw up. My heartbeat was sluggish.

At the station, I remained afraid of the monster Richard had shown himself to be and was terrified that if I told someone I'd face extreme humiliation, and lose my beloved job—the redemption of my life. I tried hard to make sense of what had happened, to accept it, to navigate working for this freak while standing my ground. And yet I felt like everyone at the station was staring at me when they saw me, even though Richard swore he wouldn't say a word. The way he looked at me, peering with expressive desire ... I convinced myself they must know.

Fortunately, within a few weeks, the other station in the building, Top 40 KROY AM, bailed me out with a job in its programming department and then the weekend overnight deejay shift. I saw Richard Irwin in the hallways from time to time but rarely exchanged more than a brief glance.

Thinking back to that locked trunk where he had stashed the photos of me shirtless, I imagined a frightening box of horrors filled with sexual paraphernalia and photos of his other victims. I retreated further into myself, tough on the outside but wounded and terrified on the inside. Every whisper in the station hallway held a potential accusation. My heart hammered in my chest in constant fear. Anger simmered beneath the surface, a bitter brew of confusion and betrayal.

But I couldn't show this, not to them. These men, with their smiles and their power, twisted everything into something I supposedly *wanted*. *If Richard and Robert John were capable of what they did, what were other adults capable of?* When Irwin's eyes met mine after, I had a cold glint replace any warmth. My body screamed its revulsion. His response, his displeasure was a tangible weight. I felt unspoken threats.

There have been times I've thought it was my fault, wishing I was someone else, someone not living with low self-esteem and depression. My relationship with both my parents was strained; I constantly felt worthless like I wasn't living up to their vision for me. With the relentless upheaval in my life—the divorces, the moves, the blended family struggles—everything felt unstable. It left me vulnerable to Robert John and Richard Irwin, both of whom groomed me to trust them. Robert John listened to me, head tilted like every word I said was a precious secret. Richard Irwin always knew the right joke, the perfect compliment to slip in. They held before me a sense of warmth and belonging that I desperately craved. At the time I felt a powerful relief of not being alone that blinded me to their true intentions.

I would end up self-medicating, misreading, avoiding, blaming myself and others, stewing over being a victim of perpetrators who were never caught, and living with many shameful flaws because of these horrid experiences. Paradoxically, for me, the deeper the trauma wound, the harder it was to recall precise details. I would eventually come to terms with these feelings. Experiencing these events would also increase my empathy toward all victims of molestation and rape.

The question that would plague me for years: *How can events from my adolescence continue to shape and define my adult life?* These people in positions of greater power, strength, authority, and experience violated my rights, my body, and my being.

16

LONDON CALLING

The townhouse into which my Dad and I moved after his final excising of Janine and her two horrible sons felt more like a prison than a home. It was just Dad and me now, and we were like ships passing in the night. He'd come home late, exhausted and withdrawn, his posture defeated, his eyes hollow.

"Rough day?" I'd venture tentatively, hoping to spark a conversation.

"What do *you* think?" he'd retort, his voice sharp with frustration. "It's always something."

Dinner was a silent affair, the clinking of forks against plates echoing in the emptiness. He was lost in his own world, his emotional pain evident. Trying to talk to him was like shouting into a void.

"Dad," I'd try again, "Is there anything I can do?"

"Just leave me alone," he'd mumble, turning away.

I felt myself suffocating in the oppressive silence. I was a latchkey kid, fending for myself with TV dinners, Hamburger Helper, and lonely evenings. I felt lost and invisible in the shuffle of Dad's workaholic life. His negativity weighed on me constantly.

"Why does everything have to be such a struggle?" he'd often grumble, his face etched with worry lines. "Why can't anything ever go right?"

His words, like a dark cloud, would dampen any glimmer of joy or optimism I tried to muster. I don't know where the spark of defiance came from, but one day, something snapped.

"I'm just ... so tired of feeling like I'm not good enough," I confessed, my voice cracking with emotion. "Like I'm always disappointing you."

He looked at me, his expression softening slightly. It was the first time I'd ever openly expressed my feelings to him, and for a moment, the distance between us seemed to shrink.

But that feeling was fleeting. He quickly retreated back into his shell, his gaze falling to the floor.

"I ... I don't know what to say," he mumbled, his voice barely above a whisper.

I couldn't take it anymore. This wasn't living; it was merely existing. I needed a change, an escape, to break free from the oppressive atmosphere, where I didn't feel responsible for him. I had to find a place where I could breathe, where I could be myself. That place, I hoped, was with my mother.

I was still working at the radio stations, but I also knew of a high school with an amateur radio station on campus. That high school was somewhat near Mom's house, and I set a target of trying to figure out how I could convince Mom and Rob that I needed to live with them and attend Rio Americano High. Having a radio station at school, I figured, would make the whole high school experience a lot more bearable. It would be a place where I could pursue my passion and connect with others who shared my interest.

Leaving was more complicated than just packing a bag, though. First, Mom's address wasn't zoned for Rio Americano High. Why move in with her just to end up at El Camino, a school without a radio station? Second, I was afraid that my leaving would push Dad over the edge.

The second divorce had hit him just as hard as the first one. We'd gone from a spacious house with a park across the street through several other moves to a musty townhouse apartment that reeked of mildew and gloom. Burnt orange shag carpeting, mismatched furniture, and an air of defeat hung heavy. It was a far cry from the life we once knew, a stark reflection of Dad's broken spirit.

Most of the familiar things that whispered of home had vanished, claimed by Mom or Janine, or swallowed by storage. We were living in a temporary limbo, surrounded by the ghost of a life that no longer existed. It felt like being trapped in a bad dream, a constant reminder of everything we'd lost.

I knew that if I "divorced" my father, I had to delicately untangle, carefully avoiding altercations. Needing all the help I could get, I had the gumption to call upon my siblings, hoping to protect myself from physical or verbal abuse.

My oldest sister, who now preferred Susan instead of Sue, was closest to Dad. He always seemed to favor her. After all, she went to his alma mater, UC Berkeley, and, in my view, provided him with moral and mental support for his victimhood.

"You're the only one who really understands me," he'd tell her.

"I'm always here for you, Dad," she'd reply, her voice soothing and supportive.

They used each other. She benefited by receiving his best side, financial generosity, and appreciation for her care and understanding of what he claimed my mom, my great-uncle Harry, and the *world* had done to him.

I confided in Susan and let her know my plan to leave our dad, move to Mom's, and change my high school to one with a radio station. I had figured out that by using my stepdad Rob's youngest son's address, I would qualify for Rio Americano and be one step closer to participating in a high school radio station.

Susan arrived early on a Saturday afternoon, as planned. We had meticulously plotted what we were going to say, how we would say it, and how I would exit from the home. Susan, Dad, and I retreated to the living room, where she stood by while I took a deep breath and exhaled words that took the most guts, strength, and courage I could muster.

"Dad," I began, my voice trembling slightly, "I know you're going through a tough time right now...."

He looked up at me. A frown creased his forehead. "What do you mean?"

"Well," I continued, trying to steady my voice, "with everything ... I think it would be best if I went to live with Mom."

His face hardened. "So, you're abandoning me too after all I've done for you?" His lament tugged at my heartstrings.

"No, Dad," I pleaded, "It's not like that. I just need a fresh start."

Susan stepped forward, placing a hand on his arm. "Dad," she said gently, "maybe this is for the best."

He hesitated, his expression a mix of sadness and resignation. "I ... I suppose," he finally replied, his voice heavy with emotion. It wasn't a full concession on his part, though the words were enough for me. *I was free. Finally. Or was I?*

Suddenly, there was utter shock on Dad's face, his jaw practically on the floor. "How could you do this to me? You're all I have."

He began to weep, which brought tears to my eyes as I thought of how he'd lost Mom, Janine (thank goodness!), his business standing, and now me, his most valued possession. Susan, my loving sis, comforted him.

"Are you sure you're doing the right thing?" Susan asked me, her voice filled with concern.

"I ... I think so," I choked out, wiping away a tear. "I just can't stay here anymore."

On the one hand, I needed to save myself, but on the other hand, I was scared I was leaving Dad to rot—or maybe even harm himself.

"He'll be all right," Susan reassured me, though her own eyes were brimming with tears.

It had momentarily slipped my mind that Dad had never taken responsibility for his outbursts of rage, violence, intimidation, and neglect, nor seemed to care what effect they'd had on my mom nor us, his children. Even now, everything is all about *him* and *his* feelings.

I made my way upstairs to my bedroom, threw my clothes and essential personal belongings into a suitcase, and plopped everything in the hallway adjoining the living room, as I heard the sniffles and gags of a broken man mingled with the pacifying words of his favorite daughter.

"It's going to be okay, Dad," Susan soothed, her hand resting on his shoulder, as she glanced at me and quietly said, "He just needs some time."

Then my brother Jim arrived.

"Ready to go, little bro?" he asked with a hint of sadness in his voice.

I nodded, unable to speak past the lump in my throat. He hugged Dad and Susan, then helped me collect my stuff, and off I went to Mom's. I now had a new burden of shame and a new narrative—I was trading my father, who had left his second wife to "care" for me, for my mother, who had apparently never wanted me to be born.

Dad's immediate reaction was to distance himself from me even further.

"I don't want to see you anymore," he spat at me one day, his voice cold and harsh. "You're just like your mother."

"And don't expect a dime from me," he snarled during one of our infrequent phone calls. "You *made* your choice." It felt as though I was teetering on the edge of a cliff.

It wasn't easy living with Carole and Rob either, but the three of us coexisted and after some time, I began to feel accomplished, independent, and stronger. I was creating a sense of self, finding it within the attention and recognition I received from being a deejay, a budding small-town quasi-celebrity with both an ego and a chip on my shoulder. On top of that, Rob, seemingly sent from heaven, was the adult listener I never had.

"You have a real talent, Robbie," he'd say, encouraging my passion for radio.

I also realized that Mom wasn't as bad as Dad said she was.

"I've always loved you," she confessed one day, her eyes filled with tears.

Those words melted me.

Rob would embolden me: "Follow your gut, go beyond what you believe is possible." He was a surgeon, skilled with his hands. He knew carpentry and helped me build a lengthy box resembling a coffin to house my very own deejay equipment system. He even let me use power tools! This unique creation housed an amplifier, mixer, two turntables, and, of course, a microphone. To protect and transport the equipment more easily, we crafted an A-frame lid, half plywood and half plexiglass, connected by a piano hinge at the peak. Sturdy handles on each end enabled two people to move it in and out of gigs.

After I got my driver's license, Rob and Mom let me use their white Oldsmobile station wagon to haul my equipment, but a taller more spacious vehicle was what I really needed. I longed for a van. Thanks to Rob, I was able to buy a new maroon Dodge van—the first automobile I ever owned. I withdrew all my savings, and he generously covered the small remainder.

Was this man the universe answering my prayers?

17

I AM A DEEJAY...

My first celebrity encounter came while still working my prized job at Sacramento's popular Top 40 station, KROY AM, and FM sister I-97. Child actor Leif Garrett had transitioned into a pop star and started climbing the charts with his first single, the disco tune "I Was Made for Dancin'." Leif agreed to appear at the California State Fair that summer of 1978 on behalf of the stations in a quid pro quo arrangement for more airplay.

I was sixteen—six months, almost to the day, younger than Leif—and excited about my driver's license and my maroon Dodge van. The station van was unavailable, and we had imprinted boxfuls of Frisbees with the logo. So, we loaded them into the back of my van, which I parked on the concrete apron on the side of the stage. The plan was to generate excitement by launching the flying discs into the crowd before and after Leif's performance. There was a shallow water-filled moat in front of the stage that meandered through the fairgrounds. The audience sat on the other side of the moat on a terraced landscaped lawn. As Frisbees flew into the crowd, Leif arrived in a limo parked near my van, just off the apron, on a patch of grass.

After the show, girls began jumping through the water and trampling across the moat to surround Leif's limo. They climbed all over it, and their collective weight caused the tires to sink into the lawn, making it impossible for the limo to leave. One of the station bigwigs urgently approached me and shouted, "Give me the keys to your van so we can rescue Leif!" Leif was pulled from the limo and pushed into my van, as the bigwig got into the driver's seat. I swiftly climbed in through the back and we departed in a hasty getaway.

A few weeks later, I found myself face-to-face with my parents' insurance agent, who happened to be a neighbor and family friend. It turned out that a girl's foot had been run over by my van, and I was being held liable. The girl had filed a claim against me through the insurance company. The agent barked at me, "Never loan your vehicle, Robbie." Lesson learned!

I would run into Leif again nearly two decades later, in 1996. At that time, he'd be plagued by drug and financial problems, while I was dating TV presenter Katie Wagner, the daughter of movie actor and TV star of *Hart to Hart*, Robert Wagner. We were at a dinner party where she introduced me to Leif.

"Leif," she said, "you won't believe who this is! This is Rob Tonkin, remember him?"

Leif squinted at me, brow furrowed. "Rob Tompkins?" he repeated, "Hmm, I'm not sure ... refresh my memory?"

So I did. I recounted the story of our brief encounter years prior—the chaotic scene with his fans that led to him being thrown in the back of *my* van to escape, the unfortunate incident where we accidentally ran over his fan, and how he ended up reuniting with his limo an hour or so later. As the details unfolded, a flicker of recognition crossed his face. "Oh wow," he finally exclaimed, a mix of surprise and amusement in his voice, "That was *you*?! Man, I can't believe it! What are the odds?" He seemed genuinely surprised and a bit embarrassed.

We spent the next several hours together in a rooftop suite of a Sunset Strip hotel, enjoying the after-party, delving deeper into the past, and catching up on each other's lives.

A year after the Leif-extraction incident, I stepped into the light as a young man with an article in a Sacramento newspaper in which I told the columnist, "I want to become another Dick Clark." Clark was the legendary television and radio personality who hosted *American Bandstand* from 1956 to 1989, a music show featuring top recording acts performing in a studio crowded with teen dancers. In its early years, *American Bandstand* was credited with introducing young America to rock 'n' roll years before TV host Ed Sullivan (famous for his variety show *The Ed Sullivan Show*) introduced the Beatles. Clark was one of my early role models, since he, too, had begun his career as a teen deejay.

As well as Dick Clark, I admired Wolfman Jack. Another icon of radio, his gravelly deejay voice was immortalized in the 1973 movie *American Graffiti*, the first big hit for George Lucas of *Star Wars* fame. During my late 1960s summer camp days, I'd listened to the howls and growls of the Wolfman on XERB-AM 1090 near Rosarito Beach, Baja California, Mexico. He'd pretended to be in Hollywood, recording his shows there and then shuttling the tapes across the Mexican border. At that time, Mexican radio stations broadcast far more wattage than their American counterparts, so the signal could be heard all over the place, and the Wolfman quickly became a household name. Somehow, at camp in the mountains, my compatriots and I had picked up the signal and listened to the Wolfman's howling show, which was definitely not allowed, making it that much more exciting.

After his appearance in *American Graffiti*, the Wolfman would pop up as a guest host on TV shows, while I-97 carried his weekly syndicated radio show. One weekend, there was a buzz around the station: the Wolfman was coming to Sacramento and would broadcast live for an hour. I happened to be working that Saturday night and got to meet him, serving as a production assistant.

Wow, it's really him, I thought, barely able to contain my excitement. I was in awe of him but also realized something wasn't quite right—he was high on something.

"Hey there," he said with a raspy laugh, as he proceeded to a nearby restroom. I saw him take a small kit in there that looked like a bag for toilet articles. I wondered what was really in that little bag. I felt a bit disillusioned but also tried to give him the benefit of the doubt.

Still, meeting the Wolfman in person, after listening to him on the radio as a small child, was simply unbelievable. It helped me believe that anything was possible and that I could achieve my dreams if I set my mind to it. And I had big dreams. I saw working at the radio station after school as just the beginning. Listening to music, being a part of it, and sharing it with others any way I could was how my spinning at parties and school dances had started—and deep down I knew there was much more to come.

In the fall of 1978, I started my junior year at Rio Americano. I continued to spend tons of time at my high school radio station and grew closer to Rob. I sometimes called him "Pop," as Mom wanted me to.

As the next school year ended and summer approached, I felt a tug-of-war within me. An invitation to join a student trip to Europe had arrived, and it was incredibly tempting. "History credits in exchange for a mind-expanding trip to Europe," the flier posted on classroom bulletin boards promised. I yearned for the adventure of exploring Europe and did want to graduate from high school. But I also didn't want to abandon my deejay business and my radio station gig.

The mere mention of a European trip sent Mom into a frenzied state of excitement. Yet she insisted that I ask my estranged father for the cash to fund this adventure. It was a bombshell that sent me into emotional turmoil.

I protested, trying to explain, "Dad will never pony up the cash."

But she stubbornly brushed off my concerns: "Your father has the money, and he should pay for this."

I reluctantly approached Dad with my hand outstretched, hoping that he would reveal a trace of humanity. As expected, he shot me down, as cold and detached as an icy volley across a tennis court. "If your mother wants you to go, she will have to cough up the dough," he declared.

Surprisingly, Mom came through. It may have been Rob's influence. Practically the same age as my dad but with grandkids my age, Rob had wisdom and patience that I never found in my own father. Maybe it was because he'd learned from his own mistakes raising his kids, but he always seemed to know how to guide me without judging me. He was there to help me build my dreams, not tear them down. He wasn't just a stepdad; he was a mentor, a confidant, and a true source of support, almost like having an extra grandfather in my corner. With a little help from Rob, whose family owned a bank, Mom scraped together the required sum and I eagerly signed up for the school-supported expedition, joining a crew of sixty-nine fellow students alongside a few teachers.

I recently found a letter tucked away in an old travel journal. It was from Mom, received in Rome, that holds the key to a turning point in our relationship:

> "Robbie dear,
>
> So far, we have thought of you constantly! We stayed at the airport and watched your plane ... with many other parents. On the way home, we stopped at the cemetery ... and put flowers there .... We returned to Tiburon, freshened up, and returned to the city ... We also called Uncle Leo to hear about your flight... Leo said you sounded so manly... Thanks for calling him."

"You *must* call your Uncle Leo," Mom had insisted. In those days, making a phone call to another state was considered long distance and cost a lot of extra money per minute, so Mom and Uncle Leo spoke infrequently. I, however, had been in Uncle Leo's home state during my layover, so I was able to call him without any long-distance call fees. Mom hadn't wanted me to miss the opportunity to connect with him. My stomach churned. While my mother adored her Uncle Leo, I barely knew the man. What on earth would I say to him? And so, armed with a handful of coins and a heart full of apprehension, I'd found myself standing at a bank of payphones at JFK airport, fumbling as I punched in the unfamiliar number. The phone rang a few times, and then a gruff voice answered.

"Hello?"

"Uh, hi," I stammered, "Is this Uncle Leo?"

"Speaking," the voice replied.

"Hi, Uncle Leo, it's Robbie … Robbie Tonkin," I said, trying to sound more confident than I felt. "My mom, Carole, wanted me to call you."

"Robbie!" he exclaimed, his voice suddenly warming. "Carole's boy! How are you? How's your mother?"

Looking back, I can appreciate Mom's intentions. In an era where communication was less immediate and often cost-prohibitive, even a local call carried a certain weight. But for me, a boy thrust into an uncomfortable situation, it was a reminder of the complexities of family obligations.

> "After a good night's sleep, we feel great and hope you enjoy Madrid. We'll follow your itinerary each day...
>
> You have a great group, and you will make new friends.... A little secret: Rob and I were teary when you left, as were the other parents... It was kind of comical. I'm just so grateful you can partake in this adventure...
>
> You will probably spend more time than you wish waiting ... but it can't be helped when you're in a large group, so try to be patient... After this first trip to Europe, you'll get the 'hang of it,' and you'll become a good 'world traveler'...
>
> I'll write you again in Salzburg....
>
> We love you more than words can express....
>
> Love, Mom
>
> PS ... don't keep the Trojans in your dop kit or bag. Keep them in your pocket... I hope this finds you full of

joy, fun, and new beginnings.
Love, Rob!"

Clearly, Carole and Rob were enthused about my adventure. Still, I suspect Rob heavily influenced Mom's letter writing, advising her to be supportive. That, and perhaps my mother was learning to be more compassionate and had missed me during the years we'd spent living apart.

The trip *was* incredible. We roamed the storied streets of England, tasted the flamenco rhythms of Spain, savored the culinary delights of Italy, toured the ancient ruins of Greece, wandered through the castles and salt mines of Germany, and basked in the musical roots of Austria, home to both Mozart and *The Sound of Music*. The icing on the cake was a blissful week-long cruise on the Adriatic Sea bordering Italy. It was a ticket to a world beyond my wildest dreams.

In addition to the profound experience of legally consuming beer, there were girls. Two girls from my school who I'd briefly dated had also signed up for the trip. One, Barry Stachelek, a stylish girl who channeled her creative talents primarily into fashion. The other girl was a year younger, a stunning bleach-blonde who looked a little like actress Marilyn Monroe, with a dash of singer and actress Debbie Harry's charm and a touch of tomboyishness.

My intentions were clear: to "conquer" these women on our trip to validate my masculinity. Rob had even buoyed my efforts by giving me condoms. But my energies were in vain. Despite passionate make-out sessions with both Barry and the younger girl, neither one shared my desire to go further.

Toward the end of our week-long cruise at sea, I spotted a stunning Italian girl. I had never seen a bikini so scandalously skimpy. Though she didn't speak a word of English, somehow we managed to communicate and spent time together by the pool and at dinner on the final night. She even invited me to her stateroom, adjacent to her aunt's room, who was her chaperone for the voyage. This was a significant upgrade from my accommodations. I was one of four high school boys crammed into a tiny room with bunk beds. It was on the bottom deck of the ship, with cold steel walls, no porthole windows nor even a baño within the room.

Conversely, Angela Carlotto's room was spacious, located on the highest deck, adorned with wood paneling, a double bed, and a separate bathroom. Angela encouraged me to stay the night, and we made out heavily and held each other, proving that language was no barrier to romance.

Awakening, I realized I had violated curfew, overslept, and nearly missed my group's disembarkation meetup. I snapped into action, rushed to my room, crammed my belongings into my suitcase, and sprinted to the designated spot, barely making it. Of course, I was interrogated about my whereabouts, but I just broadly smiled because I didn't care at all.

In Madrid, Spain, we were treated to an authentic bullfight at the renowned Las Ventas. My takeaway was that the art of bullfighting was effortless, and the lofty admiration bestowed upon the matadors was silly.

In Segovia, Spain, we ventured off the beaten path to a farm boasting a modest arena with adolescent bulls where we could witness the training of fighting bulls. When an invitation was extended to test our mettle as amateur bullfighters, my bravado took over—I would impress my trip compadres and the ladies. Knowing how easy bullfighting was, I stepped into the ring with a double-sided cape, pink on one side and yellow on the other, clasped in my hands. As I glanced upward, my eyes locked into the gaze of a brown-and-white calf, his curiosity piqued. Waving the cape to coax him forward, I turned my back with success, but the bull continued to charge toward me. This time, my cape was positioned incorrectly, leaving my body vulnerable to attack. The bull made contact, the cape remained on its head, and I involuntarily somersaulted through the air, landing with a jarring thud upon my arm, the remainder of my body crashing into the dirt. No bones were technically fractured, but a gaping scrape on the inside of my elbow and searing pain accompanied my swift exit from the ring. It was a humbling reality check.

18

SEX ON FIRE

"Mom, Rob," I began one day, my voice a mix of nerves and determination, "I need to talk to you about something important."

Mom sighed, barely looking up from her *People* magazine. "What is it now, Robbie?"

Rob, slumped in his easy chair, glued to the TV, muttered, "Can it wait? The Duke is about to have a showdown with the bad guys."

"I'm moving out," I said, my voice rising with agitation.

Mom lowered her magazine, her perfectly coiffed eyebrows shooting up in surprise. "Move out? What are you talking about?"

"I'm moving in with Jim," I declared, my voice firm. "I need my own space."

I appreciated that Mom and Rob had taken me in, but I wanted something that felt like my own. Since my parents' divorce, I had moved eight times. Just when I'd adapt to a new routine—*bam!*—everything would change again. New house, new school, new family, new rules. It was exhausting and emotionally draining. It was like building a house of cards in a windstorm. My European adventure had helped me decide it was time for a place where *I* could be in control and finally be myself. Constantly hearing Mom and Rob's bickering, witnessing their cocktail parties with my mother drunk in this "proper" house where I didn't feel comfortable bringing a girl home either was something I didn't care for anymore.

"But Robbie," Mom protested, "you have your own room here.

What's the problem?"

I did have my own room—but it also *wasn't* my own room. It was the guest room, a temporary space at Mom and Rob's. While it contained a desk Rob had helped build for me, the pussy willow wallpaper, the matching pussy willow drapes and bedspread, and even the coordinated pussy willow bathroom across the hall made it feel like a museum exhibit, a perfectly curated space where I was merely a visitor. Even the twin beds, a constant reminder of the room's intended purpose, seemed to mock my longing for a place to truly call my own.

"I need to be more independent," I said. "Jim's cool with looking after me."

Rob turned away from the TV, his expression a mix of curiosity and concern. "I understand, Robbie. If that's what you need, then we'll think about it. We need to talk to Jim first."

"And," I added, "I'd also need some financial help until I turn eighteen next year. Maybe you could pay Jim my share of the rent and expenses?"

"We'll discuss that with Jim," Rob assured me, almost sarcastically.

"Thank you," I said, not caring if he was serious or not, hope flickering in my eyes. I felt a surge of relief.

A couple of days later, I cornered them again. "Have you talked to Jim yet?" I asked, my voice tight with anticipation. Mom and Rob exchanged a glance.

"We have," Rob said slowly. "And while we're not thrilled about it, we agree it might be for the best."

"Thank you," I said, relief flooding through me.

"Just try not to be a stranger, okay?" Mom added with a hint of sadness in her voice and mist developing in her eyes.

"I won't," I promised, though a part of me knew that my umpteenth move was about more than just finding my own space. It was about creating distance, about finally stepping out of my parents' shadow and into my own light.

My new digs were the Selby Ranch apartments, a sprawling

townhouse tract community with swimming pools, a small clubhouse, and divorcées. Jim was twenty-eight and had just transitioned from working for our father for nearly a decade and a nasty divorce from a high school sweetheart who he had caught cheating on him, to being a traveling sales rep for an upstart beverage dispenser company as well as a newly single man.

Moving in with my cool older brother Jim was a definite upgrade. Our townhouse was close to both my school and the pool. Even better, the place had a spacious living room and kitchen, and we each had our own bedroom and bathroom upstairs. I also had my own wheels, job, money, and independence. I had shed the baggage of my parents and their messy lives in exchange for loose supervision by Jim, finally on my way to full autonomy.

Our next-door neighbors reminded me of Neil Simon's characters in *The Odd Couple*. They were divorced older men, cohabiting. They were both named Bill and around twenty years older than I, probably in their late thirties. Bill No. 1, newly sober with a dark tan, silver hair, trimmed beard, slight potbelly, and messy tendency, was described by my brother as "a bullshit artist," when I asked about his occupation. Bill No. 2 was a well-groomed, mustachioed big-rig truck driver resembling the actor Pat Harrington, who played the building superintendent Schneider on the TV sitcom *One Day at a Time*, complete with a jean vest over a white T-shirt, a pack of cigs rolled into the sleeve, a tool belt, and a retractable key chain.

We shared a common wall between our units, and from the closet ceiling in my bedroom, there was a hatch entry to the attic crawl space. Out of curiosity, I shimmied up into the crawl space and saw that a few feet away there was another hatch entry that led to Bill No. 2's closet.

It all started with Bill No. 1, the "bullshit artist." I told him about the attic hatch I discovered and its access to Bill No. 2's closet. While hanging out with my brother Jim and Bill No. 1 one evening, he brought up the hidden passageway. Intrigued, we investigated, and the idea, simply, emerged. It was more like a dare, a challenge whispered amid late-night conversation. Bill No. 2, surprisingly, was game. And so, with a mixture of excitement and trepidation, we took turns climbing the ladder, peering through the hatch, and witnessing a scene that would forever be etched in my memory.

I watched from a few feet away while Bill No. 2, fully aware of what we were doing, had sex with his oblivious conquest. He seemed to relish the attention, the thrill of being watched or maybe of teaching me, a young teen who was in awe of this guy and his "prowess." About two weeks later we did the opposite—our neighbors put the ladder up on Bill No. 2's side of the wall, climbed up through his closet, and watched me having sex with one of my radio groupies.

The voyeurism, I realize now, was a bizarre, out-of-bounds experience, even for a time when social norms were looser and experimentation was in the air as the "sexual revolution" was in full force between the mid-60s through the mid-80s. But in those seconds, it felt almost natural. As a teenager, I was curious, didn't see the point of many boundaries, and was living in a world where boundaries seemed to be constantly shifting anyway.

At the time, the experience felt strangely empowering. It was an adventure, a breaking of societal norms. It gave us a sense of control, a feeling of being on the edge of something forbidden. It was live pornography. Of course, looking back, I recognize the inherent exploitation and the violation of the women's privacy. Maybe if we had asked they would have agreed to it, but we hadn't given them the choice.

That same year, Jim had multiple girlfriends. One brought a female friend for a pool day and barbecue. We all got into the Jacuzzi afterward, as the sun set. The two girls began kissing one another. "Look at that," Jim mouthed to me with a smirk, nudging me with his elbow. For me, this was "erotic city," as the singer Prince would say.

Afterward, my brother played bartender while the two young women proceeded to the shower upstairs in his bathroom. "Don't get any ideas," he called out with a wink as they headed upstairs. I followed them and watched them kissing and rubbing one another in the shower. They caught me. "Whoa there!" the girlfriend exclaimed with a laugh. "Didn't anyone ever teach you about privacy?" I apologized, and the next thing I knew, the friend stepped out of the shower and motioned for me to go with her to my bedroom. "Come here, sweetie," she purred. *Oh, dear.* This was an older woman—she was in her early 20s—and she proceeded to teach me a thing or two. Once I was exhausted, she went into Jim's room, and I could hear the three of them laughing and carrying on late into the night.

These fulfilled teenage fantasy events would have a major impact on my behavior moving forward. My objectification of women unfortunately continued for decades after. Yet Jim didn't corrupt me on purpose. He was recovering from his failed marriage while living in a patriarchal world. Almost no one I came across seemed to have had positive parental or societal role models showing us what good, healthy boundaries or communication between romantic partners should be like.

After a half-year of living with my brother, I traded one party for another when I moved into an apartment on a busy street, a two-bedroom space in a new building with a pool. I was seventeen, a high school senior, living on my own, with a roommate. I began picking up women in school, at events where I worked, and through professional and amateur radio stations. I also had a few trysts with neighbors in my complex. Most of them became short-term conquests. Every woman was another way to prove to myself that I was worthy of attention, and love.

Proms? Never went. Homecoming? Nope. Football games? Skipped those too. While other kids were hanging out with friends, I worked. There were radio and deejay gigs, and I was constantly around a revolving door of people; yet, I was alone, grasping at women in order to validate myself. I was drawn to girls treating themselves as objects to be looked at and evaluated based on appearance. Some had outstanding personalities and senses of humor; some were intelligent and fun to be around. But they all had a common thread: They were beautiful, they were sexy, and they were willing.

I feel a deep sense of shame for my past behavior. I was dehumanizing women, focusing on their bodies as a way to distract myself from my own insecurities, and my own lack of self-love. It's hard to love and respect someone you see through a narrow lens. It's hard to be compassionate and kind toward someone you don't really see as a person—especially if that person is yourself.

PART TWO

...AND THEM

19

FIELDS OF GOLD

The broadcast booth was more than just a room. It was a portal to another world. As I sat behind the mic and the dimly lit studio faded away, I'd feel a surge of power. The red "On Air" light would glow, and I'd take a deep breath, the warmth rising within me. My voice, amplified, filled the airwaves, reaching into cars, homes, and workplaces. I was shut out from the rest of the world and all its horror, yet thousands of people listened to me. They gave me their attention, their time, and their respect. It was a strange intimacy, a one-sided conversation with a vast and unknown audience. I imagined families gathered around dinner tables, teenagers cruising in their cars, shopkeepers stocking shelves, all united by the sound of my voice. I felt safe and *heard*.

With each song intro, each witty remark, and each carefully crafted transition, I felt a sense of purpose, a validation that transcended the insecurities and anxieties that plagued me outside the studio. It was a heady feeling, an intoxicating connection that made the broadcast booth my refuge, my stage, my connection to a world that often felt beyond my grasp.

That world expanded when I, along with most of the KROY crew, jumped ship to join our crosstown rival, KXOA AM 1470. It was a chance to level up, to be part of a new and exciting chapter in Sacramento radio. Radio frequency numbers are like houses—sometimes they get new owners, but the address stays the same. AM 1470 had been known as KNDE or "Rock Kandie" under previous owners. As a kid I'd been drawn to the excitement, hype, and enthusiasm of Rock Kandie—the energy of the deejays, the sound bites, the musical effects used to punctuate or emphasize a thought, a program format, and more. Though it was now KXOA, landing a deejay gig at AM 1470 felt like coming home, a connection to those same radio waves that had sparked my passion.

I continued my weekend deejay gig, honing my on-air persona, as my duties expanded beyond the broadcast booth. After graduating from high school, I also stepped into the role of full-time promotion director, charged with organizing a whirlwind of events and spreading the word about KXOA. What I really longed for, however, was to become a full-time deejay, and enjoy the same pay, prestige, or endorsement opportunities as the starters.

By this time, the old saying about paying your dues had been permanently burned onto my mind's hard drive—and I felt I'd more than paid them. For years I'd been a part-timer—which was like being a benchwarmer—relegated to weekend, fill-in, and overnight shifts. On top of that, I had had to endure the violating tutelage of Robert John and Richard Irwin. *I've paid my dues* echoed in my thoughts as I began sending out audition tapes to smaller markets, hoping to land a full-time on-air position.

One of these audition tapes was sent to Mark Driscoll, a deep-voiced character, and the man responsible for Rock Kandie AM 1470. I had admired his work when I was a kid, and in the cover letter, I let him know as much. To my surprise I got a bite: He offered me a job as music director and midday deejay at KERN 1410 AM in Bakersfield, at the foot of California's fertile San Joaquin Valley, known for cattle ranching, agriculture, and oil fields—acres upon acres of "black gold." Bakersfield is ultra-conservative and famous for being the home of country music singers Merle Haggard and Buck Owens. Owens owned some of the most successful radio stations in town, including, ironically, a cool underground FM rock station.

I had a few loose ends to tie up before I left, however.

"Hey Paul," I said one day to a friend and fellow radio deejay who on occasion helped me out with gigs, "I'm thinking of leaving Sacramento. Any interest in taking over Disco Party Sound?"

He looked surprised. "Really? You're selling your business?"

"Yeah," I confirmed. "I'm ready for a new chapter. I'm moving down south for a fresh start."

"Wow," he said, scratching his head thoughtfully. "That's a big decision. But, yeah, I might be interested. What are you thinking?"

We talked it over, and I suggested he buy the name and phone number.

"I'll even throw in the customer list," I offered. "It's a great way to get started."

"That's generous of you," Paul said, a smile spreading across his face. "I appreciate that."

I sold the business to Paul but held onto all the equipment and the music library—and, of course, my beloved maroon Dodge van. It was bittersweet, saying goodbye to the deejay business I'd built from the ground up.

In June 1981, one month after my nineteenth birthday, I packed my belongings into my van and drove nearly 300 miles along Interstate 5 to Bakersfield, where the average June temperature was ninety-two degrees. I pulled into town and checked into the first roadside motel I could find. The next day, I went to work.

I was a young buck with a five-year track record of success at three different radio stations in Sacramento. Due to my young age and rapid rise from intern to deejay, I garnered heaps of publicity. Going from a metro area with a population approaching 1 million to a rural town with only about 200,000 people meant I could be a bigger fish in a smaller pond.

Mark Driscoll, who now was a prominent programming consultant, was also known as "Mr. Voice." He had opened his consultancy after many years as an acclaimed program director, Top 40 deejay, and voice-over pro. He had a wicked sense of humor evocative of The Joker in the *Batman* films. He would often call in on the hotline in his signature voice, saying things like, "Keep shootin' like a pistol, Tonkin!" My music director title meant I was one of the key decision-makers on what music the station played. Record companies paid close attention.

"Hey, Rob," a record rep would say, sliding a new album across my desk, "I think track one's gonna be huge. Give it a spin, will ya?" It was up to me to add a song to our playlist and give it crucial exposure.

Smaller radio stations and markets often influenced the larger ones. We had to be trendsetters, taking risks on new music and breaking artists before they hit the mainstream. What we played in our little corner of California could ripple to Los Angeles, shaping the sound of popular music. Our decisions had real weight, real influence.

I rented an apartment, made a few friends, dated girls, and when Labor Day weekend arrived, Mom and Rob visited me in my new home. While I worked, they helped me further settle in. After they left, I received a letter from them:

> "Rob dear,
>
> Sorry we didn't do the laundry; we were too hot and tired. You have enough T-shirts! Give some away! You could also throw away a few hangers... you are a pack rat! We couldn't hang the macramé plant because we couldn't find a drill or a hook. We thought it would look nice in the window... When you come home with your van, we can get a wicker chair for your bedroom... The two dining chairs look nice for extra seating in your living room. You were terrific on the air! We had 1410 KERN on the whole time... The lady in our motel listens to it all the time and asked me for your name. Glad to see you happy. Call when you can.

Love you, Mom
Rob too."

Being under twenty-one and living in Bakersfield presented some challenges. I wasn't able to drink at bars, but I managed to navigate around that obstacle—which helped with my social life. Living in a "cow and oil town" didn't exactly match my ambitions or vibe, yet I had a bold, cocky attitude, and had set about conquering the town. In my first six months, I enjoyed a whirlwind of romances—and unfortunately, a short-lived but unwelcome encounter with crabs.

But it wasn't all about chasing girls. I was hungry for music immersion. I hit the road, catching Cheap Trick in Fresno, a town not much bigger than my own. Then, I headed south to Los Angeles to see the Rolling Stones command the Coliseum and again to see and *meet* an all-female band that was becoming a cultural phenomenon: The Go-Go's. Around this time, I also fell hard for The Police. I loved the reggae influence, the driving rhythms, and the sense of rebellion I heard in their music. Of course, all of this took place during my days off. During work time, I *worked*.

One day at work, I had flubbed a line on air, my voice cracking with nerves. The mistake echoed in my head, a blemish on the perfect show I was striving for when Serena sauntered into *my* control room, clipboard in hand. Serena was a fiery redhead who tended to treat me like an underling and reminded me of Endora, the troublemaking mother-in-law from the TV series *Bewitched*. I was seconds from going on air again and planned to redeem myself, when Serena, oblivious, asked me something about the advertising inventory, called commercial cartridges or "carts." Suddenly my heart hammered in my chest, a wave of panic washing over me, her question like an intrusion, a violation of my sacred pre-mic-opening ritual. All the years of feeling unheard and unseen by authority figures, and the constant pressure to perform, all bubbled to the surface.

"Get the fuck out of my studio now!" I yelled.

The next day, a few days before Christmas, I came down sick, and called into work, down for the count. On Christmas Eve, I heard a knock on my front door. It was the program director, my immediate supervisor. He was holding a shopping bag in his hands. I thought it was nice for my radio station family to think of me while I was sick and alone and visit me right before the holiday. He looked nervously at me though, eked out a strained "Hello," and handed me the bag. I could see my headphones and other personal belongings peeking from the top. Then he mumbled, "Uh, sorry, Rob, but you're fired."

What the fuck? Somehow I'd thought it was okay to tell Serena to get the fuck out of my studio—that my anger at her was justified. It wasn't. She may have at times treated me in a dismissive manner, yet what I'd done definitely was *not* okay. If I could go back in time, I'd rewind to that control room moment and apologize to Serena.

I got my comeuppance. The shock of being unexpectedly fired knocked me off my pedestal and flung me through a gamut of emotions—denial, anger, sadness, shame, and worry for the future—all while suffering through the flu and crabs in cow town Bakersfield. Was this a wake-up call from the universe?

20

CALIFORNICATION

The thought of spending the holidays with my parents left me with more complicated emotions since my heart was always playing tug-of-war between them. Ultimately, I decided to head back home to Sacramento, where I would attempt to divide my time equally between my warring mom and dad.

At a Christmas party of Mom's, I ran into Tommy Bolton. Tommy was an intense character with a square jaw, a lived-in baby face, short dark brown hair flipped over his forehead, a mustache, an athletic build, and a rugged but preppy style, giving him a sense of authenticity and maturity. He was a stepcousin who took quite a shine to me. Tommy was nearly a decade older and treated me like a cool younger brother.

Tommy once took me and my sister Susan on a rafting adventure down the American River that included an area of rapids that I hadn't previously experienced. Looking back, I can't help but wonder if he had some romantic infatuation with Susan, but that's neither here nor there. What mattered was that Tommy was now in my life again. Tommy was the son of my stepfather's sister. But to me, he was simply Cousin Tommy. We hit it off right away. He was a man of intellect, energy, and drive, beloved by Mom and Rob.

Young and ambitious, Tommy had become the youngest office manager in the entire E.F. Hutton stock brokerage chain, following in the financial footsteps of his banker father and grandfather. And where did he set up shop? In Carlsbad, a coastal suburb about thirty miles north of

San Diego. He lived in a rented house near the beach, dated a woman he worked with, zipped around town in his shiny silver vintage Porsche 912, and spent time on his sailboat as though he was a James Bond character.

When Tommy got wind of my unfortunate firing, he invited me to visit him in Carlsbad once the holidays were over. The invitation was casual but held a glimmer of hope. So I packed my bags and headed south. That visit stretched into a year. Eventually, I managed to rent the house next door, fully immersed in the vibrant community surrounding this coastal haven. The beach life and the town itself fascinated me in ways I couldn't have imagined. It was wildly different from Bakersfield where I'd been a big fish in a small pond, but also very much a fish out of water.

Shortly after settling in Carlsbad, I reached out to an old buddy, Jeff Hunter. A fellow veteran of the Sacramento radio scene, Jeff had moved down to San Diego and carved out a name for himself as a deejay and program director at The Mighty 690 radio station, a popular Top 40 radio station on the AM dial. Officially known as XETRA-AM, The Mighty 690 was one of several "border-blaster" stations, transmitting on a 50,000-watt platform from a tower located just outside Tijuana, in Baja California, Mexico.

I called Jeff, desperate to see if there were any job openings. He promised to keep me in mind should anything open up. In the meantime, I worked at two restaurants and also resurrected my mobile deejay business.

One hot summer day, a whimsical girl crossed my path. It happened as a Canadian friend, Doug, and I cruised through the Carlsbad town center, searching for a spot to grab lunch.

"Hey, check out that girl on the moped!" Doug shouted, pointing excitedly.

Our attention was captured by a young blonde wearing baby-blue dolphin shorts and a white spaghetti-strap tank top speeding along on a moped. Doug yelled out without thinking, "Hey, what's up?" from the passenger side of my maroon Dodge van.

Startled, she turned her head and flung back, "Whoa, you spooked me! Not too much."

"Smooth, Doug," I chuckled, shaking my head.

Debra Nicol would go on to play a significant role in my young life. In addition to her moped, Debra Nicol's aggressive running style often took her several miles on foot from the tract-home suburbs east of the I-5 freeway to the beach where Doug and I hung out.

"She's like a gazelle," Doug would say, admiringly, "So graceful, so strong."

While Doug was infatuated with her, I was simply fascinated with her mystery. My efforts were in pursuing a tall, blonde, pale-skinned girl from the local tennis club. That is until she made it clear she wasn't interested. Then, Debra's allure grew stronger. She became a symbol of the Southern California beach lifestyle, with sun-kissed skin, flowing blond hair, and striking gray-blue eyes. For a few exhilarating weeks, Debra, Doug, and I immersed ourselves in the carefree spirit of youth, meeting at the beach and having a blast. There, amid the ocean breeze and crashing waves, Debra transformed from a serious runner to a stunning beach beauty, revealing a toned physique in a bikini that could stop the tide itself. I felt compelled to ask her out.

I was nineteen years old, while Debra was sixteen. At the time, California did not have in place a "Romeo and Juliet law" that would allow for consensual relationships between teenagers close in age. Instead, any sexual activity of a person over eighteen with a minor was deemed statutory rape, regardless of consent. Looking back, I should have considered the legal implications more seriously. But as a teenager, my awareness wasn't always the best, and my feelings for Debra overshadowed my better judgment.

Before I could make a move, I talked to Doug to be sure I wasn't stepping on his toes and violating the "bro code," which was more my legal speed at that time. He agreed she wasn't into him and cleared me for take-off.

"So," I started, my engines blazing, but trying to sound casual, "What do you think about catching a movie sometime?"

"Sure," Debra replied with a smile, "That sounds fun."

We were in flight.

She later confided that she had chosen me over Doug because I reminded her of Davy Jones, the heartthrob in the Monkees, a pop-rock band created for a TV show in the 1960s. She didn't like tall guys and loved my hair, the way it swept across my forehead like Davy's.

"You're so cute and kind. You mean the world to me, Rob Tonkin." Debra told me.

Her unique appearance appealed to me. It stemmed from her mixed ancestry—her mother, Bonnie, had Italian and Blackfoot Native American roots, while her father was a Scottish Catholic known as Scotty and shared my name, Robert. Debra grew up among five sisters, all immersed in a competitive dynamic. Debra was second oldest, with one older and three younger siblings. She seemed closest with Nicole, two years her junior. I was to navigate the challenges posed by her sister's judgments, her conservative upbringing, and the attentive gaze of her parents.

In the early years of our relationship, I lived a double life in the trenches of the service industry—from waiter to cook to manager in one restaurant and busboy at another fancier one. Then, I would morph back into a mobile deejay with my company Disco Party Sound. The entertainment gigs went well, so I eventually ditched the restaurant grind. Meanwhile, Debra was finishing high school and working for a printer toner store, then as a hostess at Fidel's Mexican, a notorious Carlsbad watering hole and restaurant.

In the spring of 1982, Jeff did me a huge favor by connecting me to The Mighty 690 where I was hired as a weekend deejay. While it wasn't in Northern California, the job still fulfilled a childhood dream I had long had of being a Top 40 deejay on KFRC-AM, The Big 610, in San Francisco. The Mighty 690 was owned by Edward J. Noble, an Irish American advertising professional who had emigrated to Mexico.

There, he founded an advertising agency that eventually grew to become the largest in Latin America, with several offices serving multinational corporations advertising to the Latino market. This successful agency was ultimately sold for an impressive sum exceeding $150 million. While living in Mexico, Noble married a Mexican citizen, and they had five children, all of whom held dual citizenship. The children possessed a license for the Mexican radio station, while their father established an American operating company to broadcast in English.

Two weeks after my arrival at The Mighty 690, Jeff exited for a bigger job in San Francisco. Thanks to him getting me the job, I was able to truly relaunch Disco Party Sound, which I renamed Party Sounds as the disco trend fizzled and died. The radio station became a pipeline for gigs when people called in wanting to hire a deejay for weddings, other events, and opening for bands or playing during their breaks. I took Party Sounds very seriously, and it became my biggest source of revenue.

With my new radio job and deejay business, my income jumped significantly, and I was generous with Debra. At Nordstrom, I bought her the first pair of designer jeans she had ever owned and got her a fancy hair salon makeover in La Jolla. I even took her to Benihana, a high-end Japanese restaurant where the meal was cooked at our table, for her birthday.

Every weekend, and often for fill-in shifts, I'd make the long haul down to Mexico—a 100-mile roundtrip for each air shift, twice a weekend—to broadcast from the control room of The Mighty 690, nestled at the base of its towering transmitter. Within a year, I was juggling those duties with the role of promotions director. The Mighty 690 was located near the coast in an area known as Baja Malibu. Driving through Tijuana during the rainy season presented various challenges as I made my way to the toll road highway along the Pacific Ocean. The dirt connector roads in the grimy border city were primarily made of clay soil, which often became oversaturated and slippery. This resulted in frequent detours that sometimes led to dead ends before reaching the highway. Traveling along these roads was always a gamble, as I never knew what obstacles I would encounter. Looking back, I realize that despite my fearlessness at the time, this was an exceptionally unsafe undertaking.

Upon arriving at the station, a sense of solitude prevailed. Typically, only one other individual was present, responsible for operating the transmitter as part of a Mexican union requirement. A few times, Debra accompanied me and basked in the sun on the nearby Baja Malibu beach while I spun the tunes for my six-hour marathon shift. Most Top 40 radio stations had on-air shifts that were three or four hours long. At the station, a thirty-pound, short-haired mutt named Gringa kept me company.

As devoted as I was to my job, I never put my relationship with Debra on the back burner. About a year into our life as a couple, I got a weekend off from work, so we took a short road trip to my hometown of Sacramento in my van. We enjoyed an adventurous day rafting down the American River. And then I introduced Debra to Mom.

"It's so nice to finally meet you, Debra," Mom said, flashing a warm smile. "Rob has told me so much about you."

"It's nice to meet you too, Mrs. Tonkin," Debra replied politely.

"Mrs. Robinson!" Mom snapped back.

During another conversation, Mom raised questions about Debra's faith and the possibility of converting to Judaism.

"So, Debra," Mom began, her voice taking on a curious tone, "I understand you're Catholic. Have you ever considered converting to Judaism?"

I shot my mom a surprised look. "Mom!" I interjected, "Where is this coming from?"

"Just curious, Dear," she replied smoothly.

This surprised me, given that Mom had never shown much interest in religion and married a gentile, also known as a non-Jew.

"Well," Debra stammered, a bit flustered, "I've always been Catholic, but I'm open to learning about other religions."

The whole encounter left me frustrated and feeling bad for Debra, to be put in such an awkward position.

We then met with my dad, who was guarded, still resenting me for the "betrayal" of wanting to live with Mom for a year after I'd lived with him for over half a decade. His values also made it difficult for Debra and me to stay overnight in his house. So we parked the maroon Dodge van in his driveway after going out in Sacramento and spent the night in each other's arms.

We approached his doorstep the next morning. At breakfast with Dad, he spoke of his work, life in the bottling plant, his many social and charitable ventures, including the Rotary Club, and the fact that he had once been named Sacramentan of the Year. He harshly criticized Debra for preferring Coca-Cola to 7-Up. Suddenly, I felt closer to her than ever.

Seeing Debra, the girl I was falling for, being judged and dismissed by my parents just like I had been, forged a bond between us. We were two outsiders, finding solace and understanding in each other's company.

When we returned to Carlsbad, I let Debra use my prized maroon Dodge van to run an errand. Unfortunately, she got into an accident, leaving her bruised but otherwise okay. The van was a total loss, all my deejay equipment and records from a gig the night before scattered across the 78 freeway. Most of it, which was still intact, I picked up using a van from the radio station that I could also borrow for future gigs. I bought a sleek new black Honda Civic, a six-speed with incredible gas mileage to get me to and from Mexico. I would eventually buy some used vans as well.

Debra and I continued our wild ride, but rough waters were ahead. I discovered that her ex-boyfriend from middle school, a surfer dude, had a grudge against me. He resented me, a "kook" by his definition, for winning Debra's heart, and took it upon himself to steal my cherished red bike, which matched a yellow one I had bought for Debra. Meanwhile, I became increasingly uncomfortable with all the looks Debra was getting from other guys. The deep-rooted feelings of rejection from my childhood made me jealous and paranoid, and the more I let my distrust known, the more she played with it, flirtatiously smiling at other men as they gawked at her.

Jealousy, however, was a two-way street. Debra didn't like my new-found Southern California fame as a deejay and viewed every friendly conversation with a girl as a betrayal. It was a vicious cycle. We would run toward one another and make passionate love right there on the spot, sometimes in the foyer or on the stairway to the bedroom, and the next minute, we'd have a terrible fight about some perceived slight. We'd call it quits two tumultuous years after I had first spotted her riding her little moped in those tiny dolphin shorts. Then spent the next four years getting back together, breaking up, then doing it all over again—until finally, we'd separate for good when I was twenty-five, and she, twenty-two.

21

BEAT IT

In the meantime, my job at The Mighty 690 had gone extraordinarily well. It was somewhat surreal to think that the station had an audience of more than 1 million weekly listeners. Most of these people were in San Diego, Orange, Los Angeles, Riverside, and Ventura counties, primarily accessing the station through their car radios.

This remarkable signal, which stretched some 200 miles north, wasn't just a job. It was the one place where I felt I belonged, where I mattered. So, from a hidden world within, achieved from the humble confines of a small, dark brown, wood-veneer-paneled studio that was really nothing more than a shack, I poured myself into it. Every on-air shift, every promotion, every listener interaction was a lifeline to a reality I craved. Yet returning home after work through the US border crossing was an incredibly chaotic and frustrating experience. Often, I waited for hours in a line of backed-up cars, breathing in their noxious fumes. It could take me a staggering four hours to travel from the studio to my house, all on my own dime, with lots of wear and tear on my precious black Honda Civic.

One of the major goals of the team that ran The Mighty 690 was to build a presence in Los Angeles, a lucrative market where the station, thanks to its huge reach, stood to gain an even larger audience, leading to more revenue. At the end of 1983, I was asked to move to LA. So, for nearly a year, I worked out of a rented apartment on Doheny Drive just south of the Sunset Strip. Each weekend, I still drove down in The

Mighty 690 van for my weekend radio shift in Mexico, which added another two to three hours, each way, to my commute. I would spend my nights in a cheap Mission Valley hotel room, fighting for sleep against the roar of the busy interstate highway just outside my window.

One of the more memorable on-air promotions I created as the promotions director for The Mighty 690 was around the popular "Weird Al" Yankovic song "Eat It," a parody of Michael Jackson's "Beat It." Listeners were asked to call in to win a copy of Weird Al's latest album, *Weird Al Yankovic in 3-D*. Their names were then entered into a drawing for the grand prize: dinner with Weird Al and his band. Al chose to have the meal at the iconic Mexican restaurant El Coyote, which years later would be featured in the Quentin Tarantino film *Once Upon a Time in Hollywood*. My real life seemed to match the film's premise as it swerved back and forth between reality and an entirely alternate universe.

Mom and Rob, lured by the bright lights of Los Angeles, made a couple of visits while I was there. The letters they sent afterward, especially the first, revealed a surprising new dimension to my mother:

> "Rob dear,
>
>   We just stopped for a bite and picked up this card—we miss you already. We loved being with you and enjoyed our stay in your comfy apartment. It's so good to see you so happy, doing what you like to do and doing it well. We have every reason to be proud—first, for being the person you are: intelligent, ambitious, sincere, diligent, persevering, polite, refined, handsome, etc., etc., etc. ;-).
> ... Love ya oodles, Mom."

Revisiting this memory surprised me because it differs from the tension I typically recall of Mom's character. During their second visit, anxiety arose when I addressed her excessive drinking and her return to smoking. I believe Rob significantly influenced her ability to write this letter, tapping into her vulnerable side.

The second letter, from Carole, was more introspective:

> "Robbie dear,
>
> Today, I received your payment, and thank you... It reminds me of the past when I have loaned you money and never asked you for a payment. I have always trusted you... You've proven that, and I consider it very special. I totally trust you in every respect... This all brings me to another point ... regarding our relationship as a mother and son. I am not asking you to approve of everything I do. All I am asking you to do is accept me as your mother, with my weaknesses and my strengths, and accept me for me... Don't sit in judgment of me as it isn't fair.... I do not consider my social drinking a problem, and I am not proud of the fact that I smoke. On the other hand, I do not approve of everything you do, nor do I have to.... So why not accept each other the way we are?... I am proud of your success and love sharing it with you, both the ups and downs.... Why do you feel you must judge me, my habits, and my life and approve of what I do?... I've found I cannot depend on anyone to defend or support me. I must do it myself and I am doing that with you now.... To my knowledge, I have been supportive and have loved you as I do today and always will.... My thoughts are sincere, and I hope you accept them. Please get in touch and let me know your feelings. Always, your loving Mom."

When I received it, I likely struggled to empathize with Mom, but now, with age and maturity, I realize that she cared deeply and was proud of me, but was also grappling with her own demons.

22

RADIO CLASH

AM radio's coolness, which once attracted me to it, had faded with the rise of FM in the seventies. FM stations lured away younger listeners by offering not just superior sound and stereo broadcasts, but also diverse music formats. While 91X, our FM station, thrived once it flipped to alternative rock, The Mighty 690, our AM station, struggled to maintain its audience. After changing formats from Top 40 to oldies, we needed a boost.

During a brainstorming session with the general manager and program director, someone suggested bringing in a celebrity spokesperson to build the station's image—a figure with widespread appeal, like Dick Clark, the timeless *American Bandstand* host. We contacted his wife and manager, Kari, regarding two TV spots that would sync the visuals to Ray Charles's 1959 "What'd I Say" and The Temptations' iconic "My Girl," two classic oldies with maximum recognition. Kari Clark liked the idea, so I negotiated a reasonable payout, and we had a deal.

Dick Clark arrived at the Hollywood studio and conducted himself like a seasoned pro. It was an incredible experience for me to meet him and play the client role while Dick approached the session with enthusiasm, reading his lines effortlessly, and reciting them in a way that showed genuine passion for the music and the station. He encouraged anyone who heard or saw the commercial to "Tune in to 69 XTRA Gold," the new name for the station that had been The Mighty 690, and convincingly noted that this was the station he enjoyed listening to whenever he was in San Diego. His endorsement was incredible, a surreal experience. I'd grown up watching him on TV, aware of his impact behind the scenes, and now the tables had turned: he was the one seeking my approval.

Toward the end of 1984, I received a job promotion: I would also become promotions director for 91X, which with its new hip format was making inroads in the ratings against longtime market leader KGB-FM, the San Diego market's longtime album-rock station. It was a big step up, and 91X's irreverence fit my young punk-ish attitude. I moved back to San Diego and settled in Pacific Beach, home to many of the city's most popular clubs and restaurants, as well as a nearly three-mile oceanfront boardwalk filled on virtually any summer day with bikini-clad roller-skaters, bicyclists, and joggers.

Heaven.

Despite 91X's steady ascent in the ratings, we had a tight budget for on-air promotions and contests. Most of our marketing dollars were spent on TV spots and outdoor billboards advertising the station to the masses. We had also printed up oval-shaped, black-and-yellow 91X bumper stickers that caught on and at one time appeared on what I estimate were about 20 percent of the cars I'd see on the road. My promotional-guru self always believed that when a sliver of good momentum occurs, it's time to add fuel. Focus on a good idea and amplify it. We ordered hundreds of thousands of additional stickers to support the sticker campaign and let our fans advertise for us. This cost money, but station management felt it was worth the investment. Attractive and long-lasting stickers meant listeners would feel good about applying them to their vehicles.

The next important step was to find a mass local distribution method. Applying some of what I had learned as a young kid in the bottling plant, I created a fashion brand to promote the station, and a good number of surf, action sportswear, record stores, and souvenir shops sold our 91X T-shirts at a hefty profit. They were more than happy to hand out our stickers, too, to help draw foot traffic into their stores, particularly since we'd mention the sticker handouts on the air. We then schemed to get the stickers into fast-food restaurants so that every bag or tray would include a sticker. Welcome to the family, Carl's Jr., our third choice after McDonald's and Burger King turned us down.

I knew that greater public awareness of the station would invariably translate to higher listenership and ratings, which, in turn, meant the station could charge more money for advertising and please my bosses. So, we upped the ante. We built a big promotion around a concert in Sydney, Australia, by Genesis, a progressive rock band that was becoming increasingly popular with the alternative rock fan 91X hoped to attract. We worked out a deal with the record company for us to receive ten meet-and-greets, and got a cruise liner to give us cruises and an airline to give us airline tickets, all in exchange for on-air mentions. Our catchy hook, "How to drive to Australia," hit the airwaves.

To win, listeners needed a 91X sticker on their car. Our street team would be out spotting cars all over San Diego County, and if they saw one, we'd announce the license plate, car color, and description on the air. The driver then had thirty minutes to call in and claim ninety-one dollars. For five weeks, ten winners each week received ninety-one bucks. We also held a random drawing where one of those winners could snag the weekly grand prize: a trip for two to Australia to see and meet Genesis, followed by an all-expense paid cruise through the Tahitian Islands. To spread the word about the contest, we printed the details on the back of 91X stickers and distributed them widely throughout San Diego County, partnering with Carl's Jr., and other businesses to reach as many people as possible.

Naturally, I had no intention of missing out on the excitement of the grand prize trip. I persuaded the station manager that a chaperone was necessary to ensure everything ran smoothly. I volunteered my services, managing to also secure a spot for a friend to accompany me. My choice of guest reflected the times: Ralph, my cocaine dealer. In the eighties, coke was everywhere, and in my circles, so was Ralph.

The trip was a blast—both figuratively and literally. Cocktails flowed freely during our long flight to Australia, and Ralph consumed his remaining amount of cocaine in the plane's restroom. We made it through Australian customs and were taken to our hotel in Kings Cross, Sydney's entertainment and red-light district. I met up with my travel agency friends, Murray and Robert, who'd orchestrated this whole adventure. We'd become friends as they'd often arranged experiences for radio stations and contest winners. They introduced me to radio people in Sydney and took us to dinner at a fancy Indian restaurant. It was the first time I had ever eaten Indian food.

The Australian radio folks also invited a few single women to the dinner, including Cassie, a slender, whip-smart, long-legged blonde, and Karen, shorter, dark-haired, witty, and *sassy*. Dinner with Cassie and Sassy! Then we met up with the winners and saw them off as they were taken to the concert. I went back to my hotel room to freshen up. Ralph was passed out on the bed—no blow, no go.

I headed off to the show where Murray and Robert, accompanied by Cassie and Karen, were eager to see how their planning unfolded. Backstage I escorted the contest winners to meet Genesis band members Phil Collins, Mike Rutherford, and Tony Banks. They politely acknowledged us, we took a group photo, and then we walked over into the main hall of the Sydney Entertainment Center, where even those of us who weren't diehard Genesis fans were wowed by the show.

After the concert, Murray and Robert whisked me away to the Kardomah Café, a hidden gem of a live music club tucked away in the city's underbelly. Australian radio folks, as well as Cassie and Karen, came as well. The club was just a short walk from our hotel, which was perfect since I had my eye on smart and sassy Karen. She was stunning, and a bit of a challenge—exactly my type. Fueled by the music and flowing screwdrivers, we lingered until the wee hours. One by one, everyone else eventually took their leave, leaving Karen and me alone, just as I'd hoped.

But the night took an unexpected turn when Karen disappeared in the restroom. After a while, I went to check on her and found her leaning over the toilet, paying the price for the Indian food and potent screw-drivers. We stumbled back to the bar, clinging to each other for support. After a couple of glasses of water, we departed back to the hotel.

Standing in the lobby, I seized the chance and invited her up to my room. To my surprise, Ralph was still passed out cold. A quick shake brought him back to consciousness where he took one look at the situation, mumbled something about needing fresh air, and made a hasty retreat. What followed was pure magic, the highlight of the night, the highlight of the trip ... heck, it was one of the highlights of my life!

Later that morning, I had to scramble. Karen left. Ralph returned, packed, and left while I was showering. Like my mad dash to catch the group during that school trip to Europe, I threw my things together and raced to the bus, disheveled and late.

"Sorry," I announced breathlessly, "I haven't been feeling well since an Indian dinner last night."

The irony wasn't lost on me—I was supposed to be the responsible one, looking after *them*. But my night with Karen had been too good to miss.

I had another gotta-go-now moment when we launched the "Louie, Louie" promotion at 91X. To boost ratings, we decided to dedicate an entire day to playing different versions of "Louie, Louie," a Black penned classic popularized by White rock group, The Kingsmen, that was a huge hit in 1963. Since then, it's been covered by tons of diverse artists like Black Flag, the Beach Boys, The Kinks, Toots & the Maytals, and Motörhead, to name a few. We played them back-to-back all day long, with no commercials, on what we called "Louie, Louie Sunday."

Coincidentally, that same Sunday in July 1987, I'd also signed on 91X as a sponsor of the Stubbie's Pro Surfing Contest. Now we had two big events, completely unrelated to each other, scheduled for the same day. *How could we tie them together?* I recalled a television and radio commercial campaign for California Cooler, a trendy alcoholic beverage known as a wine cooler—essentially, diluted effervescent sangria. The company had produced an ad that featured "Louie, Louie" as the soundtrack, with visuals of people partying and singing along as they enjoyed California Coolers on the beach. As the commercial buoyed about in my mind, a way to combine the two promotions came to me: We could recreate the commercial on the beach during the surf contest, and to take things up a notch, have the original Kingsmen perform the song live, at the end of the contest to celebrate the winners.

The "Louie, Louie" promotion was a blast and felt like I was conducting an orchestra. I was artistically adding just the right ingredients and colors to bring an idea to life. I had to persuade California Cooler to participate and soon discovered that brands plan far in advance with little room for changes once decisions are made. It was a challenge, but I secured their support. Then I located and convinced The Kingsmen to come out of retirement and play a gig. They agreed, and we found an opening act—a local novelty act featuring former San Diego Mayor Roger Hedgecock and my journalist buddy, Thomas K. Arnold, who, as The Arnold-Hedgecock Experience, had recorded "Louie, Louie" as a benefit single for a local charity. They jumped at the chance to perform a song or two before The Kingsmen took the stage. This brought in tons of additional local PR value.

But my greatest promotional triumph had come just before "Louie, Louie," in the spring of 1987. It was called "X-Pose the X" and involved getting listeners to display our logo in the most prominent way they could think of. The winners were to receive significant prizes for their bravado. The top prize of $25,000 went to an enterprising listener who spent three weeks creating four elaborate ten-second claymation commercials featuring the 91X logo—and then buying airtime on a local TV station to play them twelve times a week for several weeks.

The second-prize winner created a four-inch ceramic pin modeled after the 91X bumper sticker and got actress Valerie Bertinelli to wear it while hosting an episode of *Saturday Night Live*. She wore it first during the opening monologue, and again while introducing the featured musical guest, Van Halen (Bertinelli at the time was married to the late Eddie Van Halen, the band's guitarist). It was a moment of beautiful irony for 91x, a station known for its alternative leanings, being embraced by Valerie—one degree away from hard rockers Van Halen—on national TV.

One of the third-place runners-up painted an old Cadillac black with the 91X logo on each side. He then hoisted it up ninety-one feet in the air with a crane, revealing a giant 91X banner on the car's underside, and spent the next ninety-one days living in the car.

Another runner-up got 91X more national TV exposure during the annual PGA golf tournament at La Jolla's Torrey Pines Golf Course. He snuck in a black umbrella emblazoned with a big 91X logo across the top, which he opened and aimed sideways in the eyeline of the ball just as a golfer hit an eagle while sinking a putt. Cameras captured the rare feat, and TV news and sports announcers nationally broadcast the lucky golf shot—and the open umbrella with the 91X logo—repeatedly for several days.

Another impressive display involved 1,000 high school students spelling out the 91X logo on a football field. The "X-Pose the X" promotion still ranks as the most successful promotion in 91X history. It also elevated my reputation in radio circles across the country, fueled my ego, and my paycheck. By then, I was making enough money from my radio gig, and the mobile deejay business I had once again built up into a lucrative side hustle, that I was able to buy my first, three-bedroom, house in Pacific Beach for $187,500, a huge amount of money at the time.

Not bad for a twenty-four-year-old whose father firmly told him, "You'll amount to nothing without a college degree. Your life will be far worse."

23

FATHER OF MINE

Party Sounds had been a lifeline after my abrupt firing from radio in Bakersfield. I'd arrived at Cousin Tommy's in Carlsbad feeling lost and unsure of my next steps and needed to make money while figuring things out. I took restaurant jobs, but they'd seemed like a step backward, so I had decided to dust off my old deejay equipment and music library and resurrect Party Sounds.

In the larger San Diego market, I'd replicated the same grassroots marketing strategy I'd used in high school back in Sacramento. I placed ads in weekly newspapers, and gradually, the gigs started trickling in. Landing even one school as a client meant repeat bookings throughout the year, providing a steady income stream. Over time, I upgraded my equipment. Leveraging my connections at The Mighty 690 and 91X also vastly expanded the company's reach. Referrals and repeat business helped build a solid client base. I even figured out a way to do barter advertising with the radio stations, trading services for airtime to promote Party Sounds. It was a win-win situation, and it helped to transform my side hustle into a serious business. Eventually, I had five complete audio and lighting systems, as well as some used vans to transport it all, allowing me to service multiple events simultaneously.

Remembering the early success of using celebrity radio deejays in my Sacramento days, I incorporated that into my San Diego marketing, creating a sub-brand, the "91X Road Show," allowing us to command premium prices. To maximize profits, I also rented out our equipment and crew when they weren't booked for events. Since I also had a demanding, full-time, radio day job, I retired from personally deejaying gigs and solely hired people to spin records as well as run what had become a

management-intensive business. We used my garage to store the vinyl, sound, and lighting equipment. There was a small shed connected to the garage, and we built it out to be our office. My operations manager also got compensated with free rent in one of my spare bedrooms and the incremental income he made by booking and deejaying events.

In the mideighties, personal computers were still a novelty, like something out of a science fiction movie. But we were determined to bring Party Sounds into the digital age: no more handwritten contracts or endless phone calls to confirm music selections. We hired a programmer to create custom software that allowed us to generate professional-looking contracts, personalized cover letters, and even music lists for clients to browse and make requests in advance.

This was revolutionary. Our deejays knew exactly what to play before they even arrived at an event, giving us a serious edge over the competition. It may seem commonplace now, but back then, this technology gave us a distinct corporate image and streamlined our entire operation. Clients were impressed, and as a result, we were able to charge more and handle a higher volume of bookings with greater efficiency.

As my radio career was taking off, ambition burned within me to expand Party Sounds nationwide. We had all the ingredients for a successful franchise: cutting-edge technology, a vast music library, and a proven track record. Imagine a nationwide network of Party Sounds deejays, ready to entertain at any event! "We" included my expansion partner, Mark Rowlands, who was just as enthusiastic about the idea. Mark was key to this plan because he was an established supplier of European, Asian, and American equipment with connections throughout the budding deejay industry. He also owned an equipment distributorship in LA and his own deejay company. We worked together and became close friends.

"We could be the next big thing!" he'd exclaim, his eyes sparkling with excitement. "Party Sounds in every city!"

Together, we engaged a franchise consultant who helped us develop a comprehensive business plan. It outlined the path to nationwide expansion, but it also revealed the financial outlay required.

Even though I was only twenty-five and hadn't gone to college, I was considered a successful businessman. I'd built my company from scratch, worked for a major market radio station, and even bought my first house near the ocean in Pacific Beach. Owning my own home felt great. Through some early childhood experiences, I'd glimpsed affluence and its possibilities, and a part of me yearned to replicate that feeling of privilege, constantly seeking stability through wealth, maybe a bit like Mom.

"It's a lot of money," Mark acknowledged, "but the potential for growth is huge."

Franchising needed outside capital, a whole new level of investment. Both the consultant and Mark recommended securing an initial round of funding from friends and family before approaching institutional investors. I was living in a time before the sexiness of a startup business or the appeal of crowdfunding was a thing.

"Start with your inner circle," the consultant advised. "People who believe in you and your vision."

Hesitantly, I approached my mother first. Her immediate response was, "Ask your father, honey."

That response ached, especially considering her and Rob's financial resources.

So, I made an appointment with my estranged father.

"Dad, it's Robbie," I said on the phone, my voice a bit shaky. "I was hoping we could meet. There's something I'd like to discuss with you."

He paused, and I could practically hear the gears turning in his head.

"All right," he finally replied, his tone cautious. "How about Saturday at the office? We can meet in the conference room."

I had already consulted with my brother, Jim, about how to approach

Dad. Jim had a knack for persuasion. Sometime before this, he'd convinced our great-uncle Harry, who had been Dad's majority partner for years, to invest in a potato chip venture. It was a bold idea yet seemed like it could work. Unfortunately, the chips crumbled, so to speak, and the business fizzled out after a year.

"He's not going to be easy to convince," Jim warned me over the phone, the night before. Jim had worked for Dad for years, knew his ways better than anyone, and agreed to be present not just as my brother, but as a seasoned negotiator who still knew how to win Dad over.

And so, after a seven-hour drive from San Diego to Sacramento, I found myself at the bottling plant. Upon my arrival, I exchanged pleasantries with the financial controller, Jim, and my father. Dad sat across from me, while the other two flanked him.

"Robbie," Dad said, his voice surprisingly warm, "It's good to see you. What brings you here?"

I took a deep breath, steeling myself for the conversation ahead. "Dad, I have a proposition for you...."

Dad asked me to explain the business to him. I had copies of the business plan and started to go through a brief narrative until he interrupted me, "Uh, Robbie, I have a few questions."

As I began to field them, I shrank lower in my chair because they weren't related to the business. They were about me.

"Do you know how to read a balance sheet?"

"I think so, but please know we'll be hiring a financial person to do that. What I want to convey is how this deejay business is so fresh, we're like cowboys on a new frontier," I responded.

"Can you explain to me what a balance sheet is?" Dad quipped. The conversation seemed to be going backward.

"Well, it tells us the amounts in each account, I think...," I trailed off.

"Do you know the difference between a balance sheet, a profit and loss statement, and an income statement?" Dad snapped back.

"Well, I will learn all of that! Dad, I've been running my own business for years and managing budgets for the radio stations...."

He couldn't see my point or sense my unease at the barrage. "Do you know what debits are, what credits are?" he continued. "Have you ever operated a business in this financial way? What makes you think you can do this?"

Finally, I said, "This feels like I'm being tested about my financial aptitude. I'm seeking your advice and support on my business expansion idea!"

Jim chimed in, "Robbie, Dad is trying to help you."

My natural reaction was to explain my game plan, which was to focus on the creative and conceptual part of the business and hire people with financial competence to take care of the rest. But in my head, I kept thinking, *Who are these assholes, and why are they so mean? Why don't they care about hearing my idea?*

My years of experience and proven track record in running a profitable business while maintaining a full-time job didn't interest my Dad or the group. Nor did the fact that I had been able to buy a house without his assistance at the age of twenty-four.

The conversation centered instead on my lack of education. The fact that I didn't go to college meant, to my father, that I was unqualified to run a business and, thus, the risk of him investing any amount of money was far too great. I sensed that even if Dad had a million dollars of extra cash in his safe, which he didn't, he wouldn't have parted with fifty bucks to invest in my business. *Didn't he see what I had already accomplished?* I had artfully carved a path without any support from my blood family. Why was this man using his position of power and money over me to try to convince me to get an education? Why couldn't he see the goodness in me, my intelligence, creativity, and willingness to take risks?

Even the controller, the outsider in the room, seemed uncomfortable and embarrassed by Dad's grilling, lack of support, and disinterest in anything I had prepared or creatively envisioned. Couldn't Dad have, at the very least, complimented any of my accomplishments in a show of fatherly support? Rather Dad's words hung in the air like a thick fog, obscuring everything.

I eventually stumbled out into the hallway, each step heavy and uncertain. My chest felt constricted, my breath catching in my throat. It was like a weight had settled on my shoulders, pressing me down, down, down. All I could hear was the dull thud of my heartbeat, a lonely rhythm in the sudden silence. I felt invisible, like a ghost drifting through a world that couldn't see or hear me. My father, the man I'd looked up to, had dismissed my dreams with a wave of his hand. It was worse than rejection; it was a complete erasure.

I could barely see the road through the tears that flowed freely the entire drive home to San Diego. With my spirits as low as my visibility, the aspiration of starting a national deejay company felt like it was slipping away.

When I got back, I informed my partner Mark and the consultant we had hired that there wasn't a chance in hell my dad was going to put seed money into the business. And since Mark didn't want to be the only one providing capital for our franchising plan, the whole venture unraveled.

24

ONLY A LAD

I dealt with agonizing disappointment by throwing myself into my work, subconsciously hoping it would be my grand savior, or, at least, a momentary solace. Music and radio, too, had helped me cope with the stresses of my teenhood.

One of the most memorable events I organized for 91X was a massive festival concert designed to promote both the radio station and Mexican tourism. It was called MeXfest and was to be held in Tijuana on June 30, 1987, as something of a grand finale to "X-Pose the X."

MeXfest originated from a meeting with John Lynch, the minority owner and operating partner of Noble Broadcasting, the company that owned 91X. Raised in the Midwest, Lynch was a second-generation Irish American who had climbed the ranks in radio in San Diego. He held the distinction of being the only American in charge of Mexican radio stations. Physically imposing, John was tall, clean-cut, and slightly overweight. In his younger days, he played college football and was even drafted by the Pittsburgh Steelers. Unfortunately, a knee injury prevented him from ever playing in the NFL. On the other hand, his son, John Jr., fulfilled his father's dream by excelling in football. A multi-time Pro Bowl selection, John Jr. would go on to earn a Super Bowl ring with the Tampa Bay Buccaneers and later become the general manager of the San Francisco 49'ers. Years before that, I'd had the opportunity to deejay John Jr.'s sixteenth birthday party. I'd also booked renowned bands for the annual grad night concert at a prominent North County high school stadium in San Diego, where John Jr. attended and played high school football.

The meeting took place in John's impressive office. He requested that I keep things confidential. He then explained an interesting fact: "The radio station's license belongs to the Noble family, who are Mexican Americans. As operators of the station, we have an agreement with the Mexican FCC to promote tourism in Mexico through our broadcasts." This explained why we frequently aired public service announcements highlighting vacation spots like Loreto, Mexico, on the Baja peninsula. Then he told me, "For political purposes, we need to organize a concert in Mexico. Specific details are still up in the air. However, I'm meeting with the owner of Caliente, the dog and horse racing track just minutes away from the border in Tijuana."

Lynch invited me to join him for dinner at Dobson's, a downtown restaurant popular with San Diego's power elite. We were ushered upstairs, where within seconds, we found ourselves face-to-face with Jorge Hank Rhon, the enigmatic owner of the Caliente Racetrack. This wasn't just any racetrack; Caliente was a Tijuana institution, a sprawling complex hosting both horse and dog races. And Hank Rohn himself was a larger-than-life figure—a man who would later become the mayor of Tijuana.

Hank Rohn had long, dark brown hair and matching stubble on his face. He had an effortless sense of style, opting for casual attire, complete with cowboy boots crafted from exotic animal skins. Notably, he spoke flawless English, with little trace of any accent. He spoke softly, conveying a sense of humility, which immediately made us both like him. The three of us discussed creating a concert event at the racetrack. Hank Rohn generously said, "I am excited and honored to offer the facility at no charge, and will help however possible."

My next step was to request a site visit to familiarize myself with the venue and assess its potential as a rock concert location. Until then, there hadn't been any notable pop or rock acts performing in Tijuana, except for a Santana concert that reportedly took place at the bullfighting ring several years earlier. As I mulled over our plans, I wondered, *How can we persuade artists to include Tijuana in their tour stops even though it's not a typical destination? How do we combat the unfavorable perception of Mexico, especially Tijuana, and ensure the safety and security of artists and their teams? What factors make a racetrack an appropriate choice for a concert?* Finally, *Can we trust Hank Rohn?*

Visiting the track, I went on a comprehensive tour of every area, including the luxurious turf club, where Hank Rohn made sure that I met a couple of attractive hostesses.

"That's quite the welcoming committee," I chuckled, trying to maintain my composure amid the gigantic pack of yapping chihuahuas mixed with other rare miniature Mexican dogs that encircled Hank Rohn.

"They have a way of sensing good people," Hank Rohn said with a wink as I wondered, *Is he talking about the girls or the pooches?* Then he gestured toward a plush armchair. "Have a seat. Tell me, what are your impressions of the track so far?"

"It's impressive," I admitted. "But I'm curious, what are your ambitions for doing this concert? What do you hope to achieve?"

Hank Rohn leaned back in his chair, a thoughtful expression crossing his face. "More than just exposing racing and the music," he said, his voice filled with a quiet passion. "I want to create an experience, something that draws people from all over, especially those young Americans."

"And why is that?" I asked, intrigued.

A glint of determination shone in his eyes. "Because," he declared, "I want to elevate Tijuana's image. I want to showcase the vibrancy of our culture, the energy of our city, and the hospitality of our people. I want to change perceptions and create a destination that rivals the best in the world." He paused, then added with a serious tone, "And most importantly, I want to ensure that every visitor, especially those young Americans, feels safe and welcome here." He leaned forward, his voice taking on a conspiratorial tone. "You see, my friend, a thriving, safe

Tijuana reflects well." He winked.

I left the track convinced that it would make an excellent concert venue. After securing myself as the show's producer, the next step was to obtain technical support. This proved challenging since radio stations typically didn't purchase talent or hire crews and rig gear for concerts. Therefore, developing a thoughtful strategy became necessary to organize the staging, choose and book the artists, and create a comfortable compound for their safety.

Unfortunately, choosing one of the two local concert promoters in town would inevitably alienate the other, and regardless of who we picked, they'd likely perceive us as encroaching on their territory by taking their artists away from local venues and using them in Mexico. Also, I wasn't convinced they'd fully grasp the nuances of the situation and the importance of this particular event. They might dismiss it as unfeasible, lacking the desire to align with our political and strategic motivations driving the initiative. On the other hand, I had previously interacted with MEGA, a trailblazer in the then-new concept of music tour sponsorships. MEGA was a small New York City-based entertainment marketing agency and I knew their managing partners had formerly excelled in talent acquisition. I shared my thoughts with Lynch and "Mad Max" Tolkoff, 91X's program director, and we agreed an end run using MEGA was the best approach.

Max and I had already discussed our preferred artists, so we had a clear direction in mind. Our initial focus was securing a headliner since they typically draw the largest crowds to concerts. However, we also planned to create a festival-style show with multiple acts. I spoke with Hank Rohn about potential dates, and we settled on June 30, 1987, a Tuesday, despite my misgivings about staging an event in Tijuana on a weekday rather than the weekend.

Securing the lineup for MeXfest was a high-stakes game. Every artist we approached was a calculated risk, a gamble that could either pay off spectacularly or backfire dramatically. Finding the right headliner proved to be an even greater challenge. We cycled through a string of potential acts, some of whom, sensing the unique nature of the event, made exorbitant demands as their agents and handlers saw dollar signs in our desperation. It was a frustrating dance of rejections, floating offers, receiving counteroffers, and constantly weighing the cost against the potential return. Each inflated demand forced us to make a tough decision: pay up or move on. The tension was palpable, the clock was ticking, and the weight of expectation was heavy on our shoulders. It was a journey fraught with uncertainty and nail-biting negotiations.

Many names were being considered for the headline slot, and we eventually settled on Oingo Boingo, which at the time was popular with the alt-rock crowd through such hits as "Weird Science" and "Dead Man's Party." To round out the bill, we went with The Fixx, Squeeze, Chris Isaak, The Bangles, and the Hoodoo Gurus. It was a fantastic lineup that we were quite proud of.

My agency partners flew someone in for a site check, and we concluded that a stage facing the grandstand seating would not be as effective as hosting the show on the track's grassy infield. This arrangement would allow for an authentic festival-style experience with no seating—everyone gathered on the lawn.

As word of our festival plans spread, we attracted the ire of Avalon Attractions, the prominent Los Angeles-based concert-promoting firm that held an exclusive contract to book shows at the San Diego State University Open Air Theatre, one of the busiest concert spots in town. In the past, they'd relied on us to promote their shows, and in return, they spent money on advertising and gave us ample tickets to use promotionally.

We had a conference call with Avalon executives, and it quickly became apparent that they saw what we'd done as poaching, which they took very seriously. Concert promotion was a fiercely competitive business, and Avalon was particularly upset that our festival planned to feature multiple artists on one bill because this meant it shut them out.

Those artists could not perform or advertise other shows in our area for at least ninety days before and after our event.

To appease them, we made them part of the deal. We agreed to pay them a fee for their services as the local staging production team for the event. We reassured them that our sole intention was to promote this one radio concert event rather than to enter the concert business. Ironically, years later, radio stations across the country would organize concerts of their own without promoters, often with the artists provided free of charge by their record labels in return for guaranteed airplay.

MeXfest was a huge success, selling some 27,000 tickets. The concert began in the afternoon with Chris Isaak, who was having a breakout year with his first successful radio track, "Blue Hotel." Then came Australian rock band Hoodoo Gurus, known for their popular song "What's My Scene," which was in heavy rotation on 91X. Next up was The Fixx, a band from London with several familiar songs, including "Red Skies," "One Thing Leads to Another," "Stand or Fall," and "Saved by Zero." Then came another UK band, Squeeze, performing such hits as "Tempted," "Black Coffee in Bed," and "Cool for Cats." Right before Oingo Boingo came The Bangles, an all-female group rising high with their Prince-penned hit "Manic Monday" and their signature song, "Walk Like an Egyptian." Oingo Boingo didn't take the stage until after 11 p.m., but despite the late hour, they blazed through their theatrical styled repertoire including radio hits and fan favorites such as "Only a Lad," "Little Girls," and "Wild Sex (In the Working Class)." The entire infield was a swirl of sweating, dancing bodies.

A few weeks after MeXfest, a knock at my front door startled me. I opened it to find myself face-to-face with one of the stunning hostesses from Jorge Hank Rohn's exclusive turf club at the Calienté Racetrack. It was a shocking surprise. My mind flickered, struggling to process what I was seeing. She led me out to her car, where she popped the trunk to reveal a cooler with a bottle of champagne chilling on ice. I was utterly dumbfounded. *How did she even know where I lived? What was this all about?*

With a captivating Mexican accent, she explained, "You're really cool, and I just wanted to celebrate the success of MeXfest." We went back inside, where we spent the next several hours together. It was an unforgettable encounter that left me both flattered and bewildered. To this day, I still wonder if she acted on her own or if someone, perhaps even Jorge himself, sent her as a thank-you gift.

25

GOOD RIDDANCE

Jorge Hank Rohn may have appreciated me, but I felt Noble Broadcasting did not anymore. While for years, Noble Broadcasting had trusted me to manage budgets and create events, commercials, and promotions, things changed when John Lynch, who had risen from general manager to CEO, expanded Noble Broadcasting nationwide and brought in someone at the corporate level to oversee me, which I resented. My overseer was a man in a suit, the furthest thing from cool, questioning me about everything and taking over aspects of what I was doing. It felt like a substantial blow.

"I can't believe they're doing this to me," I fumed to my colleagues. "After all I've done for this company, they don't trust me to manage a budget?"

Though I was only twenty-five years old, the innovative promotions I had staged at 91X, including "X-Pose the X," "Louie, Louie" and the MeXfest concert, had earned me national recognition. I'd even received an unsolicited job offer from another San Diego radio station and interviews with KIIS-FM, KLSX-FM, and KROQ-FM in Los Angeles.

My frustration became obvious. *I am being singled out.* What was really going on, though, was that I was a young person who didn't have wise and supportive parents or mentors to help guide me. John Lynch was shrewd enough to know that with a large expansion, we all had to be extra careful. The person he'd brought in to oversee me was in risk management. Though we'd accomplished a lot, we needed to be vigilant, follow FCC guidelines, and cross our t's and dot our i's.

I told myself local radio was a repetitive business. National scale work, that's what I yearned for. So, when an opportunity to work at MEGA presented itself, I jumped at the chance. MEGA stood for Marketing Entertainment Group America, as the acronym also echoed the company's status as a mega player in that nascent world of entertainment marketing. A pioneer in bringing corporate sponsorships to music tours, MEGA paired up The Who with Schlitz Beer, the Beach Boys with Sunkist Orange Soda, and The Thompson Twins with Swatch Watches. I had the opportunity to attend The Who show and work with the latter two tours during their stops while I was in San Diego. Combining these seemingly unrelated entities resonated with me and became integral to my life. Working with those tours reinforced my belief in the inevitable merging of brands and musical acts. The fusion of art, craftsmanship, and commercialism, presented most favorably, offered the perfect outlet for my creative talents.

My departure from 91X was neat, clean, and anti-climactic. I made an appointment to meet with John Lynch, walked into his office and simply said, "I've enjoyed my time here, but it's time for me to move on."

He nodded understandingly. "I appreciate all your hard work," he replied. "We wish you the best in your future endeavors."

Exiting 91X and San Diego for MEGA in New York City felt like a leap of faith. I'd be leaving behind not just a radio station and people I'd loved, but also my dogs. I'd raised a pup when I bought my house, and later adopted another, so they were a big part of my life there. I was also leaving my house, and Party Sounds, which I'd been juggling for the past five years. But I felt comfort in the fact that I was leaving these in the capable hands of my Operations Manager, Kevin Lightcap. I was to move across the country to New York and do empowering work with brands and bands across America, while he effectively took over my old life and even brought in a roommate to fill the void created by my absence.

26

NEW YORK, NEW YORK

Upon arriving in New York, I luckily found an incredible apartment through a colleague, Lisa. She said, "I have this friend, a concierge at the Helmsley Palace, a fancy Manhattan hotel, and he's going stir-crazy. I think he needs to get off the island for a while." I moved into his unit as a subletter.

My new home was located on 14th Street between 7th and 8th avenues, near Greenwich Village and Chelsea, and a short commute by subway to SoHo, where MEGA was headquartered. Running east to west, 14th Street was known for a strip of cheap fabric and clothing stores on the south side of the street, where, a NYC hipster told me, "Low-income people shop on weekends for unnatural fabrics."

Just across the street from my apartment stood Nell's, a renowned, upscale club that had opened the year before. Owned by Nell Campbell, an Australian actress and singer famous for her role in the 1975 film *The Rocky Horror Picture Show*, the club was known for its exclusivity, even denying entry to several celebrities.

Previously, in my radio station roles, I had been pursued by people wanting to work with us. At MEGA, I was the one doing the pursuing. I was charged with selling or attempting to sell David Lee Roth as a spokesperson for automakers, getting shopping malls interested in teaming with the MTV Museum of UnNatural History, and promoting Swatch Watch as a tour sponsor for Lisa Lisa and Cult Jam to radio stations and concert promoters who weren't used to tour sponsorships. This was a pronounced shift in my career.

MEGA had a small team led by majority partner Danny Socolof and minority partner Whitten Pell. Working with Whit as his client in San Diego, I'd found him to be a good pal, engaging, and somewhat eccentric. Our relationship took a 180-degree turn as my direct supervisor. Whit frequently summoned me to his office: "Tonkin, show me your binder with the market updates." Then he would review it with me at his desk. "Why is so much information missing? I can't even read these!" he'd snap. Initially, I found this amusing, but over time, it became a humiliating experience. I suspect that my childhood experiences with authority figures may have triggered this. On numerous occasions, Whit even raised his voice: "I'm not interested in hearing bullshit.... I *told* you that if it's not documented on the forms, it *doesn't* exist!" He believed my perceived lack of care in filling out the forms reflected a rebellious attitude. I went from respecting him as a friend to disrespecting him as a boss.

Danny Socolof had consummated the Swatch Watch tour sponsorship deal. He called me into his office and said, "You've been hired to manage the sponsorship to ensure the brand and band are both happy." I was excited by the role and felt the timing was perfect, as Swatch Watch was one of the hottest fashion accessories of the time and Lisa Lisa and Cult Jam were getting significant airplay and rising up the music charts.

One of my duties was to travel to every major tour date. I only had to attend about a dozen shows, since the deal only covered markets where Swatch sales aligned with the crowd Lisa Lisa and Cult Jam attracted, mainly in the Northeast and along the East Coast, as far south as Miami and Atlanta. It was my first time flying to so many cities, most of which I had never been before. Since I wasn't traveling on the tour buses, it felt like I parachuted into all these different cities to spot-check the program and schmooze with the promoter, the band, and any media I could bring into the fold to make noise about the sponsorship.

One of the most appealing aspects of my job involved fashion. Though I had experience creating jackets and designing and selling

T-shirts and hats for radio stations, I was now responsible for conceiving top-notch leather tour jackets for the band, crew, and a select few clients. Swatch was known for its fashion accessories and had recently branched into apparel. It was clear that I was generating fashion for fashionistas.

"You've gotta talk to Norman," Kathy at Swatch had insisted. "He's the best in the business!"

Stormin' Norman was a fashion production icon. Norman's shop was in the Garment District on 22nd Street, eight blocks from my apartment. When I first visited Norman's showroom, I was struck by his commanding leather-clad presence. In his fifties, he was still in decent shape and sported a full head of graying hair. He came across as a character straight out of a movie.

"So, you're the guy with the hot new band," he boomed, extending a hand the size of a baseball glove. "Let's see what you've got."

Norman resembled a clean-cut version of a Harley-riding biker gang member. I couldn't shake the feeling that he might not be the most reliable person, which made me a little nervous.

The room was quite spacious, like a big hall with a hardwood floor and a somewhat disorganized appearance. Racks filled with samples, fabrics, and an assortment of stylish jackets adorned the space. The air buzzed with the rhythmic hum of sewing machines, and I could see skilled sewists hunched over their work, their needles flashing as they stitched intricate designs. Stormin' Norman specialized in satin or leather bomber jackets. Among them were works he had designed and crafted for the Hard Rock Café, the New York Mets baseball team, and the Daytona Racetrack. There were even jackets paying homage to Led Zeppelin.

Stormin' Norman didn't always provide straightforward answers, yet we had a productive conversation about my project.

"Here are the Swatch logos and imagery," I said, spreading them out on the table, "and here's Lisa Lisa's stuff, and here we've combined them."

He rubbed his chin thoughtfully. "Hmm ... interesting. How about a white-leather body with black wool sleeves? Black and white striped ribbed fabric cuffs on the bottom and the sleeves? That'd be sharp."

"I like it!" I responded enthusiastically. "And let's put this logo on the back, nice and big."

"You got it, man," Norman said with a wink. "I'll make you a jacket that'll blow their minds."

I left the showroom feeling confident that I'd been directed to the right person for the job. Norman, despite my initial reservations, had a creative spark and a passion for his craft that was contagious.

The sewing machines buzzed into action, and I would stop in regularly to approve the next steps. I found myself interacting more and more with Norman's assistant, who, it turned out, was my main point of contact throughout the project. And with each interaction, my initial attraction grew stronger. There was something about her quiet confidence and understated style that intrigued me.

A few weeks later, the fifty jackets arrived at our office in SoHo. They were even better than I'd imagined. The white leather was buttery soft, the black wool sleeves were impeccably tailored, and the Swatch logos were bold and eye-catching. The band members were ecstatic, and the crew couldn't wait to sport their new gear. Even *the* Lisa, of Lisa Lisa fame, with her discerning taste, was impressed.

"These are amazing!" she exclaimed, running her hand over the smooth leather. It was gratifying, a testament to creativity through fashion and design, all started with a chance encounter with a biker-looking, leather-clad icon named Stormin' Norman.

My infatuation with Norman's assistant led me to invite her to join me at a concert where Lisa Lisa, who had been quickly blowing up in popularity, was the opening act for David Bowie at Giants Stadium in East Rutherford, New Jersey. She agreed to the date, and I also booked a hotel room, anticipating that the concert would run late. This worked out well, as I was flown into town through the Newark airport after visiting cities for our MTV Museum of UnNatural History project, a shopping mall tour aimed at promoting MTV, its shows, and artists, and integrating some key brand sponsors. The hotel room provided a convenient place for us to sleep together in New Jersey after the show.

The next morning we shared a cab to her work, and then I continued to my place to drop off my luggage. I thought this marked the beginning of our dating journey, but it seemed she may have had a boyfriend or maybe even a connection to Norman. It was difficult to discern the truth, as she became distant once the jacket order had been delivered and our personal deal was completed. Despite this, I felt an emotional pull toward her that was hard for me to ignore. Apparently, not for her, though, as I learned about being ghosted long before the advent of texting and social media.

Even after several months, living and working in New York City still required some getting used to—and it never did feel comfortable. One night when I was heading uptown from Union Square station to attend a concert at the Beacon Theatre, I accidentally boarded an express subway train on the 6 line. At the time, I had no idea what an express train was. As the doors closed and I settled into my seat, I looked around and realized I was the only White person in a crowded train car. An older woman seemed worried as she slowly leaned in and softly questioned, "Hey, are you sure you're on the right train?" Her question filled me with dread, and at that moment, a realization dawned on me, "Holy shit, this train isn't going to make the next stop, nor the one after that." I shuddered at the thought of how far it would carry me into the unknown. Panic gripped my mind as memories flooded in: tales from a close Black friend from New Jersey, Rick Stephens, who had told me, "Even I have a deep-seated fear of venturing into Harlem and certain parts of the Bronx because the muggers will strip you of everything at gunpoint, leaving you naked and exposed on the cold street just to steal your sneakers." That thought sent shivers down my spine. When the train finally stopped, I walked with my head down, determined to find a way across the tracks to catch a train back in the opposite direction, this time making sure it *wasn't* an express.

I soon realized that there are distinct differences between New York City and Los Angeles. In NYC, individuals are straightforward when expressing their feelings toward you. They won't hesitate to let you know if they lack interest or don't like you—sometimes people call others assholes. In LA, a city heavily influenced by the glamour and fantasy of Hollywood, it's challenging to gauge where you stand with the people you encounter. They might casually suggest meeting for lunch, but in reality, they have no intention of following through; it's just their way of blowing you off. There is a concrete realness in New York and a certain fake niceness in Los Angeles. I was young, though, and just wanted to achieve.

One aspect of the Swatch Watch project that really sparked my creativity was the opportunity to create a blended show introduction. Swatch had designed these enormous Swatch watches specifically for merchandising displays in large department stores. They were about twelve feet tall, with a giant watch dial and bands on both ends. Once I saw one of these in their offices, the idea came to me to hang it over the stage during each sponsored concert date. I proposed the concept to the band, and they were open to it. I then went ahead and produced an audio introduction, a thirty-second countdown sound of a watch ticking, followed by an enthusiastic announcer proclaiming, "Swatch Watch is pleased to present ... Lisa Lisa and Cult Jam!" To enhance the effect, we choreographed the band lighting to illuminate the watch face, revealing the second hand moving inside. The result was a striking integrated art installation that seamlessly brought together the band and the brand. As soon as the band was announced, the watch was hoisted upward out of view and the show kicked in. Even to this day, I take considerable pride in the outcome. Fans saw Swatch not as a commercial intrusion, but as a way to further connect with Lisa Lisa, enhancing their experience.

Whenever I had the opportunity to go backstage at concerts, I made sure to bring along a collection of Swatch watches. These weren't ordinary timepieces—they were highly sought-after collectibles. Over time, the rarity and popularity of Swatch watches continued to escalate, making them even more valuable. During my visits to the Swatch offices, I took great care in handpicking the rarest and most impressive watches to give out later as gifts. Some I saved for the band members themselves, while others were sent to radio stations as prizes for on-air promotions, and few found their way to friends.

The end of the tour at Radio City Music Hall marked a triumph for MEGA and for me. With two of the songs on the *Spanish Fly* album reaching number one on Top 40 charts that year, Danny's selection of Lisa Lisa and Cult Jam, and our added brand marketing, it was a lesson in how to buy low and sell high. It was a methodology that would remain with me a little over a decade later when I started my own company.

What I didn't have the foresight to see was that MEGA, a small company with not another big project lined up yet, would attempt to demote me to a measly sales rep gig, cold-calling companies and pimping out artists. *I moved away from home, across the country, for this.* In frustration and anger, all I could think about was that back in San Diego, my Party Sounds Operations Manager, Kevin Lightcap, was living it up in *my* house in Pacific Beach, taking care of *my* beloved dogs. I was living a parallel existence, stuck in some twisted alternate reality.

A few times I'd managed to squeeze into Nell's, the upscale club across from where I lived. There, I took in the scene, unable to shake the feeling of discomfort. The women in the club all seemed to be tall fashion models and theater actors or hipster visual artists—the ambiance undeniably more sophisticated and expensive than what I was accustomed to in Southern California. While I had lived in the major metropolis of LA, the culture and the lifestyle of New York's inhabitants were different. New York wasn't my scene, MEGA wasn't my gig anymore, and Kevin was living the life I should be living.

The day I thought I quit, I was called into Danny Socolof's office, where he stated, "Without a tour to manage, there's no way we can afford to keep you. Whit and I like you and your work ethic, but the only option is for you to become a full-time, commission-based salesperson." Apparently, they'd hired me more for a project than a bonafide job. We mutually concluded that it was not going to work out. As a young person, I didn't realize that Danny and Whit were guiding me to quit, avoiding firing me—maybe to avert my ire. At the time, my quitting seemed entirely my idea.

I'd been adventuring it up in New York for around six months when I said, *Fuck it all.* I gave my treasured Lisa Lisa jacket to my colleague Lisa as a gift since she had hooked me up with a great apartment and shown me around the city. I called Kevin, told him I was coming home, and asked him to get rid of his tenant, muy pronto. Then I packed up the remainder of my shit, shipped it out, and hopped on a plane bound back to sunny San Diego. I wanted to be home before the snow could even think about falling on those still-foreign New York streets. As the jetliner took off, flakes started to descend from the sky. It was a practically empty flight. That's when I noticed her—one of the flight attendants. She gave me an inviting glance, and we struck up a conversation quickly. It turned out she had once graced the pages of *Penthouse* magazine as a side hustle.

When we touched down, she said, "I have a layover. How about we spend some more time together?"

"I'm in," I replied, intrigued. We agreed to meet after she finished her airline duties.

I hailed a cab, eager to settle back into my familiar space. But when I arrived, I found Kevin hadn't quite finished evicting the tenant from my room. With nowhere else to go, I called the flight attendant I'd met on the plane who I'd planned to invite over to my place. She had told me she was staying at the Travelodge near the Sports Arena.

"I'm on my way," I said, seeking refuge in her arms. From snow to sunshine, anxiety to absolute bliss, I escaped the clutches of the Big Apple. It took a bite out of me, but I was home. Back to where I belonged. Back in California.

27

WE WILL ROCK YOU

In San Diego, my first order of business was to clean the house, literally. After my airline lover took off, I kept the Travelodge room for almost another week while the usurper in my bedroom was finally given the boot, and my room was thoroughly sanitized.

Back in town, I had feelings of both shame and resolve. I felt shame because I had shot out of San Diego with dreams of making it big, really big, in New York City, only to get chewed up and spat back. But at the same time, I was determined to make a grand comeback in the city where I had really built my career in radio. It was time for Rob 2.0.

Party Sounds was on track under Kevin's watch, so I didn't have the financial concerns I had the last time I was let go. But before I could contemplate my next move, my phone rang.

"Rob?" a familiar voice boomed through the receiver. "Bill Silva here. How are you doing, man?"

"Bill!" I replied, surprised and intrigued. "Long time no talk! What's up?"

"I've got a proposition for you," he said, his voice brimming with excitement. "Something big. Something that could change your life. Are you interested?"

My curiosity was piqued. "Absolutely," I said, leaning forward in my chair. "Tell me more."

Bill, a local concert promoter with whom I had worked while at 91X, had started producing shows in the late Seventies while a student at the

University of California at San Diego. He teamed up with a fellow student, Mike Fahn, as Fahn & Silva Presents, focused on up-and-coming new wave artists at smaller venues. This gave them an edge, and when San Diego's top concert promoter fell from grace due to drug use and shady business deals, Fahn & Silva quickly rose to prominence, booking arena and stadium shows by the likes of The Who, The Police, and INXS.

In the late 1980s, Fahn, who happened to be an old family friend, moved back home to our native Sacramento, and Silva grew the business on his own. Eventually, he teamed up with a big regional concert promoter, Feyline Productions, and expanded from San Diego into other southwestern markets. Years later, he found himself in LA, promoting rock and pop shows at the iconic Hollywood Bowl and managing a roster of talented artists, including Jason Mraz.

Bill had a warm and inviting personality and was an excellent listener. While at 91X, we had worked on many shows together, and we now started meeting for lunch at a dimly lit classic steakhouse near his office to discuss possible opportunities. The waiter, who had a noticeable Spanish accent, always greeted Bill with a friendly, "Meester Seelvah!" We both found it pleasant, and it became an inside joke between us, a flash of humor in our busy days.

After a few of these lunches, Bill asked me. "I'd like you to come to work for me as vice president of Bill Silva Presents." The VP title boosted my ego and helped offset any concerns about compensation. He continued, "The position involves generating promotional ideas for multiple concerts and special projects, managing your own shows, and, most importantly, leading a new subsidiary called Impact." The vision for Impact was to create and promote a national skateboarding tour while establishing a management division to sign extreme athletes and oversee their careers, particularly in the lucrative realm of brand endorsements. As he outlined these exciting prospects, I replied, "I'm in, Bill! This sounds awesome. I can't wait to get started."

One of my first assignments had nothing to do with the action sports subsidiary we were planning to launch. I was charged with managing a speaking engagement by famed gonzo journalist Dr. Hunter S. Thompson at Symphony Hall, an old movie theater in downtown San Diego so named because it was the home of the San Diego Symphony. Thompson, perhaps best known as the author of *Fear and Loathing in Las Vegas*, was known for his outrageous, erratic behavior and riling up fans at his events into a drunken delirium. The show had been booked right before Super Bowl XXII, which would pit the Washington Redskins against the Denver Broncos.

A 1980 biopic called *Where the Buffalo Roam* follows Thompson's rise to fame in the 1970s and his relationship with Chicano attorney and activist Oscar "Zeta" Acosta. In the film, Bill Murray portrays Thompson, and Peter Boyle is cast as Acosta. One noteworthy scene in the movie shows Thompson covering Super Bowl VI in Los Angeles. Acosta unexpectedly appears at Thompson's hotel and persuades him to abandon the Super Bowl story to join his group of freedom fighters. The connection between the film and our event presented a natural marketing angle, and we billed the talk-show-style appearance as "Fear and Loathing at the Super Bowl."

I sought assistance from my journalist friend Thomas K. Arnold in handling Thompson's arrangements, including picking him up from the airport and ensuring his punctuality for the show. Thomas, known as "T.K.," had previously done this favor for another promoter more than three years before. As a young individual who had yet to fully grasp the demands of celebrities, I booked Thompson at that same Travelodge near the San Diego Sports Arena where I had stayed. I managed to secure a suite for him.

T.K., with Hunter and a young woman in tow, arrived at Symphony Hall about a half hour after the show was supposed to start. I was sweating. I had brought along Oz Medina, a popular 91X deejay, to introduce Hunter on stage and moderate a lively discussion. The audience was in a growing frenzy. Hunter immediately pointed to the unsuspecting deejay and blurted out, "I want nothing to do with that swine. Get him out of here! Go on, go!" Oz, dumbfounded, made a hasty exit. "Oh, and by the way, I want my $2,000 bonus or I'm not going on stage."

Sweat was now dripping from my forehead. "Mr. Thompson, we've done an audit and the ticket sales didn't meet the bonus threshold," I politely explained. Hunter was furious. I felt as though my head was about to explode.

T.K. took Hunter aside and said, "Listen, Hunter, I'll get you the extra $2,000, but you need to get out there!" Then, he physically pushed him onto the stage.

Along the way, Hunter grabbed Gaile, the woman accompanying T.K., and a football. "You, sit in that chair," he told her. The chair was positioned in the center of the stage, reserved initially for Oz. Gaile sat down, and for the next hour and a half, Symphony Hall descended into chaos as Hunter raged, ranted, and occasionally threw the football to Gaile.

In an article titled "Bad Time for Gonzo," Mike McIntyre of the *San Diego Union-Tribune* described the author's garish attire: Hawaiian shirt, a Los Angeles Raiders hat, and aviator glasses. He noted that Hunter arrived an hour late and maintained he "overstayed his welcome by two hours." The show's first half was complete anarchy, with around fifty audience members rushing the stage and Hunter giving barely coherent answers to their questions. However, once order was restored, the gonzo journalist occasionally displayed the brilliance that characterizes his books, albeit influenced by pharmaceuticals. He shared a story about a hunting trip in South America where he and his friends assaulted the son of the Brazilian war minister. He also referred to the first President George Bush, as a "lying, whimpering creep." He mentioned getting into trouble with the Secret Service for suggesting at Marquette University that Bush should be stomped to death.

After the show, we handed Hunter off to T.K., who took him back to his hotel room. Later, I heard that he asked T.K. if he could help him find some cocaine. According to T.K., "Hunter invited me to join him at the big game the next day." We had provided two Super Bowl tickets as part of his hospitality agreement and also loaned him an IBM Selectric typewriter, both of which had been placed in his hotel room before his arrival. When T.K. arrived at the Travelodge early, around noon, ready to pick up Hunter and go to the game, Hunter looked terrible. He confessed he had traded the Super Bowl tickets for an ounce of cocaine. Presumably, they spent the rest of the afternoon together, getting high. Still, later, I discovered that my drug-dealing friend Ralph had weaved his way into the mix as the one who had traded the blow for the tickets. He couldn't help but boast about how he had negotiated a coke deal in exchange for Super Bowl tickets and how thrilled he had been to attend the big game.

My next assignment for Bill Silva involved the Impact action sports subsidiary we were creating. Bill introduced me to a tall, light-haired, willowy guy a few years younger than me who had been the G&S skateboard team manager. John Hogan was brooding, and artistic, his voice barely rising above a whisper as he absentmindedly flicked his long bangs to the side during conversations.

It was 1988, and skateboarding hadn't yet become a global phenomenon. However, the sport was evolving, gaining wider recognition due to increased media coverage. John was to become my partner in creating a national skateboard tour and managing the skateboarders. We drew inspiration from successful one-off demo exhibitions like the "Vision Skate Escape" and "Swatch Live," which captured this burgeoning subculture's raw energy and excitement. We were tasked with developing the entire event format, figuring out the theme, the team, the stunts—the whole shebang. This ambitious tour would take the excitement of those single events and expand it across the country into a series, showcasing the skaters' incredible talent and athleticism to a broader audience.

I was introduced to such legendary skaters as Tony Hawk, Mark "Gator" Rogowski, Chris Miller, and Billy Ruff. My initial idea was to have a band on the cusp of fame, the Red Hot Chili Peppers, playing live alongside the vert ramp, but Bill deemed it too expensive and risky. We opted for a deejay instead.

John and I meticulously planned the tour, securing top skateboarders and even adding a BMX rider and an inline skater to the mix. To secure funding, I reached out to Kathy Gowland at Swatch, who I knew from the Lisa Lisa tour. She loved the idea and flew to San Diego to meet with us. Bill, John, and Kathy immediately clicked, and a few weeks later, the 1988 Swatch Impact Tour was born. John's innovative idea to use a steel ramp, easily transportable in two pieces on a flatbed truck, became a key feature of the tour.

While the Swatch Impact Tour was taking shape, I found myself navigating a complex emotional landscape. Bill's occasional flirty remarks, seemingly harmless to many, triggered some unsettling feelings within me. My teen abuse made me wary of such attention, my outlook was now distorted, no matter how innocent Bill's intentions might have been. I maintained a professional composure, but the echoes of that trauma lingered. The experience with Bill, though vastly different in nature unbeknown to him, reawakened the pain of my past, reminding me that I still had work to do to reclaim my sense of safety and agency. I needed to prioritize my well-being and find a professional environment where I felt secure.

Meanwhile, I started having second thoughts about this latest spot on my career path. The company's culture was that of showcasing and promoting Bill Silva's greatness—not of building leaders. Bill had built an impressive company, but it was centered entirely around him. Everyone wanted to work with *him* and speak only to *him*. His employees were all focused on assisting Bill with *his* vision. I had been grateful for the opportunity to learn from Bill, but I aspired to lead and create. Ultimately, my brief chapter at Bill Silva Presents was coming to a close. The tour did *not* achieve the resounding success we had hoped for.

Just before I jumped ship, John Lynch, still head of the Noble Broadcast Group where I used to work, reached out to me. He said,

"Rob, remember Robert Noble?"

I replied, "Of course, the Noble son I met during MeXfest."

He continued: "Right, and he's the owner of the FCC license for 91X in Mexico. He called asking about you. Would you meet with him?"

Curious about this proposition, I said, "I'd love to!"

John quickly said, "I'll arrange lunch for you with Robert. Let me know how it goes."

Then, I heard a click.

28

EATING BARBECUED IGUANAS

Robert Noble and I met for lunch at the Whaling Bar, a nautical-themed cocktail lounge and restaurant on the ground floor of the La Valencia Hotel, a historic pink landmark in the upscale San Diego suburb of La Jolla.

Pulling up to the hotel, I noticed a white Rolls-Royce Silver Shadow parked right in front. I parked my rust-colored Ford Bronco a few spaces down. As I entered the bar, I recognized Robert from our previous meetings during MeXfest. He had moved from Mexico City to La Jolla two years earlier. I was impressed with his selection of the Whaling Bar as our lunch spot because I wasn't used to lunching in La Jolla. The Spanish Colonial Revival-style hotel, with its panoramic ocean views, was built in 1926. It became a hideout for such Golden Age of Hollywood stars as Mary Pickford, Ginger Rogers, and Gregory Peck. Famed mystery writer Raymond Chandler lived in the hotel shortly before his death, writing his last novel, *Playback*. And, unbeknownst to me, while I was here with Robert Noble, future Pearl Jam frontman Eddie Vedder was working at La Valencia as a security guard.

Robert Noble was a slim, slight man approaching forty, with wavy jet-black hair slicked back and parted to one side. He had light eyes that shone even brighter against his dark tan and darker mustache. He had a small mouth shaped like an upside-down "U" that made even his smile appear like a frown. He wore a blue Oxford button-down shirt neatly tucked into his bright white pants that matched his Reebok sneakers.

I would learn later that this was his signature outfit and that he had a closet full of blue shirts, white pants, and white rubber-sole shoes that he rotated through.

While ordering our Caesar salads and steak sandwiches with iced teas, Noble dove right into why he had summoned me: "You did an amazing job with MeXfest and 91X. I want you to partner with me in opening a big, fancy nightclub that'll become the talk of the town." Then, he said something that still echoes in my mind: "Rob, I don't know how to work. That's why I need you."

Robert had grown up in Mexico City and enjoyed a most privileged upbringing. The Rolls-Royce parked out front belonged to him. His advertising impresario father was a close friend of Carlos Hank González, a mayor of Mexico City, and the father of Jorge Hank Rohn, my old buddy from the Calienté Racetrack and MeXfest. Robert, the fourth of five children, was around the same age as Hank and had moved in the same social circles. After completing some college in Austin, Texas, Robert decided to venture into the nightclub industry in Mexico around 1980. He and his partners successfully established and operated several high-end establishments in and around Mexico City and later expanded into the Pacific coast resort town of Acapulco.

Robert had three children who, like him, held dual citizenship. He had recently married their mother, Naomi, a Mexican woman who did not speak English. I knew Robert was wealthy, thanks to a trust fund set up by his late father, but I had no idea how rich until he casually let slip, "Rob, I believe our family fortune exceeds $100 million."

It turned out that Robert's uncle and grandfather weren't just successful businessmen. They were *ultra*-successful businessmen—the masterminds behind the iconic Life Savers candy brand. They had not only built and sold the company but also secured positions on the board of Beech-Nut, the conglomerate that acquired it. The company was making baby food in upstate New York and patented the vacuum-sealed jar process, now the industry's safety standard. Robert's family was also involved in the media industry, owning a radio station and playing a significant role in developing what would eventually become the American Broadcasting Company (ABC).

I had indirectly worked for Robert's father, Edward, the advertising and media entrepreneur, at his San Diego radio stations. And now, here I was, meeting with his son, Robert, who had inherited the family's entrepreneurial spirit, albeit with a different focus. With a deep-rooted heritage in media and advertising, Robert had developed a passion for the glitzy disco and nightclub business. But like many born into extreme wealth, he preferred to delegate. Though office computers were relatively new, operating one was not his strong suit, and he even struggled to use an installed car phone, a predecessor to the mobile phone. Consequently, he relied on others to handle his financial matters, and established friendly relationships with bankers in La Jolla.

Robert proposed that I become his operating partner while he oversaw the project and provided the funding. He even presented the terms during lunch: "We'll do a 50/50 split."

Upon hearing that, my pulse raced, and I broke into a huge grin. Believing this was likely my ticket to becoming a millionaire, I eagerly said, "Let's do it!"

Robert and I began meeting regularly to discuss ideas. Initially, it became clear that he wanted to create a club similar to the ones he had been involved with in Mexico. I had reservations about this approach and told him, "Discos, at least in the San Diego border area, are known to come and go quickly, their popularity changing with the latest trends. Let's do a live music club featuring national acts, with revenue coming from a combination of ticket sales, bar sales, and other concessions."

At the time, there were only a few locations in the city that could accommodate this concept—The Belly Up Tavern in North San Diego County, housed in a pair of converted World War II Quonset huts; The Spirit Club near downtown, across from of all things a pet hotel; and The Bacchanal, occupying the corner of an L-shaped strip mall in the middle-class neighborhood of Clairemont, sandwiched between a specialty tool store and a 7-Eleven. Except for The Belly Up, to some degree, these venues lacked excellent sightlines. They had low ceilings and limited capacity, and none were specifically designed for live music. Acoustics were also questionable.

I told Robert, "There's an opportunity to create a network of clubs throughout California, maybe even beyond, to provide a comfortable stage for rising and fading acts alike. We'll have no shortage of talent." When artists are at their peak, they tend to play larger venues, so we aimed to book them on the rise or the downswing of their careers. A packed house meant more drinks sold, and ultimately, that's where we made our money. Even with a modest crowd, we could generate substantial profits—with a 700 percent gross margin on alcohol sales, every drink poured added significantly to the bottom line.

Robert initially hesitated. "Why do people care about live music from new and old bands?" he asked.

He didn't understand the bond between artists and their fans. I took him around live music clubs in San Diego and then Los Angeles, and even San Francisco, and over time, he started to grasp the concept. "Rob, I get it," he finally told me one night after another club show. "The bands rather than the venue are the draw, and as long as we book the right artists at the right time, we can fill the places, sell alcohol, and be enormously successful." I sighed with relief.

Our challenge then became strategic: How do we break into such a saturated market and achieve success? We talked about the tremendous popularity of MeXfest and the significant number of young Americans who regularly traveled to Tijuana for their weekend fun—a destination empowered by the fact that the drinking age in Mexico was eighteen rather than twenty-one.

"If we own clubs in San Diego and Tijuana, we can leverage this advantage to book acts in both locations," I told Robert. "This will allow just a booker or two to manage all the dates."

Robert enthusiastically said, "I love the idea!"

I soon found an opportunity when I heard through the local music scene grapevine that the owner, a sailor turned nightclub proprietor, was looking to sell his club, The Bacchanal. He was in his midforties and had always yearned for more sailing adventures. He had sold the club twice before, but both deals went sour, and he wound up reclaiming the club and starting over. I felt that The Bacchanal could be significantly enhanced with some minor upgrades, the application of new energy, and improved marketing skills.

Robert described the Tijuana side of the equation to friends, family, and his bank as "a mini-MeXfest every weekend." He also reconnected with our mutual friend Jorge Hank Rohn. Jorge was developing Pueblo Amigo, an expansive open-air shopping center just south of the border, designed in the charming Mexican colonial style. We told Hank Rohn about our plans, and he immediately became interested. He took us to an unbuilt corner area of the complex, surrounded by ample parking, indicating that he believed it would be the best location for our music club, and said, "I want this to be an anchor tenant for the plaza." On the opposite end of the mall, he was nearing completion of a premium off-track betting casino. Since the shopping center was in early development, our timing was perfect, allowing us to shape the space according to our needs.

Yet I had my concerns. "How are we going to pay for everything?" I asked Robert.

"I'll speak to my family, and we'll open accounts at my bank in La Jolla." Robert's plan was that he and I would each own 16.77 percent of the club in Tijuana while his family and Hank Rohn would own the remainder. After forming Noble Tonkin Enterprises Inc., the next step was to secure an office and work out more financial details.

I met Robert's aging mother when we needed her to sign some legal papers. On a rainy day, during which Robert wasn't about to drive his Rolls-Royce, we all hopped into my rust-colored Bronco and drove through the storm from Coronado to a Mexican lawyer's office in Tijuana, where we officially sealed the deal.

The Noble family committed to contributing at least $1 million to the project. Nonetheless, Robert came to me and said, "I want you to have a personal financial investment in the venture. My brother is also pushing for this." His older brother, who controlled the estate, was someone Robert had to keep happy.

I explained, "I don't have any money just sitting around. I only managed to save enough to buy a house and operate a mobile deejay business. I thought I was supposed to be the partner who worked hard, and you're the partner providing the money."

But, still, he wanted me to have at least some skin in the game, so against my better judgment, I tapped the equity in my house to increase my ownership of The Bacchanal. We also agreed to include the existing talent acquisition manager, and gave him a token minority interest. This not only ensured our security by retaining someone capable of attracting talent to the club, but also allowed us to stretch his booking responsibilities to include the forthcoming Mexican club. The partnership agreement had Noble Tonkin Enterprises Inc. as the parent operating management company, servicing two companies and holding an interest in both: The Bacchanal and a Mexican company formed to own the Tijuana club. While the parent company was 50/50, the shares of the other entities varied.

A big cash payment had to be made to the sailor, who was selling us The Bacchanal. The deal called for a down payment and a series of monthly payments. We ran the numbers and determined that The Bacchanal's income was enough to pay Noble & Tonkin a recurrent fee and cover the monthly operating expenses, including the former owner's financing disbursements.

But how would we come up with the down payment? The sailor wanted a sizable portion of the money under the table, with no trace. Robert arranged for Jorge to have one of his guys from the track pull the cash, which became part of Jorge's investment into the Mexican club. Robert referred to this as "funny money." The club owner and five friends turned up at the leasing office at Pueblo Amigo, where I supervised Jorge's lieutenant, who happened to be the leasing manager, dropping $50,000 onto the conference room table in various denominations. The sailor and his friends' eyes lit up as they began to count it out. Each person began quivering and twitching with their $10,000 in cash to carry across the border. It felt very shady to me.

Through a close friend, I discovered an architect who showed genuine enthusiasm when presented with the opportunity to design a live music club. Coronado's Dale St. Denis, AIA, embraced our vision for the club, and his passion resonated with Robert. I named the Mexican club Iguanas, inspired by a 1982 song by the indie rock band Wall of Voodoo called "Mexican Radio." About two-thirds of the way into the tune, the lyrics jumped out at me: "I'm on a Mexican radio, I wish I was in Tijuana, eating barbecued iguana." The song was consistently played on 91X. I adored this song for a multitude of reasons. It felt as though it was speaking directly to me, resonating with my experiences working at a Mexican radio station and now constructing a club in Tijuana to celebrate rock music. The notion of a charred iguana at a barbecue seamlessly tied all these elements together.

Once we had Dale on board, we began drawing up plans for building the club, and what we would do to ensure its success. Iguanas would have a capacity of approximately 1,100. We would market it as "Baja California's Showcase Theater and Patio Bar." Spanning 12,000 square feet and budgeted at $1.3 million (equivalent to about $3.5 million in 2025), the venue would offer more than just concerts; it would also serve as a vibrant space for dancing into the late hours, giving Robert his disco. I felt one of the club's key features would be its perfect sightlines and exceptional sound and lights which were designed explicitly for live rock 'n' roll. Iguanas would stay open until 3 a.m. instead of 2 a.m., the US cutoff, which only added to its allure.

The thriving grunge music scene was erupting in the Pacific Northwest, while a second wave of alternative rock was also brewing. That meant we could catch a wealth of new bands on the way up. We agreed on a May 5, 1989, opening date, the same day as Cinco de Mayo, held each year to celebrate Mexico's victory over the Second French Empire in 1862. To headline the show, we landed Jane's Addiction, the hottest young alt-rock band from Los Angeles. Jane's Addiction was getting heavy airplay on 91X and other new music radio stations across the country and also had tons of cred, ensuring us a flawless first impression.

We hurried to complete construction, set up the bar systems, and completed all sorts of other finishing touches. But, candidly, nothing would be finished by the time we'd open, which wasn't abnormal for Mexico. As Robert Noble commanded, "We'll be opening regardless, and we'll do it Mexican wedding style, where everything looks perfect on one side of the wall, but on the other side, there are ten people holding up the wall." I laughed out loud; this much was understood.

Cinco de Mayo has long been associated with parades, street food, block parties, mariachi competitions, folkloric ballets featuring dancers adorned in shiny ribbons and braids, and vibrant, ruffled dresses. While some Americans use this day as an excuse to indulge in tequila shots with salt and lime, I saw it as an opportunity for Americans to experience Mexico, new American rock music, and to celebrate the launch of our cool new club—on a Friday party night, no less. We invited 91X to broadcast live from our patio, and we gave the station a small batch of tickets to give away as the official presenters of the show.

The months leading up to opening day were filled with memorable moments. One was a pre-opening press event that included a performance by Jack Mack and the Heart Attack, who were riding high as the house band for *The Arsenio Hall Show*. We arranged for journalists from all over Southern California to be bused across the border to attend so they could write about the club before its official opening. *San Diego Magazine* did a nice photo spread and write-up on the opening. Getting all this media attention was unusual for a Tijuana establishment, especially a club. The opening day concert sold out less than five minutes after tickets went on sale. Jorge's top lieutenant, said to me one night after drinks in his strong Mexican accent, "Ralb Tonkeen, you are bess prummoter!" Hearing this boosted my ego.

One afternoon, a few weeks before opening day, I was at the club when Jorge suddenly asked me to dinner that night. I was about to return home to Pacific Beach in San Diego, but he insisted we meet at his restaurant, Alcázar del Río, in the Zona Río section of downtown Tijuana. The anxiety began to build and I asked if my female assistant could join us for dinner since she had accompanied me to the club. To my relief, Jorge smiled and graciously said, "Yes, she is welcome."

When we arrived at the restaurant, I felt a knot in my stomach. The place was eerily empty except for a large round table that had been prepared for us. We took seats as Jorge, the top lieutenant, the leasing manager, and a few others joined us. Robert Noble wasn't there. In total, there were eight people, including my assistant, who happened to be the only female.

A blur of seafood dishes, escargot, and an endless stream of side courses followed. The restaurant itself was white-tablecloth posh, ornate inside, traditionally Mexican colonial, but with a continental modern flare, and it had valet parking—at the time, a novelty in Tijuana. Conversations shifted back and forth between Spanish and English, prompting me to wear a fake smile and avoid eye contact as I only understood about half of everything that was said. As the evening progressed, Jorge gestured to the waiter and said aloud, "We'll celebrate with a special smooth tequila, a reposado blanco." Shot glasses of the clear liquid were filled for everyone, and we raised them in a toast to something unknown, but likely it had to do with me. The clinking sound of glass echoed across the room and continued for what felt like an eternity, then more toasts and more anecdotes stretched on for what seemed like forever. Jorge was grateful for the success of MeXfest and excited about the possibilities, "Iguanas will bring young people to Pueblo Amigo, and I'm honored with patriotism for the benefits to Mexico as a whole," he said. Clink, clink again.

My assistant excused herself, "I'm heading to the baño, guys," and I couldn't help but notice that she was gone for a remarkably long time. When I mustered the courage, I said, "Seems like she's been missing from the table for, uh, forever," and Jorge broke into another wide smile and then a laugh and the whole group began laughing along. This interaction gave me a slight chill, so I decided to check the restroom area, but to my dismay, she wasn't there. Seeing danger symbols in everything, I looked outside, hoping to find her having a smoke, only to realize that my vehicle was also missing. This sent shivers down my spine. I returned to the table. Even the music playing was annoying me at this stage. I attempted to maintain a demure composure, but deep inside, I feared that something dreadful might have happened to her. To my astonishment, Jorge brushed it off and casually instructed someone to "Drive my friend to the border since his car is gone." He nonchalantly remarked, "Rob, don't worry, we'll sort out everything, mañana," and then flashed me another friendly grin.

How could I possibly leave knowing that my vehicle and the person I was responsible for were nowhere to be found? I trudged alongside some security person toward the guy's dark-colored, unmarked Ford sedan. As we drove toward the border, I noticed a good-sized pistol lying on the seat between the driver and me. That's when I started gulping down breaths to stay calm and quiet. Tijuana is said to be one of the most dangerous cities in the world, with a sky-high homicide rate. Despite telling myself I was safe under Hank Rohn's protection, the presence of the likely loaded gun within reach still sent me into panic mode. The driver took an unfamiliar route, which made me even more nervous, but then I saw we were merely bypassing the chaotic border traffic, and he dropped me off so close to the pedestrian crossway that I couldn't believe my luck.

I crossed the imaginary line between cultures and caught a taxi to my house, which cost me a ton of money. All the while, still tipsy like a bowl of drunken nerves, my anxious mind continuously looped with thoughts of my assistant. When I got home, I dialed my car phone number, hoping desperately for her to answer, so sure she had just driven that rust-colored Bronco home to her house. However, with each passing moment, my contemplations were consumed by the worst possible scenarios, especially when she didn't pick up. Perhaps someone had stolen my car, and my assistant was unknowingly caught up in the situation? Or maybe, being slightly unhinged, unpredictable, and under the influence, she flirted with one of the lieutenants and ventured off with him to an unknown destination? Maybe it was all set up with her before I was invited to dinner? Maybe she crashed? Could she be dead?

I tossed and turned that night after desperately contacting her home, talking to her roommate and explaining that she had gone missing in Tijuana along with my rust-colored Ford Bronco. I pleaded with her roommate to notify me immediately if she returned, promising to rush back to the club and Tijuana the very next day if there were no updates. The following day, I relied on someone else for a ride to the club, where I informed our general manager and a confidant of Robert Noble, about the distressing situation. His perplexed expression did nothing to ease my anxiety, but he agreed to inquire about her whereabouts. Finally, some relief washed over me as I spotted my Bronco parked in the Iguanas lot. Thankfully, I had brought spare keys, just in case. But the solace was fleeting, as she remained missing in action.

While overseeing the construction crew for a while, I concluded that it was safer for me to return to the United States, hoping against hope that she would surface there. The following evening, I received a call from my assistant as if nothing out of the ordinary had occurred. She casually greeted me and said, "Hey, Rob, I just thought I'd check in." I was dumbfounded. What on earth? To this day, she insists, "I was high and feeling the heebie-jeebies at that dinner, so I decided to take a joyride, and I don't know why I took the Bronco. I pulled over on a random overpass in TJ, and dozed off inside the vehicle, only to eventually drive it back to the club and find my way home from some guy in the morning. Then I crashed, I mean I went to sleep. I just woke up a little bit ago. My head aches." I remain unconvinced that her tale holds any truth. Unfortunately, I will never really know what happened.

There were other strange occurrences during the build-and-development process. Robert Noble once borrowed my old Bronco and returned it sans the car phone. When I asked him what was up, he shrugged and said, "Don't worry, we'll get you a new one. I just needed one for the Rolls right away." Too dumbfounded to pursue the matter any further, I let it go. He never did replace the phone.

Another bizarre incident involved my relationship with Robert Noble's wife, Naomi. While she was always pleasant, I couldn't help but sense her dislike for me through her hunched posture, drooping head, and cringing when I'd talk with her. It may have been my youthful bravado that she dreaded, or perhaps she was jealous of Robert relying on me. There was also a significant language barrier between us.

One day, when I arrived at work, something bizarre caught my attention. On my desk sat a dinner plate-sized mound of salt meticulously arranged to form an inverted pentacle within a circular pattern. As an American, I recognized it from art and fantasy realms as a pentagram associated with evil and black magic. *What the hell is that doing here?* I thought, a shiver of unease running down my spine. Perplexed, I couldn't fathom how it came to be there until Naomi's face flashed vividly in my mind. It dawned on me that she must have placed it there. *Who else even had access?*

Opening day finally came, and the intensity was beyond what I had imagined. The place was jammed, and the band positively raged, feeding off the crowd, and vice versa. The multi-leveled club was packed with a steamy twist of young bodies, moving to the music as though in a trance. It felt so raw and alive, almost as if the venue itself had transformed into a living iguana, breathing deeply, in and out, in and out....

My reverie was rudely interrupted midway through Jane's Addiction's performance when I was pulled into a meeting with Robert, Naomi, and the general manager in a tiny, empty office we had set up under the stairway. What I witnessed next left me utterly astonished. In a frenzy, Naomi was stuffing dollars into brown paper sacks. It was the most bizarre sight I had ever seen. Why on earth wasn't the general manager handling the money and depositing it into our Tijuana bank? Why were these multimillionaires looting cash? I couldn't help but ask what was going on, and Robert responded, "We need to pay bills at home. We're separating the cash into bags of $10,000, so we can get across the border." They were taking all the money. These weren't pesos, they were thousands of US dollars that were being collected throughout the entire night. My body stiffened, feeling overwhelmed and tongue-tied; I slowly shuffled back a step or two and eventually headed home alone without taking a single dollar—not that any had been offered to me. I couldn't help but wonder why my share wasn't even being considered if this was how we would run the business.

In the process of opening and operating the clubs, Noble Tonkin Enterprises Inc. had already bounced several checks. That made me uncomfortable. I had never done business that way before. Money would come into our account from the Noble trust, and Robert would withdraw what he needed for himself and his immediate family with disregard to company obligations. Now, standing in that little room under the stairs with all the chaos of our success surrounding us, with Robert and Naomi greedily pocketing all the money we had taken in, this was that split second when I decided, *This is not for me.* I had my dream come true, designing and building the space and putting it on the map. Those minutes with Jane's Addiction and the audience proved my concept worked. I didn't need to stay to count more money or to see what would happen with Iguanas in the future. And I certainly didn't need to own The Bacchanal, either. My dream of being a millionaire was just a mirage. I wanted out.

But then came the Samantha Fox concert. Samantha, a petite blonde bombshell straight out of Page Three of a British tabloid, had become a brief pop sensation, much to the delight of our south-of-the-border partners. After the show, they were eager to meet her, and who was I to deny them a photo op? So, there I was, hoisting the pop star horizontally, her outfit offering little grip, while cameras flashed, my face in a contorted grimace surrounded by excited Mexican men, capturing a series of truly awkward and hilarious poses. I vaguely recall some catchy tunes and energetic dance moves, but the memory of that photo session overshadows the entire concert. *What a thrill to own a club.*

Some days later I approached Robert and blurted, "I'm no longer needed. You now have The Bacchanal's clout and booking power, and someone capable of handling the talent." Moreover, he had the general manager, an operator in Mexico, to handle the club's logistic details and an operator/manager for The Bacchanal. Perhaps it was time for him to learn how to put in a little work. Or maybe Naomi could fill my role. Nevertheless, I had to prioritize myself and protect my reputation. I felt terrible for the people who'd gotten bounced checks from us, including the builder, and Dale St. Denis, the architect. I was young—still in my twenties—and I had trusted someone in their forties who should have been a mentor to me. Now I had people hounding *me* for payments. I knew how much money was coming in from Robert Noble's family, but no idea how much money he and Naomi were grabbing for themselves. Looking back, I should have put my foot down regarding those cash withdrawals from what was supposed to be our business. I thought about calling his brother, who controlled the family trust that was dispensing money to Robert, and wondered whether I should narc him out.

Ultimately, I didn't make that call. *Maybe he's in on it too,* I thought, as I wanted nothing more to do with Robert Noble, or his wife, for that matter. So, a few days after the club's grand opening, we met, and Robert agreed to buy me out of The Bacchanal, which released the second trust deed on my house. I hired a top San Diego attorney to paper this entire deal, and the ream of documents he produced extricated me from the whole situation, except for my ownership shares in Iguanas, which I knew would be problematic since they were in a Mexican corporation and could be easily yanked away. I was willing to walk away with nothing, but I didn't want the experience to cost me anything, either. From today's vantage point, Jorge held the answers to Iguanas. But then, his childhood ties to Robert, and the fear in his stare, kept me silent.

The Iguanas debacle left me reeling, a familiar ache of self-doubt gnawing at my gut. That old, insidious question resurfaced: "What's wrong with me?" I had opened myself up to Robert Noble, trusted him, believed in his promises—only to be let down once again. It felt like a cruel confirmation of my deepest insecurities, a painful reminder of my past vulnerabilities.

Years later, I was living in Los Angeles and came home one day to find a letter titled: "Intent to sue with settlement demand," informing me that we, Robert Noble and Rob Tonkin, personally had failed to pay on the promissory note to the Bacchanal-owner-turned-sailor-again. *What the hell?* My naive self was confident that this was all a mistake. While Robert and I had each signed the note, the money flowing in each month to The Bacchanal was more than enough to cover the monthly payments, and besides, Robert now owned The Bacchanal, not me.

I soon discovered the reason: Robert Noble had sent The Bacchanal into bankruptcy—I'm still not sure how, although I have my suspicions—and the club had closed. The sailor couldn't find Robert because he had moved from La Jolla back to Mexico, or some other hidden corner of the world. So, because my signature was still on the note, the sailor was going after me. I again wondered how this could be my problem, as I had a stack of paperwork that I had signed and Robert Noble had signed, releasing me from all liabilities related to any of the entities I had been involved in. That's when I learned an important lesson: Don't trust the attorney will do everything. Somehow, my hotshot lawyer had neglected to get a release form from the Bacchanal's former owner, removing my "personal guarantee" from the promissory note, even though Robert took over my liabilities. Therefore, the document was still valid. I got myself a litigator and ultimately settled with a sizable payment to the sailor and a judgment against Robert Noble, which I have yet to collect.

Around the same time I received the letter about that lawsuit, I was sitting on the sidewalk patio of a Mexican restaurant on trendy Melrose Avenue in LA with a couple of friends, having dinner while cars whizzed by. Our waiter kept giving me strange looks and awkwardly maneuvering around me as if he had spotted something or I smelled horrible. Curiosity got the better of me, and I asked, "Why are you avoiding me?" He looked down and, in a timid tone, replied, "Señor, I cannot say." I insisted on knowing the truth, and that's when he dropped the bombshell: "I am a psychic medium, and I can see a spell hovering over your back." At first, I thought this guy must have been out of his mind. *Maybe he's high on some substance.* But he elaborated, "Someone has placed a curse on you. Is anyone disliking you or having a reason to harm you?" Suddenly, it hit me like a bolt of lightning—Naomi and her peculiar pentacle of salt! "You are under a Santeria spell, which requires an exorcism."

I lost my appetite but ordered more margaritas. I had never really believed in supernatural spirits like this, but how could I deny it now? *How could the waiter have known? The timing of the demand letter? What would come next*, I wondered? Luckily, nothing further unfolded, and I made an effort to meditate on the situation. Eventually, I felt a release of both the spell and the unnerving events from my mind.

I sometimes wonder if I unwittingly became part of the Mexican mafia or if I was used in some way. Did my enthusiasm and willingness to be involved get me into trouble? Every so often, we like to unsee things that we see. Maybe I should have stayed at Iguanas and witnessed how things would have played out. I also wonder if my decision to leave Noble Tonkin Enterprises Inc. caused Robert to fail. Jorge Hank Rohn later became mayor of Tijuana, ran for governor of Baja California, was arrested and freed in Mexico for allegedly trafficking endangered animal species, and has since lived what appears in the press to be a lavish lifestyle. As for Robert and Naomi, I wonder where they are now. I've read that they recreated new disco-style clubs and also adopted the live music concept in Cancun and the Dominican Republic.

And I wonder if Naomi still summons Robert with that bizarre and distinctive whistle that my assistant and I used to laugh about: "Woo hoo, woo hoo." I also wonder whether Naomi cast any more spells on people she doesn't like—or if the spell she cast on me backfired, leading to Robert losing both clubs and sending him packing just a few years after I bolted.

Iguanas did become a huge success, albeit for a relatively short time, until the club's abrupt closure in 1994. During those five years, the club's stage was graced by such alt-rock luminaries as Nirvana, The Fixx, Rage Against the Machine, Sonic Youth, The Ramones, Bad Religion, Pearl Jam, Public Image Ltd., Nine Inch Nails, and GWAR. But Iguanas was more than a concert hall: It was a mecca for teens as well as tweeners, those American young people between the ages of eighteen and twenty-one who were legally adults but could not enter popular San Diego concert clubs like the Belly Up because they had not yet reached the legal drinking age. As the *Los Angeles Times* noted in a 1991 article, "Fifteen minutes from San Diego, yet light-years removed from parental supervision, Iguanas offers an ambiance of almost-anything-goes, frontier neutrality that gives underagers an intoxicating whiff of freedom...."

When I think of Iguanas nowadays, it's not the absurdity and chicanery I suffered through that come to mind. Rather, it's a sense of achievement. I created something unlike anything that had been done before, or since: a thriving nightclub right on the US border with Mexico, where the hottest bands could be seen by anyone, regardless of age or nationality. It was a bicultural sensation, a musical melting pot in every sense of the word.

29

WELCOME TO THE JUNGLE

During the height of my Mexican nightclub entrepreneurship, I'd sold my mobile deejay business, Party Sounds, to 91X to focus full-time on the clubs. I now had enough cash left over from that to tide me over until my next hat trick, but I, along with two partners, owned an investment house a block from the beach and needed to get the cash flowing again.

I sued my ex-partner, Robert Noble, for my share of ownership in Iguanas. While I had already recouped my investment and extricated myself from any financial obligations related to The Bacchanal, this was now about principle, about reclaiming what was rightfully mine. The press was having a field day with articles about it, the public attention was draining, and the whole ordeal left a bitter taste in my mouth. I was starting to think there wasn't anything left for me to achieve in San Diego. Maybe it was time for a change of scenery.

Before I had left for New York, a guy named Simon T had offered me a job as promotions director at a San Diego radio station he had just bought with the backing of the same company that owned concert promoter Avalon Attractions. He was a man of contradictions—and the first person I had ever met with a stand-up desk. He was clearly intelligent, with a mind that could dissect complex theories and devise intricate strategies. And yet he chose to live somewhat off the grid, in a figurative sense. His eccentricities were as legendary as his elusiveness. He was known for his unpredictable behavior, his unconventional attire, his long hair at times, and his uncanny ability to disappear without a trace.

Later, Simon T had grander plans in mind. He set his sights on buying KIQQ 100.3 FM radio in Los Angeles, competing for the purchase with Westwood One Companies, which wanted a flagship station in LA to add to its New York empire and thus bolster the spread of its syndicated programming. To secure their victory and neutralize a competing bid from Simon T, Westwood One offered him a compelling incentive: the position of general manager and a significant stake in the parent company through stock options. This strategic move not only eliminated a rival bidder but also ensured that Simon T's expertise and leadership would guide the station's success. Westwood One Inc. paid $56 million for KIQQ-FM, a record-breaking price at the time, making it the most expensive single radio station acquisition in US history.

Once owned by Westwood One, the world's largest syndicator of audio programming, the station underwent a dramatic transformation. Shedding its easy listening format, the station re-launched as Pirate Radio KQLZ 100.3 FM, a bold mix of hard rock, heavy metal, and alternative rock. This clever branding was a nod to the rebellious, mainly European, offshore pirate radio stations of the 1960s, which challenged government monopolies like the BBC and brought a wider range of music to eager listeners.

Pirate Radio exploded onto the airwaves on March 17, 1989. It generated a massive buzz with its bombastic, commercial-free debut, kicking off with Guns N' Roses' anthem "Welcome to the Jungle," which quickly became the station's signature song. To further cultivate the pirate radio mystique, the station deliberately misled listeners, hinting that its broadcasts were emanating offshore from Catalina Island, twenty-six miles off the coast of Los Angeles. This playful deception was pure genius. A few months after the launch, it was already a major player in Los Angeles, the second biggest radio market in the United States.

Simon, aware of my exit from Iguanas, reached out to me and pitched the idea of joining the station as promotions director. At first, I thought, *Radio again?* But at the same time, it intrigued me, and I needed a job. I also remembered how Pirate Radio's irreverence had truly captivated me. It was a rebel, shattering rules and grabbing attention nationwide. *How could I resist its allure?*

There was a catch. While the General Manager, Simon T, was eager to hire me, the ultimate decision rested with Program Director Scott Shannon. Years earlier, while launching WHTZ in New York, Scott had conceived the Pirate Radio format, though it wasn't actually used there at the time. Supposedly, the station owners found the concept too radical, so Shannon went with his second choice: Z100 and its raucous morning show, the "Morning Zoo." The station skyrocketed from worst to first in the ratings, and Shannon became a bona fide radio legend, eventually earning a spot in the Broadcast Radio Hall of Fame.

Simon T invited me to meet with Shannon in Los Angeles. The meeting was bizarre. It lasted only a few minutes, and Shannon spoke in such a soft, barely audible tone from across his desk that I practically had to pull my ears forward with my hands cupped to hear him. I later heard a rumor that his low-volume mumbling might have been a deliberate technique to ensure people leaned in and paid close attention to what he was saying, but who knows.

As I drove back to San Diego from that odd encounter, I told my friends, "There's no chance in hell I'll get that gig." Two weeks later, I received a voicemail from Shannon's right-hand man, Shadow Steele: "Rob Tonkin, this is Shaaa-doww ... pack your bags because you're coming to Pirate Radio!" I'd been dead wrong.

Landing a job at Pirate Radio was a major career rebound, and my ambition soared once I joined Westwood One, a true giant in the industry. They weren't just a radio powerhouse; they had a significant presence in the music world, syndicating live concert recordings to stations globally. Imagine a mobile recording studio capturing the raw energy of legendary artists, and I was now a small part of the big team that brought that magic to the airwaves. Westwood One's vast holdings, including NBC Radio, Mutual Broadcasting, and the influential trade magazine *Radio*

& Records, unlocked a world of possibilities.

"Katie, this is bigger than just Pirate Radio," I described to my beloved friend and cousin, who also lived in San Diego. "Westwood One is a major player in the radio world. They have affiliated stations all over the country, and they're connected to everyone who matters. I feel like this could be my chance to really make a name for myself."

Cousin Katie, always the supportive one, nodded. "I get it. You're not just taking a job; you're joining a platform."

"Exactly!" I exclaimed. "This is about aligning myself with a company that can help me reach my full potential."

After selling my San Diego home for a considerable profit (and my investment property, unfortunately, at a small loss), I found myself drawn to the storied Laurel Canyon. I rented a house perched high on a hillside, overlooking the sprawling cityscape below. The twinkling lights of Los Angeles stretched out before me, a vibrant reminder of urban energy. The canyon was the birthplace of the country-rock sound that defined the late Sixties and early Seventies, where music legends like Joni Mitchell and Jim Morrison once roamed. Now, it was home to the Hill Gang, aspiring actors and actresses striving for their big break.

Nearly all the homes on my street, Beech Knoll Drive, were hillside rentals, their caisson stilts anchoring them to the steep slopes. Each house was divided into multiple flats, occupied by these hopeful, would-be stars. They were always surprised to meet someone like me, *not* chasing a role in a movie or TV show. One of my neighbors was Jennifer Aniston, years before she'd become a household name on *Friends*. I mingled at their parties, forging friendships with several of them.

This is also where the illustrious Norman J. Pattiz enters my story with warmth and open arms. Our offices and studios were in a high-rise on Sunset Boulevard in Hollywood, but the headquarters of Westwood One was a half-hour drive away in Culver City. A brand-new building for Pirate Radio was being constructed just across the street from headquarters, as part of the Westwood One campus. We christened the new studios, a converted warehouse, with a live broadcast and a celebratory party, and that's where I first met Pattiz—or, to his friends, "Norm."

Norm had started Westwood One from scratch, from a small office in Westwood, near UCLA. He had been a television advertising salesperson with an idea. He had also grown up in LA and had good connections. Without hesitation, I saw him as something of a father figure. I was running around the event, which I had been put in charge of producing, and just as the hair metal band Warrant took the stage, he walked up to me, introduced himself, and said, "Hey, do you have a minute to chat?"

Awestruck that he even knew who I was, I followed Norm like a puppy dog across the street.

"So," he said, extending his hand with a warm smile, "you're the rising star I've been hearing so much about."

"That's very kind of you to say," I replied, shaking his hand firmly. "I'm a big fan of Westwood One."

"Well, we're fans of yours, too," he said as we headed toward the stairs. "Shannon and, especially, Simon, have both spoken very highly of you."

We climbed the carpeted staircase to his mezzanine-level office, which offered a commanding view of the floor below. "Quite a setup you have here," I remarked, taking in the spacious office and the panoramic smoked glass window.

"It has its perks," he said with a chuckle. Instead of sitting behind his imposing desk, we settled into a pair of stylish designer chairs facing each other. I was still intimidated, but his casual demeanor and friendly tone helped me relax.

"We've heard great things about your work. We have high hopes for you here." He paused, his expression turning serious. "And I want you to know that I'm available directly to you if you need my support for anything," he added, his eyes lighting up. "Pirate's my new baby, and I need someone with your talent to help it thrive."

Could I trust this man? I wondered. There was an intensity in his eyes, a sense of power that was both alluring and intimidating. But there was also a genuine warmth in his voice, a hint of mentorship that made me feel seen and supported. And his passion for the radio station was contagious. *I was blown away!*

Norm would weave his way in and out of my life. While working for Scott Shannon, who doubled as morning deejay, I had the opportunity to organize several on-site morning show events. Scott had a penchant for creating elaborate spectacles that listeners could attend in person, resulting in a vibrant variety show on air. These events typically took place on Friday mornings and occurred a few times in the year we worked together.

Scott one day asked me to find a location for an event surrounding Easter.

"Hmm, Easter...," I mused. "What about the Queen Mary?"

He raised an eyebrow. "The ship? In Long Beach?"

"Exactly!" I said. "It's iconic, it's unique, and it's got that whole nautical theme going on. Plus, there's that massive hangar next to it with the Spruce Goose. We could really do something spectacular there."

Scott, always one for a grand spectacle, was intrigued. "I like it," he said with a grin. "Let's see if you can make it happen, Tonkin."

The Queen Mary, a massive thirties luxury cruise ship permanently docked in Long Beach, was both a hotel and a museum. Next to it was an enormous domed hangar that housed, as part of the museum, the storied Spruce Goose, a towering wooden airplane built by tycoon Howard Hughes that was flown only once, earning it the status of a flying boat. Over the last decade, however, public interest had waned immeasurably. The advantage of this for us, as well as the clincher, was the operator's willingness to cover all our expenses in exchange for exposure on air and its proximity to a working harbor dock.

Shannon had a knack for curating events that were as much about showcasing his connections as they were about entertaining the audience, attracting a diverse crowd eager to be a part of his world. As the event producer taking the lead from Shannon's vision, I would bring together actors, musicians, attractions, films, and other exciting elements. This event featured a dunking booth with the Easter Bunny and some of Shannon's on-air friends. Actor Don Johnson, a personal friend of Norm, made a grand entrance, arriving with Norm in a helicopter that landed right at the site. After an on-air interview, he hopped into his impressive forty-six-foot superboat, equipped with three turbocharged engines. Don's fascination with superboats began during his time starring in the TV series *Miami Vice*, and he ended up becoming a captain and racing boat driver. As our event took place in Long Beach harbor, he set off from the dock in his boat, leaving quite an impression on everyone present. Westwood One's logo was emblazoned on a quarter panel of the boat, a nod to Norm's support for his buddy Don's activities.

Over a decade had passed since the release of the iconic movie *National Lampoon's Animal House*. The movie has a fictional band called Otis Day and the Knights, with DeWayne Jessie playing Otis the lead singer. Ron Kurtz, a developer and producer of live performance shows, managed to locate the actor and subsequently obtained the rights to the band's name from Universal Pictures. He then organized a touring show with Jessie and backup players, featuring their standout performance of the song "Shout," a notable moment in the film.

One of the highlights of that morning was a performance by Otis Day and the Knights. However, the band was not used to playing early in the day. As the members got ready to take the stage, I couldn't find Otis, the frontman. I had arranged for them to stay on the Queen Mary in the hotel, which was both rumored to be haunted and conveniently located within walking distance of the stage. I wasn't sure what time they had arrived after an unrelated gig the night before but Otis was nowhere to be found.

I made my way to his room and began pounding on the door. "Otis! I mean DeWayne, wake up! We've got a show to do!"

The door creaked open, and DeWayne stumbled out, looking

bleary-eyed and disheveled. A half-empty bottle of Courvoisier sat on the nightstand.

"Whoa, man," he mumbled, rubbing his eyes. "What time is it?"

"Time to rock and roll!" I said. "But first," I added, grabbing the Courvoisier, "this might help." I poured him a shot.

He looked at me with a mixture of confusion and annoyance. "Who are you again?" he slurred.

"No time for introductions," I said, handing him the brown liquid in a glass and taking a swig directly from the bottle to encourage him. "Just need you to channel your inner Otis Day and bring down the house." I motioned toward the bathroom. "Why don't you freshen up while I wait out here?"

He grumbled something about "early mornings" and "rude awakenings," but he took the shot and disappeared into the bathroom. As I waited impatiently, a thought popped into my head: *Was a Queen Mary ghost holding DeWayne at bay?*

A few minutes later, he emerged looking considerably more presentable, hair done up, face washed, and smelling like fresh aftershave. He still seemed a bit unsure of who I was, but at least he was awake enough and willing to follow me. I walked with a sense of purpose, DeWayne trailing as I commanded, "To the stage," and pointed ahead, leading a brigade of one: Otis, *our man*. I had Norm, Shannon, Simon, and Don Johnson to answer to that morning, and I wasn't about to let a sleepy frontman derail the event.

Some weeks later, Norm unexpectedly visited my office one day for an informal conversation. He jokingly suggested, "Tonkin, we should hire good-looking women to ride motorcycles instead of sending jocks on appearances, can you imagine?" And then he chuckled as I daydreamed of the positive publicity. Naturally, if Norm wanted it, my creative mind latched on, and the Pirate Radio Harley Girls concept was born. What I liked the most about the Harley Girls was that we planned to use them in place of deejays for personal appearances. Instead of expecting air personalities to be good at entertaining in person or drawing crowds, these women would be capable of both.

So, my job required me to hire appealing women with motorcycle riding experience as radio station ambassadors. These women would dress in alluring leather outfits—with station logos, of course—and ride Pirate Radio customized and chrome-plated Harley Davidsons. This daring strategy aimed to capture the attention of the highly sought-after eighteen-to-thirty-four-year-old male radio listeners and ultimately increase ratings. The idea seemed almost like something out of a fantasy I could never have imagined. Bringing it to life would take a while.

Scott Shannon's programming genius was undeniable, but he also possessed a self-assuredness that could sometimes be challenging to navigate. We had a complex working relationship, with moments of synergy and moments of friction, like the time my decision to book MTV comedy veejay Pauly Shore sparked a heated disagreement.

I had known Pauly from my San Diego days. I had met him while he was still a kid through a mutual friend, and I also knew his older brother, Scott, heir apparent to the family business, The Comedy Store, at the time run by their mother, Mitzi. I watched him mature—well, that's not really the right word!—from a scrawny skate rat into a successful comedic persona playing a stereotypical surfer dude stoner as host of the *Totally Pauly* show on MTV. I asked him whether he'd like to be a guest on Shannon's morning show, and he agreed to do it. Then I told Shannon about the booking, but because I had gone against protocol—I should have asked Shannon first, not Pauly—Shannon said *no*. I was standing in the soundproof production studio hallway, pleading with Shannon to change his mind because it would be embarrassing to withdraw the invite. That's when Scott Shannon lost his mind on me! He hollered so loudly that my ears rang: "Tonkin, when you get your face on billboards all over Los Angeles, you can decide who you book on your morning show!" He wasn't soft-spoken *that* day.

Pirate Radio had launched with a massive media blitz. The station erected giant billboards that screamed, "Pirate Radio 100.3, Welcome to the Jungle!" The city was awash in those striking billboards, their vibrant neon colors and bold designs impossible to miss along the legendary Sunset Strip and the city's major arteries. Those eye-catching introductory billboards were already in place when I joined the team, but now it was my turn to take the reins of the campaign.

One day, Shannon called me into his office and we chatted about his vision for the next phase: billboards featuring his own image alongside the tagline "Shannon in the Morning, Pirate Radio 100.3." It was a bold move, putting the focus squarely on his personality and star power. My task was to make it happen, ensuring the campaign captured the essence of Pirate Radio's rebellious spirit while showcasing Shannon's unique brand of on-air charisma. That was a moment when I felt the Pirate Radio ship was veering off course, but I couldn't tell Shannon that his picture was a little scary to look at. After all, it was his face, and it was clear that he wanted me to be more of a functionary than an innovator. So, same as with Norm, I did what he asked.

Almost immediately, the phones began to light up. People were calling in to express their, shall we say, strong opinions about the billboards. Word of the negative feedback quickly reached Shannon. Since it was too late to pull the campaign, he decided to embrace the controversy and even amplify it. His solution? Introduce a mascot that had proven successful in other markets: The Party Pig, a cartoon pig wearing a hat with the cheeky slogan "Bite Me."

This seemingly spontaneous addition of the pig was actually a carefully orchestrated move. Shannon was leaning into the fact that some people did not find his face billboard-worthy, turning potential criticism into a source of intrigue. He envisioned people seeing the appearing-to-be defaced billboards and assuming some disgruntled listener or rival station had vandalized them. This would create even more buzz, amplifying the campaign's impact.

My task was to bring this vision to life, striking the right balance between irreverence and recognizability. I had the image created, revised, and refined countless times until it met Shannon's exacting standards. Then, I plastered those supposedly defaced billboards across the city, each one a testament to Shannon's audacious marketing strategy. For one particularly prominent billboard overlooking one of LA's busiest freeways, I hired an actual graffiti artist to climb up and secretly spray paint the words "El Diablo," Spanish for "the devil," over his face. I felt it was a fitting touch.

Pirate Radio blazed onto the scene, a dazzling spectacle of sparks. Its rebellious spirit and unconventional programming ignited the airwaves, capturing listeners and critics alike. But that brilliance proved fleeting. By early 1991, the novelty had worn off, and ratings plummeted. Both Scott Shannon and Simon T, stand-up desk and all, exited, and the station abandoned most of its original pirate persona, adopting a more traditional album-rock format. As the *New York Times* observed, "After some initial success, the station now has poor ratings—proof that having money and a disc jockey who made it in New York is no guarantee of success elsewhere." It was a stark reminder that even the most dazzling flames can fade, leaving behind a sense of what could have been.

The Harley Girls concept, perhaps because it was Norm's idea, survived the transition. Though they hadn't materialized under Simon and Shannon, the Harley Girls were finally launched shortly after the format changed. A Riley entered the picture at this point. She was tall, slender, fair-haired with a voice that was strong and a little gruff from chain smoking. We randomly met at a concert with her friend. Our conversation revolved around motorcycles. She possessed a unique blend of toughness and tomboyishness while also exuding femininity and radiating beauty. I thought she'd make a great Harley Girl.

She had experience riding dirt bikes, liked animals, suffered huge losses in her childhood, seemed sheltered from any financial pressures, displayed exceptional intelligence, and expressed strong opinions. Every aspect of her exhilarating personality captivated me. Additionally, she was part of the Hollywood scene, with personal connections to famous band members. Riley quickly became one of Pirate Radio's most outstanding Harley Girls. She not only excelled as a skilled rider, perfectly embodying the image we desired but also possessed exceptional public speaking skills and a great sense of humor. She had confidence, and the Pirate Radio fans loved her.

I found myself growing fond of her, as well. We spent time together at parties in my home; she invited me to her home, and I attended various events where she worked.

One Friday afternoon, after she had been doing this Pirate Radio Harley Girl job for several months, the new General Manager, Roger "Rog" Morris, decided we were all going to celebrate at Gladstones Restaurant, a Los Angeles beachfront institution. "We" was defined as everyone in the building, and, of course, the whole shebang was on the station's tab because even though Pirate Radio had dropped in popularity from its peak, we were celebrating slight ratings victories in key demographics. It was time to par-tay!

We all headed to the beach from our new Culver City studio and offices, about a thirty-minute drive. We then discovered that Rog—one of the funniest people I had ever worked for, with a robust physique and presence to match—had arranged for a private room with one extraordinarily long table. The centerpiece was an enormous seafood boat filled with lobster and crab claws, prawns, ceviche, oysters, clams, and colorful sauces. Rog had already ordered shots of tequila for everyone.

After consuming multiple rounds of tequila, Rog and the majority of the twenty or so people present started challenging each other to perform various tasks, as in the game "Truth or Dare." This group of grown-ups had reverted to their teenage years, attempting to impress and outshine one another. There were no boundaries; even though he represented top management, Rog egged us on as we engaged in salacious speech and various forms of questionable behavior, all for everyone's amusement.

Being both stoned and drunk, I was a more than willing participant.

I was sitting next to Riley when we were playfully challenged to share a kiss. To my surprise, the experience turned out to be incredibly passionate for both of us. Riley and I shared a look of astonishment, but neither one of us said anything.

As the party ended, Eric Weiss, Westwood One's corporate attorney, announced he was hosting an impromptu after-party at his home, just a ten-minute drive away. When Riley and I reached the parking lot, we discovered that each of us drove similar SUV-style vehicles—mine black and hers a color reminiscent of my Dodge van Debra had wrecked several years earlier.

We arrived at Eric's place in Pacific Palisades at the same time and, as we were attempting to park our vehicles, collided with one another, resulting in minor damage but major laughs. As we inspected our injured vehicles, Riley suggested, "Let's skip going inside and, instead, head over to your place in Laurel Canyon." As our eyes met, we felt a strong connection and immediately made a wager that whoever arrived at my house first would receive oral sex from the other person. It seemed like a win-win, whatever the outcome.

As Riley headed east on Sunset Boulevard, I struggled to keep up with her. She appeared fearless while I was trying to be cautious due to my inebriated state and fear. But despite the threat of a DUI or, worse, a terrible crash, I pressed on, and we took turns overtaking each other as we navigated the twists and turns of Sunset Boulevard, a stretch of road memorialized in the song "Dead Man's Curve" by Jan and Dean.

Cruising down Sunset Boulevard in broad daylight late on a Friday afternoon, where traffic was jammed like a parking lot, suddenly Riley floored it. My inebriated senses might have been deceiving me, but I'm fairly certain she blew through a red light and, right in front of the iconic Beverly Hills Hotel, hopped the curb onto the wide grassy median! Of course, I followed suit. Cars honked in protest, people gawked in disbelief, but Riley, showing no apparent signs of being deterred by the chaos she was creating, just kept going, with me tailing her. This was no ordinary joyride; this was a full-blown spectacle, a scene straight out of a Hollywood car chase.

Realizing that a lesser-known shortcut might be my best chance to win, I turned left on Sunset Plaza Drive, winding through the Hollywood Hills. This route consisted of narrow roadways and numerous sharp turns, but the distance was shorter. As fate would have it, we both arrived at my house at the exact same moment—but she pulled ahead and reached my driveway first. Riley was reveling in her victory—even more so when I paid up.

We lay in comfortable silence, our limbs entwined, the sheets a tangled mess around us. While she smoked, her breath a soft whisper against my skin, a thin stream of smoke curled upward toward the ceiling. I followed its path with my eyes, feeling a profound sense of peace and connection.

Riley was impossible to decipher. She could be sweet and vulnerable, but at the same time give off a sense of steeliness, like a hardened warrior. I clearly had feelings for her and believed she had feelings for me. But I was too chicken to confront her directly about what lay ahead for us, so I engaged in an internal dialogue, attempting to hash it out within my mind. *Would she now become my girlfriend? How would I navigate this at work? What in the fucking hell just happened?* I couldn't shut my mind off or even put it on pause.

After that wild night, we had some more fun. We took off to San Diego for a weekend getaway where no one knew us. One day shortly after that we were in my office at the radio station chatting privately.

"So...," I began, trying to keep my voice light, "about that weekend in San Diego...."

Riley smiled a playful grin. "It was quite an adventure, wasn't it?"

"It was," I agreed. "But I get the feeling I'm not the only one you're adventuring with," I added, my heart already sinking slightly.

Her smile faltered. "Rob...."

"It's okay," I said, trying to sound nonchalant. "You don't have to explain yourself. I understand."

"Understand what?" she asked.

"That your job is your priority," I explained. "And that a relationship ... well, it's just not in the cards right now."

A wave of relief washed over her face. "Thank you," she said sincerely. "That means a lot to me. I was worried you'd be upset."

"Of course, I'm a little disappointed," I admitted, "but I'm not going to let it get in the way of your ambition. I know how important this job is to you, and I'm not going to be that guy who holds you back."

"I appreciate that," she said, squeezing my hand. "You're a good man, Rob."

"I try," I said with a wry smile, though inside, rejection's familiar sting pierced my heart, reopening old wounds and leaving me raw.

"We can still hang sometime," she offered, her voice laced with a tiny hint of mischief. "Just ... not with any romance."

"I'm okay with that," I said, though really wasn't.

The air hung a bit heavy between us, a palpable discomfort. After several months of avoided glances, I swallowed my pride and asked to visit her. She had moved into a new place and also enrolled in post-degree classes. Her house was a revelation—stacks of textbooks and notebooks filled with writings. She spoke about her studies passionately, dissecting complex ideas with an ease that impressed me. Still, for an hour or more my attempts at connection were met with polite but distant responses. As I left, the weight of my inner conflict settled back on my shoulders. Some wounds ran deeper than conversations could heal. One thing that has always stuck with me about Riley was the nickname she once gave me, which was at once insulting and endearing: The Midget Prince.

Meanwhile, my job at the radio station was becoming less enjoyable. The initial excitement had worn off, and the daily grind was starting to take its toll. I felt the familiar symptoms of burnout creeping in—the fatigue, the feeling that I was just going through the motions. After so many years in the radio industry, I was starting to question whether this was still the right path for me. The bosses who had hired me had left the building. The format that had sizzled had faded, and now I had crossed a line with an employee.

From the moment I set foot in Westwood One, I knew artist relations was where I wanted to be. I was fascinated by the idea of working more directly in the music business, with musicians and their managers, capturing their creative energy in our mobile recording studio, and sharing those live performances with radio audiences worldwide. A big part of the appeal was the opportunity to learn the ins and outs of the industry, to deepen my understanding of the complex machinery behind the music. While at Pirate Radio, I made it my mission to learn everything I could about the artist relations department. I built a rapport with Thom Ferro, a senior executive at Westwood One, discussing my aspirations and demonstrating my genuine interest in the field.

Then, a window of opportunity opened. Several top well-known Westwood One executives were let go due to the company's financial struggles. When that happens, the big salaries are often the first to be slashed, creating openings for hungry young guys like me. With a top position finally open in artist relations, I saw it as my chance to turn my dream into reality. It was the perfect opportunity to leverage my skills and passion to contribute to the company in a meaningful way. I wasted no time in expressing my enthusiasm to Thom, hoping to secure the role and embark on this exciting new chapter.

Just a few days after my conversation with Thom, he called me. "Bud, you got the job," he said.

30

BORN ON THE BAYOU

Segueing from Pirate Radio to head up artist relations for parent company Westwood One, I was riding a new high. I had a cool office with a stocked fridge and leather sofa in the headquarters building and saw Norm in the hallways daily. He would plop down to shoot the shit, and playfully ask me stuff like, "What have you done for me lately?" He liked my new artist relations role because it was fun, involved interaction with colorful artist managers, and was the core gem of how he started; he had once performed the essence of that job for the company. He knew several prominent managers quite well, including Irving Azoff, who represented the Eagles. He also developed relationships with the artists themselves over the years.

Norm ran in the Hollywood elite circle and was worth a huge sum of money. Once Norm had me accompany him to The Forum in Inglewood to entertain Madonna and comedian Rosie O'Donnell in his pricey and exclusive floor seats. It was a couple of years after the departure of Magic Johnson and the end of the team's fabled Showtime Lakers era. I sat next to Rosie, and Norm next to Madonna. It was Madonna's first pro basketball game ever. She'd go on to date a couple of players.

Some speculated that Norm had amassed a fortune of more than $150 million in personal wealth. He owned a private Gulfstream jet and a lightning-fast, forty-five-foot luxury yacht called *The Vixen*. He lived in a home in Beverly Hills purchased directly from legendary showbiz titan David Geffen. And he wore a wardrobe of designer T-shirts and jeans, the perfect complement to his coifed, graying short hair and matching beard, always with cool shades, and a trendy jacket. He also had a car collection that included a dark gray Bentley Continental, a racer green Aston Martin V8 Vantage, and a bright red Ferrari Testarossa, among others. I was impressed with Norm's lifestyle, which was everything I had ever imagined of the rich and famous.

The job had me wrangling three to four special "Live" events, featuring one megastar headliner, in each quarter of the year, and several superstars and supporting acts in random intervals. The quarterly marquee events were used to attract affiliates—subscribing radio stations, or groups of stations—and big advertisers. The others I produced were smaller in stature, but there were many more of them, filling Westwood One's "Superstar" (rock) and "In Concert" (rock, metal, alternative) series. Westwood One President Pete Janek once said snidely that these series were nothing more than "a garbage can for spots." Culling artists and content meant far more to me than that, and I took his commentary as a personal insult.

Ideas for notable productions began flying from the day I first set foot in my new office. The one I followed through on was a biggie: To obtain the syndicated radio broadcast rights for Lollapalooza and its impressive lineup of headliners. Lollapalooza began as a touring festival in 1991 as a farewell by Perry Farrell of Jane's Addiction. The lineup in 1992, the tour's second annual run, featured the Red Hot Chili Peppers, who were (and still are) red hot, along with Ministry, Ice Cube, Soundgarden, The Jesus and Mary Chain, Pearl Jam, Lush, Rage Against the Machine, Cypress Hill, House of Pain, Stone Temple Pilots, and Temple of the Dog. Some say the 1992 tour went so well that it propelled Lollapalooza to morph into the powerhouse that it is today, an annual four-day music festival in Chicago that draws upward of 400,000 attendees.

My old friend Kevin Lyman, who I'd known since our San Diego days working for Bill Silva, was now the main stage production manager for Lollapalooza. We'd become close after I moved to LA, collaborating on numerous local productions during my time at Pirate Radio. This connection gave me a direct line to the Lollapalooza organizers, including co-creator Marc Geiger, whom I already knew pretty well, and some of the other folks running the show.

"Kevin, I have this idea," I said into the receiver, my excitement bubbling over. "We take the Westwood One mobile recording truck, hit up all the bands playing at Lollapalooza, grab some interviews, and boom—a killer radio special I can syndicate nationwide."

There was a pause on the other end of the line. "Wow, that's ambitious," Kevin said, impressed. "Sounds like a fantastic plan."

"Right?" I exclaimed. "Imagine the buzz! Westwood will have exclusive content, behind-the-scenes access—we'll pull out all of the stops."

"Definitely," Kevin agreed. "But getting everyone organized, the logistics, the clearances ... that's a tall order."

"I've got it all figured out," I assured him, glancing at the scattered notes I had already sketched out. "Where there's a will, there's a way."

"I hear ya, I'm sure you do," Kevin said with a chuckle. "But how are you going to get all those bands on board?"

"That's what I'm trying to figure out," I admitted. "Any ideas?"

I could practically hear Kevin pondering on the other end. "Tell you what," he finally said. "Why don't you fly down to New Orleans for the tour day-off celebration? It's the perfect opportunity to schmooze with the organizers, crew, the artists, their managers.... Solidify those relationships and sell them on the vision. I can get you credentials to the show and set you up with a place to stay."

"Brilliant!" I exclaimed. "That's exactly what I need."

And with that, Kevin, the ever-helpful friend, had opened a door to Lollapalooza. Over the phone, he had provided me with the necessary contacts and led me to a place to crash in New Orleans, even though the project wasn't his. The rest was up to me.

I booked my flight and hotel and arrived in the Big Easy on the Thursday night before the Labor Day weekend. I met up with Kevin in the French Quarter for some drinks and dinner with a couple of other friends he introduced me to.

He said, "After dinner, we'll walk the Quarter streets with Hurricane drinks in hand; anything goes here in New Orleans. We'll head to the tour party at a club called Storyville." We joined the party, had a few more drinks, and socialized.

Eventually, a performance by The Jim Rose Circus Sideshow troupe began. This particular show was not the usual public version, as it was intended to entertain bands and crew members. One performer, Bebe the Circus Queen, conducted various stunts, such as having a watermelon placed on her back and subsequently split with a sword while she lay on a bed of nails. Another remarkable act was performed by The Amazing Mister Lifto, who suspended heavy weights from his body piercings—for instance, a steam iron—including those in his nipples and genitalia.

The most shockingly captivating move involved extra-long, clear-plastic tubing and a penis. The extended tube was pushed through an existing piercing in Lifto's member. Another guy, Matt "The Tube" Crowley, proceeded to swallow an end of the tube, while the other end remained attached to a crude hand pump. Jim Rose filled the external pump reservoir, connected to the tube, with various horrid fluids that pulsed as they were injected through the piercing and into Crowley's mouth and stomach, only for them to be puked back out, all flowing through the transparent tube inserted into Lifto's genital piercing hole. My stomach churned, but I couldn't tear my eyes away. It was a grotesque display, yet it held me in its grip.

After the party, I joined Kevin, Mr. Lifto, and one of the crew girls back in my room for a little smoke. We then went downstairs to the hotel bar and had more drinks. Lifto left, and as the clock ticked into the morning hours, the three of us who remained decided to call it a night.

I found the friendly crew girl quite attractive, and I could tell Kevin also liked her. We got into the elevator, and I could feel my anxiety growing as we passed each floor. As the door opened to my floor, I turned and said, "Goodnight. Okay, so I'll be in the reception area out front to catch the crew bus at 10:30, right?" Kevin nodded his head in agreement, as I waited to see what the girl would do. Then the universe played its hand, and she followed me out just before the door sealed, leaving Kevin all alone in the elevator.

When the wake-up call rang in the morning, the crew girl hopped out of bed. "Oh my God! I've gotta get to my room to shower and get ready for work. See you downstairs," she said, blowing me a kiss—and then, out the door, she went.

She sold merchandise for a vendor on the tour. I knew I should also be on the bus, as I had promised Kevin and myself, but my pounding head disagreed.

I thought, "Why do I need to be there so early if the concert doesn't start until 2?" and went back to sleep for a couple of hours.

Around noon, I met up with two of Kevin's friends at a bar, people I'd met the night before. Nursing a wicked hangover, I had a beer and a sandwich, and we grabbed a taxi to the venue, located on the University of New Orleans (UNO) campus. I told them, "I'm not sure how to gain access, since I didn't take the crew bus and Kevin hasn't given me any credentials, but I guess I'll hit up will-call and have him paged."

The traffic was bumper to bumper, and I began to sweat because I didn't want to miss any of the artists. I then told the cab driver, "I need to pee. It'll probably be faster to walk the remaining distance," which was not long. We got to a small parking lot, and I advised the two friends, "Wait here a second," as I ambled over to discreetly pee between two vehicles.

"Hey, boy! Stop! Hey, boy, I'm talking to you, boy," I heard a stern voice say. I turned around to see a traffic cop glaring at me.

"Are you talking to me?" I quipped back as he nodded his head and walked toward me.

"Boy, do you know where you are?" he asked.

"Yes, UNO, Lollapalooza."

"Boy, you're in the *faculty* parking lot of the University of New Orleans."

Thinking to myself, *Okay, so what,* I flippantly said, "I see that. Now, what can I do for you because I'm working here and I'm late, and we need to get our credentials." Unfortunately, I had no proof I was working there.

The officer didn't like that comment at all. He instructed me to put my hands behind my back, and as he handcuffed me said, "This is Howard, requesting wagon at the faculty lot. Send wagon ASAP!"

He is calling for backup on his radio! The next thing I knew, a Sixties old-school paddy wagon rolled up, and that grizzled traffic cop handed me off to two handsy officers, who pushed me in through the rear of the vehicle as if I had killed someone. We drove the short distance to the campus police office without a word, and then I was put into a detention room and told, "Sit here. I'll let you know what's next when I'm ready."

Though it seemed the officer guarding me preferred I stay quiet, I turned to him and politely said, "Sir, I'm here for work. Please get a hold of the concert Stage Manager, Kevin Lyman, who will confirm that I am here working." No response.

My head was pounding, and my nerves began to take over. A half-hour later, I was back in the paddy wagon on my way to Orleans Parish Prison. I thought, *Fuck! This is not a good thing.* The red light on top of the enormous roll-up garage door spun round and round while a loud alarm sounded. Then, one of the doors of the prison slowly went up. We drove in, and it immediately shut behind us as I was escorted out of the paddy wagon to join a chain gang of men from multiple paddy wagons and squad cars who were being booked on various offenses.

When my pockets were emptied, I was informed, "Your bail amount is $200."

The cash I had was just under $100 and they did not accept American Express cards. As a result, I found myself in the first prisoner-holding cell, waiting in line to use the phone on the wall. I planned to call the hotel and request a bellman to bring cash charged to my Amex on file. There were at least ten guys ahead of me.

The cell was the size of a small bedroom, with windows looking out over the waist-high counter where I had been booked. The walls were pale green, chipped, and covered with dirty stains. There were at least twenty other people in the crowded cell. I was one of two White people. In one corner stood a rank and foul toilet in plain sight.

When it was finally my turn to use the phone, I rang my hotel front desk and in a low voice so nobody else would hear me, asked the clerk to, "Please send someone to Central Lock Up at Orleans Parish Prison with $200, and I'll tip them and approve the charges on my Amex card."

But he said, "I'm sorry sir, we can't do that for you. We are not allowed to, legally speaking, you understand."

Fuck! Fuckity fuck! I had no idea who else to contact to help get me out of jail. I couldn't let my family know about my arrest, and I didn't trust anyone else, either. I was hoping that Kevin's friends would tell Kevin, and he'd somehow get me released.

About an hour later, I was called back to the counter where I had been booked. I had no idea why I was being summoned. Then, I was asked a strange question: "Sir, when will you be leaving New Orleans?"

I responded truthfully, "My flight is set for Monday."

Unfortunately, my answer resulted in me being returned to the over-crowded holding cell. I later learned that Kevin had called to arrange for my release and promised that I would leave immediately. But how the hell could I have known that?

After another hour, miserable, hungry, and thirsty, I was moved to another smaller cell that was filthy and packed with menacing-look-ing characters. The hum of inmates smoking and gabbing incessantly vibrated through the walls. Some spoke in low whispers.

My heart pounded. "Who *are* these people?" I thought to myself.

In a sea of faces, mine was now the only pale one. I realized I was now the minority. A cold knot formed in my stomach. I hadn't had much exposure to Black people while growing up, and I was afraid of unintentionally offending them.

"Hey, Goldberg, how's your schnoz?" someone called out, followed by huge laughter.

All eyes were on me. Some seemed bemused. Others were angry. But most were vacant and cold. I forced a smile as the memory of the anti-Semitic physical assault I endured as a child washed over me. *Shit. Not this again,* I thought, while my heart pounded even harder. *Keep your head down. Don't make waves.*

Someone offered me a hand-rolled cigarette. To fit in, I accepted, though I didn't ordinarily smoke cigarettes. The first drag sent me into a coughing fit. The smoke, acrid and harsh, scratched at the back of my throat. It was unfiltered, potent stuff. The smoke, sweat, and smell of alcohol breath hung heavy in the air, making my hangover even worse—much, much worse. *God, I need to get out of this jail.*

I made my way to another line for a phone. This time, I called my office at Westwood One and got in touch with a woman who used to work for me. Unfortunately, I had made her cry on a few occasions with some asshole comments.

"Eileen, please help me on the down low; this is serious," I pleaded.

She said she would, but my fear and the guilt for the way I had once treated her supplied more distress.

After waiting in line all over again, I called once more an hour later, and she said she had contacted Eric Weiss, the head of legal and business affairs and a good friend of mine. If I was son number five or seven of Norm's, he was son number one.

She also informed me, "You're being held on soliciting prostitution and lewd conduct charges. Is it true? I need the truth, Rob."

Of course, that was a revelation to me since all I did was demurely relieve myself between two cars so that nobody would see my banana. I was in the South, though, and quickly seeing that certain people were to be treated differently. That old traffic cop saw some kid in shorts and a rock T-shirt, Doc Marten's, long hair, and a hooped earring, and said to himself, "Why, that SOB just pissed all over *me*!" Yes, he took it personally. In his mind, a college faculty parking lot was to be respected and protected by men of the law.

As I was waiting for Eric to do something, anything, I was moved into yet another holding cell. It was beginning to feel like my childhood all over again with all the moves. However, this one was the most disgusting. It was the drunk tank—a dank, smelly, tiled cell with a floor drain. The cell was full of drunks, one of whom had no teeth and a badly deformed cocked arm who hopped around in a limp dance.

He introduced himself to me, "I's go by Chick-un George."

Then, the staff began to hose down the floor because it was covered in vomit.

It was now about 11:30 p.m., and Chicken George and my other new cellmate friends told me, "Joint's full up 'cause the holiday. We all headin' to tent city," and George pointed with his bum elbow, "It's over yonder, fenced and all, cross the street outside. Git's hot."

The other prisoners seemed to know how to disguise their emotions and concerns, but I was having difficulty trying. I had gone beyond nail-biting and was now chewing my fingers in a panic. There was no place to spread out and rest or relax, even though my nerves wouldn't have allowed that anyway.

I cleared my throat, slowly turned, and, in a meek, shaky voice, asked, "Uh sir, guard, uh, could I please be let out to get in line for another call, sir?"

He agreed and temporarily released me from that drunk detention cell. I walked over to the phone line, once again patiently waited my turn, and finally connected with Eric Weiss, who ended our call with, "Don't worry Robbie, my boy, I'll find a way to get you out." His assurance was a Band-Aid on a gaping wound, a temporary fix for a seemingly larger problem.

About an hour and a half later, I ended up alone in a tiny single cell, opposite the area where people were being hosed down and given jail clothing. This wasn't just a standard shower. It was a delousing pressure hose to be sure there were no lice infestations in the jail. Every time they opened the door and someone else was taken in to be stripped and cleaned I got a glance of what was going on in there. The combination of freezing water and harsh, chemical-laden soap made the process a brutal ordeal, judging by the screams echoing from the shower room.

It was now about 1 a.m. I had missed the entire concert, and my ordeal had lasted for over twelve hours without being offered any food or water. Was I next to go into the wash, or would Eric come through for me?

Then bam, a guy came over to the cell and opened the door. I started hesitantly stepping toward the entry to the delousing room when he grabbed my shoulder and redirected me down a different hallway.

"Whew," I exhaled, the sound echoing in the stark corridor. *I can't believe it,* I thought, my mind reeling. *I'm actually getting out of here.* I felt a surge of disbelief, followed by a flood of pure joy.

I almost skipped back to the counter where they booked me. There sat a tray of my personal belongings, a symbol of hope and liberation. I was very close to being uncaged.

Fifteen minutes later, I stood outside in the humid dead of night, wondering how to get a cab. It wasn't like taxis were circling for fares around Orleans Parish Prison. I walked a while, clutching my belongings, feeling liberated, but not knowing where I was going, or where I was, until by a stroke of luck a cab came by and dropped someone off. I took the chance to hop inside and pointed that driver to the Omni Hotel. The elevator took me to my room where I crashed almost immediately.

The following day, I spoke with Eric. He had found me a local attorney. He also explained how he got me released.

"Robbie, my boy," he said, "I searched and found a nice old New Orleans judge who was at home recovering from some severe illness. I got his home phone number from the White Pages of course, and then worked my charm with his wife, who had answered the phone. She passed the horn to him, and since Westwood One owns the vital NBC Radio Network, I used that name because I thought it was probably the most recognizable to him. I explained that a colleague from that NBC Radio group was falsely jailed. Then I intimated, not in a threatening way, that this wouldn't turn out to be good press for New Orleans because the charges didn't match the crime, and the prisoner, a Mr. Tonkin, was on assignment at the time of arrest."

Eric's magic was beyond amazing. The judge agreed to call the jail and have me released. Later that day, the lawyer called me at the hotel.

"Mr. Tonkin," he began.

I interrupted him and said, "Please call me Rob."

He went on, "Okay, Rob, my advice to you is to please leave town as soon as possible. I'll attend your arraignment on Tuesday morning." That was the only music to my ears I'd hear on that trip.

Back home in LA and at my office at Westwood One, I received a call from that New Orleans attorney.

"Rob, all the charges have been dropped, and I was able to destroy the record of your arrest; it's called an expungement." He also said, "You'll receive an apology letter from the city of New Orleans."

The arresting officers had falsified my crime—urinating in public, a misdemeanor—because they decided I needed to be locked up. Corruption at its finest. It made me angry. Yet, I also played a role in what had happened to me. The day I'd been arrested, I'd woken up late recovering from a night of partying and had arrogance in my voice when speaking with a law enforcement officer. These were realizations I wouldn't make until decades later.

Grateful to leave it all behind me, I told the attorney, "Send me your bill," to which he replied, "There is no bill for something like this. I'm ashamed of this city for what happened." *Praise the Lord.*

"Do your kids like music?" I asked.

"My daughter is a *huge* Red Hot Chili Peppers fan," he gushed.

So, I procured and mailed him an autographed picture of the Chili Peppers, along with a heartfelt thank-you letter, and that was the end of that.

Yet still, I had an empty feeling in the pit of my stomach, knowing that I would need to discuss the incident with my boss, Thom Ferro, who had approved the expense and the purpose of this trip. I thought, *What will he think of me now?* I wondered if my next meeting with him would be my last.

Fortunately, when I met with Thom later that day, he gave me a stern lecture, "Robbie, Robbie, Robbie ... Tonkin, you have to meet commitments," but he also seemed to sympathize with my treatment at the hands of the New Orleans police. "I've been arrested before, probably for a worse offense," he said. "Luckily, you had Eric in your court. Shit happens, bud."

Unfortunately, I was unable to wrangle any deal out of Lollapalooza. As for Kevin Lyman, a small part of me thinks he decided to teach me a lesson for sleeping in, missing the crew bus, and winding up with the girl.

31

DON'T STOP BELIEVIN'

The trip to New Orleans had me strutting the halls of Westwood One with a newfound confidence knowing I had their support. This sense of family, fostered by my colleagues, was a comforting feeling. I also had music. Music had always been my refuge, especially growing up in Northern California amid the rise of such bands as The Doobie Brothers. Their music, in many ways, felt more soothing than actual memories of those years. The Doobies held a special place in my heart. They were *the* NorCal band of my generation. "Listen to the Music" wasn't just a song; it was an anthem to the power of music to transcend boundaries and touch lives, a testament to why music was my salvation.

It was around this time when Martita—at twenty-four, six years my junior—crashed into my life. I met her when she was working as a waitress in a cocktail bar (cue The Human League's "Don't You Want Me"). One night, we started talking, and I learned she had this insatiable desire to capture life through the lens of her camera. She had studied at the Cal Arts School of Film/Video, where she immersed herself in the art of visual storytelling through film. It was in her blood. Her father invented the revolutionary Panavision lenses, which gave filmmakers an expanded panoramic perspective.

Martita and I began dating, and the more I dug into her story, the more I realized she was no ordinary woman. Her mother had passed away when she was just a young girl, leaving her wounded. Her father wasn't exactly the ideal parent. Like my own father, he was cold and distant. He spoiled her with lavish gifts, horses, and an expensive education, but he wasn't always there for her.

I met him shortly after Martita and I began dating. He appeared guarded and plagued by faltering health. He owned a sprawling hacienda in the vast expanse of Santa Clarita Valley, northeast of Los Angeles. Martita lived in a little outbuilding on her dad's ranch. She was part cowgirl, part tomboy, and part seductress. The woman could handle a horse and tear through the countryside on her motorcycle. She seemed to defy every gender norm, effortlessly blending toughness and femininity into one captivating package.

Martita always wore a cinematographer's monocle around her neck. It was an adjustable apparatus you could raise to your eye and peer through, recreating the magic of framing a shot and playing with the lens's focal length. This little gadget had once belonged to her father. She cherished it as an accessory and a tangible link to her roots. Martita was a true artist, a soul bursting with creativity and an avalanche of emotions. Being with her felt like stepping into imagination, where reality and fantasy intertwined in the most electrifying way. She taught me that there's beauty in darkness and that true art can stem from the depths of pain.

But Martita wasn't just some dreamer lost in whims. She was fiercely driven by her desire for a career in the film industry. Even though Daddy was happy to provide for her, she refused to conform to the drudgery of being, in her words, "a mere house mouse."

Martita's softness and tenderness charmed me, but little did I know about the wild lover within her, until, with a mischievous glint in her eye, she confided in me, "I have an affinity for both men *and* women." The mere thought of it sent my mind spiraling into a world of untamed possibilities, especially when she nonchalantly mentioned, "I'm fond of threesomes." We embarked on a journey of sexual exploration, inviting other women to partake in our passionate rendezvous. It was a thrill beyond words, leaving me feeling like the luckiest guy alive. Martita breathed life into my most intimate and fiery fantasies, taking temptation to consummation.

But there's always a "however" in my stories. I discovered that when I initially crossed paths with Martita, she had still been involved with another man, probably equally attracted to her as I was. She neglected to disclose this information, hastily leaped into my world, and abruptly ended things with him without bringing it to my attention. Later, she repeatedly alluded to his persistent pursuit of her, expressing guilt for leaving him behind. There were also certain nights when she failed to show up as promised. Not only did this raise concerns for her safety, since it typically followed her shifts at the club where we first met, but it also fueled suspicions about her actions, especially considering her constantly shifting moods.

Despite her appeal, I couldn't accept this behavior. I confronted her about it, and she replied, "Babe, your jealousy is baseless." The excruciating fear of betrayal and abandonment I'd felt as a child gutted me. To avoid experiencing these emotions, I sabotaged the situation and pushed her away. Four months after we met, the relationship was toast.

As in the past, I clung to work and music. I had what seemed like family now in Westwood One. When the opportunity arose to record The Doobie Brothers' reunion show at LA's Greek Theatre for our "Superstar" series, I knew Westwood One's affiliates would be ecstatic. The Doobies were a radio staple, with a catalog of hits that would resonate with listeners across the country. This October 1992 concert was even more meaningful as it was a benefit for the young sons of their percussionist, Bobby LaKind, who was battling terminal cancer. This reunion, a rare occurrence since the core members disbanded in 1982, was charged with emotion, and I felt honored and excited to be a part of it.

The Greek was one of my favorite venues, and seeing The Doobies there brought me back to one of my first memorable concerts: Seeing The Doobie Brothers at Sacramento Memorial Auditorium in December 1978. I was sixteen, and the experience was a revelation. I had tagged along with a deejay friend who was introducing the opening act, and I still remember the thrill of walking backstage and witnessing the spectacle unfold. California Governor Jerry "Moonbeam" Brown and legendary singer Linda Ronstadt introduced the band, and when The Doobies hit the stage, I was mesmerized.

The benefit concert at the Greek was organized by Bruce Cohn, who had managed The Doobies since 1969. I had heard of Bruce, but we had never met. So nearly fourteen years after that concert in Sacramento, my position at Westwood One made it possible to arrange a meeting, and we hit it off. He was very enthusiastic about the idea of recording the concert for posterity using our thirty-two-track mobile recording studio. And he graciously accepted my offer of a $10,000 contribution to the LaKind Foundation.

The band rehearsed in the San Fernando Valley to prepare for the concert, and Bruce invited me to come by. I brought along a friend, and Bruce led us down the hallway into the rehearsal room where The Doobies were practicing. I had assumed a small audience would be present, but to our surprise, it was just the three of us positioned against the back wall about fifteen feet from the band, which at the time consisted of founding members Tom Johnston and Patrick Simmons, plus Michael McDonald and several others, including at least three percussionists.

Bruce casually offered me a joint during their practice performance, and we lit up right there. I couldn't believe it—I was smoking a doobie watching The Doobies! I liked the weed so much that I asked Bruce if I could buy some. He agreed, and two nights later, someone handed me an ounce at the Greek.

About the time of that Doobies show, I reached out to Martita in a moment of loneliness. I hadn't spoken with her in about a year.

"Yes, I had betrayed you, and I'm sorry about that. But I also still have feelings for you," she confessed. We agreed to meet for dinner, and she brought along a girl I had met at her birthday party, a lavish affair aboard her daddy's colossal motor yacht, moored at Marina del Rey. The three of us went back to my house—and let's just say we had a most satisfying reunion. Then Martita left, while the other girl stayed the night. She and I dated for a while, but the chemistry wasn't there and that ended, too.

One night, several months later, while I was sound asleep, I was startled awake by my two dogs, barking furiously. I distinctly heard a voice utter menacingly, "I'm gonna get you. I'm gonna kill you." To make sure it wasn't a dream, that this was really happening, I looked out my window. There was a person outside the fence surrounding my yard. I let the dogs out, hoping to deter the prowler while I dialed 911. I would soon learn a valuable lesson: Unless someone has actually broken into your house, the police don't see it as an emergency. The dispatcher merely advised me, "Keep an eye on the situation and call back if he breaks in." Desperate for help, I contacted one of my closest friends with an urgent plea to come over or get help. He dismissed my distress: "Dude, it's the middle of the night. I'm exhausted." Then he hung up. I called him again, and again, and he didn't pick up. So much for close friends.

The intruder eventually befriended my dogs through sweet talking and treats and found a way to jump over the fence, entering—trespassing—in my yard. Because my house couldn't be seen from the street or by neighbors, I only had window coverings in the bedrooms. There were no curtains in the living room and hence the intruder had a view right inside. I was terrified when I saw a figure in the darkness peering into my window and heard someone trying to test if any entry points were unlocked. I hurriedly took refuge in the hall closet, which had a deadbolt, clutching the cordless phone with me.

I called 911 again, this time forcefully telling the dispatcher, "Hey this intruder is armed, on my property, and attempting to break into my house, posing a serious threat to my life!"

The dispatcher took me at my word because I dropped the correct terminology. She responded, "Sir, stay on the line. Police have been dispatched, and they're on their way."

As I heard the officers tackle the intruder in my backyard, I sprang from the closet. I ran out through the front door nearest the closet and immediately intercepted more officers while the interloper was being apprehended and handcuffed.

The morning light revealed a chilling sight—a .22 caliber pistol and a hunting knife stashed in the bushes of my backyard. With a trembling hand, I brought them inside and placed them on my dining room table. Surveying the scene, I then walked out to the front, where I spotted a parked car I didn't recognize. *It must belong to the intruder!* Curious, I walked up to the car, and, to my surprise, it was unlocked. Under the driver's seat, I discovered a stash of unused syringes and registration papers. The car belonged to Martita's ex-boyfriend, the very same person she had dumped when she met me and then went back to. *This is getting out of hand,* I thought. I immediately called the police and handed over the weapons I'd found.

I wondered whether he had heard about our "reunion" and flipped. Or whether Martita sent him in retaliation for me going out with her friend, even though she had been a willing participant and "blessed" our initial encounter. I was still debating all this in my head when the phone rang. It was the guy calling from jail, "You know who I am, and I'm coming for you. You put me in jail, you asshole. That gun was just a prop. I wasn't going to hurt you." *How did he even know my address and phone number?*

I went to work and told a select few what happened. I informed Norm because I knew he carried a gun with a permit and Thom because he needed to know why I was acting edgy, unable to think straight. Norm's chauffeur fancied himself as some sort of law enforcement figure and had a concealed weapons permit. I asked him if he would accompany me home that night as protection. I knew the guy had been released from jail and feared he would return. Maybe he'd even be waiting for me at my house since he had left his car there—and his weapons. But when we got home, the car was gone. Even so, I was still rattled and asked him to secure the property. He covered the perimeter, moving from room to

room with me in tow like in the movies, all with his not-so-concealed and
loaded weapon drawn.

That night I decided I needed to buy a gun. The cops suggested a
shotgun. The dramatic sound it makes when cocked can have a deterrent
effect on potential criminals. Additionally, shotguns have a wide range,
making hitting the target easier. The investigating officer told me, "The
mere presence of a shotgun may intimidate and scare away your would-be
assailant, reducing the likelihood of a confrontation. It's the safest thing
to do."

This unnerving encounter made me realize the importance of making
healthier relationship choices. Martita may have appeared extraordinary on the surface, but who knew what darkness lay within her? Her
ex-partner was unstable, and I thank my higher power every day that he
never returned to cause me any further harm, psychological or physical.
Regrettably, during my research for this book, I came across more sadness—an obituary for Martita. She died less than two years after our final
encounter, just twenty-seven years old.

32

MYSTERIOUS WAYS

After The Doobie Brothers, I had my share of successes, but targeting and landing U2 would be a whole new level. They were arguably the biggest band in the world, at their absolute peak, and securing a live concert from them wouldn't be easy. But that's precisely what fueled my ambition. It was a chance to add to Westwood One's already impressive cachet, and at the same time, raise my profile. This wasn't just another deal. It was a statement.

I had several years of experience with the Irish group U2, dating back to 1985 when they had been dubbed "the band that matters most, maybe even the only band that matters," by *Rolling Stone* magazine. I had seen them play in a small club on the campus of San Diego State University. During their 1987 tour in support of the *Joshua Tree* album, I organized a fifty-passenger party bus road trip for 91X contest winners through the Joshua Tree National Park desert to their Las Vegas concert. Then, I saw U2 again for two sold-out shows at the San Diego Sports Arena. By that time, I had become a huge fan. At one point during an East Coast trip, while working for 91X, I had even dropped into the Island Records headquarters in New York City to meet with their head of promotion to underscore our commitment to the band and their record label.

Now I was at Westwood One, and I'd become a master of strategic persistence. If the squeaky wheel gets the grease, I was prepared to dive headfirst into a vat of Valvoline. I knew that sometimes a little—okay, a lot—of tenacity was needed to get the job done. So, I began a calculated campaign of calling and faxing Principle Management, U2's management company, helmed by Paul McGuiness, determined to make myself heard. They eventually assigned someone just to handle my inquiries. Then, in late 1992, a wonderful, saintly woman by the name of Sheila Roche gave me a crucial tip: "Paul will be attending the annual Midem Music Conference in Cannes, France, in January."

I quickly learned that the conference consisted of a European-led contingent of global music biz heavyweights meeting in the South of France for a giant party camouflaged as an industry convention. The parties compete to lure the most influential recording, publishing, and music management executives. Champagne on yachts, concerts in hotels, cocktails seaside—sophisticated socializing at its finest.

After hearing Sheila's assurances that Paul would be receptive to meeting me, I requested a meeting with my boss, Thom Ferro. I requested "budget approval for a trip to Cannes, where I'm going to have an in-person chat with Paul McGuiness to deliver the U2 deal. I'm on Paul's calendar and know his hotel, and maybe you'd like to join me." The next thing I knew, Thom had booked us a hotel and flights through the company travel agent. We were on our way to the South of France to take in Midem and hang with Paul McGuinness, who not only made U2 a household name but also made them the second highest-grossing Irish export, just behind Guinness beer.

We landed and checked into our hotel. The next day, we went to the conference. After, I slipped out and walked over to the Carlton Hotel on the prestigious Boulevard de la Croisette, where Sheila had told me Paul would be staying. At the front desk, I asked the clerk to ring his room but was told he had been delayed due to a "family emergency." I was used to setbacks, but this one was on a new level. I had flown all the way from Los Angeles to France—with my boss, no less—to make a deal with Paul, and he was across the English Channel in another country.

In the evening, Thom and I had dinner at a nearby restaurant and decided to walk back to our hotel. On the opposite side of the waterfront, away from the main harbor area, I spotted what appeared to be a cool, unmarked little bar at the base of the hillside leading up to our hotel. Thom agreed that we should stop off and have a drink to check out the scene.

In the South of France, one drinks champagne as if it were sparkling water. We ordered our first bottle at the bar, looked around, and saw a dark, subdued place with a few men and some gorgeous young women who seemed quite friendly. They were wearing sexy outfits and serving drinks. Our server ensured our eyes connected as she poured us two glasses from the bottle and sashayed back to her post. Within an hour or so, I was in a semi-private booth with our server, and we were each about a bottle of champagne deep. What kind of place had we stumbled into? I had been to strip clubs in the United States where drinks were not a factor. It was all about cash for attention, which made the transactional nature immediately obvious. I found this French connection very different. I was unsure if the pretty young women in this place were just friendly waitresses, or something else.

Thom was in the next booth with another server. He leaned over to me and said, "Hey bud, I'm gonna run back to the hotel to grab some weed because my waitress wants to get high with me." *He had weed after flying across the ocean?* His international smuggling maneuver dumbfounded me, albeit risky during the nineties, but a quite typical Thom move. Nonetheless, I couldn't have cared less what he wanted to do as this French woman had momentarily stolen my heart. I bought bottles of champagne as she gave me her undivided attention, and management turned a blind eye to her fraternization. In fact, they had moved us to the curtained booths. We had fun trying to communicate with one another, me attempting to speak to her in French, and she attempting to reciprocate in English. We had what felt, to me, at least, like a genuine connection. I'd consumed an ample amount of inhibition-lowering champagne and I made a pitch to her to join me at the hotel at the end of her shift. We were kissing and rubbing up against one another and things began to escalate—until I fucked it up.

While making out with her, I slipped out of my petite wooden French bistro-style chair and fell backward, knocking over the bucket chilling our champagne. Broken glass flew everywhere.

"Merde, merde homme Américain!" the manager screamed, which translates to "Damn American!" My "date" quickly excused herself, and the manager motioned for me to pay the check and exit. Thom had rung up a few bottles, as had I, and that's when I noticed the price of each bottle included the friendly company. Thom hadn't returned from his weed run, so it was up to me to pay over a thousand US dollars on my credit card, an expense I knew he'd approve, as he was complicit. The girl I had been making out with, the one with whom I had felt such a real connection, was gone.

The next day, there was a thick fog over the sea and an even denser fog in my head. As the fog lifted, I looked out of my hotel window at the Mediterranean sunshine floating above, slowly dissolving the marine layer. *Was Paul's emergency real?* I decided to take one last crack at finding him before our scheduled departure later that day.

I called the Carlton and asked the hotel operator to ring Paul McGuinness's room. I fully expected the operator to say he had not yet checked in or that his reservation had been canceled. Instead, I heard a ringing sound, and then a man in a deep Irish brogue said, "Hey-low?"

I immediately launched into my pitch: "Paul, this is Rob Tonkin from Westwood One. Sheila told me you were open to meeting with me. So, could we set a time to discuss the live concert broadcast rights to the Zooropa Tour from U2?"

He replied, in a friendly tone, "Tanks, Robe, yaas, I remember Sheila tailin' me you'd turn oop in Cannes."

I interjected, "I'm happy to come to your hotel now, but my flight is leaving soon."

Paul said, "I caint now but troost me, Robe, eef U2 duss a bro'd cast eet'ill be wit shoe."

"Thank you, Paul. Thank you! Let's keep in touch."

Beyond thrilled, I hung up the phone. I dashed outside with my bags. Thom was already there, waiting for our ride to the airport. "Hey, man, I met with Paul and we're all good," I said excitedly. "They aren't sure they're up for a broadcast, but if they do one, we'll get it." I sensed a bond between us, knowing we'd somewhat unnecessarily flown all the way to Cannes, yet had still accomplished something great, even though it came down to the wire. *Hallelujah, praise be Paul!*

A few weeks later, I received a handwritten fax on Principle Management stationery in my Westwood One office, scribed in big letters, "Hi, Rob, how much will you pay?" Signed, "Paul."

Direct? Indeed—but we both knew what each of us wanted. Paul McGuinness kept his word, and we wound up getting the deal. I flew to Paris for a preview of the show and got to meet with the crew and stay at the same hotel as the band on the Champs-Élysées. Then I flew to Dublin to check out the location for the show we were planning to broadcast. I had dinner at Bono's brother's restaurant and picked up a waitress who wound up taking me to the club where U2 got their start.

I flew to Dublin again for their two-night stand at the RDS Arena and was on hand as we beamed the second night for our Westwood One "Live" satellite broadcast and recording. One highlight of those shows was access to a little VIP hospitality room tucked beneath the stands, for special guests of the band, where I had the honor to briefly chat up one of the most extraordinary music men in rock 'n' roll: Chris Blackwell, who signed U2, among other such fabled acts as Bob Marley and Roxy Music.

33

BAND ON THE RUN

There were plenty of other close encounters with famous musicians. In 1993, my friend David Saltz landed a gig as a tour producer for Paul McCartney's "New World Tour." He scored Blockbuster Video as a sponsor and Fox TV to broadcast one of the shows live. Then, he brought me on board to spearhead the radio promotions across Westwood One's affiliate stations and through our network. I even managed to snag the audio broadcast rights for the TV show, giving our affiliates a *simulcast* opportunity. The chosen concert was in Charlotte, North Carolina, just before Labor Day.

I was whisked away to Charlotte on Norm Pattiz's private G3 jet, along with the heads of affiliate relations and a top media buyer. To my surprise, David invited me and two of my bosses to a meet-and-greet with the man himself! It would turn out to be an encounter with an iconic figure who would stand out above the rest. I met Linda McCartney first, and then, there he was—Sir Paul.

"So," he said with a grin, "I hear you're the one responsible for all this commotion about my little concert."

"We're just trying to make sure everyone knows about it," I replied, feeling a bit flustered by his attention.

"Well, it seems to be working," Sir Paul said with a chuckle. "Everywhere I go, people are talking about this broadcast. Makes me feel famous again!"

We all laughed, and I felt a surge of warmth toward this music legend who could still poke fun at his fame. The whole encounter was captured by a photographer who later sent me a print, which remains one of my most treasured career mementos, reminding me of how genuinely kind and well-informed Paul McCartney was about our efforts.

My next adventure involved another of my all-time favorites, arguably America's biggest rock band—the Eagles. Founding member Don Henley was organizing a benefit for the Walden Woods Project, an ambitious undertaking to preserve "the land, literature, and legacy of author and philosopher Henry David Thoreau to foster an ethic of environmental stewardship and social responsibility," according to its website. Henley launched the project in 1990 with the goal of buying and protecting historic Walden Woods and Thoreau country property in Concord and Lincoln, Massachusetts. Henley's benefit included performances by himself, Elton John, Sting, Jimmy Buffett, Aerosmith, and Melissa Etheridge. Irving Azoff, the fabled music industry heavyweight derided in a book as "The Poison Dwarf" because of his demeanor and height, was my main point of contact, and we discussed broadcasting the show and raising awareness in advance through special programming on Westwood One.

Despite his reputation, Azoff never came across as condescending. I actually found him quite pleasant. He always returned my calls promptly and was terrific to work with—*not* an asshole. He and Henley had agreed to Henley's set being broadcast and recorded, and Azoff said he and his charge would help get the other artists on board. Westwood One offered to publicize the concert nationally—drive the big-rig mobile recording studio across the country from Los Angeles to the Boston area, pay for all of the production necessary to capture the concert and interviews, and beam the show live via satellite to radio stations as a special event. Westwood One also agreed to donate a large variable sum of money to the charity, which depended on how many other artists also allowed us to record and broadcast their performances. Azoff knew that not all of the artists were willing to let us do that, but he still quoted the best-case amount to Henley. Unfortunately, when Henley discovered the actual amount would turn out to be a lot smaller, he was furious.

One afternoon, my office fax machine spit out another important letter, this one personally signed by Henley and addressed to yours truly. My excitement at getting a personal missive from the co-leader of the Eagles soon turned to dismay when I read what Henley had written. He wrote that he was "disgusted that you reneged on the deal" and called me "shameful." Before receiving the letter, I had never met him or spoken directly to him, and at the time had no idea what he was talking about.

A short time later, while the deal was still in play, Norm, always a mover and shaker, attended the wedding of Bernie Taupin, Elton John's longtime songwriting partner. At the reception, he ran into Don Henley and chatted about the upcoming Walden Woods charity concert event. Henley began badmouthing "Mr. Tonkin" about my supposed betrayal. But Norm, privy to the deal points, immediately set him straight.

The following week, Norm came down from his mezzanine office with a letter and tossed it on my desk. I noticed it was addressed to him from Don Henley. I picked it up and began to read under Norm's watchful gaze. After several sentences about how wonderful it was to bump into him at the wedding and other small talk, Henley wrote, "Please apologize to Mr. Tonkin on my behalf. Sometimes, because I get my information second hand through Irving, it isn't always clear to me."

I flew to Boston over the 1993 Labor Day weekend for The Concert for Walden Woods at Foxboro Stadium (now Gillette Stadium). I made sure to stop at Walden Woods so I could see why Henley felt so strongly about preserving the area. As Henry David Thoreau wrote about Walden in 1854, "I went to the woods because I wished to live deliberately, to front only the essential facts of life, and see if I could not learn what it had to teach, and not, when I came to die, discover that I had not lived." My takeaway was that Henley related to Thoreau as a writer. At the show, while I didn't get to meet or talk with Henley or the other artists, I was able to spend time with Irving Azoff. Everything went as planned, we wound up with another great recording and Henley thanked Westwood One in the printed event program and "*especially* Rob Tonkin."

I framed all three of Henley's acknowledgments of me together. It's a favorite bit of memorabilia from my music business days, up there with the McCartney pic, definitely besting my gold and platinum record awards collection.

34

LIKE A ROLLING STONE

I have always felt that The Rolling Stones signify pure and simple irrever-ence. "Satisfaction" is pushing sixty, and while I'm a couple of years older than the song, it neatly sums up my life. Abandonment issues trigger re-bellion, psychologists will tell you, and as I discovered music, I came to idolize those lanky, sneering Brits who did what they liked regardless of what anyone thought.

The first time I saw the Stones in concert was in the summer of 1978, at the Oakland Coliseum. They headlined a show billed as a "Very Special Day on the Green" because the band initially did not have a tour date in the Bay Area. Bill Graham, the promoter who set the standard for well-produced, large-scale rock concerts, organized daytime Day on the Green stadium shows there every summer, this Rolling Stones' one being the fourth that year. I still remember my amazement when I saw Mick Jagger, wearing a tight T-shirt and American-style football pants, running from one end of the stage to the other. With Keith Richards and Ronnie Wood wailing on guitars and Charlie Watts and Bill Wyman driving the beat, the band blazed through their set under the midday sun in front of 60,000 raucous fans, me included.

Since then, I'd seen the Stones a few more times. And when the chance to work with them presented itself, I was beside myself. Having scored deals with many superstars of rock, including Aerosmith, Tom Petty and the Heartbreakers, Bruce Springsteen, Paul McCartney, Rod Stewart, The Doobie Brothers, U2, and the Eagles (at least Don Henley),

I was on a roll and excited to keep on rolling with another "Live" score—hopefully, this time featuring the world's greatest rock 'n' roll band.

In early 1994, The Rolling Stones were ramping up for the *Voodoo Lounge* album release and tour, and I figured now was as good a time as any to snag the rights to a live broadcast. The tour was produced by Canadian promoter Michael Cohl, who, with some pretty hefty financial backing, was able to go after top-tier superstars and offer them oversized guarantees of $100 million or more in return for the right to promote their entire worldwide tours. He then got 100 percent of the ticket proceeds and was able to sell the rights for television, radio, merchandise, and other creative endeavors.

Michael had pulled off a tremendous coup in snagging the Stones, beating out none other than Bill Graham. Getting a meeting with him was like getting a meeting with God, but I was determined. Michael's assistant heard from me so many times that we became friends. Jaye was the neck that turned the head, and eventually, the head agreed to meet with me. So, off I went to Toronto. Michael chain-smoked his way through our one-hour meeting, which ended with us agreeing on a price as well as on which show location and date made the most sense to broadcast live. We settled on the band's October 10, 1994 performance at the Louisiana Superdome in New Orleans, a city I already knew too well.

Michael limited our rights to the United States so he could sell radio rights to the remaining territories within the world. We usually obtained global radio rights, but my bosses didn't want to rock the boat, so we settled for what he would give us. The night of my visit coincided with a David Gilmour-led Pink Floyd concert Cohl was promoting at the CNE Stadium, and I was invited to join Michael in his skybox. It was a fantastic way to end the day.

Once the deal was signed, I arranged to attend tour rehearsals at RFK Stadium in Washington DC. I spent a week at the historic Ritz-Carlton on Embassy Row, where the band was also staying. Inside the hotel was a bar and restaurant called the Jockey Club, one of the city's most famous watering holes for the rich and politically powerful, named after a renowned club in London. I spent evenings in the bar drinking and chatting it up with crew members and supporting musicians such as Bernard Fowler, who would go on to be a backup vocal singer for the Stones for over thirty-five years.

My days consisted of taking the Metro to the stadium near the Anacostia River and the DC Armory. Once inside, I watched the run-throughs, got to know the touring crew, met actor Dan Aykroyd, who was hosting a VH1 tour preview, and reported back daily to company headquarters. We also managed to garner interviews for our own syndi-cated radio tour promotion. While some might view this extended trip as an unnecessary indulgence, I believed these experiences were essential investments in building relationships and expanding my horizons.

The week culminated in the opening show of the tour on August 1, 1994. The concert was a blast, and while I had watched their rehearsals, seeing them play live and feed off the full-house audience was a whole other experience. The Rolling Stones opened their twenty-plus-song set with a dragon spitting flames as they broke into "Not Fade Away," the classic Buddy Holly song that became their first UK hit in 1964. They proceeded to play songs from throughout their career supported by astonishing lighting, video, and other effects, including their newest song from *Voodoo Lounge*, "You Got Me Rocking," plus a whole string of clas-sics: "Tumbling Dice," "Shattered," "Satisfaction," "Beast of Burden," "Wild Horses," "Street Fightin' Man," "Honky Tonk Woman," "Brown Sugar," and more. Then, for the encore, "Jumpin' Jack Flash."

Mick Jagger, as expected, stole the show with his boundless energy and physical explosiveness, his sinewy, oddly youthful strutting body commanding all eyes—including mine. Then, accompanied by sound from each side of the stage, the sky burst into color with a dazzling fire-works crescendo to the night's revelry.

The next time I saw the concert was at the New York Giants Stadium in New Jersey, about two weeks after the opener, where I produced a pre-concert party for advertisers hosted by Westwood One President Pete Janek, my *least* favorite boss. The party came off well because it was held indoors, just before the clouds moved in, and an unexpected summer storm poured on the outdoor concert for nearly the entire performance. My date, Traci Collins, a music industry manager I had met in Los Angeles but who had since moved to New York City, was dressed in a crushed velvet Betsey Johnson outfit with Manolo Blahnik heels. By the end of the show, even after Cohl's rep, John Meglen, gave us tour rain jackets and found Traci a spot to dry off temporarily, we were soaked to the bone watching the show from our seats. But it was a sort of magic to watch the crowd get rained on and hear the thunder of the band.

Afterward, we rolled back to the city, still drenched, and ended up at the midtown Four Seasons on 57th Street, where most of the band stayed. There was a reception in the lobby, but we headed to my room first to dry off. Traci disrobed and I saw her entire lower body was indigo colored because of the garment dye bleeding from her leggings. We both erupted into laughter. Her shoes were utterly trashed.

Upon my return to Los Angeles, I was summoned by Norm: "Tonkin, I want to go to the Stones show in Chicago. Bring it!" Later, his assistant, Alexia, informed me that he also "needed" to meet Mick Jagger, one of the few rock stars he hadn't yet met. My job was to make shit happen, and Norm was used to being treated as a VIP. Michael Cohl was gracious and agreed to arrange a pre-show meeting at the tour stop in Chicago in mid-September, about a month before our live broadcast in New Orleans.

We boarded Norm's private G3 jet at the Van Nuys airport, a busy general aviation airport in the San Fernando Valley, and flew to Chicago, where we were picked up from the tarmac by a stretch limo. We checked in at The Ritz-Carlton and then returned to the limo for the short drive to the restaurant for dinner. There were four of us: Norm, Alexia, and I, who had flown in together from California, and Pete Janek, who had flown in from New York City on a commercial flight. Pete, the head of our division, was a man whose abrasive management style and penchant for taking credit annoyed me enough that I privately referred to him as "the bad apple." The prospect of spending an evening with him, even amid the excitement of The Rolling Stones concert, was less than appealing.

After dinner, the limo took us to Soldier Field, where I had arranged for backstage parking, high-level credentials, and reserved "family and friends" seats on the mixing board platform. This was proper VIP treatment; of the kind I had rarely experienced before.

Backstage, we were ushered into the Voodoo Lounge, a sprawling tent transformed into a rockstar oasis. The carpet beneath our feet covered the blacktop below it, and the air hummed with anticipation. Pool tables gleamed under soft lighting, sofas invited relaxation, and a well-stocked bar promised a good time. Every detail, from the spiked tongue artwork to the music pulsating through the speakers, echoed the *Voodoo Lounge* album's theme.

A few moments later, Norm was introduced to Mick Jagger and they spoke briefly. I was an afterthought in terms of intros, but before Mick strutted out, we were quickly introduced, and I managed to shake Jagger's hand as well.

By the time the tour rolled into New Orleans, appropriately the home of voodoo folklore, zombies, and queens, I had seen the tour a couple more times. Ironically, I never made it out to New Orleans for the show we broadcast live. My prior experience in that city had left me with a bad taste, and I had no hankering to return to the Big Easy anytime soon. But the broadcast went off without a hitch, and Westwood One scored a real coup.

35

WHEN THE MIGHTY STRIKE OUT

After bringing the world's greatest rock 'n' roll band to the world's largest syndicator of audio content, I felt invincible—and indispensable. Big names brought in big audiences, big audiences led to big advertising dollars, and big advertising dollars led to significant spikes in year-over-year sales.

And yet, the company's stock price languished. Some joked that its name had changed to "Westwood One and a Half." Investor sentiment and market dynamics had depressed the share price, though I walked the hallways of Westwood One with my head held high, making direct eye contact with everyone. Shmoozing coworkers, I'd say stuff like, "Hey there, keeping those stations happy? Don't worry, I'll keep bringing in the big names so you have something to brag about!"

I dove headfirst into the music industry, only to find it teeming with *assholes*. Desperate for recognition, I mirrored their toxic behavior. There's an old Southern saying, "He's gotten too big for his britches." It essentially means that someone has become conceited or thinks too highly of themselves. My britches had been getting tighter and tighter with each big act I signed, but when I secured The Rolling Stones, they burst apart. I had unwittingly used The Rolling Stones to prop myself up, to soothe those pesky wounds from years before. My true self was buried somewhere beneath layers of ambition and insecurity, a ghost haunting the halls of my success.

In the weeks leading up to my delivery of the Stones, when I was sure we had the deal in the bag, I felt confident enough to ask for a raise. A friend from San Diego had also moved up to Los Angeles, where he was working as an artist and repertoire (A&R) executive for a major record company. I was making just under $100,000 a year, and he easily made nearly four times that amount. One night we talked money, and he was aghast at how little I was making. "Rob, you need to go in there and ask for more—a lot more," he chided.

I discussed the matter with my direct boss, Thom Ferro, who encouraged me to write a memo directly to the company President, Pete Janek. I carefully laid out the value I felt I had brought to the company in securing all these big-name acts, noted we were on the verge of signing the Stones, and asked them to double my salary. I knew this was a daring move, but Thom assured me he had my back, so I sent the memo to Pete in New York.

A few days later, the memo came back. I wish I had saved it. Pete had used a blunt pencil to draw a diagonal line all the way across the page, topped with "NO" in large capital letters. He had depressed the pencil with such force that it had embossed the paper and nearly torn it. It was an angry and revealing childish response to what I had felt was a fairly innocent request for compensation I deserved.

I was astonished—and embarrassed for him. I was close to inking a deal that would make the company money, generate gobs of publicity, and please my bosses. And yet I had been snubbed, even humiliated. I went to Thom and showed him the memo. He laughed, and prompted me to cast aside my anger and confusion and let out a halfhearted chuckle, primarily at Janek's expense. That was indicative of how Thom would play all sides of everything. A week later, Thom summoned me to his office and said, "Tonkin, don't worry about that response from Janek—you know how he is. I've got you covered, and we're going to give you a raise—not what you're asking for, but we'll meet you close to the middle." They increased my salary by about 60 percent. I was ecstatic and felt that I had won the lottery. But, more importantly, it gave me a feeling of being supported.

At times, Thom rang me himself on the intercom. Such a summons was invigorating because I'd enter his office to hear another crazy personal story or an affirmative suggestion for a project I was working on for the company. His stories ranged from tales of jumping through plate-glass windows just for fun to throwing television sets into the ground-level pool from the nineteenth-story suite of the posh Century Plaza Hotel in Century City to sexual exploits with *Playboy* centerfolds, complete with graphic details. It was early 1995, within months after The Rolling Stones broadcasted from New Orleans, and after my big raise. All of a sudden, Thom Ferro's assistant rang. She was always cold toward me. It was mid-morning. "Thom wants to see you immediately." This was different.

I arrived at the opposite end of the building where my boss's not-so-friendly assistant, who sat in a cubicle outside his office with the demeanor of an armed security guard, motioned for me to open the door and enter. A solid, hunter-green wooden door led to Thom's stately, split-level office, complete with a mirrored wall, sitting area, and a private bathroom with shower.

I walked in and saw Thom behind his large, elevated desk, waiting for me. Our corporate controller, who doubled as head of human resources, sat in one of the two leather club chairs across the desk from him. I thought, *Oh, it's a budget meeting*. I took a seat in the other club chair, and the woman welcomed me.

"Hi, Rob. How's your day going so far?"

Thom, rife with facial tics, began meandering through more small talk. Then, shifting to a more somber tone, he said, "I'm sorry, Bud, but they want me to let you go. I tried to convince them not to, but you know how it is.... We're gonna publicly call it a separation by resignation to help you get another job, and I'll give you a great reference."

All I could hear at that moment was piffle. I was in total shock. I glanced at the woman, who smiled and explained the next steps in my dismissal. I deciphered that to get my final paycheck, I had to sign a waiver.

I felt an adrenaline rush, and as the hormone rushed into my blood, I could feel my heart rate rising.

She continued talking: "You've got X many accrued vacation days, and your final check will include these, but there's no severance because the company is not in a financial position to pay."

I walked out of the office in a shameful stupor. *Everyone here knows I've been canned*, my mind told me. I made my way back to my office cave, attempting to mask my disbelief with a calm demeanor. My office had no windows, and I felt the walls closing in as shock turned to panic. I had a reputation, a house, a mortgage, a car payment, insurance, and credit card debt. How would I survive this? What did I do to deserve it?

This guy, the one who just orchestrated my downfall, was supposed to be my friend. We'd traveled together, partied together, and shared personal stories. Had it all been a lie? Was this real life, or some twisted nightmare of betrayal? It felt like both.

Had asking for a raise been a mistake? I wondered. Or was it just the excuse Pete needed? Maybe he resented my youth, the ease with which I connected with people, especially women. In Dublin, Ireland, when a girl chose me over him when he wasn't given an "all access" laminated pass, could that have festered, leading to whispers and backstabbing? That night U2 had only given me a certain amount of all-access passes and since I was one short, I left out my least favorite person—Pete. Or maybe it was that thousand-dollar bar tab in Cannes. Had Thom blamed me for that? I also wondered where Norm stood on all of this, even though by this time he had sold about a quarter of the company to Infinity Broadcasting, one of the largest owners of radio stations, and turned over management to them. Still, he remained chair of the company, and I wondered why he didn't protect me. I still don't know.

As I gathered my belongings, I noticed the facility manager—who, oddly enough, was also the drummer for "Weird Al" Yankovic—hovering nearby. Apparently, someone had instructed him to supervise my exit. *The same guy who had dinner with me and those contest winners a decade earlier was my escort out of the building....* It felt brutally unfair. Maybe I had been naive, too trusting. After all, this was a corporation, a machine that often prioritized profits over people.

The drive home was like a movie reel playing continuous clips from the five years I loyally served that company. I had been rewarded along the way, provided with major career advancement, benefits, creative leeway, music industry perks, a big travel and expense budget, encouragement, meaningful friendships, and additional salary. *Where, when, and what did I do wrong?*

What followed was terrible resentment toward Westwood One—and disappointment in myself. The trauma from this sudden separation from my workplace, my coworkers, my daily routine, and my social environment was deeply unsettling to the rattled little boy deep inside of me. Not knowing exactly why I had been fired gnawed at my gut. *Was I confused about their expectations? Did I overperform at my job as a way to control and manipulate them to give me more needed assurances and compensation? Where was the communication breakdown?*

I thought back to my request for a raise, Pete Janek's angry "NO," and then Thom Ferro's assurance that my request would be granted. I imagined what had gone on behind the scenes, a conversation between Thom and Pete after I showed Thom the returned memo response from Pete. Ferro likely began with something like, "I can't believe Tonkin would ask us to double his salary at a time like this. He knows the company's stock is in the toilet, but clearly, that arrogant little fucker only cares about himself. We need him to bring this deal home, so let's give him the raise and blow him out when it's over." And Janek retorted, "Yeah, that's a good plan. And let's keep that little shit on a tight string until the day we can celebrate his death. Who does he think he is?"

The next important step was finding another job. I kept trying to remind myself that being let go from a prized position that I thought I loved was simply a temporary setback. It had nothing to do with a lack of ability or being liked. At the time, though, all I could see was red. Deep inside me lurked a sense of inadequacy, a feeling that I had been fired because I wasn't smart enough, because I didn't know enough, as Dad's critical voice fired over and over in my head, "No college, no success! Do you finally see it now Robbie?"

36

FREE BIRD

Almost immediately after my surprise firing from Westwood One, I joined The Album Network Group. This influential company wasn't a radio network in the same way as Westwood One, but it held significant sway in the music industry. It published trade magazines that were essential reading for anyone in the business, and it also offered a curated suite of promotional services to record companies, including nationally syndicated radio special programming events to launch new albums. They sold advertising space in their magazines and compiled CDs of the latest music for radio programmers. Most importantly, their team had strong relationships with hundreds of radio stations across the country. They directly influenced which songs got added to playlists—a crucial factor in an artist's success in those pre-internet days. Every Tuesday, radio stations reported their top songs and key "adds," and The Album Network published these lists.

I was excited to be part of a powerful player in the industry. The Album Network was owned by brothers whose family had emigrated from Lebanon via Cleveland. The Album Network's president, a non-related part of the family named Steve Smith, had been brought in several years earlier and grew to oversee the company's new offerings and all business operations. When a major new album was about to be released, Smith and his team would either acquire the rights to a live concert broadcast or present an exclusive interview featuring music from the new record, or both. So, when Smith called me and invited me to lunch with himself and his "rock" lieutenant Tommy Nast after hearing of my departure from Westwood One, I figured he was interested in hiring me to manage rights acquisition and supervise content production for their syndication, much as I had done at my previous employer. He, however, had a much different role in mind for me.

Smith and The Album Network had gotten involved with a secret new venture called 1-800-MUSIC NOW, which was majority owned and funded—to the tune of $50 million—by MCI Communications. This big phone company later morphed into Verizon Communications. In those pre-internet days, the new service would allow people to preview music over the phone and then buy the record, with the tagline, "You call, you listen, you like, you buy." MCI would also customize the service in thirty different radio markets. My job would be to select, convince, and enroll multiple radio stations in each of these markets, signing them up in advance of the service's November 1995 launch. To tackle this challenging task, I hired staff in Los Angeles and New York City and produced a roadshow.

I identified a posh, centrally located hotel in each market and then scheduled radio stations, generally ten per market, for presentations. The stations that signed up would get a share of sales revenue and receive incremental increases in ad buys from MCI in exchange for on-air promotion.

Steve Smith had an enormous task on his plate to build and get this startup to market and simultaneously run day-to-day operations at The Album Network. A few months into the job, I had a new boss. She was a former radio deejay and, with her husband, they owned a small radio syndication ad sales firm that had partnered with The Album Network to manage the new venture.

Almost immediately, my new boss began to undermine me, make changes without discussion, and effectively diminish my role. I saw that once again, even in the glamorous world of music, office politics and power struggles were all too common as we started to clash. One day, I was on the phone with my assistant, when she told me about something she had asked her to do that was completely contrary to what I wanted her to do. I blurted back, "Fuck her!" My assistant and I talked for a few more minutes and then hung up. About an hour later, her business partner, also her husband, called me and unemotionally said, "Rob, we're letting you go effective now."

Unbeknownst to me, my assistant had conferenced my boss into the call—a silent audience to my professional undoing. The betrayal of the eavesdropping didn't surface until days after the axe fell.

That familiar tightness in my chest, mixed with uncertainty about my future, returned. I had been let go on the eve of the service's launch, after about five months of hard work I had put into 1-800-MUSIC NOW. This was the second time in a year I had been unexpectedly betrayed by someone close to me at work. Ironically, I'd wanted to work on The Album Network's syndicated productions and only took the position with the phone company record store because Steve convinced me it was good for *my* career. He was projecting. It was good for *his* career.

But 1-800-MUSIC NOW didn't last much longer than I did. Initially, it seemed the venture went quite well; within the first four months, the 800 number received over 400,000 calls a day. But calls are one thing, and sales are another. A year after launch, the service was abruptly shut down amid reports that the highest-selling album had sold a grand total of just 400 units.

Being let go twice in one year was not good for my ego or my finances. After getting the big Westwood One raise in 1994, I had gotten rid of my human roommates and remodeled my house, which felt great because I was able to live an unfettered life with my two dogs, Hank, a liver-spotted Dalmatian, and Sybil, a brindle Staffordshire terrier. Yet that left us entirely dependent on my salary. With it gone, and no job in sight, I made the difficult decision to sell my cherished Laurel Canyon home at a loss.

37

WALK ON THE WILD SIDE

After the sale of my house, I began preparations for a move into a stylish rented loft in Venice Beach, famous for its eclectic beachfront boardwalk—a spectacle of humanity where people from all walks of life converge to express themselves, entertain, and soak up the unique atmosphere—equal parts sand, sun and surf.

Then, I received a game-changing phone call from a British music Manager friend named Tony Dimitriades. Tony had had a hand in shaping the careers of many famous musicians, from Tom Petty and the Heartbreakers to Billy Idol, Lindsey Buckingham, and members of Yes. He invited me to lunch at his favorite spot, the little Italian café inside the trendy Fred Segal store on Melrose Avenue. There, he told me, "I want to connect you with a music TV content producer who's a friend of Billy's and planning a new music TV series that might be great for you." I knew this meant it would somehow be good for him, too.

John Diaz had produced several Tom Petty and Billy Idol music videos. Tony set up the meeting, which took place in John's office, an upstairs loft over a vacant retail storefront, also on Melrose. John was proof that good things come in small but mighty packages. He'd done the Big Easy, conquered the Big Apple, and finally landed in the City of Angels.

"So, Tony tells me you're putting together a pretty groundbreaking show," I said, extending my hand to John. "*On Tour*, right?"

"Yeah, that's right," he replied, shaking my hand with a firm grip.

"And I'm hoping you're the one to help me make it bigger."

"I'm intrigued," I said, taking a seat. "Tony gave me a brief overview, but I'd love to hear more about your vision."

I knew *On Tour* involved filming concerts by popular bands around the country and had support from PBS, which would broadcast the shows on public television stations across the country, with underwriting from AT&T.

"Well," he began, leaning forward with enthusiasm, "it's all about capturing the true essence of live music. We're going on tour with these bands, embedding ourselves in their world to capture the energy ... the real deal."

"That's what makes it so unique," I added. "It's not just another sterile studio performance for TV. You're capturing the raw energy of these artists in their element."

"Precisely," he said. "And we're not just talking about any bands," he added with a wink. "I'm hoping for some decent names."

I raised an eyebrow, intrigued. "Oh yeah? Like who?"

He leaned in conspiratorially. "Well, let's just say I have my sights set on some big acts."

"I can't wait to see who you land," I said, my anticipation growing.

"And that's where you come in," he said, his smile widening. "I want you to be the talent executive. Tony says you're hot shit."

My heart skipped a beat to both points. "Really?"

"Absolutely," he confirmed. "You'd be responsible for selecting and acquiring the artists, managing their legal rights, and cultivating those relationships."

"That sounds amazing," I said, barely able to contain my excitement. "I'm in!"

This role aligned perfectly with what I had done at Westwood One, with the added bonus of moving beyond audio and into visuals. I would be working with the same network of top-tier talent managers with whom I was already familiar.

Three months into *On Tour*, John called me into his office. I had a feeling this wasn't going to be our usual check-in.

"Robbie," he began, a broad smile spreading across his face, "I'm absolutely thrilled with how things are going. You're killing it."

"That's great to hear, Diaz," I replied, feeling a surge of pride. "I'm really enjoying this project and pouring my heart into it."

"It shows," he said, his voice full of sincerity. "Your dedication and creativity are evident in every aspect. And your knack for securing those high-profile artists? Awesome."

"Well, I do have a certain gift of persuasion," I said with a slight grin.

"Indeed," he chuckled. "Which is why I've decided to promote you to co-producer."

"Co-producer?" I exclaimed, trying to mask my surprise. "That's ... that's quite a leap."

"You deserve it. You've been instrumental," he said, and then proceeded to delineate my expanded responsibilities. "I want you to oversee the filming itinerary, manage the audio recordings, secure more brand sponsorships ... basically, do everything you can to enhance the longevity of this project."

"Consider it done," I said, confidence radiating from my voice. "I'm ready to take *On Tour* to the next level."

"I know you are," he said, beaming. "That's precisely why I'm paying you."

My Westwood One experience provided very valuable knowledge about the audio recording process that I was able to apply to the TV show. I understood the line feeds from all the instruments and vocal sources, additional microphones to capture the ambiance of the crowd, mixing the show on-site, remixing afterward as needed, the approval processes, and ensuring that the final product was suitable for broadcast. At Westwood One, our recording setup featured two large digital audio tape machines, playfully named Fred and Ethel, after characters from the *I Love Lucy* television show. Working alongside an experienced team had taught me invaluable lessons about the art of recording live music.

On Tour was a startup company with a small staff. The production company, Sunshine TV, had limited resources, a makeshift office, and non-traditional workspaces. My workstation consisted of a metal folding chair and a six-foot wooden folding table. On the bright side, the talent reps I reached out to expressed interest in what I was offering. Diaz had high hopes but never expected the caliber of big-name artists I was able to secure. In just a few months of pre-production, I had agreements in progress with a highly diverse roster of artists, including Beck, Cypress Hill, Robert Cray, Taj Mahal, No Doubt, Bruce Hornsby, Lou Reed, Meat Loaf, Ozzy Osbourne, Lenny Kravitz, Metallica, The Cure, Steve Earle, The Smashing Pumpkins, The Cranberries, Bad Religion, Bob Weir, the Indigo Girls, Pantera, Tears for Fears, Sting, and many more. Instead of recording in a sterile studio, we filmed on the road, and as we followed the artists on tour, each venue became our "set." From April to August 1996, our crew crisscrossed the United States and then Europe.

One of the advantages of working with PBS was its status as a nonprofit organization. When I contacted artist managers, they were aware that there would be no compensation. It was their responsibility to help convince the record companies and music publishing entities that the rights would be provided free of charge, in return for massive exposure via the nation's most prominent provider of programming to public TV stations in the United States, distributing shows such as *Frontline*, *Nova*, *PBS NewsHour*, *Masterpiece*, and *Sesame Street*.

To complete our cross-country journey, we needed a mobile recording truck, a video control room truck, a truck for lighting and camera gear, and a tour bus for the crew. Additionally, we needed meal catering, credentials, an on-site office, and showers. At each of the thirty-four venues where we collected artist footage, there were numerous moving parts to manage. We not only filmed the headliners but also captured performances from the support artists. Moreover, we successfully included concerts from various festivals such as Lollapalooza (yes, I was finally able to land a deal and not end up incarcerated) and Reggae Sunsplash. Aside from broadcasting the concerts on PBS, we also offered them to international TV networks, each requiring its own negotiation and contract. John primarily handled the international deals and acted as the main contact with the affiliate station KCET in Los Angeles, who dealt with PBS, although I also communicated with public TV executives.

On Tour provided me with an extremely relaxed work atmosphere. John was a big proponent of smoking weed in the office, using profanity, engaging in interoffice relationships, and other unconventional behavior. Among the crew was Misha, John's assistant. Misha was strikingly attractive—half Mexican, half Scandinavian, with piercing blue eyes and pale, almost translucent skin. She oozed charisma. Linda, the associate producer, managed all of the taped assets. John, Linda, Misha, and I bonded over long lunches, fueled by laughter, creative brainstorming, and the occasional recreational substance. The three of them often playfully teased me for being "tightly wound." Misha frequently made sexually suggestive jokes. Despite the laid-back vibe, we had an immense workload to tackle, and my determination to complete the tasks and ensure the venture's success was unwavering, which John liked.

Misha and I started going out for dinner and drinks together, mostly when I was entertaining managers or record label executives. Misha proved invaluable to our entourage due to her engaging conversational skills and infectious sense of humor. On several occasions, the men we had entertained contacted me to inquire about her availability and willingness to socialize without me.

Misha had all sorts of delicious stories about dating celebrities such as the late Matthew Perry, Jim Carrey, Emilio Estevez, and others. At first, I wondered whether these stories were true. But as time went on, I came to discover that she did, indeed, know these men and had been involved with them in some fashion. Misha lived in Studio City, in a small, one-story, multi-unit building with paper-thin walls. She had no father figure, a distant relationship with her mom, and frequently brought up her sister, who was living in Mexico and had dual citizenship.

Our relationship was very close, childlike in its boisterousness. One day, while joking around in the office, Misha followed me into the bathroom.

"Hey, wait up!" she called out, a mischievous look on her face.

I laughed as she caught up to me and playfully held my penis while I urinated.

"Whoa there," I said, trying to maintain my balance. "A little help here?"

She giggled, her cheeks flushed. "Just making sure everything's working properly, Mr. Co-Producer."

It felt like an innocent, albeit hilarious, moment of best-friend-type bonding. We would occasionally flirt, but it never seemed likely that either of us would take it further.

Meanwhile, it had taken me some time to realize that Katie Wagner, a friend of the head of our film division, was interested in me. We would casually chat whenever she visited the office, which was frequent.

"You're really funny," she'd say after one of our office chats, her eyes sparkling. "We should hang out sometime."

"I'd like that," I'd reply, though it took me a while to work up the courage to actually ask her out.

As I mentioned earlier, while describing my encounter with former child actor Leif Garrett, Katie was a TV presenter, primarily hosting music-related programming. She belonged to a well-known Hollywood family. Her father, Robert Wagner, was a famous actor who had appeared in numerous films and television series. Her half sisters, Natasha and Courtney, were the daughters of the late actress Natalie Wood. Katie was from Robert's first marriage. We eventually began dating, and during our time together, she introduced me to her dad, sisters, and other celebrities like Justine Bateman and Leif Garrett.

Growing up in the industry, she was well-versed in the Hollywood dynamic and had interviewed many celebrities for various programs.

Katie was warm and sweet-natured, with an occasional wild streak. I found it amusing when she casually bought a new Cadillac on a whim.

Katie and I were never serious, though, and as time passed, Misha and I began flirting more and more. I agreed on an official date with Misha as her guest to a Fourth of July party hosted at comedian and commentator Bill Maher's modest home in one of the trendy LA canyons. When we got to Bill's house, an enticing aroma of freshly made tortillas greeted us. As we entered the living room we heard the distinct sound of a record skipping, coming from a nearby room, repeating the same few notes over and over. It was a jarring contrast to the festive atmosphere but immediately clued me into the casual nature of the party. Bill had arranged for his Mexican cleaning lady to cater and help with the event, serving tasty tacos for the all-American holiday. A small self-serve bar was set up on the patio.

The sound of footsteps revealed Bill, who warmly welcomed us and took us on a brief house tour, beginning with his office den where the vinyl record played. "Damn thing is so sensitive, it skips too easily," he said. We continued and ended up in his bedroom, where it was evident he lived alone. The three of us and another one of Misha's girlfriends shared a joint.

As we returned to the patio where most of the guests, around twenty including us, were gathered, I was amazed at what I can only describe as a Mount Rushmore of elite comedians. They included Jerry Seinfeld, Gary Shandling, Bill, and the influential talent Manager Bernie Brillstein, who were all deeply engaged in lively conversation. They laughed and shared stories with one another. It was my first time interacting with a small group of highly prominent individuals on a casual level. As the drinks kept flowing and the effects of the weed kicked in, my inhibitions vanished. Misha and I snuck off to a secluded corner and had a long conversation—about us. We ended the night at my place in Venice and woke up the next morning as boyfriend and girlfriend.

From then on, we spent our days together at work and most of our nights at one of our homes. One of the highlights of that summer was a trip to Cabo San Lucas, Mexico, where her sister lived—and where she had many friends. Overall, Misha was delightful to be around, though there were moments when her flirtatious nature triggered my insecurities. I vividly remember one night when we decided to visit the Cabo Wabo Cantina, where I once worked on a Westwood One syndicated special featuring Owner Sammy Hagar and several of his biggest-named musician friends jamming in concert.

"For this occasion," Misha commanded with a purr, "I want you to look your absolute best. Wear that Paul Smith suit I made you bring, please."

We had a table reserved for us, and I, dutifully following her request, was wearing a trendy suit in the resort atmosphere of Cabo, feeling quite out of place. I sat at the table and watched Misha dancing, fully aware she wasn't wearing any underwear. Some guy she knew was dancing with her, being very touchy-feely, and she responded in kind. At that moment, a few unfamiliar people approached our table and asked if they could join me for drinks. I didn't mind until they demurely asked, "Hey man, can I score from you?" They assumed I must have been some drug kingpin. It was both amusing and uncomfortable.

Our romantic relationship did not last more than a few months, but it was long enough for Misha to break my heart. I inadvertently introduced her to a rock star, Roger, the keyboard player in The Cure, and off she went to Europe to elope with him. As in so many other relationships, I was crushed, abandoned, and alone.

In retrospect, I should have seen this coming. Misha didn't seem to have much of an attention span when it came to relationships as she was always looking for the next mountain to climb. After Misha returned from Europe, she maintained a long-distance relationship with her rock star boyfriend, but we remained friends. We also continued to work together at *On Tour*.

Around that same time, fate brought Norm Pattiz back into my orbit.

We found ourselves in the same social circles, and from time to time, I would accompany him on his weekly Saturday afternoon yacht trips to Catalina Island. We'd gather at the California Yacht Club in Marina del Rey, board his powerful boat, speed to the island, anchor, explore, dine onboard, and then return. It was a casual, easy friendship now, a world away from Westwood One. On one of those luxurious outings, I brought Misha along. It seemed natural, a way to share a piece of my life with a friend. That simple act, it turned out, was the catalyst for their connection—a brief affair. It was a strange, almost inevitable loop.

Her romance with the rock star didn't last long, either. Within a couple of years after that, Misha married Patrick Wayne, son of iconic actor John Wayne, and for a while, she included me in family events at their house in Toluca Lake, an LA neighborhood consisting of a cluster of homes on large lots, many owned by celebrities, around a small man-made lake. Maybe I came around too early in Misha's life when she was not yet ready to settle down. Or maybe it was me....

My relationship with Misha wasn't the only drama I was involved in during that first *On Tour* summer of 1996. I organized a two-week run in Europe to film live shows by such prominent artists as The Smashing Pumpkins, Meat Loaf, and Lou Reed. My journey began with a flight to London and a short plane ride to Scotland for the Lou Reed concert. My crew caused a small electrical fire in the Glasgow Royal Concert Hall, resulting in several fire trucks racing to the scene.

My next stop was Dublin for a sold-out show by The Smashing Pumpkins and Filter at a 7,000-seat venue called The Point Theatre. About four songs into The Smashing Pumpkins set, the moshers surged toward the stage and began trampling each other, despite the presence of 110 security guards and singer Billy Corgan warning the audience, "Listen, there's a bunch of people down here who are falling down and getting crushed. Please move back." I don't want anyone getting hurt."

A seventeen-year-old girl named Bernadette O'Brien was trapped in the chaotic pile-up near the stage and so seriously crushed that she suffered a heart attack. I watched two security guards carry her over the barricade backstage as Corgan stopped the show and announced, "A lot of people got hurt. Somebody may have even died. We are totally freaked out. We are human beings, and we cannot stand up here and continue to play." Young Bernadette was rushed to a hospital, where her death was announced the following day.

From backstage, I will never forget watching the medics give Bernadette a shot of adrenaline as she lay on the ground before she was placed in the ambulance. It made me think of the scene from Quentin Tarantino's *Pulp Fiction*, where Uma Thurman's character, Mia, suffers an overdose but jumps back to life after John Travolta's character, Vincent Vega, plunges a huge hypodermic needle into her heart, after first marking the spot with a Magic Marker. It was a difficult scene for me to watch on film, and then it was repeated in real life in front of my eyes, with a horrifically tragic outcome. I felt just as helpless as I had as a young teen witnessing Dick Fleming's death during my deejaying days. Not knowing what else to do, I found myself contemplating the next steps, when I was handed a phone.

"Rob?" a voice boomed from the other end. It was Peter Mensch, the band's manager.

"Peter," I said, trying to maintain my composure. "This is a terrible situation."

"It is," he agreed, his voice heavy with concern. "We're all in shock." He paused, then continued, "Listen, I need you to do something for me."

"Anything," I replied.

"I need you to surrender all the video and audio recordings you have of the concert," he said. "We have to figure out what to do with this footage."

I felt a hesitation inside me. This concert was supposed to be a big part of our *On Tour* European package. But then a memory from a few years earlier flashed through my mind.

While working for Westwood One, the management company that

Peter was a partner of, Q Prime, had requested several tapes that were in our tape vault of the Suicidal Tendencies' live concerts. I had to convince Westwood One's management that it was a goodwill gesture to surrender the tapes and the rights to that band, with the hope that Q Prime might someday provide us with an opportunity to record live concert audio with one of the other big acts the company represented, such as Madonna, Def Leppard, Metallica, The Smashing Pumpkins, or Hole. *This gesture is a way to build trust.*

"Of course, Peter," I said. "You'll have everything we've got."

"Thank you," he said, his voice softening slightly. "I appreciate that. We'll be in touch."

Peter called me back a few hours later.

"Rob," he said, "The Pumpkins won't be playing in Belfast tomorrow. They're taking a few days off to process this tragedy."

"I understand," I said.

"But," he continued, "they still want you to capture their next performance. They want to have a record of it, and they want you to have it for *On Tour.*"

"That's incredibly generous," I said, surprised by their willingness to continue filming.

"They appreciate your professionalism and discretion," Peter explained. "They know you'll handle this situation with sensitivity."

We handed over the recordings and set our sights on their show at Brixton Academy in London a few days later.

The next day while in Dublin, I sent the crew to film our third show, a solo performance in Gent, Belgium, by Maria McKee, formerly of Lone Justice. From there they were to drive to Munich for a Meat Loaf show. Then came The Smashing Pumpkins' London show. This meant our crew labored back-to-back every day, traveling, with no days off. They were growing increasingly restless due to being overworked and lacking cash per diem and a paycheck while in Europe. Figuring out how to get them paid was my own personal challenge. I reached out to our accountant in LA, and we devised a plan for a funds transfer to a London bank. A couple of days later, carrying a duffle bag, I hopped into a cab and made my way to the bank in South London, where I collected approximately £40,000 in cash. South London is a rough neighborhood, and there I was, lugging around a bag full of money. I was a bit nervous, but fortunately, I made it through unscathed and we avoided a crew mutiny.

The Smashing Pumpkins show at Brixton Academy was absolutely phenomenal, their energy and performance spectacular. The audience was fully immersed in the music, moving rhythmically in sync with the beat. The lighting design against that venue's architecture was superb, and the band's spirit was immensely uplifting, possibly a reaction to a renewed appreciation of life's beauty.

The funds provided by AT&T were running short, however. We needed additional underwriters, as they are known on public television. Back in the United States, I spent the next few months making fundraising calls. While many advertising agencies and brands expressed interest, there were challenges due to the restrictions on advertisements on PBS stations. Any depiction of a person using the advertised product or service was not allowed, which meant we couldn't use existing auto commercials, which typically featured a driver. That meant the advertiser would have to create an entirely new commercial at a significant additional cost. Another constraint was length. A standard TV ad was typically thirty seconds, while PBS restricted them to a maximum of fifteen seconds. I kept striking out until I eventually struck gold with America Online, which, in those early days, was the dominant portal on the internet.

Securing AOL as an underwriter for *On Tour* left me with a great sense of accomplishment. Having them on board gave the show a cutting-edge feel—a feeling that was amplified when we secured The Athletic Footwear Association as an additional underwriter at a time when sneakers by such brands as Nike, Adidas, and Reebok were the latest rage among young people.

Even so, it became clear that *On Tour* would have a limited lifespan.

The difficulty in getting underwriters and the big expense of travel, filming, and production were heavy. So, two years into the project, I informed John Diaz that I wanted to go fully freelance, and he was agreeable. I would still honor my contract as producer of the series but would also take on other clients.

38

GO AHEAD AND JUMP

My freelance career took some exciting turns. I co-produced a Rolling Stones concert film that aired as a PBS pledge drive special. I also produced concert films for The Smashing Pumpkins and The Cranberries, both destined for DVD release. And for a brief, surreal period, I even joined the circus.

No, it's not what you're thinking. I was introduced to Kenneth Feld, who owned the Ringling Bros. and Barnum & Bailey Circus, and was hired to work on a new project his team was developing to compete with Cirque du Soleil. The new tent show had no ringmaster, just a dramatic clown and his foil introducing acts and performing between them. The production consisted of sixty-two performers, fifty-four crew members, eight horses, and twenty-seven geese, along with fifty trucks to move them around the country, from city to city. I had a blast immersing myself in the world of the circus, especially working with the clowns. They were all European, a breed apart from the typical American clown—more whimsical, more theatrical, and masters of subtle humor.

Alas, after a $15 million investment, what was called "Barnum's Kaleidoscope" was scrapped after less than a year on the road due to a lack of profitability.

I was still living and working in my swanky Venice Beach loft and had started seeing an equally swanky psychotherapist in Beverly Hills. I was running for exercise, plus I'd begun yoga, all part of my journey to build a better me, to overcome the emotional and psychological damage caused by abandonment, shame, assault, sexual abuse, as well as the traumatic deaths I'd witnessed.

Professionally, I was at a crossroads. Freelancing offered exciting projects but lacked financial steadiness. A regular job was tempting, but trying to please others who held gargantuan power over me had always backfired. At thirty-six, I felt adrift, unsure of how to reconcile my ambition with my need for security.

Desperate for advice, I turned to Dad. He had softened a little over the years, yet his response still caught me off guard. Instead of offering encouragement or exploring options within the entertainment industry, he suggested I open a franchise—a UPS store, a Quiznos, anything that, in his words, "would provide stability."

"But Dad," I protested, "that's not *me*! You know I thrive on creativity and pushing boundaries. Franchises are all about following someone else's rules."

"That's the point, Robbie," he countered. "It's a proven system. The parent company helps you minimize uncertainties."

"It just feels so ... limiting," I argued. "Where's the room for innovation? Where's the excitement?"

He sighed. "Look, if you choose a franchise, I'll invest in it. You were never invited into the family business," he added, a hint of regret in his voice. "This is my way of supporting you, of being a part of your success."

His words were double-edged—part of me was grateful, and part of me stung. I struggled to understand if his advice stemmed from a lack of understanding or a desire to keep me close and under his influence. I felt like a child again, his love and respect conditional on following a path he deemed suitable. The idea of moving back to Sacramento to manage a sandwich shop, a far cry from the vibrant world of Hollywood, filled me with dread. The situation held a certain irony, a fact that became clearer with time. I remembered a period when I'd been excited about launching a Party Sounds deejay franchise and had looked to him for guidance and backing. His reservations then mirrored his current stance, highlighting a recurring theme in our relationship: my aspirations often seemed to clash with his vision.

In contrast, my stepfather, Rob, always offered sound advice. "Do what you know," he quipped. "Keep moving, or the grass'll die."

Years earlier, during my time in Bakersfield, he'd sent a letter that perfectly captured his unwavering support. He wrote:

> "Dear Robbie,
>
>   I've not had a chance to talk to you, but I understand from talking to Jimmy, Sue, your mother, and Uncle Harry that you are very happy in your new job and, to this date, you are enjoying Bakersfield.... I also understand from the 'grapevine' (lousy pun) that you have probably found a place to live, two bedrooms with a garage. I suppose your house and garage cost you $400. I would suggest that you subtract about $75 a month as a business expense from your van and deejay business... It would seem that your move was a good one and that you are closer to your final goal of radio, TV, movies, etc., in San Diego and Los Angeles. Play your cards, keep it cool, and always remember that we love you and really have all of your concerns at heart.
>
> Love, Rob"

His voice was like that of a good supportive friend, always there with a reassuring word and a gentle push in the right direction. He'd always been so attentive, so genuinely interested in my life and my dreams, even down to the details of my living situation and my fledgling deejay business. He'd encouraged me to keep detailed tax records. He'd understood my ambition to work in entertainment, and now, facing this professional crossroads, his belief in me fueled my own. He'd instilled that confidence in me years ago, and it resonated now more than ever. I knew what he'd say without even talking to him: *Keep moving, trust your instincts, and find a way to make your passions a reality.* Was it him or a higher power?

I started exploring ways to leverage brands' growing interest in music marketing. Perhaps I could develop programs that connected them with music fans in meaningful ways. I had been calling myself The Marketing Factory for freelance gigs, and so I decided to use the same name for a company of my own, incorporated as Marketing Factory Inc., which would focus, as its tagline said, on "Connecting Bands and Brands."

The seeds for my new venture had been planted more than a decade earlier when an abstract idea called the "Tour Annex" began to take shape in my mind. The concept centered on allowing classic rock and legacy music artists to connect with brands in a more engaging way. Many artists had hesitated to embrace corporate sponsorships due to concerns about compromising their authenticity. They didn't want to be seen as sellouts. However, I believed there was a way to unite bands and brands without this stigma. I pictured a dedicated section at arena concerts, like a cool tent outside the venue, showcasing interactive memorabilia and historical displays about the artist. This immersive experience would be open to the public, including non-ticket holders, all day before the show, free of charge. Radio deejays would broadcast live from this area, promoting the brand and its added value to the concert. It combined a bunch of things that I had mastered over the years.

I'd been inspired by The Rolling Stones making history in 1981 by being the first major artist to sign on with a tour partner, Jovan Musk fragrance. The same entrepreneurs behind that deal forged a groundbreaking relationship between Michael Jackson and Pepsi that lasted nearly a decade, laying the foundation for incorporating popular music into modern brand integration strategies. Before too long, more and more brands began associating themselves with pop artists, and the practice was still on the upswing. The Tour Annex idea had been on my mind for quite some time, and I felt now was the time to act. I saw the opportunity to further refine what came before. The hardest part was getting over my innate fear of failure. Without a written business plan or much money, I created Marketing Factory using a bootstrap approach.

I left my rented loft, moved into a tiny apartment, and opened an office with the money I was saving. I hired four full-time staffers, developed a stable of program producers and consultants I could call on as needed, and stylishly built out and furnished the office in anticipation of potential clients—complete with a kitchen, conference room, private offices, workstations, high-output printers—and all the necessary computer and content capture equipment.

How did I pay for it all? My landlord financed the "tenant improvements," I was able to lease a good amount of the gear at a fraction of what it would cost to buy it, and a cash windfall came my way when a publishing company hired us to market a new travel-oriented magazine, canceled the project just a month later, and insisted we keep the entire $15,000 deposit.

Our next client was the Vans Warped Tour, a traveling music and extreme sports festival featuring mainly punk-ish bands such as blink-182, Fall Out Boy, and Bad Religion. They say it's who you know, and I was able to land the tour because I knew Kevin Lyman, the tour creator, even though he'd been unable to get me out of jail. We initially met when I was working on the Swatch Impact Tour. We remained friends as our respective careers took off, and when I struck out on my own with Marketing Factory, Kevin was more than willing to work with me again.

Our goal was to provide additional value, beyond the physical tour, for sponsors. To achieve this, we came up with the idea of Vans Warped Tour Radio, intending to help the tour, as well as its sponsors, gain media exposure on commercial radio stations. We created engaging content by interviewing action sports stars and punk bands. We also enlisted a host from KROQ radio in LA, and Kevin joined us as the color commentator. This gave him a platform to directly connect with fans and share his thoughts. We produced a kick-ass, one-hour, weekly show, burned the episodes onto CDs, and shipped them via FedEx to affiliated stations across the country, just like Westwood One and Album Network were doing. These stations got great content and, in return, aired our commercials and sponsor mentions built into each episode. I also found a boutique sales company that sold ad spots while Marketing Factory and the tour shared sponsors. We had around thirty stations on board throughout the country, garnering millions of listeners each week. We also implemented on-air promotions on the affiliated stations for sponsors like Diamond Rio, the first MP3 player, Sony Electronics, Mountain Dew, PacSun, and many others.

It was ironic that the punk community was so accepting of sponsorships, to the extent that the actual Vans Warped Tour resembled a trade show, with various sponsors setting up booths as a big part of the concert's footprint. The fans loved it, and Kevin found ways to seamlessly incorporate the brands in a way that the attendees found acceptable. We kept doing the Vans Warped Tour Radio show for a few years until Kevin decided to sell the tour to a new internet company called Launch. While they had no interest in continuing a program geared toward traditional broadcast syndication, they believed that the radio show could be automated and streamed on-demand through their service.

We also created another show called Chick Click Radio inspired by a trending new website which had a more female-centric appeal and was broadcast on Top 40 pop stations. These two shows were Marketing Factory's specialties, and we put a lot of effort into promoting and generating buzz around them.

The next audio production we worked on, in early 2000, was a celebration of *Spin* magazine's fifteenth anniversary. We created a four-hour special that featured artists from every cover of *Spin* over the years, including new interviews and exclusive audio clips that we gathered. We also coordinated promotions with the fifty radio stations that aired the show over Labor Day weekend. The show was sponsored by an early dotcom music streamer, Listen.com, and the lifestyle brand OP (Ocean Pacific).

As more brands became title sponsors for tours, the more successful Marketing Factory became. We even facilitated a tour sponsorship connecting Yahoo!—the dominant search engine and online platform after the AOL era, but before Google—with Moby, one of the most important dance music figures of the time.

My home life was also filled with music. One benefit of living in that nanoscopic duplex apartment was the fun shared with neighbors on the other side of our common wall—Simone and her boyfriend, Rory. We each had dogs that liked to play with one another, which naturally brought us together. Most Fridays after work, Simone and Rory would play music on the porch of their unit and invite me over for beers. I learned that she worked at an ad agency central to American Honda Motor Company's national advertising. She learned that I was plugged into the music world. She would complain about Honda not taking enough chances. She said she was always harping on them to get involved in music, but they kept rejecting her suggestions.

In the meantime, I was introduced to outspoken singer, songwriter, and guitarist David Crosby. He co-wrote a book called *Stand and Be Counted*, focusing on how artists and causes influenced America through music. Given Crosby, Stills, Nash & Young's involvement in political activism, it made sense for him to tell these stories. Crosby was working on turning the book into a documentary, supported by Norm Waitt, brother of the founder of Gateway computers. They were interested in my expertise with public television. One option we discussed was premiering the movie on PBS during a high-exposure pledge drive, which would require finding a well-heeled corporate sponsor. I suggested Yahoo!, but Yahoo! wasn't interested.

I eventually shared a VHS preview copy of Crosby's documentary with Simone, who absolutely loved it.

"This documentary deserves a major sponsor," I explained to her. "It's powerful, important, and aligns perfectly with the growing awareness of social and environmental issues."

"I agree," she said, nodding thoughtfully. "Have you considered Honda? Their corporate culture is all about sustainability, and they're making big strides in hybrid and electric vehicles."

"I know," I said, "but they haven't been receptive to music-related projects in the past."

"That might be true," she countered, "but this documentary isn't just about music. It's about activism, social change, and making a difference. That might resonate with them," she said. "You absolutely have to get this in front of Honda." She paused, then added, "I have a contact at my ad agency who handles the media for Honda for this type of thing. He might be receptive. Let me make an introduction."

I was thrilled and able to secure a meeting. Yet my pitch went nowhere. Even though he was a music fan, was named Steve Perry (just like the singer in Journey), was gracious, and was in a position to champion our proposal—nada. In the business world, it generally takes an internal promoter to make things happen, sort of like a politician sponsoring a bill. Steve made it clear that he was not my guy.

"They just don't get it!" Simone said to me, her voice laced with frustration. "I've been trying to explain how powerful a music tie-in could be for Honda, but they're stuck in their old ways of thinking." Simone also happened to be a singer-songwriter, which further fueled her belief in the power of music.

"I know," I commiserated. "It's frustrating when people can't see the bigger picture."

"I'm not giving up," she insisted. "I'm going to keep pushing until they understand the value of music and its ability to connect with people on a deeper level."

It was at that moment that I realized she could be my sponsor, with the motivation and disposition to make things happen. It was either the universe or luck coming together for me again by giving me Simone as a next-door neighbor.

Of course, I'd not been able to find Mr. Crosby a sponsor for PBS, yet he and his team would ultimately find a television network to buy and broadcast their program. Despite his reputation for being difficult, I found David to be warm and down to earth, and very appreciative of our efforts—even if things did not work out as I had hoped.

Not long after, Simone told me of a meeting she had boldly set up with her boss. The three of us would meet in her office and casually talk about Honda and music. With no idea where the discussion would lead, I didn't formally prepare anything. Upon arrival, I sat down in Simone's office, and after the obligatory small talk, she apologized and told me the meeting would actually be held in the agency's conference room. I was ushered in and took a seat. Then, about a half dozen ad agency folks entered the room and I realized there was nothing casual about this meeting.

They soon began peppering me with a barrage of questions. One I'll always remember is, "You can really get an artist like blink-182 to link up with Honda?" I wasn't sure if the woman who asked was questioning my ability and contacts or Honda's image. Regardless, I had to assume she needed convincing that I was legitimate and could deliver nearly any artist they wanted. I spent much of that meeting listening as the agency people rambled on and on about the all-new Civic model and how they needed to make the vehicle seem cool and acceptable, as they were aiming to attract a younger audience in the hopes of lowering the average buyer's age by at least a few years. Another key insight was their need for something beyond traditional advertising because their research indicated a shift: Young people were becoming increasingly difficult to reach with TV ads.

At the time, MTV was nearly twenty years old. Everyone thought MTV represented the music generation, but the dirty secret was the ratings were lousy and there was hardly any music left on the channel. Advertisers would check the MTV box and think they were connecting through music, a sort of perception versus reality situation. Wrong! The ad agency Honda used was not ready to walk away from MTV, but they were open to discussing new ways to reach people. They mentioned college campus gift packs, playing commercials before movies in theaters, and other new ideas for that era. I had to come up with something far better. I recognized their hunger for the right concept to take to Honda. The meeting adjourned, and my head was spinning with data on the Civic model and their needs. They asked me to think about it and return to them if I had something tangible. That's when a new door swung wide open.

I was running on the soft sand of Venice Beach early one morning, as I often did, meditating on my newest concern—Civic and Honda—when the seed of an idea began to germinate. I reflected on the everlasting Absolut Vodka print advertising campaign, which began in 1986 when Andy Warhol painted his interpretation of the Absolut Vodka bottle. Over the next twenty-five years, there would be 1,500 variations of the original ad, and Absolut would go global. The campaign was so successful it spawned a coffee table book chronicling the long life of the world-famous bottle. The upshot: Alcohol was interpreted as art, and a brand was elevated because it became an integral part of pop culture.

I was intrigued by something I noticed about the new Civic. Many kids were customizing their new cars with imaginative paint schemes and custom wheels, lips, tips, and exhaust systems. A light bulb came on in my head. If music artists would customize a Honda Civic to go on tour with them, fans would experience the vehicle as part of pop culture. I envisioned the Honda Civic Tour as a multi-artist touring concert series under Honda's banner, with each headlining artist accompanied on the road by their own customized Honda Civic. *This is a perennial franchise opportunity.* I imagined promotions with MTV, radio stations, websites, and magazines.

My next meeting with the ad agency included even more agency folks. After I presented my Civic Tour proposal, they asked a ton of questions. More meetings followed, each with a different set of people. I had to sell my proposal to the national advertising group, which focused on building up the Honda brand, and the regional advertising group, which was more focused on selling cars in twelve distinct regions, each with its own tailored ads and messaging style.

After six long months of that, I got a green light from both advertising groups. Then I had to sell the concept to Honda itself. To mitigate any concerns around blink-182's appropriateness for Honda, given the band's pop, punk, and potty-mouthed image, the ad agency reps had reviewed and edited my proposal and even rehearsed a meeting with me. Concerned that Honda might find blink-182 too edgy, at the agency's requisition I'd also obtained a letter from the band's agent from California's Paso Robles Fair that stated how compliant blink-182 had been for a family performance.

Armed with carefully culled goals, explanations, and supporting facts, it was showtime: I was to pitch my idea directly to the head of national advertising for Honda. His name was Eric Conn, and the agency had drilled me on who he was, what he was like, as well as how to approach him. The room was small, and every seat was filled—about twelve people, with Eric at the head of the table. I was on one of the sides, in the middle. All were silent as I gave my proposal. Eric Conn himself wore a mask of indifference, his body language suggesting a complete lack of attention. I carried on. And on.

"Eric, you don't need to worry, these guys can do a family-friendly show. Here's a letter from the Paso Robles Fair explaining...." With that, Eric finally perked up. I'd learn his apparent disinterest concealed a sharp mind.

"If we do this, and I'm not saying we are, we will not edit an artist and tell them to be something they aren't," Eric said.

He then allowed me to proceed—until I got to the word "turn-key." He interrupted me: "That's preposterous. Nothing is turn-key, Rob. Let's be real." Eric hesitantly laughed, then related, "I had to bring a hairdryer to Christina Aguilera, who was having a meltdown when she performed a song for the NCAA halftime show we sponsored."

I left that meeting knowing that the Civic Tour was going to happen.

39

ANOTHER BRICK IN THE WALL

The Honda Civic Tour would turn out to be a nearly twenty-year phe-nomenon, a testament to the enduring power of music and marketing. Marketing Factory Inc., my company, which was behind this ground-breaking campaign, navigated countless challenges: regime changes at the ad agency and at Honda, a war, an economic meltdown, an evolving music industry, fierce competition, demanding artists and executives, and relentless attempts by rival firms to sabotage our efforts. But through it all, the Civic Tour thrived.

The magic? Each artist, from Linkin Park to Fall Out Boy, lit up when they first laid eyes on their customized Civic. It was a tangible sym-bol of the collaboration, an extension of their artistry on wheels. This, I realized, was the heart of the campaign: the car as an authentic canvas for self-expression.

Like the Absolut campaign, the Civic Tour proved its adaptability. It morphed and shifted with the times, responding to market trends, evolving attitudes, and the natural progression of the music industry. It was proof of the power of a strong concept and the enduring appeal of connecting with consumers through the universal language of music.

After the first few years of working through Honda's ad agency, on my way to another meeting, I once found myself sharing an elevator at Honda with Eric Conn, the carmaker's national advertising chief. In his hand was a ukulele, oddly out of place amid the corporate environment, especially when held by his exceptionally large, puffy fingers.

"Heading to a jam session?" I asked, curious.

"Just finished one, actually," he replied with a smile. "We have a little music group here on campus. It's a great way to de-stress and connect with colleagues."

I was impressed by Honda's commitment to fostering a creative and engaging work environment.

As we reached the third floor, Eric turned to me, his expression turning serious. "Rob, let's step into a conference room for a sec," he said. There, he continued: "I've been incredibly impressed with your work on the Civic Tour."

"Thank you," I replied, feeling a surge of pride.

"Honda recognizes the value you bring," he continued. "We believe that collaborating directly with Marketing Factory would be more efficient and mutually beneficial."

"That's fantastic news!" I exclaimed.

"It is," he agreed. "Though I suspect it might ruffle a few feathers at the ad agency." He winked. "They won't be able to filter our communication anymore."

I grinned. "I'm sure we can handle that."

This surprising shift to a more direct role as a specialized vendor was a significant win. It elevated our status, allowing us to operate with a similar level of trust and collaboration as their agency of record, but with a different area of expertise. A streamlined approach also benefited Honda, saving them significant costs.

Our strengthened relationship with Honda opened doors to new opportunities. We expanded our services to other Honda divisions, including multicultural marketing, motorcycles, Canadian Honda, and Honda Financial Services, and took on new programs beyond the Civic Tour. At our peak, our billings more than tripled. We consistently won Honda's vendor excellence awards and external marketing accolades, solidifying our position as a key partner. We even became gatekeepers to others, fielding calls from countless companies eager to sell their ideas and "media inventory" to Honda.

But Honda became our 800-pound gorilla—a blessing and a curse. Landing a Fortune 50 super-brand like Honda was a major coup, but our reliance on them became absolute and I constantly strived to exceed their expectations to maintain their interest. To the outer world, this may have seemed positive, but it came from a place of fear. I'd done the same as a child to try to gain the love of my dysfunctional family.

I continued to see my therapist, do yoga, or hit up the beach. After our first five years, year-over-year auto sales boomed, and my relationship with Honda deepened. The dotcoms were blossoming as Yahoo! gave way to Google. My company did so well that in 2003, I bought my fourth property, a Craftsman-style duplex built in 1910 two blocks from the beach.

By this time, I had fallen in love with Venice. The little beachfront community south of Santa Monica is world-famous. Venice sits on a giant marsh, and developer Abbot Kinney originally built the canals that gave it its name to drain the marshy land so he could build a walkable seaside resort town. What was initially called Venice of America was established in 1905 and included an amusement park, a dance hall with a salt-water plunge, and a business street with Venetian architecture.

When I moved there, Venice was a mix of welfare housing, homelessness, and mega-wealthy homes fronting the ocean. It exuded a bohemian spirit, with funky shops, renowned visual artists, palm readers, and the famous Muscle Beach outdoor gym. It was artsy, eclectic, edgy, and a little weird. Sort of like me.

Around this time, I established a link with an entrepreneur named Kevin Wall, an investor, activist, and Emmy Award-winning producer of global events such as Live Aid, Live Earth, and Live 8. As CEO and founder of the investment fund PTK Capital, Wall would eventually finance companies focused on social and environmental issues with a commitment to gender equality. I found him to have extraordinary charisma, intelligence, and sharpness. When I first met him, his reputation preceded our discussion. I knew he had been a major producer of Live Aid, which alone was impressive. Live Aid was a multi-venue benefit concert held in July 1985 to raise funds for relief of the famine in Ethiopia. It was orchestrated by Bob Geldof and Midge Ure as a follow-up to the Band-Aid charity single, "Do They Know It's Christmas?" Live Aid was held simultaneously at Wembley Stadium in London and John F. Kennedy Stadium in Philadelphia. It was televised and broadcast on radio, reaching a vast global audience. I was in awe of what Live Aid accomplished. It united a huge throng of pop music artists into a massive movement to end world hunger.

When Live Aid happened, I was still at 91X and we managed to secure broadcast rights to the show. To expand the reach and be certain 91X was credited as the station bringing this to San Diego, we not only aired the concert but also produced and sold a record album featuring San Diego musicians and personalities. We called our effort Sand-Aid and donated to local charities, played the songs on-air to support the cause, and contributed some of the proceeds to USA for Africa. Being part of this experience was truly heartwarming.

Kevin, at that time, ran a media company called Radio Vision International, whose offices were in West Hollywood, on the edge of Beverly Hills. The facility consisted of an expansive multi-level room with glass separations adorned with music memorabilia from Kevin's past work. When my company was starting out, Kevin and I discussed working together due to my creation of audio programming that could be streamed online. People talked about the potential streaming audience, but the timing and technology limited bandwidth to dial-up in most cases. But everyone knew that one day, expanding broadband capability would blow the lid off traditional audio and video, providing access directly to consumers. Kevin was savvy to the potential and had segued into developing and producing entertainment websites. He led the strategic acquisition and organization of forty-two internet design and consulting companies and eventually built BoxTop Interactive, a public company with 3,000 employees, thirty-eight offices, and annual revenues of more than $400 million. Unfortunately, our discussions about working together never led to anything concrete. Years later, we talked again. But, for the second time, nothing ever came of those talks.

In the early 2000s, I spent a couple of years educating myself about a trend that I felt was inevitably invading all of us on planet Earth. This was a few years before Vice President Al Gore's *An Inconvenient Truth*, a landmark 2006 documentary film that brought the urgent issue of climate change to the forefront of public consciousness.

What I saw was more than just the environmental movement—it was a shift in consumer lifestyle to health and sustainability. I read countless books on this, but the one that resonated most with me was *Mid-Course Correction: Toward a Sustainable Enterprise* by Ray Anderson. He wrote about a "dream team" of consultants and advisers he engaged to overhaul industrial flooring manufacturer Interface Carpet, focused on environmental sustainability.

Within my company, I put together a dream team of my own, including one of Ray's team members, and before long, we had drafted a concept for a series of festival events in green parks and fields featuring authors, speakers, futuristic exhibits, and acoustic daytime concerts by big-name music artists, all integrated with forward-thinking brands. I called this concept "Organik" and divided the mission into body, mind, spirit, and music. The opportunities, I felt, were endless.

I hired a couple of guys to help me sell the Organik concept to brands, and one of them was Jim Garfield, a personal trainer for Bob Iger, who at the time was president of The Walt Disney Co., and later became CEO—twice. The next thing I knew, I was in Bob Iger's office in Burbank, surrounded by a fleet of assistants. This was Bob Iger, the man who had greenlit films like *Pirates of the Caribbean* and went on to acquire Pixar and Marvel. He was a legend in the entertainment industry, and here I was, sitting across from him, about to pitch my idea.

The office was bright, natural, and comfy, with white shabby chic style sofas mixed with a minimalist aesthetic. Bob came out from behind his massive desk and sat casually on the edge of it while we sat facing him before he moved into a large high-backed upholstered chair.

"So, Rob," Bob began with curiosity, "Jim tells me you have a fascinating idea to share with me."

"I do," I replied, feeling a little nervous excitement. "It's called Organik, and it's all about connecting brands with consumers in a more healthy and sustainable, authentic and engaging way...."

I walked him through the concept, explaining how Organik would leverage music and entertainment to create unique experiences that resonate with audiences.

"It's quite impressive," Bob commented, nodding thoughtfully. "I particularly like how you're integrating music and immersive activities to create a sense of community."

"Thanks," I said. "We believe that by tapping into shared passions for the environment and health, which I know you are familiar with since Jim has told me, we can piggyback a burgeoning trend."

"I agree," he said. "And I can see how these events take consumers and brands closer to environmental sustainability both now and in the future." He paused, then added, "I'm curious, how do you envision this playing out on a national scale?"

I outlined our strategy for expanding Organik's reach, emphasizing the importance of partnerships and strategic alliances. After about twenty minutes, his assistant interrupted to let him know his next appointment was ready. I braced myself for a quick dismissal, but Bob surprised me.

"Tell them I'll be a few minutes late," he said with a wave of his hand. He turned back to me, a smile on his face. "Now, where were we?"

We ended up talking for another half hour, and by the time I left his office, I felt energized and inspired. We'd spent nearly an hour together. Bob Iger, the head of Disney, had not only given us his time but also his genuine interest and encouragement.

A few days later, a Disney card arrived addressed to me, handwritten by Bob, thanking *me* for meeting *him*. I fell off my chair. I literally could not believe the head of this powerful, iconic company had taken the time to write me a longhand thank-you note. I was elated; it made me feel validated in every sense.

The following weekend, the trainer Jim had a big birthday bash in Malibu at a rented house on the beach. I brought a young date, we smoked a good amount of weed, and into the party we went. Jim introduced me to a few of his friends, and I recognized others I knew. And then, out of the corner of my eye, I spied Bob Iger, with his wife, journalist, and TV personality Willow Bay, from across the room. I should have made a respectful beeline to him to say hello. Instead, Bob Iger, the nicest of nice guys, saw me and immediately began to walk toward me.

"Hi, Rob. Bob. Remember we met? This is Willow. How are you?"

I could barely speak. Not only had Bob Iger—*the* Bob Iger—remembered me, but he remembered my name and thought enough of me to approach me from across the room at a party with dozens of guests. Trying to find my voice and introduce my date was beyond difficult. I stammered something of a response, and he went on with more polite small talk as if we were best friends reconnecting. Then he asked if it was raining in the Venice area where I had come from.

I responded, "No, I didn't see any sign of rain, Bob."

He continued: "It's going to rain tomorrow," and added more details about the upcoming weather.

"No, it's not going to rain, Bob," I blurted out without thinking. "I'm not sure what weather report *you* saw."

Bob gave me a quizzical look, cocking his head like a dog, and I didn't know what to say next. I don't remember even saying anything before Chelsea, my date, grabbed my hand and dragged me outside to the beach.

"Wait," I whispered, nudging Chelsea. "Do you know who that was?"

We were sitting on a driftwood log on the sand, watching the waves reflect the warm glow of the house lights.

"Who?" she asked, her brow furrowed.

"Bob Iger," I breathed, still in disbelief. "The *president* of Disney. The chief operating officer, expanding Disney into China and India and revitalizing the ABC Network, Disney Parks ... he's becoming a legend!"

Her eyes widened. "Oh wow! *That* Bob Iger?"

A beat of silence. Then, we both erupted in laughter.

"You're kidding me," she gasped, wiping a tear away. "You talked to Bob Iger about ... the weather?"

I groaned. "I know, I know! I completely froze, I was too stoned."

"Well," she said, her voice laced with amusement, "you certainly made an unforgettable impression."

I wanted to bury myself in the sand. "Do you think I could go back in and try again?"

"Maybe tomorrow," she snickered. "He's probably had enough excitement for one night."

As we talked, I flashed on something that had completely escaped my mind: Bob Iger had begun his meteoric rise within ABC, a subsidiary of Disney, as a weatherman! This guy knew the weather backward and forward, and I had been arguing with him.... *What the fuck was wrong with me? How could I sabotage a business relationship with one of the highest-ranking executives in American business and entertainment, who was not only gracious but also clearly interested in me?* Bob Iger spoke to heads of nations, Steve Jobs, celebrities, authors, and Nobel laureates—this was the most connected of connected humans I had ever met. But because I was insecure and socially awkward, higher than usual, and, beyond doubt, off my game, an opportunity to know Bob Iger escaped me as fast as it had presented itself.

Not long after, I had a third business meeting with Kevin Wall, this time for my presentation of Organik. I believed he could be a catalyst to help the concept succeed. He was supposedly sitting on a pile of cash, had remodeled his large Beverly Hills estate, and invited me to his home study. It resembled a library with built-in fancy wooden bookshelves, overstuffed dark brown leather club chairs, and a relaxed designer feel. He was dressed in a tight, short-sleeve silky polo shirt tucked into tapered chino slacks with no socks. His thin leather belt matched his leather loafer shoe color.

He listened intently as I went through the deck. Yet he was distracted by his wife once, the housekeeper another time, and someone working in the backyard a third time. Then his smoothie was ready, and he paused and walked into the kitchen. I followed as he grabbed it, and we continued. Kevin was living well, sober, in better physical shape than I had remembered, and seemed hungry for the next step. What I noticed during this meetup, though, was that he had trouble paying attention. Later, I learned that he did, in fact, experience ADHD. He was also a challenging read. He showed consideration, yet didn't express an overwhelming interest.

We stayed in touch, and about a year later, in 2005, he was on another rise. The wave he was riding was brilliant. He had developed an alumni event, repeating his success with Live Aid. He dubbed it Live 8, a string of benefit concerts in the G8 countries and South Africa. They were timed to precede the G8 conference and summit in Scotland in July. Kevin revived his career with a sequel, with the bonus aspect that technological advances allowed for a truly global event. It also coincided with the twentieth anniversary of Live Aid. The Live 8 lineup featured more than 250 musical acts, including Madonna, U2, Destiny's Child, Jay-Z, and Pink Floyd, who performed within twenty-four hours of each other at concerts on seven continents. Utilizing legacy and new media, Live 8's live multi-feed webcast attracted an estimated audience of 2 billion people, a then-record for online viewership. As the executive producer of Live 8, Wall won the first Emmy for content delivered via the internet. This was later described as a "tipping point" and the "defining moment" in online content distribution.

I most admired Kevin Wall's ability to turn his activism into a business for himself, a way to get brands to use their resources to greatly help, inspire, and entertain others, while also supporting him and his family. He created Network LIVE, a joint venture with resources and funding from AEG, the global sporting and music entertainment presenter; AOL, the largest web portal and online service provider; and XM Satellite Radio, the most listened-to satellite radio network. These three entities had been core distributors of Live 8. They represented a powerful backbone to deliver more events on a smaller scale, emulating Radio Vision, but with global reach in the dotcom era. Kevin was reinventing himself, as himself, in a new chapter. He made seductiveness both an art and a skill. He could articulate concepts easily, and intimidate, even threaten, in the kindest way I've ever seen. People would say yes to him and not even realize why, which was Kevin being Kevin.

He decided to invest in a company called Ignition, which did experiential marketing similar to Marketing Factory. They brought ideas to life in physical form for brands by creating and producing interactive exhibits and human touch points. The Ignition piece of his puzzle enticed me. When he called me for a meeting, I went to his new office in Beverly Hills, cloistered near the Civic Center, Live Nation headquarters, Gibson Guitar's VIP lounge, and what had been Madonna's Maverick Records. It was way more stunning than his old office suite in West Hollywood and was filled with a staff of people busily doing things. If I was "visioneering" my future, it would have looked like what I saw, with me at the helm, but somehow I knew that wasn't possible.

Kevin moved in a different orbit, effortlessly navigating the constellations of power and celebrity. Bob Iger, the Disney visionary; Tom Freston, the mastermind behind MTV; Mick Jagger, the rock 'n' roll legend—these were the stars in his universe, and he seemed to effortlessly gravitate toward their light. While I had met each of these people, he could discuss ideas with them, hang out with them, and even go on vacation with them. This was the ultimate access, and it's what I mean when I say Kevin was being Kevin. He's one of a kind.

We flew to Atlanta to meet the owners and team at Ignition. Kevin's idea was for me to insert my agency into Ignition to help develop deeper tentacles in entertainment than they currently possessed. We would combine our strengths: Kevin's high-level contacts and Ignition's resources, along with my established relationship with Honda and my track record in the industry.

When I met the other Owner, Dill, I recalled seeing him speak at a marketing conference about Coca-Cola's Olympic torch relay across the globe. He made a strong impression on me because of his evangelical allocution style. Dill had extraordinary passion.

"Well, Rob," Dill boomed across the table, a gleam in his eye, "Kevin tells me you're quite the marketing whiz."

"Lucky," I said with a laugh. "I've had some successes, but I'm always eager to learn more."

"That's the attitude we like to see!" Dill exclaimed, raising his glass. "To collaboration and growth!"

Kevin and Dill talked about their private jet memberships and their Indy racing team at dinner.

"You know," Kevin remarked casually, "we should really consider sharing fractional ownership of the jet and the race car. We could both benefit from the convenience and cost savings."

"I'm in!" Dill declared, a broad smile spreading across his face. "I'm always up for a good investment, especially when it involves speed and convenience."

Ignition had a couple of primary clients in Coke and Delta Airlines, both headquartered in Atlanta. Dill and his wife Susan ran the company, with other family members in pivotal roles. The deal they offered me for the acquisition of Marketing Factory included ownership in a bigger entity that Kevin was going to grow through more mergers and investment, using the same roll-up strategy executed for Box Top. The team was excited to meet me, and we spent the night, the next day, and subsequent hours on the phone, learning about one another.

The biggest appeal for me was on the execution front. If I was free to focus on relationship management and creative development, with another entity managing the back end, it would free up my time and relieve the stress from detail-oriented production work, also known as fulfillment. It also offered me a more extensive playing field with an engine room behind me, an open doorway to Coca-Cola and Delta to develop entertainment properties for them, and room to breathe with an infrastructure handling financials, human resources, logistics, legal and risk management, business operations, and all the other responsibilities of ownership. I envisioned Kevin and Ignition sending me into "warm doors," corporations they had prospected, being greeted enthusiastically by their prospects, and using my creativity to develop outstanding campaigns involving music, extending to any form of entertainment.

They guaranteed me a salary, a bonus structure, and a future where I would own a more minor part of a watermelon versus all of an orange. It also allowed me to work closely with Kevin, someone I admired, on the direction of the company and the acquisitions it would make. I reviewed the deal. Beneath the veneer of a very smooth operation, I saw some disturbing signs and tiny cracks that gave me doubts. I checked in with my gut and decided to ignore the doubts and instead combine efforts.

I informed American Honda that I had made a deal and we would need to sign over the contracts to the new company. This was the biggest risk I had taken since starting my business. I had worked for decades to have the wherewithal to acquire Honda, and for no money down, I handed it to Kevin, Dill, and the company. There were stipulations in my agreement with Ignition that gave me some leverage, but the risk was still there.

Once inside the system, the cracks rose to the surface. I quickly learned that Ignition's staff didn't have the capabilities to fulfill the needs of Honda. The deal included some employees from Marketing Factory, but since Ignition wanted my focus elsewhere, I had to hire people and train them. It was literally like starting over again.

I chose some good people and some people who were not so good.

My time was spent indoctrinating them to Honda's systems, my systems, and the overall expectations. I was allegiant to Honda and could not let them down or lose them as a valued client. It was a slog because, at the same time, I was learning how Ignition did things and how Kevin operated. There wasn't time for me to find my place in the new order of business. Sometimes, I felt lost in the shuffle with no control.

A shared vision is essential for common goals. But in this case, Dill had his vision, Kevin had another, and I found myself somewhere on an island between them. Dill and Kevin began to talk about one another to me, not in a direct derogatory manner, but some frustrations were vented in both directions. I traveled back and forth to Atlanta several times. I consciously decided to support Kevin, aligning with his vision of Ignition. Dill and Ignition had strong Christian religious tenets. It wasn't unusual for a chaplain to lead the Ignition team in prayer or deliver a sermon as a motivational exercise. One or two other Jewish people were in the company, but the overwhelming majority were Baptist or some other Christian denomination. Then Dill made an anti-Semitic remark about ten months into the blended company structure. The assault I'd suffered as a child was still inside me, and I felt in my gut at that moment that I needed to find an exit.

There was a clause in the contract that allowed me to unwind the deal and retrieve Honda within one year, at Honda's and my sole discretion, and the year was nearly up. My attorney advised me to get out quickly. On a Sunday, I emptied my office, took my server with all my Honda Civic Tour data, and fled. The next day, Kevin made an angry call to me.

I knew that if I gave him advance notice, there was a risk that Dill or Kevin would try to block me through some shenanigans. A few months before my departure, we had a horrible meeting at Honda with Dill. He was obsessed with Indy racing, had done work within the Indy Racing League (IRL), and had gone forward and invested in an IRL car team. While Honda dominated the IRL, all my contacts at Honda had no active role in that division. I clarified this to Dill when he asked me to bring him to Honda to introduce him and Ignition to my contacts. And yet, thirty minutes into the allotted hour-long meeting, Dill began to discuss racing.

"Now, about this exciting opportunity in motorsports...," Dill began with an almost manic intensity.

My jaw was on the floor as he droned on and on about something no one in the room had any interest in or connection with. There was no way to stop him. I was angry but held my composure. Luckily, we had taken separate cars and the drive back to my office gave me time to breathe and calm myself with a little weed.

According to my calculation, Ignition—Kevin and Dill—owed me significant money. I remember my lawyer, Keith Holmes, talking me off the ledge. He told me they were "behaving like thugs" and encouraged me to walk away from the money but to "keep the golden goose happy." By that, he advised me that Honda was far more valuable than a fight with Kevin and Dill. He was considerate and right about everything. He and his partner Peter Paterno even provided me and my three-person staff office space on their floor in a Century City high-rise while I rebooted what was left of Marketing Factory.

I wanted to move back into my cool office on Abbot Kinney Boulevard in Venice, but over my year with Ignition, rents had more than doubled. So, I did the next best thing: Since I owned a duplex in Venice and lived upstairs, I decided to pay off the tenants downstairs to move out and use that as my new office space. It certainly made the commute more effortless.

40

YOU'VE GOT A FRIEND

During the time that my company Marketing Factory had been doing well, my stepfather Rob had been failing. His medical practice had slowed considerably over the prior twenty-plus years, and he'd mostly participated in surgeries as a consultant to younger doctors, a role that allowed him to forgo malpractice insurance—something he strongly opposed, believing insurance companies shouldn't dictate the cost of medical procedures such as hip replacements. His health had been further declining for several years, and my mother also suffered from the stress of watching her John Wayne slowly wither away. He began to zone out mentally as well as physically. I knew he was not long for this world. I remember wanting him to just be with others with no need to fill the silence, just a peacefulness, an unhurried exit. Some say that reflecting on the inevitability of death can help people appreciate the beauty of life and be thankful for people and experiences. This is called *memento mori*, which can help people savor simple pleasures and return to peace and joy.

Rob's life was filled with simple pleasures. He enjoyed watching news and nature programs on television and sharing stories of his hunting adventures. He was a fan of conservative commentator Rush Limbaugh, who had first made a name for himself as a local radio broadcaster in Sacramento before achieving national fame. He had a collection of guns that he eventually passed down to his nephew, Tommy Jr., with whom I had once lived in Carlsbad. Honesty was paramount to Rob, and he despised catching people in lies. He held strong opinions on a wide range of topics, often saying, "I know a little about a lot." When it came to medicine, he was pretty knowledgeable, particularly about surgery. He didn't believe in cortisone or chiropractic treatments, instead preferring exercise, therapy, and surgical interventions. It was likely his expertise in surgery that honed his precision with tools. Among his favorites was the band saw, which offered him dexterity when working with wood. He even taught me how to use one, creating cherished memories from my childhood and strengthening our bond. There was talk in our family that he had constructed one or two entire houses by hand before he'd hooked up with my mother.

Yet I held conflicting feelings toward the good Dr. Robinson. Though he had become a source of support and comfort, I still harbored some lingering distrust. My mother's betrayals and my father's constant attempts to brainwash me against him had left their mark, making it difficult to fully let my guard down. That aside, Rob was an inspiration to me in so many ways. Unlike anyone in my immediate family, he'd taken the time to get to know me and understand my most profound dreams and aspirations. When it came to being a parent, he surpassed my biological parents. Having him in my life provided much-needed support.

One thing that stood out about Rob was his understanding of my desire to become a mobile deejay. We'd worked tirelessly together to make it happen—from acquiring the necessary equipment to setting up the systems and finding a suitable vehicle for transporting everything to gigs. His level of generosity toward me was truly incredible, not just because of the financial aspect, which I primarily funded on my own, but because of the time and dedication he invested. No one had ever been there for me in that way before. It felt like a miracle, and I am forever grateful for his assistance, even if I didn't express my appreciation to him as much as I could have.

Losing him in May 2002 stung. It also added a whole new dimension to my responsibilities in life. While I had casually taken on an advisory role for my mom's finances, along with Rob's oldest son, my stepbrother,

Rob3, there was a big shift at foot, a metaphorical and financial rebalancing. Rob3 and I met with Rob and Mom's accountant who was also failing physically and unable to work at the pace he once did. There was a split—with my stepbrother overseeing Rob's estate, and I assuming a much more active role in Mom's.

41

WAITING IN VAIN

Six years had gone by since Rob had passed. I was in my downstairs office in Venice one day when I received a call that Dad, at eighty-nine years old, had been hospitalized after experiencing extreme shortness of breath while barbecuing. It was around 2008, and Dad loved to grill. My sisters, who lived nearby, told me he was in the ICU with a grim prognosis. The thought of his death sent a jolt of anxiety through me, and memories flickered through my mind: the night he came home with his teeth filed down, Mom laughing at his appearance; his threat of suicide if I didn't live with him; the smirk before handing me the phone to speak with my mom.

As a small boy, I'd longed for him to connect with me, to share my love for music, but it was as if he saw me only as an extension of himself, not as an individual. Dad never seemed genuinely interested in my passions, or my feelings. What I found most difficult to understand was the way he was a pillar of the community, admired and respected, but at home, he was a strict, often intimidating figure.

Whenever I displayed behaviors or interests that deviated from his expectations, he made his disapproval known. Dad had a transactional approach to our relationship—rewards were contingent on obedience. But the price often felt too steep, the tasks required to please him too arduous. It made me feel as if authority figures could never be satisfied, no matter what I did. As I grew up, a sense of emptiness grew within me, a persistent feeling that others mattered more than I did.

Letters from Dad written when I was between thirteen and twenty-seven were strikingly formal and businesslike, typewritten on his company letterhead. One was a response to a letter I'd sent at fifteen after I'd left to live with Mom and Rob. In my letter, I chose my words carefully, tiptoeing around his emotions as I expressed my desire for better communication and asked for information about the college fund he'd mentioned. He responded sporadically over the next two years, only providing the financial information after I graduated from high school.

Dad's letters often reiterated his disappointment in my decision to leave:

> "Remember, Robbie, you elected to leave your Dad. The deep hurt ... is still there and nothing I know of will ever change that short of you returning to me."

He criticized my grades, my study habits, and my choices, always emphasizing that his intentions were for my benefit. He even recounted my various living situations, lamenting my lack of communication, and seeming to blame me for the strained relationship.

He cautioned against buying a car at my age, suggesting I wait until I was eighteen. He even instructed me to have my mother contact his attorney if we disagreed. His controlling behavior and insistence on putting me in the middle of his conflict with Mom infuriated me.

Before graduating, I sent him interviews that local radio and TV stations had aired about my burgeoning career. I craved his approval, but his response was dismissive:

> "Whether you continue in this chosen field or select another one is not the important point."

He still didn't grasp that I was actively pursuing my dream. He went on to reiterate the importance of a college degree, his advice sound but his tone condescending.

He questioned my decision not to invite him and Lillie, his third wife, to my graduation, further solidifying his perception of my lack of interest in a relationship. At the time, I didn't know how to respond to his accusations. Now, I realize I should have simply told him the truth—that as a young teenager, I was afraid to have to deal with his rancor toward Mom and be caught in the middle of them both on *my* graduation day.

At twenty-one, I'd already spent seven years working in radio when I considered supplementing my experience with some formal education at the La Jolla Academy of Advertising and Art. I told Dad, hoping, finally, for his approval. Instead, he bluntly stated, "A liberal arts college education is most valuable." I bristled at his disapproval, a sense of injustice rising within me. Why bother trying to please him if he couldn't see the value in my hard work and accomplishments?

As I entered adulthood, my relationship with Dad remained a struggle. He rarely reached out and revealed little interest in my life or pursuits. Despite my attempts to connect, our relationship remained inconsistent and emotionally distant. I longed for an apology, for some acknowledgment of the pain he'd caused. I even asked him to help pay for my therapy, but his contributions were sporadic and unreliable. Eventually, I gave up on trying to change him and focused on acceptance.

After Dad was hospitalized, his condition deteriorated rapidly. Seeing him in that dimly lit, cramped ICU, hooked up to machines, was a shock. Despite everything, he was my dad. I sat with him, and told him I loved him with tears streaming down my face. He squeezed my hand. The doctor's words, "This is about as sick as anyone can get," echoed in my ears.

I went home, knowing that I had said goodbye to him. He lived for a few more days and then was taken off the machines and allowed to pass in peace. I felt a sense of relief. However, the funeral proved to be highly emotional and quite painful because it highlighted the stark contrast between the admiration from others and the emotional void I felt inside.

The outpouring of support at his funeral was overwhelming. The temple overflowed with mourners, the sanctuary expanded to accommodate the crowd. He was honored by the temple, the military, Rotary International, the Masonic lodge, and the Boy Scouts of America—a testament to his impact on the community.

The irony was that Dad, Millard, the local public figure, sought love from the world. While I, the private individual, craved only his. As I wept uncontrollably, I couldn't help but feel the emptiness of being cheated out of the availability and care he'd given others.

42

HERE COMES THE SUN

The year that followed the extrication of my company from Ignition was a trial by fire, a struggle to regain control after a period of professional and personal instability. As always, I hurled my heart and soul into work. I was determined to right the ship, to steer the agency back to its winning ways. And when Honda chose to stick with us, rejecting the advances of Ignition, it was a powerful validation.

Relief washed over me as we re-entered the game. I felt reinvigorated and had a terrific core staff to move into the next chapter. The revenue from Honda and the number of projects we were doing both soared, despite the economic downturn that happened to be going on around us. I condensed the company to a sustainable level and re-expanded it to even greater heights. Getting through the muck of the divorce from Ignition wasn't fun, but it was the right decision. I developed close relationships with key Honda executives and managers and was sometimes even able to introduce divisions for collaboration when they didn't even know one another. Marketing Factory 2.0 was a significant upgrade, a leaner, meaner machine built on the ashes of the old.

The stage lights blazed, the bass thrummed through my chest, and the crowd roared as the headliner launched into their hit song. Another Honda Civic Tour concert was in full swing, another city conquered. But for me, the real thrill wasn't just the electrifying atmosphere or the screaming fans. It was the knowledge that this tour campaign, year after year, was more than just a spectacle. It was a finely tuned machine designed to drive results.

Sure, we measured success by the packed venues and the enthusiastic response from concertgoers. But the real measure of our impact lay in the numbers that mattered most to Honda: the uptick in Civic and other model sales. We weren't just creating a buzz; we were moving metal. Our team meticulously tracked the data, analyzing everything from email sign-ups and social media engagement to DMV registrations. We correlated the number of concert attendees with the number of Hondas sold in those same demographics. The results were undeniable. The Honda Civic Tour was more than a marketing campaign. It was a sales engine, fueled by the power of music and our strategic approach.

We were laser-focused on making young adults—licensed drivers—aware of the coolness and relevance of Honda. Cars are a high-ticket item; they need to resonate with consumers long before they walk into a dealership. Our goal was to plant that seed, to make Honda synonymous with youth, excitement, and possibility. And the "cool factor" we brought to the table was undeniable. While Honda's exploration of music began in 2000 with the development of the Civic Tour, by 2009 we had extended Honda in another unique way by integrating the company and its line of vehicles into music festivals.

Success in my personal life, however, remained elusive. I was in my early forties, unmarried, lived alone, and was consumed mainly by work. Had I, perhaps unconsciously, become my father in that regard? He and my mom separately and quite frequently had inquired about whether I had a "significant other" in my life. This often made me feel uncomfortable, as if I was being judged for not meeting certain expectations—just as Dad always looked down on me for not getting a college degree. I would manage to pull off a "plus one" for events and dinners, but I had yet to find the partner I was longing for.

To soothe my overworked mind, my daily morning routine consisted of either invigorating surf or the tranquility of yoga, which helped me regulate my nervous system. The sessions started early in the morning. I had practiced yoga for many years and after some time became friendly with the woman who would often be the one to open the studio doors, Dawn. She even referred to me as "7 A.M. Rob." Sometimes, I would arrive early and wait outside for her to come and unlock the door. I would even lend a hand with the opening tasks on those occasions. Gradually, we started talking more and more, and I found myself profoundly admiring her.

My palms felt sweaty as I approached her before class one day. Months of shy smiles and casual conversations had built up to this moment. "Um, hi," I began, feeling a bit flustered. "Would you maybe ... want to exchange numbers?"

She smiled warmly but didn't answer. My stomach lurched. *Was that a no?* I thought, trying to hide my disappointment.

Later, as she prepared the room for the next session, she walked up to me and discreetly handed me a folded piece of paper. Excitement surged through me. It wasn't a phone number, but her email address, written in elegant cursive. This was her way of saying yes, her way of opening a door.

I began corresponding with her, and she responded readily. In person, both of us tended to be reserved and shy, yet through writing, she appeared much more at ease in expressing her thoughts and emotions, which also resonated with me. We continued to communicate through email for a few weeks, regularly seeing each other at the yoga studio. It felt somewhat awkward as if we each had dual identities—one in writing and one in person. Our communication delved deeply into our families, our interests, our hobbies, and our goals, effectively revealing our life stories to one another. I told her about my dysfunctional family, from Mom kidnapping me when she left my father, to Dad's disapproval of pretty much everything I ever did. She told me about her family's strong entrepreneurial background, but she was still finding herself after school and wanted to get some other experience before she joined the family business, which is why she was working at the yoga studio.

After a month of these emails, we finally decided to meet for a picnic lunch on the beach to explore the possibility of further developing our face-to-face connection. We were both nervous about this step, yet also eager. We set a specific day and date, and she kindly offered to bring lunch for us. I anxiously awaited our meetup.

A few days before our lunch, I was stripping out of my wetsuit after a surf when I saw her leisurely strolling along the sidewalk near the beach with a dude and a canine companion. We greeted each other awkwardly, and she continued without pausing.

Recounting this peculiar encounter with my confidant, Jay, I couldn't help but express my confusion about her early morning visit with a male friend. Later that afternoon, a cryptic email arrived from her.

"When I saw you this morning," it began, her words dancing across the screen. "I should have introduced you to ... someone."

Someone? I thought, a knot formed in my stomach. *Why so vague?*

She continued, "He's more of the live-in kind. An old flame. But it's complicated."

The recollection of her words, specifically "the live-in kind," continues to reverberate through my mind years later. Though I felt a pang of betrayal, my traumatized psyche yearned for more. It was almost as though I craved the intensity of that familiar sensation of abandonment, of being forsaken for someone or something else. In my distorted subconscious, it seemed like a sanctuary, a place I could call home.

All signs pointed to a confused person who was dealing with her own issues and unable to be honest. Yet, instead of backing away, I pressed on.

"Does this mean our emailing must come to an end?" I wrote, trying to sound casual despite the turmoil inside me. It was my sly way of keeping a crack open in the door that had only been partially closed.

Her reply came quickly. "Of course not," she assured me. "Our emails are ... special. They're a place where we can truly be ourselves."

I felt a surge of relief, a mixture of excitement and guilt. She had taken the bait.

Thus, though the sack lunch date didn't happen, our relationship continued along its familiar path—the awkward in-person encounters in the yoga studio and our significantly more intimate virtual interactions via email. Then, a few weeks later, another email arrived, this one filled with unexpected news.

"Guess what?" she wrote, a hint of excitement in her tone. "My ex just moved out!"

My heart leaped. *This could be it,* I thought. *A chance to finally move beyond emails and into the real world.*

"And guess who's moving in?" she continued. "My coworker from the studio."

I didn't know quite what to think. Should I ask her out for another picnic lunch, or was I now firmly in the friend zone? Then, one day not long after the new roommate email, Dawn nonchalantly hinted that we should grab dinner together.

We are on. I organized a real-life date where we met up at the yoga studio on our bicycles and proceeded to walk to a nearby restaurant. To my surprise, she had dressed up beautifully in a way I had never seen before. She wore a sexy, black, gauze-like, sleeveless dress with a prominent back-shoulder design that almost looked like angel wings. It was edgy, incredibly unique, and cool as hell.

We took a short walk to Warren Cuccurullo's Via Veneto, a chic Italian eatery where I had reserved a table for us. Cuccurullo, a former member of Duran Duran, and a guitarist known for his virtuosity, also performed with Frank Zappa and co-founded Missing Persons.

Dawn and I savored a charming, shared meal of roasted branzino, accompanied by a bottle of wine.

"I have a confession," Dawn said after dinner, her cheeks flushed.

"Oh?" I replied, intrigued. "What's that?"

"I might have ... overdone it with the wine," she admitted, a giggle escaping her lips. "I'm not much of a drinker."

I smiled, taking in her slightly uncoordinated movements and rosy coloring. "Well, you're certainly holding it together admirably."

"I'm trying my best," she said with a playful wink. "But maybe we should switch to water for the rest of the evening."

Several days later, I texted Dawn and received a response telling me she was at home. I kept texting. Nothing but silence followed. Her apartment was a mere three blocks away. I knew this as I'd once walked her home and she had invited me in for some tea. So, I mounted my beach cruiser, embodying the spirit of Venice Beach's pedestrian-friendly vibe, and pedaled my way to her door. Ascending the stairs, I peered through the open screen door and what I witnessed left me dismayed. There sat Dawn with her fellow yoga associate and roommate, and a guy—someone she had mentioned in passing as an odd suitor she had no intention of pursuing.

I found myself enveloped in a haze of awkwardness, unsure of how to proceed. He was also a coworker of hers from the yoga studio who had recently conveyed his admiration for her through a heartfelt love letter, complete with prose and illustrations. She had divulged the entire incident to me, assuring me that she had no interest in reciprocating those feelings and, in fact, found it rather amusing—even unsettling. Yet, I couldn't help but question the authenticity of her words. Why was he there, looming? This incident should have been a clear indication to me. It was the second time she hid her interactions with other men from me. That very day I should have had a frank conversation with Dawn about how unacceptable her communication and behavior with me had been in the past, and how I expected better in a potential partner. Instead, I ignored this ominous cosmic sign.

These early instances of betrayal by Dawn stirred up a familiar feeling of abandonment and mistrust, just like my childhood. *It was the devil I knew.* After a few intense encounters and even more personal interactions, I felt the need to plan a romantic weekend escape. Considering Dawn's preferences, I booked a stay at the Big Sur Lodge, opting for a modest yet cozy experience. We indulged at a nice restaurant, explored the untamed wilderness through rigorous hikes, and lounged at the beach for a day.

While the biting, chilly water and relentless wind bothered me, Dawn found them the perfect opportunity to show off her provocatively sexy bikini. As I gazed upon her, warmth spread throughout my entire being, and our eyes locked in a deep, electric connection. Yet, after engaging in passionate kisses and intimate caresses, we were consumed by a wave of anxiety that often accompanies the exhilarating beginnings of a bond with someone you are irrevocably drawn to.

We did not have sex—at least, not in Big Sur. That came later after we had gotten back to Venice Beach. Each time we were together, it only got better and better. The conversations, the touch of our bodies, and the sharing of stories intensified our feelings for each other. We immersed ourselves in art shows, visited museums, strolled along the beach, practiced yoga, rode bicycles, watched movies, and even read to one another. We met each other's family members and spoke of our dreams. Yet despite our fun, at times Dawn still seemed tied to her ex, and emotionally unavailable to me.

I invited Dawn to join me for my annual end-of-the-year holiday on Maui. Specifically, we would stay in a laid-back town on the north shore, where I had rented a beautiful beachfront house for the past few years. I often brought along a couple of friends to use the extra bedrooms and keep things lively. It also helped split the cost of the accommodation. Our private, primary bedroom offered stunning ocean views and its own bathroom. Each day in Maui was packed with activities to keep us busy— yoga sessions, invigorating hikes to waterfalls, sightseeing, thrilling surf sessions, refreshing swims, lazing under the sun, shopping for trinkets, dining out, and whipping up delicious meals together. It seemed we had an absolute blast, although the damper was Dawn's worry about coursework that she had to complete for an online college course she was taking.

To make matters worse, her ex-boyfriend from three months before kept pestering her with texts and calls. He still owed her money for rent, and it was driving her insane. I didn't particularly appreciate hearing about it, especially when it started interfering with our vacation. It was a real downer that she would let her mindset shift to a crappy place when I had done my absolute best to give her a fun vacation. I wanted her to enjoy it.

After spending Christmas together for a week, I lobbied Dawn to stay for New Year's Eve so we could ring in the new year together. But she opted to leave to deal with her ex, study, and take a shift at the yoga studio to cover for a coworker, and flew back to the mainland. To say that I was disappointed was the understatement of all understatements. Knowing I'd be solo on NYE, when I'd had the love of my life with me in paradise, made me feel horrifically abandoned.

Coinciding with Dawn's departure was the arrival of Pedro, my South American friend, who joined me, and the other two staying in our rented beachfront house, my old friend Julia and her gay buddy. Pedro was supposed to bring his girlfriend, but they had gotten into a quarrel right before he left, so he decided to leave her on the mainland and come alone. When New Year's Eve rolled around, we decided to have our party in the house, and we invited a few people over, including Skye, the property manager who lived in an attached guest cottage with a separate entrance. We rarely saw her, but I had met her the year before, and on this trip, we had talked in passing a few times while Dawn was with me. She had met Dawn and was cordial toward us, extending island hospitality on behalf of the owners and the rental agent I dealt with.

After dinner, as midnight approached, we polished off a 1.75-liter bottle of tequila and smoked a few joints. Then, following the countdown, our guests departed, and with my two friends retiring for the night, it was just Pedro, Skye, and me left to ring in the new year. In our inebriated state, we decided it was the perfect moment to immerse ourselves in the Jacuzzi—a sanctuary of hot, bubbling water, basking in the moonlight while looking out over the dark ocean. We made sure to bring along stiff libations, and when the ice melted and we had finished most of the booze, Pedro graciously volunteered to replenish our drinks.

"I'll go open another bottle," Pedro announced. "What'll it be, folks?

Same?"

"Definitely," I replied, handing him my half-empty glass. "The night is young."

Skye nodded in agreement, her eyes sparkling with mischief. "Don't hold back, Pedro. Bring out the big guns," she blurted out as she passed him hers.

I had been sensing a connection between Pedro and Skye, feeling his pain that his girlfriend got left behind due to some stupid argument. I lounged on one side of the Jacuzzi while Pedro and Skye cozied up on the other. But just as Pedro stepped out of the hot tub to make his way to the kitchen, Skye shot me a seductive glare. Slowly, tantalizingly, she migrated from her spot to mine until our lips met, and her body wrapped around mine.

Surprised, I pulled back slightly, my mind foggy but my conscience nagging.

"Skye," I said softly, "I think you've had a bit too much tequila."

"Maybe," she buzzed, her voice husky, "but I know what I want."

"And what's that?" I asked, trying to maintain my composure.

"You," she breathed, her lips brushing against mine.

I gently pushed her away. "Skye, I'm with Dawn. And I thought you and Pedro...."

"Pedro who?" she slurred, her words laced with a playful defiance.

Right then, Pedro discreetly returned.

"Whoa," he said, his eyes widening in surprise. "Looks like I've got some competition."

He smirked and handed us fresh cocktails. "I'll just leave you two lovebirds to it," he said, turning to leave.

"No, Pedro, wait...," I started to explain, but he cut me off with a wave of his hand.

"Don't worry about it, man," he said with a sneer.

And just like that, I was left face-to-face with temptation, a danger I knew all too fucking well. I didn't have any rational thoughts. My mind was racing. While I was angry with Dawn for abandoning me on New Year's Eve, it wasn't right for me to succumb to this temptation. Or maybe it was? She'd not been fully honest and transparent with me about her ex, nor the suitor she'd flagrantly invited into her home. I was torn between conflicting emotions, intoxicated, high, and filled with desire. With Pedro out of the picture, Skye and I engaged in a more intense session, which ultimately led me to make a decision. Either I would retreat to my bedroom and indulge in some self-pleasure, or I would extend an invitation to her to join me.

"Skye," I said, gently pulling back, "I ... I can't."

She looked at me, her eyes searching mine. "But...."

"I have a girlfriend," I reminded her, my voice barely above a whisper. "And even if I didn't...."

"Even if you didn't, what?" she asked, her voice soft and inviting.

"Even if I didn't," I repeated, my resolve wavering, "we can't act on ... on what we're thinking about."

A flicker of disappointment crossed her face, but she quickly masked it with a smile. "Right," she said softly. "Of course."

But that setback only fueled her desire more. As I emerged from the water and entered the living room, she trailed behind, drying off.

"Come with me," she whispered, her voice low. "To the guest house."

I hesitated, unsure. "But...."

"No buts," she insisted, her eyes locking with mine. "It's the only way we can have some real privacy."

Her seductive gaze and the promise of intimacy were hard to resist. I followed her, stepping cautiously and slowly, almost like a zombie under her spell. As we walked through the lanai outside the front door, past Julia's bedroom window, Skye uttered the line that broke me.

"Rob," she commanded, her voice a mix of urgency and desire, "you're coming with me. Stop resisting. *Did I mention I'm a nymphomaniac?*"

Women don't usually ask a man to have sex with them. I often had to put in days, weeks, and months of effort to get a woman to sleep with me. Yet here was an exquisite woman not even asking but *demanding* sex—from *me*. It was like I was in a primal, animalistic, alternate reality. Any resolve I'd had was demolished.

"Okay, okay," I stammered, my heart pounding in my chest.

Skye squeezed my hand, a triumphant smile spreading across her face. "Good," she hummed. "Because I have plans for you."

Once I stepped foot into her oceanfront lair, with just a sliver of a view of the water from the living room, the conversation took a turn toward an abusive ex and various unrelated subjects—all under the watchful gaze of her feline protector. Just moments later, Skye and I stumbled into the bedroom, which seemed to spin as I tried to steady myself, and our passion rekindled. There may have been an encounter, or perhaps two, but I honestly can't remember. Even so, the morning sun woke me up and I was immediately overwhelmed with guilt and remorse. I retreated to the main house, only to be met by Pedro and my other two roommates. Their knowing looks felt like spotlights, exposing my shame. Julia, my closest confidant, urged me to bury the secret. "Deny, deny, deny!" she insisted. They offered an escape to a distant beach, but I was too exhausted, too hungover, too confused.

Dawn's absence, the sting of her rejection, and the lingering thrill of the forbidden encounter twisted into a knot of loneliness and longing. The shame of betraying her warred with a perverse sense of justification. *I'd already crossed the line, hadn't I? Men don't turn down sex, right? Get it while you can.* These toxic societal messages echoed in my head, drowning out any sense of reason. I opted for a nap instead, but sleep offered no solace.

Upon waking, a desperate craving pulled me back to Skye's. It wasn't just about the sex; it was about numbing the pain, chasing a fleeting high to escape the emptiness Dawn had left behind. I told myself this time would be different, that I could control myself, that Skye and I could just talk. But as soon as I stepped into her bungalow, I knew I was lying to myself. Denial is an elusive trick.

She welcomed me with a knowing smile, and within moments, we were back in her bedroom. The experience was undeniably thrilling, a temporary balm for my wounded ego.

43

LOVE WILL TEAR US APART

After my descent from the dreamlike paradise of Maui, I found myself back on the mainland, reunited with Dawn. The gears in my mind, all associated with her, seemed to grind slowly, burdened by an overwhelming sense of shame. Any pleasure I'd experienced with Skye paled in comparison to the shame over the love for Dawn I had jeopardized. Though my heart never strayed from Dawn, another part of my anatomy had found its way to Skye. Of course, I uttered nothing about that encounter to Dawn.

And then, like a bolt from the sky, a beautiful thing unfolded. My relationship with Dawn took a turn for the better, surpassing even the halcyon days before we vacationed in Hawaii, where she was tormented by her past love and seemed seldom fully available to me. Now, she appeared undeniably committed, something entirely new to me. We thrived with no interference from the outside world, forging a connection that placed me firmly in her priorities.

One Friday date night at the end of January, we arranged a rendezvous. I had given her a set of keys to my house. She rode her bike into my backyard and ascended the stairs to my place. I stood waiting in the kitchen, eagerly anticipating her entrance.

But the Dawn who appeared through my back door was not the Dawn I expected. She had a fury etched on her face that jolted me to my core. The keys, hers and mine, sailed through the air like a missile, propelled by her anger and aimed squarely at me. They struck me in the chest, and when I asked her what had prompted her to act this way, she shrieked at me, "You know damn well why! How *could* you?"

But I *didn't* know damn well why. I had no idea what she was screaming about. What had happened in Maui eluded me in that moment. I had pushed the shame so far down inside me, that I'd nearly convinced myself Skye had never even happened. Now, it all came back—someone had blabbed. Dawn knew what happened on New Year's Eve, but apparently not New Year's Day. It was impossible for her to know about it since my roommates were unaware. Then, I thought Skye might have told her, but even that seemed extremely unlikely.

Two things raced through my mind. The first was the word "deny," which Julia had repeated. I held Julia in high regard. She had brains, hailed from a seemingly caring family, and remained well-grounded. Another individual who had incessantly drilled the word deny into my psyche was Thom, my boss at Westwood One, who eventually gave me the boot. His go-to defense was always, "Robbie, you must master the art of denial: deny, deny, deny."

A pathological response took hold in my brain, and I began denying that *anything* transpired in Maui. *If I deny it ever happened, perhaps I can make that be the truth.* In my mind, the distance between Maui and Los Angeles felt like a chasm, and what had happened between Skye and me seemed private, distant from Dawn's reality, as well as from the deep desire for closeness I wanted with Dawn right here, right now.

But Dawn flew into an even more frenzied fit of rage. Over the next few days, she wouldn't let up. Day after day, she bombarded me with relentless questions. It felt like she kept throwing her keys at me, as she screamed accusations of infidelity. After several days of this, however, her tune started to change, bit by bit. Feeling like now might be a safe time to start telling the truth, I confessed that something passionate did happen with Skye. However, I adamantly refused to admit to full-blown intercourse, let alone the outrageous world of anal—which Skye had made imperative during our fling.

Dawn was torn. On the one hand, she felt she couldn't trust me any-more and was ready to call it a day. On the other hand, she felt deeply attached to me. She told me she might forgive me, but on one condition: I had to join her on an upcoming road trip to Arizona for training related to her family's empire. We were to crash at her brother's condo, sharing his guest room. I thought of how he'd be sizing me up and question-ing my intentions with his sis, probably suspicious of the fact that I was twenty-one years older than her—not to mention judging me for the infidelity she'd likely spilled to him. It made my skin crawl.

"Look," I said to Dawn, my voice heavy with guilt and uncertainty, "I understand why you'd want me to come along. But meeting and facing your brother ... I'm not sure I'm ready for that."

"I know it's awkward," she admitted, her voice soft. "But it's import-ant to me. It's a way for me to keep an eye on you, for us to start rebuilding trust," she said, embers still in her voice.

I hesitated, weighing the potential discomfort against the possibility of reconciliation.

"Okay," I finally agreed, "I'll go. But it won't be easy."

I hadn't slept well during the nights since that Friday evening. I was exhausted. But like any anxious and attached human, I agreed to the road trip because losing her would be even more excruciating. It would awaken the subconscious pain of childhood abandonment all over again.

I endured the car ride with Dawn, who treated me like Satan them-self. The anxiety I felt nearly sent me hurling. After seven long hours in her zippy little import, with me driving most of the way in the dark, we finally arrived. I faced her brother, and we crashed in his guest room as planned.

I continued to apologize and pleaded for her forgiveness.

"Dawn," I begged, my voice cracking with emotion, "I know I fucked up. I'm so sorry. Please, give me another chance."

She looked at me, her eyes filled with hurt and anger. "How could you do this to me?" she asked, her voice trembling. "We were just starting to build something real."

"I know, I know," I said, tears welling up in my eyes. "I was weak. I made a mistake. But I love you, and I'll do anything to make things right."

Eventually, she said she *might* forgive me, but she had conditions: couples therapy, severing ties with *all* female friends, maintaining *constant* communication, and adhering to myriad other actions to suppress her doubts.

"I need you to prove to me that you're serious," she said, her voice firm but laced with a hint of vulnerability. "I need to know that I can trust you again."

I agreed, knowing her lack of trust was warranted. I had violated our bond and felt awful for hurting her.

"There's something else I need to tell you," I confessed, my voice barely above a whisper. I *had* to come completely clean. "I ... I slept with Skye."

The color drained from Dawn's face. "What?" she gasped.

"I'm so sorry," I said, my heart sinking. "It was a mistake. It meant nothing."

My confession detonated like a bomb.

"How could you?!" she cried, tears streaming down her face. "You *betrayed* me in the worst possible way!"

I reached for her, but she pulled away. "Don't touch me!" she sobbed. "I need some time to process this."

Eventually, Dawn told me she appreciated my honesty, but she needed time to decide whether she *could* forgive me. She insisted that I call Skye with her and confess everything, putting me in the excruciating position of being shamed in front of both women. The Dawn-Rob-Skye saga was a tangled mess of emotions and misjudgments. I felt terrible for Skye, but perhaps she deserved this, considering that she had encountered Dawn and knowingly contributed to the complications of our budding romance. Skye was a drunk/high fuck; Dawn was my true love interest.

A few months later, our relationship took another twist.

"Rob," Dawn began hesitantly, her voice barely above a whisper, "there's something I need to tell you."

My stomach tightened. "What is it?"

"A few days after you told me about Skye...." She paused, her eyes welling up. "I ... I slept with my ex."

A wave of shock washed over me, followed by a strange sense of relief. "I deserved that," I admitted, my voice heavy with guilt. "I have no right to be angry."

Then came another bombshell.

"I'm moving," Dawn announced, her voice firm despite the tremor in her hands.

"Moving?" I echoed, my heart sinking. "Where?"

"Just a few doors down from you, actually," she said, a flicker of mischief in her eyes.

A mix of excitement and foreboding washed over me. "Why?" I asked.

"Because," she said, a sly smile playing on her lips, "my lease is up at that awful, noisy, shared space. Time for me to get my own place—a little studio all to myself. And since I practically live at your place anyway...." She trailed off, letting the implication hang in the air.

Her words felt like a warm embrace, a validation of my worth. But a shiver of unease ran down my spine. *Was this truly about convenience?* I wondered. *Or was she finding a way to keep me close, to keep an eye on me?* The thought was both flattering and unsettling. Now she was getting closer to the real me, the one who had betrayed her trust.

The rest of the year was a whirlwind of ups, downs, and many in-betweens. It became painfully apparent that our future together hung by a slender thread. I endured the fierce grip of her punitive decrees and was periodically confined to the figurative doghouse, where my spirit was continually crushed. So, a bit past the one-year mark of my monstrous indiscretion, I presented her with an ultimatum. I couldn't take any more of the constant back and forth. One minute she was open and vulnerable, sharing her heart with me, and the next she was cold and distant, her resentment a barrier between us. I was in love with her, and it was tearing me apart to be with someone who purported to love me but continued to punish me.

Surprisingly, Dawn promised to work on genuinely forgiving me. We talked and agreed that she should move into my house. To further solidify our unity as a committed, cohabitating couple, we acquired a puppy, Milo, a feisty Australian Shepherd.

Things went quite well at first. We went through the usual fluctuations of a relationship, although I remember mostly favorable times. I took Dawn on an epic two-week vacation to Asia, a destination she selected. We flew business class and stayed at three different Four Seasons resorts. We had a romantic blast. It felt like the dream honeymoon I never had.

We settled into a routine. Dawn would leave early in the morning for the West LA office that served as the central hub for the family business where she worked while I ran my enterprise just down the street from our beach house.

One spring evening after work, we engaged in our typical sharing of what our respective days had been like. Dawn gleamed with exhilaration as she recounted being invited by her older brother to explore a private art collection belonging to an entertainment industry titan who founded a major talent agency and served as president of a large media company based in California. He had become one of the world's top art collectors, with upward of 3,500 works by such iconic artists as Pablo Picasso, Jasper Johns, and Willem de Kooning. He showcased his collection in a white-box gallery space in his stately home. Dawn's brother, Ethan, an alum of a prominent art school, served as the mastermind behind the design, art, and furnishing aspects of their family's enterprises, adorned with genuine artwork and designer fixtures.

The wild card of our evening chat came when Dawn told me about some shady, obsessive figure who trailed her throughout the gathering, supposedly serving as some legal or business emissary for the power broker turned collector. A few days later, Dawn came home from work and told me the guy had reached out to her brother, eager to secure a date with her. I asked about Ethan's response, and she told me he had informed the guy that she was in a relationship and lived with her boyfriend. The peculiar character somehow slithered into our conversations several times over the following months as somewhat of a paranoid joke, tossed around when my own insecurities would rear their ugly heads, leading me to make ridiculous comments like, "I wonder if the *attorney* would appreciate that humor?"

One day I was enjoying a midday meal with a business associate at my favorite lunch spot, an outdoor patio in the heart of Venice called Axe, when I received an urgent call and text from a concerned neighbor, alerting me to a distressing spectacle unfolding at my house: My place was being looted by a group of strangers carrying valuables to vehicles parked near my garage. I quickly settled the bill and ran the few blocks to my house. As I approached my open garage door, I collided with one of Dawn's brothers, accompanied by his fiancé. The next instant, I was face-to-face with Dawn, carrying a huge box that obscured her vision.

"What is happening here?" I cried out.

"Isn't it painfully obvious, Rob?" she responded. "I am moving out. I'm leaving you."

Shock reverberated through my very being, rendering me speechless and powerless to intervene. With no words, I retreated to my office, consumed by disbelief and the agonizing sting of abandonment.

Later that day, over the phone, I implored Dawn to reveal the reasons behind her decision, although I knew deep down it didn't matter. She assured me that there was no other suitor vying for her affection. It was simply that she could no longer bear to coexist with me. I was crushed. We had literally made love before work that morning as if nothing was bothering either of us.

I rode with her to her mother's storage facility the next day. We were there to exchange some items. As a parting gift, she gave me a vintage designer furniture piece—an iconic Le Corbusier tubular and black-leather armchair. During the drive, she was gentle and understanding. I found myself sobbing at times, though I tried my best to hide the depth of my pain. Looking back, I realize that it was my family's abandonment that was triggered at that moment. So, yes, I was heartbroken and shocked by Dawn's actions, but the wound was already there, festering inside my soul. It had been suddenly ripped wide open once again. My buddy Jay and his trusty surf bus eventually arrived at the storage facility. We loaded the items and hit the road. Jay helped me tend to my emotional wounds through his kindness and spirit.

Over the next few weeks, I had to ask Dawn to stop contacting me. Every time I started to heal, she would reach out. Maybe it was guilt, per- haps it was something else. But I couldn't stand the constant reminder of what we once had. So, I made it clear that I would contact her if, and when, I was ready. She agreed to those terms.

About five months after our sudden—and to me, at least—unex- pected breakup, I called her, and right away, she said she wanted to have dinner with me. In my distorted perception, I saw this as an opportunity to reconnect and maybe even rekindle our romance. We met at a nearby restaurant, and the moment I saw her, I felt my heart race and my face grow flush as I experienced that familiar, intimate connection once more. Then she dropped a bomb on me.

"Rob," she began, her voice hesitant, "there's something I need to tell you."

My stomach tightened as it always did. "What is it?" I asked, a knot of anxiety also forming in my chest.

She looked down at her plate, avoiding my gaze. "I've been ... seeing someone."

The words had crushing disappointment. "Seeing someone?" I echoed, my voice barely a whisper.

"Yes, and I think we're in love," she said softly, finally meeting my eyes. "His name is Mark, and we met at that massive private art collection tour, the attorney guy you used to joke about."

She spun some elaborate tale about randomly bumping into him at a coffeehouse, and it all just clicked. Likely story. I knew immediately that I had been taken for a fool. From the moment she first met this guy at the private gallery tour, I had felt something.

Intense rage surged through me. I'd not only accepted her constant flagellation but had done everything she'd ever asked of me to do to make amends for my own cheating—while she slept with her ex out of revenge. I had stopped talking to every female friend I had, taken her on the best vacations imaginable, moved her into my home, and spent as much time with her as I could. Meanwhile, she abandoned me, deceived me, and on top of it was now here to lie about it to my face, when at this point she could have just let me be. I looked at her in disbelief, motioned for the waitress, literally blurted out a cliché, "Check, please," and quickly paid.

I walked out as Dawn had the audacity to ask me to escort her to her car. I ignored her.

"I hope I get raped walking alone to my car, so you'll feel like shit, you asshole!" She screamed down the sidewalk as she turned away. Her words cut deep, especially that last one, echoing in my ears and dredging up a childhood of feeling attacked and mistreated, then blamed for it all. I'd been abused by assholes, worked for assholes, and now, in her eyes, I had become one, too. The realization hit me like a heavyweight punch to the gut.

44

MAMMA MIA

After that fateful dinner with Dawn, I did what I always did after a traumatic event: I buried myself in my work. By 2010, the economy was recovering from an economic collapse, and Honda was increasing budgets and expanding entertainment marketing programs. By spearheading the addition of music festivals to their portfolio, we'd driven significant expansion in this area.

One of the first festivals we did was, ironically, Lollapalooza, in Chicago. It had morphed from its early days as a touring caravan into a massive multi-day music festival with Soundgarden and Green Day among the headliners, and Lady Gaga, still somewhat of a newcomer, playing a small stage. This was the same Lollapalooza that, years earlier, had sparked my ambition at Westwood One, where I'd envisioned producing a special radio program featuring the tour and its artists. Later, it became a highlight of the *On Tour* series, capturing Metallica's explosive performance. And now, here I was, working with Lollapalooza yet again. It was like coming home. We set up an "eco-village" featuring Honda's hybrid cars, promoting the company's early commitment to sustainability. The crowds ate it up.

Another festival we did was called Sasquatch! The event was held over the 2012 Memorial Day weekend in a gorgeous outdoor venue near Seattle called The Gorge. It was the first music fest we worked to allow stage naming rights, and where we initiated the term "Honda Stage." We also turned cars into photo booths and printed the pictures on branded bandannas attendees could wear as they walked around the festival, which featured performances by such trendy stars as Jack White, The Roots, Beck, and Childish Gambino.

The location was stunning, perched on a cliff with views of the Columbia River Gorge near the tiny town of George, Washington. The convenience of staying just a few hundred yards away at an upscale winery resort connected to the venue was a big plus. The winery had a gourmet restaurant, and once while dining with clients, I looked over and noticed Jack White sitting at an adjacent table having dinner with Producer Danger Mouse.

I had relocated Marketing Factory from my duplex to a nearby office, a rental owned by a well-known metal sculptor. There was a shared outdoor atrium between his studio and ours. He often worked with metal fabricators who ground, sanded, and cut steel outdoors, creating a constant noisy distraction. I eventually started looking for other spaces and decided it made more sense to buy a building. This way, Marketing Factory could pay *me* rent, and I would be my own landlord. In early 2011, we moved into our new offices, also in Venice, but closer to Abbot Kinney Boulevard, a mile-long road lined with shops, restaurants, and galleries once called "the coolest block in America." I curated a collection of fine art and furniture, creating an office environment that exuded creativity and refinement.

Around this time, my responsibilities for my mother grew. She needed more support, and the assisted living facility in San Francisco could only do so much. I felt the weight of being her sole caregiver, especially as her demands increased. My siblings, though they still loved Mom, had built walls around their hearts. They kept her at a bit of a distance, a way to protect themselves from her occasional harshness and the unfairness they sometimes felt. I, on the other hand, had somehow managed to let my guard down. Maybe it was because I still craved her approval, or maybe it was just the way our personalities meshed. Whatever the reason, I was the one she leaned on, the one who became her caregiver. It was a strange echo of my childhood; when I felt the responsibility for my father's emotional well-being. Now, with Dad gone since 2008, Mom was my new burden.

"Robbie," she'd say, her voice sharp with impatience, "I need you to come up here right away. This place is driving me crazy!"

I'd sigh, already anticipating another emotional issue at the assisted living facility. It was a constant balancing act, trying to meet her needs while also managing my own life and career. But I knew I owed it to her to be there, to provide the care and support she needed in her later years.

Her older voice had a deep, throaty New England accent, and while she didn't read books, her pronunciation was precise—with one exception: She would say "heelie-oh-copter" instead of "hell-uh-copter." Still a natty dresser, she had an inherent sense of style generally found in the Northeast or the Bay Area, where she had spent virtually all of her adult life. Whether embarking on a mundane trip to the grocery store or gracing a grand charity ball, Mom was always dressed to the proverbial nines, the veneer of a flawlessly styled, self-assured woman. I often wondered whether this was just a product of her upbringing or a subconscious way to mask the timid little girl inside of her grabbing at alcohol and cigarettes.

Ironically for an orthopedist, Rob hadn't taken very good care of his own bones. He didn't exercise, he drank and smoked too much, and eventually, his body just gave out. He'd died at eighty-four from organ failure, leaving my mother, for the first time in her life, alone and untended. She had relied on him in many ways; one might even say she was co-dependent. She'd wanted him to be part of almost everything she did.

After his death, Mom immersed herself in creative pursuits: planning and helping with parties, remodeling homes, and arranging flowers for herself and others. But her planning skills fell short in two areas: her finances and her health. She entrusted these matters to others, first to my stepfather and then, after he died, to his oldest son, my stepbrother, Rob3, as well as myself.

Rob3 was highly educated and had established a successful career as a tax attorney and self-professed business junkie. He was still in charge of his father's estate and said he had meticulously designed a comprehensive trust and estate plan for my mother, but it was time for me to be fully in charge of her finances on a day-to-day basis.

Ah, the cycle of life. Our parents take care of us, and then we take care of our parents. I began by reviewing all of my mother's investments, her annual budget, spending patterns, and income sources, and set out to put some controls into place. There was irony in this exercise since my father had once chastised me for not knowing accounting and finance.

I owned my business and had an in-house business manager who did my books. We took on my mother the same way we would address a project or client. My goal was to ensure her money would last for her lifetime. Carole couldn't balance a checkbook. She knew how to write a check, use a credit card, and phone the bank to see if there was money in her account. Passed that, she would lean on me. This added pressure because I constantly had to advise her to "spend less, spend less, spend less!" I even asked her to return certain items she had bought because I felt they were either too similar to something she already owned or too outlandish.

But trying to "control" Mom's spending became a joke. My mother was a heavy consumer of alcohol, vodka in particular. I never knew how she could consume sometimes ten or more ounces of it daily and seem fully functioning, energetic, and organized. "I'm on a budget, tee hee," she'd joke, her childish sarcasm dripping with a sense of entitlement that made my eyes roll.

One day I got a call from a friend of hers that Mom was in the hospital and had suffered a stroke. She was about seventy-five years old at the time. I flew to San Francisco and went to the hospital to visit her. Other than a slight sag in her face and a slur in her speech, she was alert. And yet, *Is this my mother?* I thought to myself. With the after-effects of the stroke and without her hair done up and heavy makeup, she looked ancient to me.

"No more drinking," her doctor bluntly told her. She quit immediately, just as she had quit smoking years earlier. I was genuinely impressed by her commitment to sobriety. It made her more attractive, and I empathized with her, wanting to help her however I could. Thankfully, she had support at home for rehabilitation, and within six months, it seemed as though she had fully recovered and was unstoppable. It felt like she could live forever. Of course, with that came concerns about her money.

During the first dotcom market bust, Mom had lost a significant amount of money and the Great Recession housing market crash didn't help either. The way Rob3 had set up her finances was a complicated morass for me to manage. With the market downturns severely affecting her net worth, I worried she would deplete her funds and need to tap into my stepdad's estate. This would involve his adult children and potentially trigger legal battles over inheritance, a scenario I desperately wanted to avoid.

My mother had improved the rented apartment she was living in, with its stunning views of the San Francisco Bay, spending massive amounts of money to remodel the kitchen and bathrooms and generally change the unit for the better. However, these improvements were lost when I moved her to a smaller apartment in the same building, overlooking the park, to cut her rent by more than half. This move, while financially sensible, was a difficult adjustment for her, as she had grown attached to her previous home and the enhancements she had made.

But still, every month was a financial tightrope walk. Mom, accustomed to a life of luxury, felt entitled to spend freely, seeing her trust fund as a seemingly bottomless well. Around 2009, the reality of her dwindling resources finally forced me to take serious action. Her lifestyle was simply not sustainable. I turned to Rob3 for help, and together we explored the option of assisted living. But Carole refused even to entertain the idea, making me promise she wouldn't die in "an old folks' home." The prospect seemed especially horrifying to her, as she never saw herself as an old person. She would readily label others as old, but not herself. She was completely dissociated from aging, a trait I seem to have inherited.

We wound up buying a condo in an assisted living facility and paying monthly dues that covered most of the services, including meals and entertainment. She acclimated to the community and made friends immediately. She also embraced her role as the weekly Friday cocktail party hostess, maintaining a cheerful demeanor despite not partaking in the drink. Greeting residents and guests with genuine warmth, Mom ensured everyone felt comfortable and included. It was the perfect segue for her. Until it wasn't.

Mom was still going a million miles an hour around 2011 when she began to show telltale signs of mounting confusion. She was eventually diagnosed with early-stage dementia. I began getting more frequent calls from the general manager of the facility, notifying me of her behavior. I felt like the principal's office was calling, and she was my daughter, who had misbehaved.

On a Friday evening, the phone rang, and it was Mom. "That nurse!" she shrieked into the receiver, her voice a furious rasp. "She's incompetent! Get her fired!"

Before I could even process her words, another call came in. This time, it was the general manager of her assisted living facility. "Mr. Tonkin," he said, his voice grave, "I regret to inform you that your mother has ... well, she's assaulted a nurse."

My stomach dropped. "Assaulted?" I stammered. "Carole? She wouldn't hurt a fly!" I knew Mom could be demanding, but violent? It seemed impossible. This was my mother, who once sent back a bowl of soup at a restaurant because it wasn't *smiling* at her. She didn't have a violent bone in her body.

But this same scenario repeated itself several times. Each time, I found myself playing mediator, defusing the situation, and even flying up to San Francisco to meet with the increasingly exasperated general manager. It finally dawned on me: I wasn't just Mom's financial manager anymore. I was her manager, period, responsible for every aspect of her life—like a parent to a young child.

Desperate, I called my siblings. "Look," I pleaded, "can anyone possibly take Mom in? Just for a little while?" The response was a chorus of weary sighs and hesitant no's. It wasn't that they didn't love her, but Mom, even before the dementia took hold, had a unique talent for pushing people away. As my sister, Susan, put it, "We love her, but she stirs the pot too much for us."

It was all going to be up to me, and me alone. So, in 2011, I moved Mom close to me, to Los Angeles, which to her was like a foreign land. I relocated her to Marina del Rey overlooking the harbor, just south of where I lived and worked in Venice, in a secure building that had been highly recommended to me by several friends who had gone through similar situations with aging parents. Before the move, I had taken advice from social workers and doctors from her care team up in San Francisco and arranged her new home to mimic the setup of her previous assisted living condo, which she referred to as "my doll house." This was an attempt to provide her with some semblance of normalcy and consistency.

Considering her previous marriage to a doctor and her VIP status at various medical offices, I aimed to find a similar quality of care. Finding trusted doctors for her in LA was challenging, not because of a lack of qualified physicians, but because of her expectations. She was accustomed to preferential treatment and personalized attention, a level of service that was difficult to replicate, even in a city known for its high-end healthcare. It was a constant struggle to find doctors who could meet her exacting standards and cater to her, shall we say, "unique" personality. After all, this was a woman who, in her mind, had once been royalty. "I was probably a queen in a past life," she'd declare. Her self-importance was nearly comical.

Fortunately, I got her admitted into UCLA Health, a renowned medical system known for its expertise in neurology. Dr. David Reuben, an exceptional practitioner in geriatric medicine, possessed extensive knowledge of Alzheimer's, dementia, and associated behavioral issues. Getting accepted was quite an achievement, but I found a way. Hey, if I could convince the dunking Easter Bunny to share their holiday event with Shannon in the Morning and Don Johnson, I could surely navigate the complexities of the healthcare system.

As time passed, the weight of Mom's medical needs, her care, and the management of her affairs grew heavier and heavier. Desperate for guidance, I enrolled in UCLA-sponsored support sessions for caregivers. It was in one of these sessions that I met Patti Davis, daughter of President Ronald Reagan. She spoke with raw honesty about her father's battle with Alzheimer's, calling it "The Long Goodbye."

Patti, who had famously taken her mother's maiden name to forge her own path, shared her complex family history. Her political views had diverged sharply from her parents, leading to a period of estrangement. Yet, in the twilight of her father's life, she found herself drawn back into the fold, becoming a caregiver during his long decline.

Her insights, born from personal experience, were invaluable. She spoke with empathy and understanding, sharing anecdotes about her father that were illuminating. One that stuck with me was about the five-dollar bill he always carried, even as president—a man who never needed cash. It became a running joke between them, a touchstone to his past.

"Dementia patients crave routine and nostalgia," Patti explained, "but as their filter fades, they become like children, blurting out whatever comes to mind." She emphasized the importance of avoiding arguments, of letting them be right, even when their reality was skewed. This advice proved crucial as my mother's mental capacity diminished. The woman who once relished oysters on the half shell and delicate pieces of sushi now declared them "disgusting." She'd never touched a pancake in her life, but suddenly, she was clamoring for a short stack at IHOP. It was a constant negotiation, a delicate process of preserving her dignity while navigating her shifting reality.

One Friday in November 2013, I had just returned from my morning surf and was preparing for a client meeting at the office when the phone rang, bringing with it a chilling sense of foreboding. It was the caregiver, her voice frantic. "Rob, it's about your mom. She's fallen, and she won't get dressed for her doctor's appointment. She's slurring gibberish and not making any sense...."

My gut clenched. "Is she hurt from the fall?"

The caregiver replied, "She doesn't appear to have been injured."

Something's terribly wrong. My voice tightening, I said, "Call 911 immediately!"

An ambulance took Mom to UCLA Santa Monica Medical Center. After examining her, they determined she needed more specialized neurological care and transferred her to Ronald Reagan UCLA Medical Center in Westwood.

By the time I arrived at Ronald Reagan, around four in the afternoon, Mom had been settled in the intensive care unit. I found her there, enclosed in a large floor-to-ceiling glass room overlooking the atrium. The sight was agonizing. She was writhing on the bed, strapped down for her safety, yelling a stream of unintelligible babble. She was completely out of it, unable to recognize me or understand what was happening. My heart ached for her, lost in the fog of her condition.

After what felt like an eternity, the doctor emerged from examining her brain scan and showed it to me. "Mr. Tonkin," he said, his voice somber, "Carole has suffered a cerebral hemorrhage. It's not an aneurysm, but...." He paused. "There's likely significant brain damage due to lack of oxygen."

He explained that surgery, while routine to aspirate the blood, was risky at her age and given her existing condition. "The best-case scenario," he said gently, "is that we get her back to where she was before the fall, but it will also take considerable rehab."

But where she was before wasn't good. At eighty-seven, with

dementia progressing rapidly, she was fading fast. The thought of putting her through a major surgery, with minimal chance of improvement, felt unbearable. I was torn, caught between hope and the harsh reality of her situation. There was a real risk that following surgery she would have to be put on a breathing machine and a feeding tube, maybe indefinitely, so I decided against the operation. Mom had always told me she did not want to be kept alive artificially, and I had a legal document that said as much. Dr. Reuben endorsed my decision, given her wishes and condition, and eventually, she was transferred to a quiet room and put on palliative care. This meant she was given morphine and taken off all fluids.

Dr. Reuben told me that Mom would likely live two to four days. He arranged a private room—this is something she had drilled into me—and I was very grateful. I went to see her the next day, and she was in a coma. After about four nights, Reuben called me and politely informed me that the hospital requested that Carole be discharged to a convalescent hospital. I was confused and disturbed by this news because I felt she was in the best place under the best care. I pleaded with him and learned then that hospitals have a specialized job. They are designed to save lives, and when it becomes clear that a patient is going to die, they don't want that on their record. I quickly searched for and found a convalescent hospital in Santa Monica with an available bed. I went for a visit to confirm that it was appropriate for Mom, and once I had done that, I arranged for a move the following day.

The next day, I arrived at the convalescent hospital to prepare for the move, only to find Mom had already been dropped off by an ambulance, with the nurses still waiting for delivery of the morphine drip. I couldn't believe that this hadn't been arranged beforehand! And to make matters worse, Mom, still in a coma, seemed terribly uncomfortable, trembling and softly babbling incoherently. Since the morphine had been taken away before the transfer, it had been hours since she had received any relief. When I went to the nurses' station to inquire about this, the nurse casually said the driver was "stuck in traffic." *LA! Great, just great.*

As if that wasn't enough, Mom was assigned to a tiny, shared room, even though I had explicitly arranged for a private room during my tour of the facility the day before. The cramped quarters, the constant presence of a stranger—it felt like an intrusion on her dignity, even in her unconscious state.

Eventually, the morphine arrived, and I was able to have Mom moved to a private corner room. The space was larger, quieter, and more peaceful. A sense of calm settled over me as I watched her rest, her breathing finally more even and relaxed. Perhaps, in some way, she felt it, too, a subtle easing of the distress that had clouded her final days.

After that, I would visit Mom daily, just for a few minutes. It was truly unbelievable how her body refused to shut down—a testament to the strong woman that she was. Another week went by, where she existed in this half-dead state. Then one morning I received a call as I was about to leave for work. I was informed that her breathing had slowed, and they believed she would pass soon. I hurried over, only to find she had died thirty seconds before I walked into the room. It felt strange to stand over her bed, looking at her stiff, lifeless body and the absence of breath. This was my mother, the woman who had given me life. And now, she was no more. I was an orphan. I stood over her, knowing the grief would come, but right now feeling only a sense of utter relief.

Managing another person's life is a profound responsibility, one I hadn't anticipated when I initially agreed to oversee Mom's finances. Yet I, the youngest of her four children, had found myself at the helm of her care, managing her life, navigating the turbulent waters of her declining health and the complexities of her personality for nearly twelve years. There wasn't much left in the end, but Mom didn't run out of money.

In a strange twist of fate, I became the parent she'd never quite been to me, maybe one she herself didn't have either. Perhaps I was more patient, more understanding, and more attuned to her needs. Or maybe, in caring for her, I was unconsciously seeking the love and acceptance I craved as a child, the validation that had always seemed just out of reach.

Whatever the underlying reasons, those years were a poignant blend of duty, love, and a lingering sense of longing. Caring for an aging loved one is never easy, especially when dementia casts its long shadow. It's a journey fraught with challenges, heartbreak, and unexpected moments of grace.

PART THREE

ME AND
YOU...

45

DRIVEN TO TEARS

November 2013, the month Mom passed, was the month I realized I'd become a master of not just the music biz and automotive marketing, but also elder care, medical bureaucracy, real estate, managing a trust fund, and navigating family matters. It was an education forged in the fires of experience, an MBA in the school of life, with a minor in managing Mom's eccentricities. Oh, and I'd also grasped a world of numbers that would have made Dad do a backflip in his grave.

And through it all, Marketing Factory flourished. Our marquee event, the Honda Civic Tour, was riding high on two incredibly success-ful years. In 2012, we featured Linkin Park and My Chemical Romance, and in 2013, Maroon 5 and Kelly Clarkson.

In January 2013, I orchestrated a press event at the Sundance Film Festival in Park City, Utah, for Acura, the automotive sponsor of the festival, to launch the premiere of the documentary *History of the Eagles, Part One*. Serendipitously, I found myself sitting next to Don Henley, who was seeing the finished film for the first time. Before the movie began, we struck up a conversation. I was tempted to mention that I was the guy who'd worked with him on his Walden Woods benefit concert some twenty years prior, and the letter he'd written, acknowledging me. But I resisted. Instead, we talked about his excitement for the new doc. "I'm eager to see how it all came together," Don confessed, a hint of ner-vousness in his voice.

I mentioned something about the Austin City Limits Music Festival, knowing his daughter was working for the promoter. He lit up, a proud dad, and launched into a story about her. "She was an English major at Emerson," he beamed. "A real chip off the old block, though she's thankfully chosen a less chaotic path than her dad." It was surreal, sitting there with a rock legend, making casual conversation. And it was a testament to how far I'd come in the entertainment industry.

Marketing Factory was on a roll. We were arranging unique offerings for Honda at three music festivals annually, producing entertainment for their annual dealer meeting, and landing a variety of other high-profile assignments.

Toward the end of 2013, we were gearing up for the 2014 Honda Civic Tour and had tentatively secured a coup, Kings of Leon as the headliner, just as a new head of marketing arrived at Honda. He was eager to make his mark and felt it necessary to stress-test every existing program, including ours. I strikingly remember him slamming his hand on the table during a meeting, his face contorted in rage.

"I heard the singer's a drunk!" he roared. "They're on my iPod and I'm not in the demo! Those are just two reasons we're not fucking doing Kings of Leon!"

No one from Honda had ever spoken to me like that, pretty much like, well, an asshole.

"But..." I tried to reason, "they're a huge draw! Tons of cred. They'll bring in a massive audience!"

He just glared at me. "I don't care. Find someone else."

Unfortunately, he forced us to revamp the tour campaign. This resulted in three smaller tours with lesser-known, less impactful artists. More than a decade later, I'm still bummed about the loss of Kings of Leon.

It was that year, in August 2014, I purchased a retreat in Topanga Canyon, a beautiful and rugged area just a few miles from the coast in the Santa Monica Mountains just south of Malibu. With its steep, sage-covered hills, majestic oak trees, open grassland, and lush streams, Topanga teemed with wildlife and had a rich history as the home of a who's who in music and Hollywood. The house was built in the 1970s and occupied a large plot of land, providing a secluded—and welcome—respite from city life. Mom would have loved it.

As for Honda, with new management in place, we rebounded in 2015 with our most successful Civic Tour ever, featuring teen sensations One Direction on a fifteen-city stadium outing. We followed that with Demi Lovato and Nick Jonas in 2016 and One Republic in 2017.

Marketing Factory was a magnet for talent, a dynamic mix of personalities and ambitions. Some, like Natasha Hamidi, became integral parts of the company's fabric. Natasha, with her unflappable calm and genuine warmth, managed our finances and HR for years. I watched her family grow, offering her the flexibility to bring her newborns to the office and creating a private space for her in our new location. Back then, that kind of support was rare, but it felt essential to me, a way to acknowledge the *person* who was the employee. It cemented a loyalty and trust that proved invaluable.

Our early success was a rush, fueled by a team of dedicated individuals who threw themselves into the chaotic energy of a burgeoning company. Jason and Horacio were indispensable in those startup days, their combined expertise laying the foundation for our growth. Jennifer and Jamie, with their infectious enthusiasm and sharp minds, were instrumental in getting us off the ground. Victor, our side-hustling initial IT guru, kept our systems humming in those first few years, a quiet force ensuring that the technology never faltered. He passed the baton to Clifford, who brought his own brand of tech wizardry to the team for over a decade.

We even had two exceptional Matts. The first, a UCSB grad with a knack for numbers and deejaying, was a client services whiz. He juggled budgets, exceeded expectations, and kept Honda happy. Alongside him, Russell navigated the complexities of artist relations, ensuring smooth operations on the ground. The second Matt, an entrepreneurial USC alum who also deejayed and ran his own record label, brought his creative flair to production and design, his skills evident in every sleek marketing campaign.

The years had brought a stream of talented individuals: the ambitious Heather, who produced events with tireless energy. Sydney and Shaelen, whose contributions in the later years were invaluable. Our road warriors, Dan, David, and Max, kept the tours running smoothly, their resilience tested on countless highways and in countless venues. And then there was Levi, a rising star recommended by Bob Dylan's manager. I saw a spark in him, a potential successor, but the allure of a major global opportunity in Texas proved too strong.

Marketing Factory was a crucible, forging skills and ambitions. It was exhilarating to witness the growth and to see employees blossom into confident professionals. Some moved on to major corporations like Apple, Harman Kardon, and Universal Music, their Marketing Factory experience a steppingstone to bigger things. Others embraced the entrepreneurial spirit, launching their own multimillion-dollar ventures with the same passion and drive they'd honed in our small office.

But managing people wasn't always a success story. It was a mirror reflecting my own shortcomings and my struggles with communication and connection. There was the brilliant strategist, paralyzed by his fear of failure, unable to step into a leadership role. His timidity frustrated me, a stark contrast to the bold, decisive action I craved. Then there were the imitators, mirroring my every move, seeking validation through mimicry rather than forging their own paths. It was unnerving, this distorted reflection, and it saddened me to see their unique talents suppressed. Those in need of constant handholding, who seemed incapable of independent thought or action, drained my energy and patience. Their need for incessant reassurance felt like a weight on my shoulders, a burden I wasn't always equipped to carry.

My own anxieties fueled my not-always-perfect boss status with my employees, as well as certain decisions I made. I expected people to read my mind, to anticipate *my* needs without clear communication. I often projected my insecurities onto them, creating an environment of tension and unmet expectations.

I also had my personal life to manage. I was in an on-and-off dating relationship with someone who became difficult to be with. She suddenly decided to get an Australian Shepherd puppy, just like mine. It was tough for her to keep him in her apartment with no yard, so he mostly stayed with me. I named him Ernest, but she called him Ernesto. He was born in 2016 and is still my loyal best friend today. The girl? Her life took a different turn after that.

By 2017, I was fifty-five and was being peppered with questions about why I hadn't married yet by friends, clients, and even random people I met at parties and work functions. Each time someone asked me that, I thought to myself, *What an asshole for asking something so personal,* while I would matter-of-factly answer, "Because I haven't found the right person yet—you know how that works."

During those conversations, I never imagined that Layla, a beautiful young woman from the Canadian province of Ontario, was even an option. We'd first met in 2003 when Layla visited my old friend Chelsea in Venice Beach. Layla, at 5'11, towered over me. At the time, she was in her early twenties, and I was in my early forties.

Fourteen years later, Chelsea, who had long since left Venice, came to visit me over the summer. One day, she happened to be video chatting with Layla, who I definitely remembered, and Chelsea brought me into the conversation. Later Layla and I friended each other on Facebook and started messaging. Over time, our conversations became increasingly intense. We talked about our lives, goals, philosophies—you name it.

Layla had been abandoned at a young age by her mother. Her father, Phil, was a farmer, and he had stepped up and raised her with unwavering love and support. Layla had lost her sibling in an accident. She studied topics related to the environment and the impact of human activities on it and possessed a captivating sense of confidence and beauty. Her unique physical features included high cheekbones accentuating her exotic, luminescent blue eyes. Her olive-toned skin was a testament to her external radiance, with inner strength and incredible poise despite a slightly wild side she occasionally exhibited. Though our communications were those of friends, my attraction to Layla grew as I discovered how much we had in common and how interested I was in her story.

Some months later, I confided in Layla, "I wish I could find someone like you in LA. Someone who shares my passions, someone who's kind and compassionate, someone who understands me."

Her response: "Why not *me*?"

Dumbstruck, I revealed my intimate insecurities: "Seriously, I never imagined you would have any interest, given your towering height over me and the fact you live in Canada."

She responded, "So what?" and suddenly, all was right with the world. Within the next few days, we made plans for her to visit me. I hadn't been this excited since I was a little kid, waiting for Santa.

The day finally arrived. Layla walked off the tarmac and into my arms, then my car. We engaged in the obligatory banter about her flight and the events of her day. Finding someone who shared my eclectic mix of interests felt like discovering a rare gem. We connected on everything from music and fashion to politics and spirituality. We were both early risers, energized by the morning light and fueled by healthy meals. We even shared a similar sense of style—casually smart, with a touch of individualized flair. And when she expressed her desire to learn how to surf, I knew I had found someone truly special. We hooked up, and our bond rose to unprecedented heights. Celestial bodies collided, and pyrotechnic displays flashed in my mind. It felt *so right*.

We floated between my Venice Beach place and my mountain hideaway. She didn't care about sightseeing LA. But when we cruised toward Malibu along the Pacific Coast Highway one day, with the ocean beside us, something outrageously whimsical went down. Layla and I had been intimate for only about two weeks at this point, and as she leaned into me, she let slip, "I would *marry* you."

Well, fuck me running! I almost crashed the car. I had to ask her to repeat herself, to make sure my mush of a brain wasn't just messing with me. Was she speaking metaphorically? Was she trying to get me to propose? Was she proposing?

She paused for a second and said, "Yeah, I want to marry you, Rob."

Holy fucking shit. My blood started racing through my veins. I didn't have a clue what I was feeling at that moment. It was like some out-of-body experience. This nearly-perfect creature just waltzed into my life and straight-up asked me to spend the rest of my days with her. *Pinch me, tell me it's all just a dream.*

It *wasn't* just a dream. After returning to my place, we had a conversation fueled by the intoxicating effects of sexual desire and love in which she affirmed her sincerity. I couldn't help but chime in and enthusiastically agree. Within three months, I bought her a diamond engagement ring, and she continued to fly back and forth from Canada to Los Angeles every two weeks.

I had finally found Mrs. Right. Or had I? I forgot to mention that she had two young daughters, five and seven years old, and was embroiled in a nasty custody-divorce battle. Regardless, she created a scenario in which the two girls spent two weeks with her, then two weeks with their daddy, and on it went. In the meantime, I was spending two weeks with Layla in the flesh, and then we'd chat daily long-distance. I felt connected and faithfully engaged. We made plans together.

One day, at the mountain house in Topanga, as I shared plans for a total demolition and rebuild, Layla's face lit up. She was completely on board with the idea of transforming the house into a modern, spacious haven. The Venice Beach house, though charming, held little appeal for her.

"This place has so much potential," I said, gesturing toward the sweeping views. "Visualize: natural privacy, floor-to-ceiling windows, a chef's kitchen, a pool overlooking the canyon...." I imagined clean lines and rustic modernist aesthetics.

"It's perfect," she agreed, her eyes shining. "We can really make this our dream home, a place where the girls can grow up with space and freedom."

The girls had loved their summer camp experience in LA, and the thought of enrolling them in a local school and providing them with a stable, loving home filled us both with joy.

Layla's property in Canada, however, was a different story. While she acknowledged its beauty and potential, she spoke of it with a touch of detachment. The remnants of that idealistic time, the space dedicated to her former passions, the physical manifestation of her abandoned plans—it was a life she was ready to redefine.

"It's beautiful, of course," she admitted, "but it's also a lot of work. And to be honest, I'm ready for a fresh start, a simpler life."

The idea of selling the Canadian property and focusing all our energy on Topanga resonated with both of us. It felt like a clean break, a chance to build a new future together, unburdened by the past.

"This is where we belong," Layla said, taking my hand. "This is where we'll create our happily ever after."

And with that, we delved into the details of the renovation, our hearts filled with dreams of a married future filled with love, family, and the promise of a life well-lived in our mountain haven.

Layla painted a picture of her ex-husband's imminent return to the US, her words imbued with a hopeful certainty that I found infectious. Apparently, he had often spoken of missing the spirit of the West, the landscapes of his youth, and she seemed convinced that his Canadian chapter was coming to a close. His residing back in the US would make it that much easier for Layla and the girls to relocate to California and build a life with me.

I hung on her every word, eager to believe in this future she painted so vividly.

But even in my optimism, a flicker of doubt remained. Was this truly his plan, or simply a hope that Layla clung to? A seed of unease was sown, but I quickly buried it, choosing to bask in the warmth of her conviction.

Within the initial three months, with the massive renovation of our mountain house, Layla and I moved into temporary quarters down the street in Topanga. To ease the burden of managing the remodeling project, Layla stepped in to assist me as I juggled my full-time job and other responsibilities. To offset the monetary impact of this endeavor, I decided to rent out my beach house, allowing us to break even financially.

Throughout our relationship Layla and I went on several wonderful trips. Our early days were a whirlwind of adventures. We explored New York City, a dizzying maze of energy and excitement. We took a California road trip on which I introduced Layla to my family, their warm embraces a stark contrast to the pesky uncertainty in me that lay somewhere beneath the surface. We even escaped to France for a week, enveloped in the beauty of Provence. We stayed in a friend's magnificent château, where lavender fields stretched toward the horizon, and the air was filled with the scent of pine and warm earth. We dined on exquisite meals under the shade of ancient trees, explored charming villages, and wandered through sun-drenched vineyards. The week culminated in an unforgettable night, with The Rolling Stones belting out their iconic anthems under the starry sky of Marseilles.

But perhaps even more memorable were our two cross-country road trips from Texas to California. We piled into a tour van, my two dogs jostling for space, and set off with a driver/tour manager at the wheel. Dibs, as I came to call him, was more than just an employee; he was our navigator, our resident comedian, and, increasingly, my confidant. He handled every detail, from booking hotels to navigating winding roads, allowing Layla and me to simply enjoy the ride.

Looking back, I realize the immense privilege of it all. To travel with such ease, with someone else managing the logistics, was a luxury I'd never experienced before. It was breathtaking freedom, a sense of being utterly cared for. Layla's love and devotion, amplified by Dibs's attentiveness to every detail, created a bubble of blissful ease, plus we could pour cocktails and smoke weed along the road.

And what a ride it was! The blistering heat of Austin gave way to an unexpected flurry of snow in Waco, leaving us ill-prepared but exhilarated by the wildness of it all. We found ourselves in Marfa, Texas, a dusty oasis and artistic haven, where we bunked in a vintage Spartan trailer—a quirky coincidence considering I had recently completed a renovation of a Fifties Spartan, transforming it into a stylish guest retreat on the Topanga property. In Taos, New Mexico, we indulged in glamping, soaking in pristine hot springs as the first snowflakes of October dusted the high desert. Every day and night was a new adventure, a kaleidoscope of rugged campsites, extravagant escapes, and comforting stays at roadside motels, punctuated by the occasional Ritz-Carlton splurge. A road trip is far more than a journey, it is a profound means of truly getting to know another soul. With every mile traveled, we grew closer. Layla also spoke to me of her children.

Over time, I forged a deep bond with Diana and Renee, Layla's two daughters, and found myself morphing into a paternal figure, a role I'd never envisioned. My connection with Diana, the eldest, was particularly strong. We formed an inseparable alliance, a world of inside jokes, shared secrets, and endless laughter. It was exhilarating to be their mentor, their protector, their confidant. I cherished every moment, every question, every silly story. I didn't just talk to them; I truly talked *with* them. I assumed the role of mentor and shepherd, grateful for each interaction. I thoroughly felt like a parent to children for the first time in my life.

Then subtle shifts began to emerge. The ex-husband refused to grant the girls dual citizenship, dampening our dream of a shared life in LA. Layla, wrong about him returning to the US, was now burdened by the strain of her divorce and her ex-husband's obstinacy. She grew increasingly anxious. The carefree joy of our early days started to fade, replaced by a growing undercurrent of worry and frustration.

Doubts now clouded a future that had once seemed clear, and my attempts to balance my conflicting emotions strained our relationship.

On the one hand, I loved Layla deeply and cherished every moment we spent together. On the other, I began to question the feasibility of our fantasy due to logistic challenges. Layla mentioned moving to LA and figuring out how to bring the kids later, which triggered deep-seated abandonment issues within me. There was no way I was going to be the cause of her leaving her children. I firmly told her that was out of the question.

I thought about moving to Canada, but the construction of the mountain house was well underway, leaving little room for turning back. Furthermore, I had Marketing Factory with clients and employees, making it challenging to abandon everything. We often began to argue about things unrelated to the issues at hand. The intensity of our bickering escalated due to our built-up frustration.

Our life together, woven with threads of adventure, laughter, and love, unraveled with a final, heartbreaking tug. After two and a half years, the impossible truth lay bare: we were a beautiful impossibility. The realization pierced me like a shard of glass, leaving a wound that would take far longer than two and a half years to heal.

46

THE SOUND OF SILENCE

Losing Layla ripped open the scars of abandonment, leaving me raw and back in therapy. As the fog of depression began to lift, my vision became astoundingly clear. It dawned on me that while I was so focused on my relationship with Layla, Marketing Factory, once a formidable force, was slipping through my grasp.

Honda was my primary client, and the financial rewards were quite lucrative. I was a supplier of ideas. Each time Honda agreed to one of my ideas, my team and I brought it to life in the best conceivable way. Through the years, I had creatively collaborated with artists such as blink-182, Incubus, Maroon5, One Direction, Demi Lovato, Fall Out Boy, Black Eyed Peas, Paramore, OneRepublic, Panic! at the Disco, Charlie Puth, and many others. I also was able to partner with music festivals such as Lollapalooza, Sasquatch!, Governors Ball, Austin City Limits, and Music Midtown. I interacted with such top acts as John Legend, Steve Miller Band, The B-52's, Kenny Loggins, Train, Zac Brown, Ziggy Marley, Pitbull, Jewel, Paul Simon, Santana, Brian Wilson, Eagles, and Foo Fighters.

I even had an opportunity to work with historically black colleges and universities for an annual pilgrimage to Atlanta, where their marching bands participated in a Battle of the Bands, which was a rewarding and emotional experience. The students' enthusiasm, dedication, and skill filled the Georgia Dome stadium, and I produced a performance video titled "Stompin' at the Dome" to capture and commemorate the event.

My career relied on a fluctuating knowledge of artists. I had to predict which artists or music properties were on the rise. Like a worthwhile investment money manager, the goal was to buy low and sell high, providing returns along the way. The buying centered around negotiating at the right time while they were trending, and the selling was the marketing program—centered around public messaging and interaction—which was meant to happen at their peak.

But my productivity was declining with age. I was probably at my peak around age thirty-six, which was near the beginning of my company. Then, I had a knack for knowing what worked. It was like when I was a mobile deejay, years before I could read the crowd and know exactly which song to play next to keep the energy high. This felt similar, but instead of music, it was bands and marketing campaigns. But by fifty-six, that instinct wasn't as sharp. It was harder to connect with the new bands, now mostly pop, rappers, and deejays, and I relied on research and my staff as much as my intuition.

Simultaneously, Honda was shifting its internal priorities. A new Japanese CEO was brought in to oversee American Honda and several executives who were loyal to my programs and who knew their origin, efficiency, and value either retired or were pushed out.

When Honda held a dealer meeting event, I was responsible for securing the entertainment and producing the concert for the final night's celebration. This is a common practice among auto manufacturers to show appreciation for their franchised dealers. Owners and general managers of most of the brand dealerships from across the country fly in for a few days to hear the general plan for the future year, see the newest physical vehicles and prototypes, preview new commercials and marketing campaigns, and schmooze with one another. Honda paid for everything except for their hotel rooms and flights.

Each year dealers looked forward to a private concert by some big-name artist on the final night. We also always arranged a band meet-and-greet with top Honda executives and their guests, usually a handful of particularly prominent dealers. In the year in question, One Republic was the band and the Japanese CEO of American Honda was among the VIPs in a private room before the show. Somehow, a conversation began between Mr. Iwamura—all Japanese executives are referred to as Mister, "insert last name here"—and me. I asked him how he liked the Civic Tour and thanked him for continually renewing it and being supportive. Some small talk ensued, and then he turned to tell me he was not happy about the Honda Civic Tour logo because the "H" was too close to the other elements in the logo. There was supposed to be an isolation area, and he found the logo disrespectful to Honda. I thanked him for his input and quickly moved on to schmooze with someone else.

Shepard Fairey, a famous American contemporary artist, activist, and founder of the OBEY fashion brand, was the person who had designed and blessed the logo. As far as pop culture goes, he is likely more well-known than the Civic Tour. Honda's marketing staff that happened to be in the United States understood the value of the logo, and while I told them of Mr. Iwamura's dissatisfaction, nothing ever changed.

What was essential to Mr. Iwamura was thought-provoking. In his culture respect is paramount. When greeting each other in America we shake hands as a way to show peaceful intent, to *connect*. When greeting each other in Japan, Japanese people bow as a way to show *respect*. In America, if I gave my business card to someone, they might glance at it and then smile at me to connect with me. In Japan, the expected protocol is to receive a business card with both hands and study it carefully to show respect. At the time, I felt Mr. Iwamura didn't fully appreciate how effectively the tour campaign connected young people with our brand. Yet he was concerned with what made sense to him culturally—outward-facing respect for American Honda.

Loyalty in a Japanese company was always important, too, and it worked both ways. I was willing to bleed for Honda, and they were supportive, as long as the campaigns were measurably successful.

Unfortunately, under the new Honda with new executives who barely knew me, loyalty became less important. Ideas, even good ones, had less value. Morale sunk.

My company had survived several minor regime changes over the previous two decades, but this was a top-down adjustment. Each department was challenged to cut spending to become more efficient and reevaluate everything. The management team took control of our Honda Civic Tour and immediately disagreed with our artist recommendations. We presented them with what I felt, what I knew, were some stellar options within their budget range, but they didn't like any of them. They wanted someone bigger, something better.

I developed and delivered a white paper showing that their proposed investment was far below the going market rate for what they were seeking. In the twenty years since our launch of the Honda Civic Tour, many more brands had entered the music market, which kept prices soaring. On top of that, in the early years of the Civic Tour, Honda's promotion of artists meant a lot, but with time, the flood of brands and bands crowded the market and made such exposure less valuable to artists. There were other factors, too, that made pulling rabbits out of hats more complicated, including relationships I had with some music managers who had aged out.

Honda was not impressed by my financial white paper report and solution-based narrative. I don't know if they even read it. Unbeknownst to me, they decided to entertain proposals from other entities that they determined might be better at serving the Civic Tour. Word of this leaked back to me almost immediately. I confronted them and they divulged their plan of putting my project out to bid, telling me that I was in consideration but would have to answer their request for a new proposal the same way as the other new potential vendors.

My heart sank when they told me. If Honda was a romantic partner, they had just said they wanted to take a break and maybe see other people. Was this the same as being fired? Was it what happens in a romance when one partner isn't "feeling it"? I had conceived of the Civic Tour, nurtured it for two decades, and ridden its mostly highs and a few lows. And now, it seemed to me, they wanted someone else to take over. My company was vulnerable because it depended on one big company for 85 percent of its revenue. I had attempted to expand our revenue stream by prospecting for new clients in the hopes of securing another brand or two that would hire us on the same level as Honda. None of it worked.

Life was pummeling me down all at once. My girlfriend, who had become my first-ever fiancé, was gone; Honda was on the cusp of leaving me; and all of this was coming at me at a time when I'd undertaken a weighty financial commitment to remodel my home, turning an undeveloped property with a cabin and swimming pool into a cherished compound. I just wanted to bury my head in the sand.

But I had to make a gigantic decision. Did I want to continue with Honda or not? We had made history together and I had thought our relationship meant something. For the very first Civic Tour in 2001, we filmed content with blink-182, in which they showed us their customized Honda Civic for the first time. I hadn't met the band prior to that shoot, but we agreed to do everything in San Diego out of convenience for them since they were based there. Mark Hoppus and Tom DeLonge were on set, and we were all waiting for Travis Barker. I went with my friend Alli McGregor from Creative Artists Agency to his dressing room area to find him, and he was walking down the hallway toward us as we headed toward him. I immediately noticed a huge, shiny belt buckle that was the Cadillac crest.

I announced, "Hey, Travis. I'm Rob. Is there any way you could wear a different belt buckle?"

Those were my first words. Alli looked at me in horror! How could I have said that to him? I just glared back and told her, without him hearing, that if it's visible, the footage won't be able to be used. He didn't remove the buckle. Somehow, we salvaged the content, and it didn't appear as a recognizable item in anything.

Ten years later, when blink-182 returned to headline the tenth anniversary of the Honda Civic Tour, we finished our final show at the Hollywood Bowl. I went backstage afterward to thank the crew for their hard work and stopped into Tom's dressing room since I had developed a relationship with him. We chatted for a bit, and I was able to thank him. Then I said hello to Mark and thanked him as well—we had worked together on other projects, so we knew each other as well. I didn't think Travis would have any idea who I was, but as I passed him in the hallway filled with people, he turned around and stretched out his arm to shake my hand, looked me in the eye, and said, "Thanks, Rob, I appreciate the opportunity. We had fun, man!"

Being recognized by the band's most famous member, whom I insulted on day one, was confirmation that things were going well. At the time I felt great about Honda, the Civic Tour, Marketing Factory, and myself. Now, not so much.

There might have been some truth when the head of national advertising at Honda told me our incumbency would undoubtedly be considered during the request for proposal process. Still, it struck me as more than a little bizarre to hear him say, "If you want to continue to operate the successful campaign that you [conceived of and] produced for Honda over the past twenty years, you have a good chance, but management above me wants to open bidding to others."

Unfortunately, I never had intellectual property rights to my creation, thanks to corporate America. Honda's legal team had advised them to own everything. In working this program for Honda, I had to hand it over to them for no compensation other than the hiring of my company to operate it, and each year, that contract was up for review and renewal. Honda had nineteen previous opportunities, one each year, to reach out to others before renewing our contract, but they had not done so. The executives I worked with before the most recent regime change expressed gratitude and appreciation for our work. There were even times when they had funds left over in their annual budget that they needed to spend, so they booked purchase orders for us that required little work in return. It was just one more way of saying thank you.

Running a small business in general had been tricky. I'd dealt with subversions, a merger, an acquisition, planning, building, rebuilding, financing, firing, rewarding, operating, promoting, creating, coaching, defending, leading, and unwinding. In starting Marketing Factory, I followed an inner sense, a vision. It sounds corny but there's a scene in the 1989 film *Field of Dreams* in which Kevin Costner is walking through a cornfield at sunset with a shovel and hears a voice speaking to him that says, "If you build it, they will come." It repeats a few times, haunting him as he checks back with people on the porch of the nearby house and asks them if they heard the voice. Of course, they had no idea what he was talking about because the voice came from within him.

Through my own experiences, I've come to realize that many of us possess an inner voice capable of answering our questions. If you stop and carefully tune in to what's inside of you, you will develop a reliance on yourself to guide you. With Marketing Factory, I listened to that voice when starting the company, like the time I was running on the soft beach sand and the idea of customizing the Civic came to me. Over time, I became so stressed and pressured that I stopped listening to it and let my anxiety take the helm. Each time I did this, a new challenge developed.

After sleeping on it for two nights, I made my decision. I told Honda that while I appreciated the opportunity to bid on the Civic Tour alongside such heavyweights as Live Nation and iHeartMedia, "we have decided not to accept or respond to any request for proposal regarding the Honda Civic Tour. Further, I've given the other major project some thought as well. We would also like to formally resign and exit our agreement as music fest program producers." There are times in your life you just have to move on.

The newest head of marketing was silent for a moment, thanked me, and told me someone would be in touch to begin transitions. I walked away from not only the opportunity to fight to retain the Honda Civic

Tour but also from the music festivals, a sure thing. Had I cut off my nose to spite my face, as they say? Had my anger over Honda's decision not to automatically renew the tour agreement caused me to make a rash decision I would wind up regretting? Was my fear that they would abandon me so great that I walked away from what could have been an opportunity to make my relationship with Honda even better?

Six years later, I'm still not sure what the answer is. Live Nation, the world's number one live music brand, with annual revenue of more than $10 billion, won the bid to manage the Civic Tour. Yet maybe it was fortunate that Honda was to move forward without me. The winding down of the company happened throughout 2019, with our final project in September, a private concert with Weezer for the annual dealer meeting in Washington, DC. Just a few months later, in the spring of 2020, the world stopped, changed, and adapted to a new normal due to the COVID-19 pandemic. My business would have been suspended and possibly even wiped out had we continued to work with Honda. My sudden and unexpected retirement, and adjusting to a life with no work after nearly forty-five years of almost nothing *besides* work, could not have been better timed had I tried to step off the bus at any other point.

The music business, and the music itself, had evolved dramatically over my career. I went from funk, soul, rock 'n' roll oldies, and Top 40 to new wave, then grunge, hip-hop, rap, electronic, and deejay-produced beats. Along the way, I had an eclectic personal taste in music, with favorites running the gamut from Sly and the Family Stone to The Clash to Willie Nelson to U2 to The Rolling Stones to Die Antwoord. Endorsements and sponsorship have also evolved, from none to many, a veritable plethora of what are now called "ambassadorships" and "exclusive collaborations."

I, however, took the right offramp, retreated to my mountain home, and planted veggies, poppies, and fruit trees.

47

FAME

It's been said that people who are driven, like me, are generally motivated by fame, fortune, or both. I suppose there's a fair amount of truth in that. While my career has certainly allowed me to enjoy a higher standard of living than my dad ever had, even without the college degree he valued above all else, I ventured into entertainment because I wanted to be somebody. I wanted to be seen; I wanted to be heard.

Fame. That's what I wanted; that's what I was drawn to. I never did manage to become the next legendary promoter like Bill Graham, or prominent entertainment business titan like Irving Azoff. But I did rise high enough in the music industry hierarchy to be in a position to rub elbows with some of the most influential figures in the history of rock 'n' roll and popular music, like Paul McCartney, Brian Wilson, and Mick Jagger.

I'd met and had drinks with hot actress Diane Lane alongside the infamous record promotion man Charlie Minor at Le Dome Restaurant, at one of his Tuesday night affairs. A few years later Charlie Minor would be murdered at his Malibu home.

I'd spilled a beer on Billy Idol's leather pants, got bitched out by Lou Reed and Gene Simmons, and drove Kenny Loggins around Napa, looking for a good hiking trail. I sat between Don Henley and Glenn Frey at the Sundance Film Festival premiere of the Eagles documentary as they chatted and reminisced about the celebrated band's rise to glory. I drove an almost-passed-out Steven Adler, the original Guns N' Roses drummer, in the back of my SUV from Orange County to Laurel Canyon. I played golf with Counting Crows guitarist Dave Bryson, went to a theatrical performance in Venice Beach with U2's the Edge, and almost went to the Super Bowl with Hunter S. Thompson.

I had drinks with Keanu Reeves, got booted from a strip club while hanging with Eddie Van Halen, shook hands with Donald Trump at the Caribou Club in Aspen long before his presidential days, and hung with Cuba Gooding Jr. at a Christmas party at Adam Sandler's producing partner's house.

On a personal note, I recently dated an actress whose father was an A-list celebrity in the 1970s.

Casey Kasem, also of that era, hosted the nationally syndicated *American Top 40* countdown show and its various offshoots for upward of three decades. But I first knew him as the voice of Shaggy on the *Scooby-Doo* cartoons, which I watched religiously as a child. Years later, in the 1990s, we met while I worked at Westwood One, the syndicator of his second countdown show, *Casey's Top 40*. The program aired on Sunday mornings across many Top 40 stations in the United States. I had the opportunity to meet Casey a few times and even created some promotions that were featured on the show. Writing promotional copy that Casey delivered in his famous voice was a career highlight for me.

Another icon I also had the good fortune of meeting was Prince. My connection to Prince's music dates back to late 1979 when he released, "I Wanna Be Your Lover." The sheer freshness of his sound captivated me, and I was astounded to discover that he wrote, performed, and played every instrument on the track. As a sixteen-year-old radio deejay spinning his records, I felt a kinship with him, similar to Dick Clark and the Wolfman. We were both achieving great things at a young age, and I marveled at his ability to forge his path and create such daring music.

At the age of nineteen, I had the chance to see Prince in concert. In 1981, he was opening for The Rolling Stones at the Coliseum in Los Angeles. The crowd's response to his performance perplexed me: they hissed, booed, and even hurled stuff at him. He, however, remained unfazed, standing tall and proud in his extra-high heels and a long trench coat as he fearlessly rocked the house. I remember feeling bad for him. Evidently, people were not yet prepared for an artist of his skin color, his gender ambiguity, and his unique dance music.

As time passed, all of that changed. Prince became one of the biggest superstars of the eighties and nineties. I vividly recall seeing him perform at The Forum and later at an outdoor venue in Irvine, California, during the peak of *Purple Rain*, his highly acclaimed 1984 album. He dominated an entire era of music. The song "1999," in particular, was a stroke of brilliance, captivating listeners for seventeen years leading up to that fateful year. Although the predicted apocalypse did not happen, the song remained a classic. Prince always managed to stay relevant, committed, and unique in our chaotic and complex world. He sold his tickets and music without the need for agents, a genuine artist, with a capital 'A.'

We crossed paths in 2006 at a post-Grammy Awards party, hosted by the William Morris Agency in an elegant Bel Air mansion. I was walking on this narrow second-story hallway, almost like a catwalk, connecting two house sections. I noticed a person with a hat walking toward me from the other end, whom I immediately recognized as Prince. At one time I had a roommate who was Prince's chef, and he had told me many stories about The Purple One, including how employees were not allowed to ever look him in the eyes. If he caught anyone looking at him, they were fired on the spot. I moved to one side to allow Prince to pass by me and he looked straight at me, into my eyes, and even gave me a nod, a tip of his hat as an acknowledgment. It made me feel as if he saw me as something of an equal—a warm and lasting memory.

Prince's untimely death in 2016 at the age of fifty-seven transported me back to the moment I first heard his music. I reflected on how music today has shifted its focus from substance to performance. We seem to have skipped over the essence and gone straight for the flash.

My encounter with Lou Reed, leader of the legendary avant-garde group The Velvet Underground, and later a hugely successful solo artist, was not so warm. He was known as much for his experimental and influential songwriting and guitar playing as he was for his abrasive demeanor. In 1986, while I was promotion director at 91X, management wanted me to secure Lou Reed as a spokesperson who would appear in a television commercial for the station. Lou Reed was based in New York City and his influence extended beyond his music. He was deeply intertwined with the glam rock, Andy Warhol, art, and cultural scene, making him the epitome of cool. 91X was known as "The Cutting Edge of Rock and Roll," and no performer was more cutting edge than Lou Reed.

When I contacted his manager, he suggested Lou might be open to the idea if we funded the production of an MTV public service spot in which Lou would appear on behalf of Rock Against Drugs, or RAD. Reed had been a heavy user of alcohol and methamphetamine and occasionally dabbled in heroin; he had weaned himself off drugs and was eager to proselytize about his newfound sobriety. I willingly seized the opportunity and enlisted a producer in New York City, who in turn found a director. Together, we developed a storyboard and a script to present to Lou's manager for Mr. Reed's consideration.

To everyone's delight and surprise, Lou agreed to participate free of charge. Filming took place at the director's studio, where I, as the client representing the station, supervised the production. Our director would be the same talented individual who had received Clio Awards for directing the iconic 1971 "Crying Indian" keep America beautiful TV PSA. That ad featured an actor, an Italian American from Louisiana who called himself Iron Eyes Cody, dressed in stereotypical Native American garb and shedding a tear when he saw someone throwing trash from a car window.

Our 91X commercial was filmed against a red brick wall, featuring the station's yellow logo spray painted onto it with just enough light to see it. Lou Reed, wearing a black-leather jacket and aviator shades, stood in the dimly lit room in front of the wall, basking in a soft blue light. The focus was mainly on his upper body, from the waist up. Watching the scene, I felt that Lou's delivery lacked the necessary punchiness for the copy. I approached the producer, who suggested I speak with the director. I asked the director if I could request Lou to "give it more energy," and surprisingly, he agreed to let me ask Lou. Unfortunately, it didn't go well. Lou was so insulted that he almost walked off the set. Though young twenty-four-year-old me beat himself up over that, it wasn't like Lou had a reputation as America's sweetheart.

Another legend, albeit from the world of film rather than music, who I briefly interacted with was Dennis Hopper. Hopper will forever be remembered as the director and star of the notorious Sixties road movie *Easy Rider*, in which he and Peter Fonda play a couple of bikers who travel throughout the Southwest with the proceeds from a cocaine deal. I discovered *Easy Rider* years after it came out theatrically and it immediately became one of my favorite films. I was captivated by Hopper's freewheeling, devil-may-care persona and his status as a counterculture rebel. Hopper's life had its share of challenges. Known for his temperamental nature and struggles with addiction, these obstacles undoubtedly affected his career. Yet much like his friend Jack Nicholson, he embodied cool. We both lived in Venice, and I was well aware that Hopper lived a few blocks away, on Indiana Avenue. Designed by the renowned architect Frank Gehry, his compound, not unlike him, stood out as a testament to Gehry's bold, unconventional style, which blended common materials with dynamic and intricate structures. I drove by often just to appreciate the architectural beauty—although a part of me was hoping for a chance encounter with Hopper. Later, I discovered Hopper's passion for fine art, which led me to become a fan of his photography. I attended exhibitions showcasing his work and found myself truly appreciating his range of artistic talent.

My random encounter with him in the spring of 1992 at an LA Sports Arena concert remains a cherished memory. After the show, I found myself standing next to him at a VIP bar. Empowered, as I so often was in those days, by alcohol and assertiveness, I extended my hand and introduced myself, offering to buy him a drink. Hopper courteously informed me of his sobriety, so I bought him a Pepsi instead. As we waited at the bar, I had the chance to express my profound admiration for his work, his creative spirit, and his refined taste. He was gracious and appeared genuinely thankful for my comments.

Jack Nicholson, I met a second time, some two decades after my first encounter with him on that eye-opening New Year's Eve in a fancy Aspen restaurant where I'd overheard him charming a woman. I'd been invited to a Lakers game at The Staples Center to enjoy championship-level basketball. It was late March 2011, and Kobe Bryant and Pau Gasol led the team against the Clippers. I had been told to arrive early and meet in the Wells Fargo Room, which I had never heard of before that night. The directions were a bit sketchy; you had to know the secret door to enter a stairway to get to a private level in the bowels of the building.

After a few wrong turns, I made it. Upon entering, I was transported to a dark, upscale lounge with a generous, elegant buffet of meats, vegetables, cheeses, sweets, fruits, and nearly every alcoholic beverage imaginable. Best of all, this smorgasbord was free in a building that charged twelve dollars for a sixteen-ounce beer.

Living in LA, I was no stranger to celebrity sightings. Out of the corner of my eye, I saw the exalted heartbreaker himself, Tom Petty, saunter past me and head for the exit. I got the signal that it was time to head to our seats. But first, I had to empty my bladder. I walked over to the door in the corner of the room, which led into a small foyer and, in turn, a lockable restroom. It was locked, so I stood in the foyer and waited. About thirty seconds later, the door was thrust open, and out walked ... Jack Nicholson—older, with less hair, a bit puffier, but instantly recognizable with his trademark sunglasses, stubble, and unconscious smugness.

I had to say something to him. My mind was racing to come up with an opening line. I abruptly said, "Mr. Nicholson, may I tell you a quick story before you go to your seat?"

He responded in full Jack mode with, "Of course, but make it fast because there's a game to see."

"You, sir, had the best line I've ever heard a man deliver to a woman," I blurted out.

To my relief, Jack broke into his signature smirk and smile. "Oh yeah, remind me—what that was?" he asked.

I told him the line I had overheard on that fateful New Year's Eve twenty years earlier: "Listen, puss, you know where to find me. If you need me, I'll be at my post."

It was a story I'd been telling for years, using my lousy but discernible "Jack Nicholson" voice. Now, though, telling *the* Jack Nicholson the story to his very face, I *didn't* use the voice. I was sure my delivery was flat as I thanked him profusely, and shook his hand.

"Good thing you reminded me so I can use that line again," Jack said.

Time stopped ... just as it had two decades earlier. Was it a coincidence or divine intervention that the one celebrity who sat at the top of my wish list granted me an almost accidental, one-on-one meet-and-greet in a small private foyer to a bathroom? I was elated. Maybe it was validation that I had obtained enough status to rub elbows with a megastar. Or, perhaps, it was something deeper. A yearning for recognition, not just from a megastar, but from the world at large. A whisper in my ear: *I matter, too. I have a voice, a perspective worth sharing.* It was a fleeting moment of connection, a reminder that we all seek a sense of belonging, a reassurance that our existence holds value.

And then there was the heiress and socialite Paris Hilton. My nephew, Jess, visited me in Los Angeles during his summer break from UCSB in early August 2007. I hadn't planned anything exciting for his visit, but I felt I had to keep him entertained. After reaching out to some friends, one of them came through with a brilliant suggestion. He was involved in a film project with Paris Hilton and mentioned that she was hosting a beach party over the same weekend. He invited us to join him. Paris, already a socialite, rose to global notoriety when her porn producer boyfriend, without her consent, leaked a video of them having sex. This became one of the first online sex videos of its time and turned Paris into a household name, as she followed it up by starring in a reality TV show.

Jess and I drove to Malibu, where Paris had a beach house. As we arrived and parked, we noticed that the entrance seemed unusually quiet for a big party. We made our way through the lower level of the narrow long house, its interior a surprising contrast to the laid-back beach location. The furniture, upholstered in busy patterns, exuded a sense of plush, over-the-top luxury, bringing to mind a baroque bordello. Large, gilded frames showcased photos of Paris in various modeling poses, dominating the walls. I couldn't help but think that her name, Paris, was rather fitting for the decor. The overall impression was one of ostentation, a stark contrast to the relaxed beach vibe we stepped into outside.

A deejay was spinning tunes, and a woman behind a barbecue was grilling away. There were only about twenty-five or thirty people at the party. After searching for my friend, I noticed that the person behind the turntables was none other than the talented recording artist and actress Macy Gray. The menu consisted of ballpark franks being grilled by Ms. Hilton's cleaning lady. *Hot dogs? Really, Paris?* I half expected her to pull out a can of spray cheese and a bag of Cheetos to complete the gourmet experience. I'd anticipated more from a star and hotel heiress.

Later, I went to use the restroom and noticed a red velvet rope blocking the stairwell leading to the upstairs area. I managed to find my friend and he introduced us to Paris, who seemed polite but uninterested. Observing her and her close friends' high energy and overt talkativeness as they went up and down the stairway with her, I suspected they were high on cocaine. In any case, for a teenager like Jess, meeting Paris and spending time at her beach house was quite cool.

As we were about to leave, my friend mentioned that he was planning to head east to a massive amphitheater nestled in the hills of Glen Helen Regional Park in San Bernardino, a blue-collar town about 100 miles from LA in what's known as the Inland Empire. This amphitheater, with a capacity of 65,000, holds the distinction of being the largest outdoor music venue in the entire United States. On this particular day, Rage Against the Machine was headlining a sold-out, day-long music festival. Would I by any chance like to come as well? The look in Jess's eyes when he heard the invitation was enough for me to respond with an eager, "Yes."

After nearly two hours on the road, we reached our destination well after dark. By then, Rage Against the Machine had already taken the stage. Accompanied by my friend, we wasted no time in obtaining our credentials and finding a parking spot. My strategy was to park near the edge of one of the many dirt lots, with the hope that it would provide us with a quicker exit and allow us to beat the post-concert traffic. Although I had seen Rage Against the Machine perform before, experiencing them at a huge outdoor venue in front of a wild crowd that had had all day to consume alcohol and various other mind-altering substances under the hot inland sun was something else. It felt quite intimidating to even step into the audience, so I chose to remain backstage for almost the entire show. Even my nephew, usually fearless, seemed a bit overwhelmed.

As the band played its final encore, it was already late at night, and I was eager to leave. However, my friend insisted that we stay a bit longer so he could say hi to his buddy Tom Morello, the celebrated guitarist and songwriter of the band. So now, after meeting Paris and Macy earlier in the day, Jess was about to meet Tom as well. We met with Tom, took some photos, and had a brief chat. Afterward, we embarked on a mission to find our car among the crowd of intoxicated concertgoers exiting the venue. I estimated that it had been at least half an hour since the band left the stage. *Surely, finding our car should be a breeze.* I was wrong. We walked this way and that, over here and over there. And when we finally did locate our vehicle, it was blocked in by a long line of cars waiting to exit.

It seemed futile to try to leave, so we decided to take a rest and wait. Half an hour later the line was still stuck though, so my bold friend from

Staten Island, who had an audacious personality typical of a New Yorker, decided to investigate the hold-up. With a burst of courage, he climbed on top of a nearby car and began shouting traffic directions to the drivers. Feeling embarrassed by his behavior, I slouched further into my seat, hoping not to contribute to any road rancor. But then, almost miraculously, people started listening to him. The cars gradually started moving forward, and an hour later, we were finally on the highway, making our way back home to the beach.

Music and film stars—and Paris Hilton—aren't the only celebrities I had the opportunity to meet. Shortly after launching my company in Venice in 1999, to specialize in audio content, I attended the MultiMediaCom conference in San Jose, in the heart of Silicon Valley. The internet was all the rage, and I wanted to learn all I could about the possibilities that might present themselves.

To my surprise, the familiar faces and names from traditional radio broadcasting were absent. Instead, the event was full of aspiring entrepreneurs eager to leverage the emerging technologies that allowed for streaming media, despite bandwidth limitations. A brash young entrepreneur named Mark Cuban was generating significant buzz. He had founded a startup called Broadcast.com that provided audio and video programming. Essentially, he took existing AM and FM broadcast radio signals, mainly sports events at the collegiate and high school levels, and rebroadcast them through the internet instead of terrestrial radio.

Cuban was on the verge of selling Broadcast.com to Yahoo!, which at the time was the titan of the internet, for a reported $5.7 billion in stock—most of which he'd fortuitously hedge or sell just before the dotcom bubble burst later that year. At the conference, held in March, he was one of several keynoters, and his remarks made headlines. He talked of advances in compression technology and said the day would soon come when streaming media would be so easy, and so successful, that it would spell the death of network television. He said Broadcast.com was even exploring an "all-you-can-eat" subscription service for content delivered over the internet. At the time, we had no idea how prophetic his words would be. Netflix was just a startup itself, focused on renting DVDs by mail. The move to streaming was still eight years in the future.

Following his speech, Cuban randomly sat down for dinner in an empty chair next to mine. Perhaps he was drawn to the presence of a very attractive woman at our table, who certainly stood out in a room otherwise full of mostly nerdy men. We started talking, and after enjoying our rubber chicken, a group of us, including Cuban and the woman, wound up in my rental car. Our destination was the bar at the exquisite Fairmount Hotel. We indulged in celebratory shots he bought for us while he told us of his impending payout with Yahoo—the deal was set to close on April 1.

What entranced me, though, was the story he shared with us at the bar about his humble beginnings as a door-to-door vacuum cleaner salesman. Setting up shop in a garage and without spending significant money on Broadcast.com, he achieved remarkable success. At that moment, he exuded humility and gratitude for his incredible stroke of luck. Reflecting on it, I couldn't help but think he hadn't created or sold anything tangible; his art was looking toward the future and selling that *idea*, impeccably timed. To this day, I am still trying to understand how he persuaded Yahoo! to acquire his company. Of course, he was capable of being an acerbic businessman, investor, and entrepreneur who would go on to achieve fame as one of the lead "sharks" on the ABC reality television series *Shark Tank*. Meeting him and witnessing his extraordinary triumph were truly serendipitous experiences for me.

Why am I sharing these encounters with the glitterati? Because there's a part of me that wants to share in the magic and offer a glimpse into a world that many people dream of. It's fun to recount those chance encounters, those moments when my path intersected with the orbits of stars. I was lifted off the ground by Mike Tyson and chilled with Jennifer Aniston before she was *the* Jennifer Aniston.

But there's something beyond the mere allure of celebrity, that compels me to share these stories. These encounters, however fleeting, have become part of my story, inseparable from the experiences that have shaped who I am.

48

DREAMS

About that movie star I dated...

One warm spring day in 2023, I was lounging around my pool, quietly enjoying the warmth of the sun. I heard a voice, followed by footsteps, coming up the garden path. I felt a twist in my throat as I heard Gemma—not her real name—my girlfriend of eight months, casually recounting an incident to someone on the phone: "Have I ever told you about the time when I was with this guy I used to date and we were stuck in an elevator together?"

That guy she used to date? That guy was me. Why was she speaking about our relationship in the past tense?

I peered out over my shades just as she walked along the pool deck, not realizing I was there. I cleared my throat, and she jerked her head back and gasped once she realized I must have heard what she said. My stomach was in knots as she blurted out, "Oh, uh, hi, uh, I was talking to my writing partner...."

Yeah, right! I had never been her public boyfriend. I only met her immediate family, and a few of her friends, much less any of her fellow movie stars. And while her Instagram account, with millions of followers, was filled with photos of past relationships, generally in a state of fantastical bliss, I don't think I ever appeared in a single one. Maybe it was the more than twenty-year age difference; maybe it was because I was more of a comfort boyfriend, filling a void so common among women with daddy issues. And she certainly had those....

Now, going back about a year to when Gemma and I first met. It had been a similarly warm day in late spring, and I was caught up in the spirit of love during a wedding reception for a neighbor friend who had found happiness with his new wife. The only problem was that I was sitting at a table solo, curiously observing his colleagues and other neighbors, while being sandwiched between a married couple. Two seats away, on the other side of the husband, was a woman by herself with a broad, warm smile. She spoke in a commanding tone. She had shoulder-length blondish hair, blue-green eyes, and a model's facial features and demeanor. She wore designer high-top sneakers with a posh pantsuit.

"Hi, I'm Gemma, and I work with the groom—he's my manager," she chirped, introducing herself to me and several others sitting at our table. The moment she mentioned the groom and the word "manager," I knew she must be in the entertainment industry; everyone else at the table seemed to recognize her too.

She turned to the husband and began a spirited discussion with him while I chatted up his wife about who knows what. I couldn't help but catch fragments of their conversation: "Listen, Jim, when you've been doing this as long as I have, the game gets good, and I'm happy to be here and easy to work with," she told him.

Which game? What work? I was intrigued but with more questions than answers. It wasn't just her profession that lured me; there was a spark in her eyes, a confidence and energy that drew me in. As I engaged in more small talk with the wife next to me and, across the table, a couple who worked in talent management with the groom, I found myself drifting off into a brief fantasy, longing for a conversation with the woman two seats away.

The next time I saw her was when I invited the newly married groom to a small pool dinner party after his whirlwind European honeymoon. Unfortunately, during their trip, his bride's father passed away in Germany, so his new wife stayed behind to be with her family. He needed a spiritual lift and asked if he could bring his youngest daughter and her friend. I agreed and mentioned that woman from his reception, Gemma. I told him, "Invite her if you think it's appropriate," and he chimed back, "Great idea!" When he confirmed she was an actor, director, and producer, my curiosity deepened. Even though I wasn't familiar with her fame or body of work, I was already drawn to her personality and spirit.

While I held in high regard certain stars I didn't truly know, I had plenty of experience working with celebrities and tried to avoid dating them. Most seemed to be seeking admiration to fill some kind of void. They often played roles different from their true selves, which I felt was their way of escaping their real identities. Commonly, the pursuit of success early in life leads to sacrificing experiences and feeling broken later. Many modern stars entered the industry through nepotism or started as children and relied heavily on parental support. Many celebs appeared to mask their pain through varied compulsive behaviors.

On the day of the pool party, Gemma was the last to arrive. A tall female companion with long flowing hair accompanied her. She brought wine and vanilla ice cream, hugging, giggling, and babbling as she made her entrance. That reminded me a little bit of Mom.

I opened my arms and home graciously, noticing that neither she nor her friend had brought appropriate swimwear.

"You didn't tell me this was a swimming pool party!" Gemma joked with my friend, her manager.

He promptly reminded her to check her text messages.

She read the message aloud: "It's a casual gathering around his pool. Damn, you're right," she said. I admired her for instantly admitting her mistake.

Wanting to help, I offered Gemma a brand-new bikini with the tags still attached. It had been given to me by a friend who rallied for her twin daughters' bikini company. Gemma went to change but returned fully clothed, playfully teasing me about giving her an "inappropriate" bikini in front of her manager's sub-teenage daughter. She accused me of having "mischievous" intentions.

I laughingly refuted her claim, asking, "Do you think I tried on the bikini before giving it to you?" I then offered her a pair of my board shorts and a T-shirt, which she gladly accepted.

After changing, she joined everyone else in the pool, and I appreciated her ability to go with the flow. *This girl is amazing. She's not affected by Hollywood at all—she's so down to earth.* I thought.

After the swim, I served dinner, and we all sat around and engaged in more small talk, including an animated discussion about the tenderness and taste of grilled chicken breasts and the peach pie I freshly baked from fruit grown on my land. Gemma's vanilla ice cream made the perfect accompaniment with each slice.

Gemma informed us that she was about to make her directorial debut, a comedy loosely based on her own dysfunctional family. "I'm not going to hold anything back," she exclaimed excitedly, "no matter how bad anyone looks—even me." I found myself disarmed and refreshed, silently applauding her audacious ability to confront her truth. I told myself, *This girl is for me—she is a bit damaged but so authentic!*

Not long after, we had our first dinner alone. We found ourselves saying "Me too" and "I agree" so many times that I felt drawn to her, despite my inner voice telling me to take it slow since I barely knew her. With each subsequent encounter, my attachment to her deepened, and when I happened to touch her arm, it was as though an electric charge shot through me. She looked up at me at that moment, and from the look in her eyes, I saw that she felt the same way. Then, she said, "I feel like I can be myself when I'm around you." This revelation was as exhilarating as it was daunting because she was a celebrity with millions of social media followers, a veteran of movies and TV shows, and the daughter of a high profile actor and a model mother who had dated a few A-list celebs. And yet, she seemed unaffected by her Hollywood royalty lineage and her "star" status. She gave off a striking sense of self-made perseverance and humility intertwined with childlike wonder and innocence.

I tried to resist her allure, mindful of the many times I'd been hurt before and even more hesitant because of our age difference. She was thirty-eight; I had just turned sixty. I feared being labeled a creepy old guy, and at the same time, I didn't want to leave her alone one day.

Gemma herself insisted, "Age is nothing more than a numerical construct. You, Rob, are simply irresistible!"

Then we kissed. That was it. I was in love.

There were nights when I found myself mesmerized by watching her sleep, melting when I saw her face, stimulated by her constant compliments. I kept feeling like she unlocked me and was leading me into the life I had always dreamed about. She seemed spiritual, more of the "Hollywood woo-woo type" as she referred to herself. Once she moved into my life, and quickly into my home, I was drenched in crystals, repetitive fractal organic matter. There were about a thousand pounds worth of varied forms, orbs, spheres, big and small chunks of tourmaline, amethyst, citrine, anthracite, rose quartz, tiger eye, and the list went on, and on, and on. She wanted us to be covered in their energy, open to receiving the patterns and signals synchronized with our physical beings. Sometimes my body trembled a little in gratitude for her and all that she brought.

On a sweltering day in San Diego, with temperatures soaring into the nineties even at the beach, my Cousin Katie, much like a sister to me, treated us to a delightful feast of fresh lobsters flown in from Maine. Gemma and I stayed at a resort on nearby Shelter Island. I remember taking in the sunset from Cousin Katie's oceanfront balcony, before the other guests arrived, and tilting my head back and looking Gemma in the eyes with a playful grin as I asked her, "May I introduce you as 'my person'?" She responded with a wink, a hug, and a warm kiss while squeezing my hand and responding, "Yes, I'd like nothing more. You are 'my person,' too."

After dinner, we walked around the block and then entered the elevator taking us back to Cousin Katie's third-floor condo. No sooner had we pressed the button and watched the doors close, however, that we heard a loud, jerky thud—and everything came to an abrupt halt. I immediately used the emergency call box, thinking it would connect me with 911. To my surprise, the person who answered was only an operator from the elevator service company. She assured us she would notify a technician immediately but couldn't give me an ETA. It was a Sunday night during the Labor Day weekend, so we were understandably concerned about how quickly someone would come to help us, if at all. The elevator was suffocatingly hot, and we shared the small space with two panting dogs. The operator refused to contact 911 on our behalf, saying, "Sir, our protocol does not allow us to contact emergency services." I leaned against the wall, unsure what to do next.

That's when Gemma sprung into action. "Rob, I'm an actress. I know stunts and how to get us out of here!" She wanted to stand on my shoulders to reach the roof hatch to get air from the elevator shaft and find an exit.

"Bend down," Gemma barked as she pushed me into a squat and climbed onto my shoulders.

I stupidly peered upward as she pounded on the ceiling hatch, which was painted shut. Dust and particles flew into my eyes, and I had to look away and clear them without dropping her. She got the hatch open.

"See, I know what I'm doing!"

It was time for a dismount. I told her to push her hands against the side walls for balance while I slowly crouched down.

"I will signal you when to slowly get off my shoulders," I said.

Yet I had barely begun crouching when she suddenly sprung forward to jump off. I fell backward, she fell forward, and we both broke out in laughter—until we realized she had either sprained or broken her wrist. She began to cry.

I told Gemma I was going to ring the fire bell. If a neighbor could hear it they might call 911 for the fire department, and get us the fuck out of there.

"Don't ring that goddamn bell!" she screamed at me, likely not wanting to deal with piercing noise, on top of pain.

After a few minutes, however, she agreed that it was a good thing to do. I rang it, and then we heard people, my cousin, and her friends loudly shouting down the shaft from the third floor to us trapped between the first and second floors. They said they would somehow try to manipulate the elevator manually.

The elevator car suddenly jolted a few times, causing Gemma to shudder in discomfort, but unfortunately, nothing happened to relieve our situation. We were as frustrated as ever. After about thirty minutes, the fire department arrived, but they were unable to open any doors or free us. Then, a miracle happened. After approximately forty-five minutes of being trapped, the technician from the elevator company, who we didn't expect to see, arrived and was able to release and reset the elevator manually.

Back at Cousin Katie's condo, we carefully fashioned a splint for Gemma's arm and wrist. The pain was intense, and we suspected a fracture—which would ultimately turn out to be the correct diagnosis. Gemma inquired about pain medication, and Cousin Katie offered a few pills left over from her recent back surgery. I urged Gemma to go to the ER for an X-ray, but she was adamant about waiting until morning to see an ER doctor friend back in LA.

Reluctantly, I agreed. Gemma took the pills, and we headed back to the hotel. She soaked in a warm bath to ease the discomfort, and we both fell into an exhausted sleep.

A few months later, right before Christmas, Gemma gave up her condo and moved into my house. I wondered how strange it might feel to suddenly share a living space after having lived alone for many years, but it felt surprisingly natural. She introduced several bedtime rituals that quickly became shared routines. I would fill a giant insulated jug with ice and electrolyte-infused spring water and place it on her bedside table, next to an eye mask I had secured for her. I'd fill her facial humidifier with the same special water, remedies for the day's indulgences, and a promise of a brighter morning. She'd treat that water jug like a long-lost friend, embracing it with a thirst that could only be quenched by a guzzle of electrolyte-infused goodness. She liked to chew the ice loudly, which drove me nuts. If she wanted intimacy, she would give clear signals, her terms prevailed. Occasionally, I felt like I had stepped into someone else's life, which wasn't always comfortable, but overall, I was enjoying the relationship.

But then things went downhill—rather quickly. I had not anticipated the extent of personal space Gemma would require. She took over half my closet and most of my drawers, peppered the entire house with her accessories, and commandeered my vintage Spartan trailer, which I had hoped to rent out as an Airbnb, as her office. Within weeks of her move, we began to bicker and snipe at each other, which is not uncommon when two strong-willed, independent people cohabitate. We said things out of anger, and feelings were hurt on both sides. This led us to seek a couples therapist, as we both vowed to work things out.

Eventually, an opportunity arose for Gemma to co-star in a sentimental romance film. Although she was initially reluctant to accept such a formulaic role as she preferred edgier fare, I persuaded her. It paid twice as much as her previous film. I saw it as a lucrative offer that could enhance her career by expanding her range and fan base.

She was going to spend three winter weeks away for the shoot. First, though, she was to stay with a friend for a week. The day before the morning she took off she asked me to help her prepare for the trip and assured me with a warm hug and kiss as I saw her off that we would get through it together.

I expected her to text or call daily while she was shooting, but I didn't hear much from her. When we did talk, she seemed disconnected or rushed. I knew she was busy filming, but my sixth sense told me something wasn't right.

Gemma returned to LA after the film shoot but stayed at a friend's home. We continued to spend time together, had overnights at my place, and took a bath together, but she made it clear that we would not be having sex. I felt confused at the distance she was deliberately creating between us. After the pool deck incident where I overheard her speaking of me as her "ex," I confronted her with my suspicions, but she denied there was anything amiss. Still, I knew better. The friction between us intensified, and one day, on a Zoom call with our couple's therapist, we amicably agreed to break up.

A few months later, the film's publicity campaign unveiled a love-at-first-sight story between Gemma and her co-star. A headline in a media magazine screamed about two co-stars who had a secret romance on set while filming said romantic movie. Somehow though, they failed to mention me, her supportive boyfriend who'd been left behind, whose distrust she'd dismissed.

To be fair, Gemma had come clean about a week before the stories broke, confirming my suspicions. Yet she'd downplayed the seriousness of the romance: "We're in different stages of life and you're just too complex for me right now. I never intended to hurt you, Rob, which is why it's been so hard for me to tell you that what you suspected was true. But who knows what's ahead."

The press didn't downplay *anything*. Reports blasted about the stars of an upcoming release, "which are now dating in real life after the initial sparks started flying between them while filming," one story read. "Their love story sounds like a cheesy [romance] movie in the making while on the set... Having a secret relationship may be tough at times, but it does sound like it actually worked for the duo...."

Another magazine story made me especially cringe. The story noted that Gemma "revealed the relationship turned romantic after the pair shared a meal together during the second week of filming the upcoming romance film. 'I think we went for lunch or something, and I noticed his crystals,' she told the outlet. 'I love crystals.'" *Of course, that's what she would say!* "And we started bonding over spirituality and I started to get to know the real co-star, and I was very smitten."

There was no mention of me. Me, the guy she was living with, who squatted as she stood on my shoulders when we were trapped in an elevator, who served her evening water butler-style, who let her use every inch of my home for whatever it was that she needed. I had gotten to know Gemma as a civilian, a citizen, not a star—just a regular person—but then the fame, through her attitudes and actions, crept up on me and I got caught up in making excuses for her bad behavior toward me.

The end of our relationship, though not entirely unexpected, still hit me hard. I had recreated an unhealthy situation from childhood where I was with someone to whom I was a second thought, a familiar and comfortable place to my subconscious self. Gemma's reassurances had temporarily quieted my doubts, but the familiar sting of betrayal resurfaced, a reminder of past hurts and unresolved emotions. I was left to confront the fallout, to pick up the crumbled pieces of my psyche.

This was also my first love affair without the crutch of alcohol or weed. I was completely sober, my eyes open to the fact that most of my previous romantic and sexual encounters were substance-induced trysts. Dating Gemma, albeit briefly, taught me invaluable lessons, particularly in understanding the effects of fame and adulation on individuals. I saw firsthand how the constant attention and praise could distort one's sense of self, sometimes fostering a degree of narcissism or detachment from reality. Despite my best intentions, I recognized that I had placed Gemma on a pedestal, allowing her celebrity status to overshadow a truly objective view of our connection.

The experience also highlighted my tendencies in partnerships. I discovered a deep satisfaction in caring for someone and being part of a team, whether it was helping with her nightly rituals or encouraging her career choices. Seeing my patterns helped me understand my past relationships and set healthier expectations for the future. I realized I had never truly grasped the distinctions between falling in love, being in love, and sustaining a long-term relationship. Thanks to our experience together, I gained clarity on how to navigate each of those stages.

I also learned that blaming myself or her was a massive waste of energy. Although there were some unhealthy moments throughout our time together, the unexpected insights gained from the relationship were truly remarkable, maybe even a way for me to mend my past.

49

YOU'RE MY BEST FRIEND

Dogs, often more significant and soothing to me than humans, have long played a key role in my life. Each of my dogs has had different traits and personalities, evident in their reaction to similar situations, ability to obey, level of affection, and communication techniques.

Over the years, I have become convinced, from personal experience, that canines can feel emotions and are extraordinarily capable of intuitively connecting without words. They offer solace, protection, and friendship. They can also understand and learn vocabulary, making them amazing companions. Similar to humans, they can sulk, show dominance, and be submissive, but most importantly, they exude unconditional love.

Milo was born on December 20, 2007. On several occasions, I had seen a neighbor walking a thin Australian Shepherd near the beach in Venice, and one day, I stopped her and asked her where she had gotten it. She pointed me toward a nearby salon, Rock, Paper, Scissors; one of the stylists was a breeder. To check out the new litter of pups, Dawn, my girlfriend at the time, and I visited the hair salon on a Friday evening. I was drawn to a docile female pup hanging out in the corner, not bothering anyone. But rambunctious Milo, the troublemaker of his litter, caught Dawn's eye. He was *the one*. I made a deal with the breeder that this was a test, though, and if we couldn't handle him, on Saturday or Sunday we could return him.

When we got home, we showed tri-colored, mini-Aussie Milo around.

"Look, Milo, stairs!" I said, pointing to the staircase. He was fascinated by them, his little wiggle butt wagging furiously.

"He's so cute," Dawn cooed, scooping him up. "But are you sure about this? He seems like a lot of work."

"He'll be fine," I assured her. "He just needs some love and training."

We placed his crate in the bedroom. On the first night, he whined and cried like many new puppies.

"Oh, Milo," Dawn sighed, rolling over. "Do you think he'll ever stop?"

"He'll settle down, eventually," I mumbled, half-asleep.

On Saturday morning, I put him in my bike basket, Dawn mounted her beach cruiser, and we set off.

"Look at him, Dawn!" I called out. "He loves it!"

"He looks terrified," she laughed.

Suddenly, Milo jumped out of the basket, slammed headfirst onto the street, and began peeing upside down.

"Milo!" I yelled, rushing to his side. "Are you okay?"

He whimpered and looked up at me with wide, frightened eyes.

"I think he's damaged merchandise," I said to Dawn, my voice filled with worry.

"He was already too much work," she replied, shaking her head. "We need to bring him back to the breeder."

"But...." I started to protest, but Dawn cut me off.

"No buts," she said firmly. "This isn't going to work."

I looked at Milo, his tiny body trembling, and sighed. "Okay," I conceded. "You're right."

So, we took him back.

"Are you sure you want to do this?" I asked Dawn, my voice barely above a whisper. Milo whimpered from his crate in the backseat.

"I don't know," she admitted, her voice wavering. "But it's the right thing to do, isn't it?"

The breeder agreed to take him back, even after I told her about the bike mishap.

"Poor little guy," the breeder said sympathetically, as Milo shyly peeked out from behind my legs. "He just needs a little extra patience."

"We tried," I explained, "but...."

"I understand," she interrupted gently. "It's not always the right fit."

"Wait," Dawn said suddenly, her eyes welling up. "I can't do it. Look at him!"

Milo, sensing the shift in mood, wagged his butt and tail stub tentatively.

"I know," I said, feeling a lump in my throat. "He's already part of the family."

"He is, isn't he?" she said, a smile breaking through her tears.

We were already attached.

"Let's go home, Milo," I said, scooping him up. He licked my face and snuggled into my arms.

"We'll make this work," Dawn said, her voice filled with newfound determination. "We'll figure it out together."

And as we drove away, with Milo curled up contentedly in Dawn's lap, empty crate in the back, I knew we had made the right decision.

From that moment forward, Milo took pole position as my best friend. We were inseparable; I spent more time with him than with any other animal or human in my life. My relationship with him far outlasted my relationship with Dawn. In Venice, Milo was my constant companion, joining me for daily surf sessions, invigorating morning beach romps, and even thrilling games of fetch at dawn, right on the beach where dogs were strictly prohibited—a rule he seemed to relish breaking almost as much as I did. He even came to work with me, his presence a comfort. While fiercely protective of our workspace, he also had an unconditional, loving, soft side that charmed everyone he met. Milo had a knack for endearing gestures, like gently placing his paw on the bed to wake me up or surprising us with sudden leaps onto our laps. His unwavering loyalty and playful spirit meant we never had to worry about locking up, even in

Venice—he was the best security system a guy could ask for.

As a puppy, Milo hiked a steep mountain in Oregon, got chased by a wolf and a pit bull, and discovered snow, the mountains, and the ocean. He flew first class across the United States and enjoyed a van trip back. He even accompanied me to the Austin City Limits Music Festival, where he spent nearly two weeks at the Four Seasons Hotel.

Milo's favorite activity, though, was catching a ball. As a young dog, he could quickly launch himself high into the air and snag the ball with impeccable precision and coordination. Regardless of expensive one-on-one training and repetition, he never quite picked up on returning the ball to me with the same precision. Always, always, he made me walk at least a few feet to retrieve the ball once he dropped it. And he didn't wait for me to pick the ball up; no sooner had he discarded it near me than he was already running off, waiting for the next throw.

Milo lucked out when I bought a house with a pool. He became the ruler of the pool and the acreage. If a ball got anywhere near the water, he immediately launched himself into the air with the grab timed perfectly, just before landing in the water. He would come up for air with the ball in his mouth every time. Eventually, I developed a way to communicate that the session of pool time fetch needed to end. I came up with a hand gesture, like a football referee calling an incomplete pass, along with a firm "Game over!" Milo came to accept this with dignity and even learned to dry off on a towel.

Dog parks were another story altogether. Getting Milo to leave was a challenge that invariably led to a fair amount of frustration on my part. He also wanted nothing to do with the other dogs—only his ball.

As his years turned into teens, which for him was a transfer to senior status, he became a bit feisty. He bit a dog sitter and pulled out her nose ring. He bit friends, family, girlfriends, and their kids. While we were at the Austin City Limits Music Festival, I wrangled a service dog tag for him so he could hang out with me backstage. A drunk kid got in his face; Milo nipped him.

A few days later, I went to see Ringo Starr and His All Starr Band at the Moody Theater and came back to the hotel where, coincidentally, the band sans Ringo poured into the lobby at the same time I did and then into the elevator as I was heading back to my room. I retrieved Milo and headed downstairs to give him an evening walk before turning in when Ringo's drummer passed us in the lobby. Milo decided he looked tasty and snapped at him, although he didn't draw blood. The drummer poked his finger into my chest and said, "If I were someone else, you'd be paying me millions, maybe billions of dollars!"

Milo also bit several other musicians and the hand that fed him: me. I couldn't count the number of times that he snapped at me and drew blood, bruised my skin, and even ripped my lip, which required sutures. I made many excuses for Milo's bad decisions over the years, which were all legitimate. He had some tooth abscesses, and each time they occurred, his cheek swelled up to the size of a golf ball. The vet dispensed antibiotics, the abscesses healed, and the swelling disappeared. The root issue was unbeknownst to me or the vet. It took a few years and dental cleaning, during which the doctor thoroughly examined his rear molars and gums and uncovered the culprit: foxtails. These pesky, barbed seed heads from grasses had burrowed into his lower gum line, causing chronic pain and infection. Foxtails are a common hazard for dogs, especially in areas like California. Their barbed structure allows them to easily penetrate fur and skin, migrating deeper into the body and causing serious complications if left untreated. The vet extracted the foxtails and a few teeth, finally addressing the *root* of Milo's discomfort.

Milo's aggression had likely been a reaction to his pain, yet when the pain went away, his temperament remained the same. As a person who loved Milo more than anyone, I told myself it was a sign of his protective nature. Either that or, as they say, old habits die hard. Cousin Jim DeLaurentis called Milo, "The loaded gun—he could go off at any time." As the years went by, I began to caution people who saw a sweet-faced dog and wanted to touch, pet, or cuddle him that they needed to heed my warnings. Many of them brushed me off because they thought of him as cute and themselves as dog people. At times, Milo was provoked, like when someone accidentally stepped on him. But at other times—well, as Cousin Jim said, he'd just go off.

After fourteen and a half years together, Milo finally succumbed to an inflamed abdomen and chronic kidney disease. He'd started going downhill right before his fourteenth birthday. For the final six months of his life, I knew the end was near, so I tried everything possible to keep him comfortable and content. He endured discomfort, but his stoic nature prevailed. He bounced back several times and surprised me with his energy and enduring will to keep going. Seven weeks before Milo passed, I went to the vet to euthanize him, thinking that I was saving him from any further pain and suffering.

The vet first said, "Are you sure you want to proceed with this?"

I lost it at that moment. I got choked up, tears fell from my eyes, and I said in a warbling voice, "No, I'm not sure."

The vet sent us home. From that day on, I focused even more energy on Milo, trying to tune in to know when he was ready. We spent virtually all our time together, playing ball and going on walks, and he even went for a swim in the pool, which had been one of his favorite activities.

Everyone has different relationships with their animals. For me, Milo was a child substitute, since I've never had children, and to some degree, he replaced a loving partner as well. I cared for him as I would have cared for my child or partner. While I wasn't the type to cart him around in a stroller, he was always well cared for and loved.

Losing Milo was particularly painful because this dog, for all his quirks and faults, was so much more than a pet. We were so tight that girlfriends sometimes got jealous of our close relationship. I can't blame them; I often put him above everyone else, even myself.

The growth I achieved while this dog was my best friend and partner was epic. He inspired me. Milo possessed both independence and inter-dependence, but above all else, he knew how to have fun. He lived life on his terms and didn't care what anyone thought about him—in that way, he became a wise role model for me. He became an old guy before I did, and I learned through him that the transition is symbolic and tolerable. Watching him deal with illness and imminent death gave me insight into my future, the inevitable. He assuaged many of my fears. Knowing Milo was an honor. I will forever miss his dominant presence, tricks, bark, licks, and maybe even bites. They were there to remind me that life is not fair and that sometimes shit happens. Milo was my hero and trusted best friend. Witnessing his transition was a bittersweet experience that punctuated an unforgettably meaningful partnership. People learn how to live a good life; dogs already know how, and maybe that's why they don't have to hang around as long as we do.

After Milo died, I was left with Ernest, another mini-Aussie Shepherd. He, too, has become my best friend and constant companion.

And now there's a third inhabitant of my Topanga Canyon hideaway. After Gemma and I broke up, she traveled a lot and had trouble with one of her cats not getting along with the others at the boarding facility. Mom always said, "People with cats are sneaky—they can't be trusted." I held onto that belief and had never owned a cat—until my frustrated ex handed Cooper over to me.

So, now I have a cuddly cat friend, too. Cooper is a baby-faced Tonkinese—no lie, look it up—who sleeps in my bed and gets into frequent scraps with Ernest. The two of them keep me occupied and amused, and the reaction I get when I come home from somewhere, even if I've only been gone for a few minutes, is so joyous I can't help but feel truly loved.

50

THE SEEKER

In the late 1990s, as I was preparing to launch my company, Marketing Factory, I innately knew I had to save myself. In addition to seeing a therapist weekly, I gravitated toward individuals who had committed themselves to promoting peace, calmness, healing, and the well-being of mind, body, and soul. My goal was to find a path to myself through spirituality, without religiosity. I wanted to know why I was different, what I could do to feel normal, and what would make me better.

One night, I went to a popular neighborhood bar and grill called Hal's. It's not exactly a temple of enlightenment, but hey, even a seeker needs to unwind sometimes. I noticed a thin, blonde woman with magnetic blue eyes and floral vine tattoos on both of her arms. Within a few minutes, we were out in front of Hal's, having an increasingly intense conversation.

Just a few minutes into our conversation, she leaned into me and said, "Rob, you and I will not be dating if that's what you had in mind. You are far too confrontational for me."

Being put in my place by her so quickly knocked me down from my confident demeanor. I respected her straightforwardness. Andrea and I exchanged phone numbers and became fast friends. I learned she was a yoga instructor and had trained in India with a world-renowned guru of Ashtanga yoga, Sri K. Pattabhi Jois, and a few other yoga instructors, which impressed me at a time when yoga had not yet become a trendy exercise fad. She was trim, solid, and well-versed in everything yogic. I was fascinated and open to learning from her because she had calm strength and confidence, something I desired.

Andrea began giving me private yoga lessons in my loft. She opened doors to worlds I had never known, not just through whispered encouragement, but through structured learning and shared experiences. I enrolled in one of her teacher training courses, where she seamlessly wove the wisdom of Siddhartha, the epic narratives of the Mahabharata, and the transformative power of yoga, as taught by Iyengar and Patanjali, into the curriculum. These weren't just abstract concepts; they were living principles, brought to life through practice, meditation, and insightful discussions.

Andrea Brook was meticulous, observant, and intelligent. She encouraged me to delve deeper, recommending books and studies that further illuminated profound teachings. Anodea Judith's work on the chakra system added another layer of understanding, revealing the intricate energy centers that shaped my being. I was particularly intrigued by the concept of the third eye, the seat of intuition and inner wisdom. *Perhaps with a deeper understanding of this energy center,* I mused, *I can unlock a greater sense of clarity and purpose.*

The teachings began illuminating a path toward greater self-awareness and inner peace. I felt a growing sense of connection to something larger than myself, a sense of wonder and possibility that had been dormant for far too long.

Since I had accumulated an extensive collection of CDs, primarily promotional copies sent to me by record companies, I offered to create a yoga mix tape for Andrea. I spent hours culling through my stash to find the right audio mixture to accompany her teaching style and rhythm. This was the least I could offer to this fascinating new person in my life. She appreciated it, though she wasn't enamored with my musical selections.

Initially, yoga proved to be more physically demanding than expected. It required my body to stretch in ways it never had before. Being a precise teacher, Andrea didn't tolerate excuses when my discipline and attention faltered. However, she had a talent for keeping me engaged. Andrea told stories about gurus and teachers she had encountered who had hit her with objects when her attention drifted and her āsanas—yoga poses—weren't to form.

As I improved my flexibility and muscle memory, the Sanskrit āsanas of Ashtanga yoga became deeply rooted in me. Andrea, whom I nicknamed "Yoga Girl," gave me lessons several times a week for six years. As we progressed in the physical practice, I trusted her enough to share my inner self, more of my truth. We began each session by discussing what I had been noticing in my life, similar to what a psychologist would do in talk therapy. And then, like magic, she took the essence of what I said and created a unique āsana sequence. Feelings came rushing through my body and mind, accompanying her instructions and my conscious breathing. After Savasana, the final resting pose, I would be energized through insights, more inner peace, physical strength, and reflections on the session. The yoga I got to know was incredibly transformative somatic therapy.

We flirted with a business relationship, with me as her manager. We met with television network executives and attorneys to determine how someone like her could enter mainstream media. In 2000, I visualized yoga becoming very popular, with Andrea as the host of a weekly unscripted TV show where she would travel, interview gurus, teachers, and purveyors of progressive metaphysical, scientific, and similar spiritual lifestyle movements. She would educate the viewer on what each discipline offered while simultaneously immersing herself in their expertise. In hindsight, we were trying to accomplish something ahead of our time, as the healthy lifestyle movement had not yet become mainstream.

While taking yoga lessons from Andrea, I met another woman who caught my attention from a romantic perspective. Ashley Turner, born an identical twin, came to Los Angeles for college from the Midwest and was chasing the road to stardom through acting while her twin sister pursued a law degree. This meant she needed a job to make a living while hunting for acting gigs, so she slung cocktails at a bar in Santa Monica owned by friends of mine, and that's where we met.

As Ashley and I spent more time together, she became very curious about yoga. I introduced her to Andrea, and she eventually let acting go, turned all her energy to yoga, and wound up getting a degree in psychology and a therapy license. Today, Ashley is one of the top names in the yoga world, known for combining psychotherapy with yoga practice. I take pride in having played a small part in her success. By making the connection, I facilitated a union, which embodies the true essence of yoga.

I also found that my dedication to yoga improved my ability to stay calm under pressure. Venice was fast becoming a yoga mecca, and a large, beautiful studio opened about a mile away from me. I ultimately overcame my self-consciousness about being the only man I knew who practiced yoga, much to my benefit. For centuries, men have dismissed women's knowledge, intuition, and wisdom. Some still do. Having grown up in a patriarchal society, sadly, I may have done the same at times. Now though, I couldn't help but admire these women who seemed to be pioneers, embracing yoga long before it was commonplace, especially for men. It made me reflect on the remarkable women in my own life: my mother, bursting with artistic talent; my past romantic partners—well, at least some of them—with their unique strengths and emotional intelligence; my sisters; my Cousin Katie; and Andrea, who first introduced me to yoga. It was a powerful reminder of the often-underestimated capabilities and quiet resilience of women.

I signed up for group classes and soon became a regular in the seven-a.m. class. The instructor, Jo Tastula, had an angelic appeal with her Australian accent, background in film production, and illuminating expression. Her sequencing and enunciation, manner of speech, and clear directions, sprinkled with pearls of wisdom, made her classes incredible. I spent a decade practicing at that location, mostly with Jo, sticking with it through big-money investors' gradual corporate takeover of independent yoga studios—including this one. Over time, the classes got shorter and pricier, the store out front became more prominent, the instructors had less experience, and the center began to resemble more of a spa. Then, it abruptly closed.

It was then I decided to venture out and find a new place to practice yoga. I found a new home at a studio two miles away, even though the early morning classes began at six fifteen rather than seven. The instructors were more gym-like in their delivery, the crowd was younger, and I felt like an older, experienced practitioner—a yogi. The teachers would frequently shower me with compliments and even use me as an example to demonstrate postures for new students. I was a regular until the 2020 pandemic struck, and the studio went bankrupt.

Over two decades, yoga helped me maintain a certain level of steadiness in my life. I began going to bed earlier and not staying out late partying as it wasn't fun to do strenuous focused movements with four hours of sleep and a hangover. My eating habits and diet improved, and I felt better, all around.

Those who contributed to my growth became significant mentors to me and it was a two-way street. I became a loyal supporter of Andrea, Ashley, Jo, and Jessie, providing occasional moments of comic relief and valuable friendship. They benefited from the business and career guidance I offered them. Andrea sold the Yoga Girl URL for $25,000. The concept of karma suggests that positive actions yield positive outcomes, while negative actions lead to repercussions. Ultimately, how we treat others determines the results we experience—and I saw it.

Life catalyst Andrea, whom I'd admired since the day we met at the bar and grill, would go on to teach celebrities such as actors Antonio Banderas, Marcia Gay Harden, and Owen Wilson; musicians Simon Le Bon and Ziggy Marley; and athlete Marcus Allen. She'd also develop and tour as an original musical dance performing arts solo act called Sonic Butterfly.

As Andrea had shared yoga with me, I did so with my niece. Allison, who was in college in Central California, joined me for a weekend retreat in Ojai led by Ashley. The retreat took place in a stunning craftsman home nestled on a hillside with breathtaking views. The property had a pool, grapevines, wine vats, a carriage house, guest cottages, and even a yurt. The meals were all made of nutritious, plant-based ingredients. The yoga sessions were physically demanding, held multiple times a day with breaks in between for free time.

Ashley introduced a special guest to the group. Bhagavan Das, with his remarkable background and presence, captivated everyone's attention upon his arrival. With his gray beard and tangled dreadlocks, this larger-than-life figure wore loose white caftan-type attire, exuding an aura of spirituality. Bhagavan Das led a kirtan, a spiritual gathering involving Sanskrit singing and chanting. The women were enthralled not by his physical appearance but by his role as guru, author, and performer. Early in his life, he achieved some fame as one of the first Americans to travel to India in search of yoga, abandoning his previous conventional lifestyle to join the guru circuit.

The retreat was an incredible life experience, deeply impacting not only me, but also my niece Allison, who eventually earned a psychology degree and pursued a career as a yoga teacher. Now a licensed somatic psychotherapist and artist living in Portland, Oregon, she credits the immersive yoga retreat for helping her connect with an intrinsic part of herself, which she successfully channeled into a rewarding life and a thriving business venture.

51

CATCH A WAVE

Surfing was another pastime that helped me momentously grow and understand who I am. But I didn't take it up until long after I moved to Venice because I first had to overcome one big obstacle: I was terrified of the ocean.

Back when I lived in San Diego, I spent a gloriously warm, blue-sky summer afternoon at La Jolla's famed Windansea Beach, immortalized in Tom Wolfe's 1967 pop culture essay, "The Pump House Gang." Despite heavy swells, my friend T.K. suggested we go for a swim. We had been up nearly all night, snorting coke and drinking. I followed my friend out into the water and went out into the waves. Suddenly, I felt something rubbing against me. *A shark!* was my first panicked thought. I thrashed around and realized I was caught in a kelp bed. I turned to warn my friend, but he had already retreated to shore, making his way back to his beach blanket. I bobbed up and down, and with each crashing wave, my legs became more entangled with kelp, which began to drag me down.

I yelled to T.K., but he was lying on his stomach, reading a book. We seemed to be the only ones on that little stretch of beach, a secluded spot between the sandstone bluffs. I began to panic because I was about seventy-five yards from shore and was quickly becoming worn out. How would I break free from the heavy kelp that by then had wholly enveloped my body? As a kid, my body had been thrashed around by a tire—now, this. I wondered if I should start screaming for help as loudly as I could, but my pride told me, *Don't you dare!* After about five minutes of this pounding at sea, my life began to flash before me as if this was going to be it—the end.

I gave up and stopped thrashing around. And that's what saved me. By not fighting the kelp or the current, the kelp somehow disentangled, and I made my way to shore. Gasping for air, I told T.K. what had happened, and he broke out in the most unsympathetic laughter. It felt like when I'd told my dad about the tire event. I was now angry, insulted, and offended. I stormed off to the car, with a severe fear of the ocean.

After I'd moved to Venice, in the mornings, when I wasn't practicing yoga, I would run on the soft sand. I often observed people carrying surfboards, and sometimes, after my run, I would walk over to the Venice breakwater and watch the throngs of surfers compete for the best waves. I had heard horror stories of thuggery surfing, erupting tempers, and people fighting over waves and territory. But, similar to yoga, when surfers finished a session, I noticed how they all glowed and smiled and seemed to exude a spirit that was at once energetic and calm. I sometimes wondered what it would be like to be out there among the surfers, but I could never bring myself to try. The mere thought gave me shivers. Until Jay talked me into it.

Jay Resnick was a colleague of mine at Westwood One. He was born and raised in West LA, graduated from Venice High School, and learned to surf at a very young age. He still had this laid-back surfer vibe, and it was not uncommon to see him roaming the office barefoot, with shaggy hair, light stubble, a T-shirt, and board shorts. *Fast Times at Ridgemont High* is a classic American film featuring the character Spicoli, who was essentially Jay, except Jay didn't use drugs. He seemed unfazed by anything. Despite working in the rather dull compliance department, he had a far-from-compliant personality.

Jay was kind and soulful and was always willing to lend an ear or share a meal. He had a photographic memory and could effortlessly recall everything from phone numbers and birthdays to obscure details about anything and everything. While we didn't form a super close bond, we got along well. Jay also showed a keen interest in my role and artist relations and eventually took over that role a few years after I was dismissed. More than a decade later, Jay worked as the facility manager for a group of radio stations near his home. One of these stations was KROQ, a trailblazer in alternative music.

After we stopped working together, Jay would call me on my birthday each year out of the blue, ask how I was doing, and suggest lunch. Jay was a food connoisseur. His lunch appointments were methodically planned and never a disappointment.

Then, whenever we caught up, Jay inevitably would suggest, "Robbie, let me take you for a surf." Each time, I hastily dismissed the idea. As if the angry, hungry sea wasn't enough, the sight of surfers riding waves and defying gravity seemed impossible.

One day in 2005, at the age of forty-three, I was thumbing through a yoga magazine and an ad in the back pages caught my attention. It was advertising a yoga and surfing retreat in Mexico. I heard a forceful voice in my head: *You live so close to the ocean, but you haven't swum in it in twenty years. You've seen surfers, watched surfers, thought about surfers— it's time to face your fears, dude.*

I signed up for the trip. It was scheduled for the fall, which gave me an excuse not to spend Thanksgiving with my family. Holidays have always been a painful experience since my parents divorced when I was a young boy. Since then, the holidays required making hard decisions, seeing family I didn't want to see or didn't even know I had, and sometimes attending multiple events in one day. The pressure of the entire season, from Halloween through New Year's Eve, made me want to bury my head on a sandy beach somewhere. The warm sand of the small village of Sayulita, Mexico, where waves were abundant, yoga had a view, and the hotel was named Via Amor, sounded like a pretty good plan to me.

I still remember the first time I set foot in the surf. I felt my blood pressure rise and my heart rate quicken as I romped in the warm water. The instructor was patient and kind, and I could stand up in the whitewash pretty quickly. Then my inherent impatience took over, and I paddled beyond the wash to the actual waves, where I got pummeled. Surfing wasn't just a physical exercise. It was a serious mind game. The ocean was unpredictable, and a keen understanding of weather, wind, tides, swells, and wave size, as well as what all this meant for *me*, a person on a board out in the middle of the ocean, was important. It was knowledge that would only come with time and experience.

Upon my return from Mexico, Jay was stoked—"excited," in surfer talk—that I was now open to surfing. My desire to surf—my "stoke"— increased with every session. Jay would pick me up in his old white fifteen-passenger van full of surfboard gear, and we'd head into the water, many times in the darkness of early morning. He liked to say, "Lead a kook to water, but you can't make 'em sink." He would point me in the right direction and give me supportive high-fives and comments when I did something correctly. This form of genuine encouragement was radically new to me. What did Jay have to gain from bringing this non-surfer to his beach? Nothing but good karma.

Even though I was regularly surfing with Jay and on my own, it took a couple of years for me to feel comfortable in the water. I stepped on fish, surfed with dolphins, and was startled by seals. I also accumulated a collection of wetsuits. Still, it took me five years to fully conquer my fear of the ocean. Jay upgraded from his van to an old diesel school bus that he converted to run on vegetable oil. He would collect me and my dog Milo behind my house in an alley while it was still dark so we could be the first ones in the water. The bus exhaust reeked of french fries or cod or whatever the oil that now powered it had been used for before its transformation into fuel.

Jay's encouragement was essential to my progression as a surfer. Eventually, I made friends in the water and connected with a group in Venice who accepted me into the surf community. We used to surf mostly at the Venice Fishing Pier. It was a bit chaotic as people were casting their lines right where we were surfing, and occasionally, someone would get hooked or tangled, but that never happened to me, and it never stopped us.

Beginning to surf in my midforties was a significant achievement for me. I built enough confidence and skill to join experienced surfers, even some professionals, on a few occasions. I broadened my surfing horizons to various locations along the Southern California coastline, Maui and Saladita, multiple times, before eventually exploring a state not known at first blush for wave surfing: Texas.

Throughout my Marketing Factory days, one of my favorite annual events was the Austin City Limits Music Festival. After I took up surfing, I surfed at a man-made wave pool three times and even got to experience tanker surfing on the Houston shipping channel. This fifty-mile-long waterway sees heavy traffic from large ships carrying petrochemicals, grains, and other goods between land and the Gulf of Mexico.

Intrigued by the unique experience of tanker surfing, Jay stumbled upon Captain James online, the same Captain James featured in the 2003 surf documentary *Step into Liquid*. It turned out he owned a small surf shop in Galveston and offered tanker surfing excursions. Excited, we booked a trip through his website. True to his on-screen persona, Captain James slipped right into his role as our guide, organizing a surfing outing for Jay, me, and two others after the festival one year. In Galveston Bay, which is part of the channel, passing tankers create well-shaped waves that can be surfed for incredibly long durations—sometimes extending beyond ten minutes on a single wave, a stark contrast to the shorter rides of five to thirty seconds typically experienced in shore-break surfing.

Our day began at dawn when we stopped and fueled ourselves with Texas kolaches, a regional favorite consisting of sausage surrounded by dough that the Captain procured for us at his secret spot. We then boarded his small speedboat to search for tankers. Equipped with a radio, Captain James monitored tanker movements to ensure we positioned ourselves correctly to anticipate the wakes, catch their refractions from the shoals and the man-made jetties, and surf them.

Halfway through the day in his distinctive Southern accent, Captain James warned us, "Guys, don't mean to scare ya, but when we get back to shore, make sure to clean up good, because there's been cases of bacterial infection in these warm waters." This precaution hadn't been mentioned on his website. All four of us city folk were taken aback, as each of us had some cut or skin wound, increasing our risk of contracting necrotizing fasciitis, more commonly known as the flesh-eating disease.

Our first stop after reaching shore was the local CVS, where we bought rubbing alcohol, antiseptic, and hydrogen peroxide. As one of the other members of our foursome so eloquently stated, "Why take a chance with only one choice when we can use all three?" Once back at the hotel, we passed the bag of bacteria-reducing wound cleaners down the hallway from room to room so each of us could douse ourselves head to toe after a hot shower.

Despite it all, at some point, surfing became an obsession—maybe even an addiction. It complemented my yoga: I gained core strength in yoga that I used in surfing. It's hard to say which activity I did more often, as I alternated my morning routine between surfing, yoga, running on the soft sand, and sleeping in. But there's one thing for certain: surfing was the most fun. Jay became a trusted friend, probably my best friend, through the ritual compulsion of surfing. We traveled, dined, surfed, and talked about many aspects of life. His daughter Brooks calls me Uncle Rob and his wife puts up with our time in and out of the water. The most important life lesson I gained from surfing is one that evaded me for decades: how to have pure fun.

And for that, I owe Jay Resnick a hearty debt of gratitude. It could even be said that he saved my life through surfing. At the very least, he rescued me from living in the shadow of a dysfunctional childhood, which kept me from wholly enjoying life. If yoga cracked open the door to a new me, it was surfing—and especially Jay—who flung it wide open.

Through a quirk of fate, just as Jay saved me, I was able to save *him*. We were both backstage at a music festival near Seattle in 2013. Jay was in charge of the barbecue. We were all gathered around the smoking grill, enjoying beers, while Jay grilled up hearty portions of pork, beef, and chicken. In a moment of enthusiasm, Jay picked up a piece of pork on a fork directly off the grill and popped it into his mouth. The meat was scalding hot. Jay began choking and struggling to breathe, his face turning a frightening shade of blue. He couldn't speak. I had no training in the Heimlich maneuver but positioned myself behind him, wrapped my arms around his chest, and jerked his solar plexus and abdomen in an attempt to dislodge the obstructing chunk of pork. On the third try, the small piece of meat flew about six feet out of his mouth, nearly striking a musician just hanging out.

"What the fuck just happened?" the band member said. "That was nuts!"

Jay regained his breath, and we were all relieved that a crisis had been averted. However, to this day, Jay still says, "Thanks to your quick thinking, you saved my life, Robbie!"

Maybe he's right. The nearest hospital was miles away, and finding on-site medical assistance would have been challenging. But my response is always the same: "No, Jay, we saved each other."

52

ONE LIFE, ONE LOVE

It's a warm weekday afternoon in the spring of 2025. I'm watching Ernest, my beloved mini-Aussie Shepherd, jump into the pool each time I lob a ball into it from the chaise lounge on the pool's edge, occasionally shifting my glance to the towering coast live oaks and western sycamores that form a natural tapestry against the crystal-clear blue sky, the chaparral-covered foothills of the Santa Monica Mountains off in the distance.

I can't help but draw comparisons between Ernest and Milo, my previous dog, best friend, and constant companion. Ernest doesn't jump nearly as high, and his enthusiasm for the ball is not quite as intense as Milo's. And yet Ernie brings the ball back and places it at arm's length for me to throw again, a simple lesson that Milo never learned.

It's almost like the new Rob versus the old Rob—a little slower, a little less excitable, but somehow wiser, calmer, and more in sync with the ways of life. Milo bit people, sometimes for no reason, while Ernest is less temperamental and much more self-assured—at least, most of the time. He can still be reactive and rash, particularly toward other dogs or when the pool guy wanders into the backyard. I suppose deep down he's still a work in progress, much like me.

My home is very important to me. I purchased a cabin with a pool in a field overrun with thistle, black mustard, and other weeds. Remodeled and transformed, the house and grounds now have a beautiful park-like atmosphere, with golden poppies, pink ladies, violet lupine, sturdy oaks, and lots of fruit trees and even a vegetable garden. The two-acre compound provides a sense of solitude, safety, and security that I didn't have growing up. Nestled in a rural area of Los Angeles, until recently I felt I had the best of both worlds—a secluded and very private hideaway minutes away from the Pacific Ocean and the bustling San Fernando Valley. This idyllic, peaceful setting served as the perfect backdrop for writing this book, an integral part of my journey of self-healing.

The Los Angeles fires in January 2025 changed my perspective. I've known for years that living in this wildland-urban interface comes with a price—the ever-present threat of wildfires. Over the years, I've weathered the Woolsey Fire, a previous Palisades Fire, and the Owen Fire. Each brought its own wave of anxiety, but nothing prepared me for the intensity of the January blaze, which leveled the communities of Pacific Palisades and Altadena and came dangerously close to blazing through my area of the Santa Monica Mountains, as well. I was forced to evacuate for more than a week and watched with horror as the security cameras in my driveway broadcast images of sheriff cruisers with red lights blazing and sirens blaring, shouting "Leave now!" to the few brave souls who had opted to stay behind and help protect our little enclave.

Despite having invested in fire-resistant materials and a robust fire prevention system, I feared that this time, my number might be up. As it turned out, the fires that consumed more than 50,000 acres—an area bigger than all of Washington, DC—was thankfully halted less than two miles from my home. But the vast acreage of destruction I hiked through when I was at last allowed to return home had an impact on me. *Do I really need the stress, the constant worrying, the ever-present threat of having to pack up and evacuate and maybe next time not having a home to return to?*

And yet, this uncertainty—which would have driven the old Rob crazy—somehow doesn't bother me. I have come to terms with the fact that my youth was chaotic, fraught with emotional challenges and turmoil that shaped what I became and who I still am, in many respects, to this day. The lack of love, the inability to be seen or heard, and the sexual abuse caused my childhood to evaporate much more quickly than it does for most people as I reached for independence as early as I could. Between the ages of ten and eighteen, I moved nine times, and amid the tumult that surrounded me I was always in fight or flight mode—sometimes both, at the same time.

As life progressed, I realized I had to make changes, as the pressure became too overwhelming. I now try my best to navigate life without adopting a victim mindset, and at a much slower pace. I'm no longer running. I know I'll end up somewhere, and that's all right.

Music and radio helped me survive. Those youthful moments when I listened to the radio or heard my name on the air brought a sense of magic, transporting me into a different world where I mattered.

Trauma's invisible force carries immense power. What's painfully ironic is that if you had met me at almost any point in my life, you might not have been aware of my inner struggles because I usually projected a happy and fun persona. One question people constantly ask me is, "Why did you get sober? What was your addiction?" I have no answer other than, "I wanted clarity." Being able to see clearly for the past five years has been a blessing.

Without fully realizing the process or outcomes as they were happening, I found myself engaging in self-healing through yoga and surfing. Establishing a routine helped regulate my trauma; it brought a sense of order into my life, in contrast to the havoc of my youth. Trauma can be like an injury or a wound. Given the proper treatment, it can heal, but it can also scar over and become desensitized. The protective barriers I developed at times blocked my empathy. My core was sometimes even impenetrable to myself. But that core was hurting. It was sensitive and it was vulnerable, and this conflict sparked periods of instability.

As I searched for ways to heal, I explored an array of self-help, neuroscience, and mental health literature. They offered enlightening perspectives and information but not tangible transformations in real-life situations. That required reprogramming. To that end, I invested a small fortune in psychotherapy over the years, beginning in San Diego in my late twenties and continuing off and on to the present day. I found talk therapy valuable in identifying issues within myself and others, recognizing patterns, and making breakthroughs. My therapy experience was different with each of the seven therapists I have seen, depending on their methods and approaches.

In recent years, I discovered Eye Movement Desensitization and Reprocessing (EMDR). It is well-known for its success in treating post-traumatic stress disorder (PTSD) and is also beneficial for anxiety, depression, addiction, behavioral challenges, and relationship issues. EMDR adeptly improved my conditions related to traumatic events.

At the suggestion of a recent therapist, Dr. Mari Murao, I started writing to find catharsis. I brought pages I'd written to our sessions. They detailed past wounds, stories, and even dreams that triggered strong emotional responses, resulting in highly effective EMDR sessions. Dr. Murao sometimes incorporated guided somatic experiences, a body-mind therapy focused on healing trauma through touch, movement, and meditation.

There were times when therapy left me feeling like a lost and hopeless case. Oftentimes in those moments, I felt deep shame and blame, even over things that had nothing to do with me. Dr. Murao consistently suggested that I join a twelve-step group like Alcoholics Anonymous (AA), but I balked at the idea. "Those are for people with *real* problems," I'd think to myself, clinging to a misguided sense of superiority. I'd heard whispers of cult-like practices, of trading one addiction for another, and the whole concept scared me. I was afraid of what I might find lurking in the shadows of my own psyche.

It took three and a half years of stubborn resistance before I finally relented during a period of intense personal turmoil and discovered a fellowship. Founded in 1978, oddly enough at the same year my childhood was imploding, Adult Children of Alcoholics and Dysfunctional

Families (ACA), builds on the principles of twelve steps and its traditions. Many members come from AA or other twelve-step groups and appreciate that ACA delves deeper into healing emotional wounds that trigger unwanted behaviors by providing tools for a better life. It hosts over 2,750 meetings globally.

There are millions of unwitting "adult children" in our society today. By offering a platform for individuals to share their experiences of growing up in abusive, neglectful, or traumatic environments, ACA acknowledges the profound influence these experiences have on our lives. In ACA, I found a nurturing environment to confront my childhood pain, reflect on myself and my family honestly, and address and heal from deep-rooted traumas. The program promises liberation from shame and abandonment, guiding individuals to be compassionate caregivers to themselves.

Despite my initial resistance, after attending ACA meetings for two years and completing all twelve steps, I noticed a positive change in my life and found immense value in this community. This fellowship has been a cornerstone in my healing journey, and I happily recommend it to those seeking healing. However, a word of caution—while rewarding, ACA requires time, perseverance, and dedication. In other words, it requires painful fucking work!

One of my biggest triumphs on the path to healing is that accepting the truth is becoming easier. If an automatic thought pops into my head such as, "I should not have spoken like that," or "Rob, you always seem to stir up trouble!" I am now able to recognize them as an inner dialogue of a critical parental figure or an upset child. I can change them, and respond to myself with compassion and understanding, directed toward myself and the young boy who lacked attention, safety, love, and support. This approach may sound unconventional, even bizarre to some, but it has proven effective.

Other improvements have included an ability to stop blaming myself and others. Although this sounds simplistic, achieving it continues to take wrangling. Manipulating situations to gain what I subconsciously desired—control—was standard behavior and a way to keep myself safe. I was always looking ahead and preparing, planning every way to avoid falling. But now I am choosing to let go, take the falls, and let life take me where it may. I also have grown to believe that all the answers to my questions are within me; and when I quiet my mind, I can hear them.

Since the age of ten, I'd danced with alcohol, cocaine, and marijuana addiction. At the mature age of fifty-seven, I decided to stop using drugs and alcohol to gain clarity. Marijuana, in particular, had become a crutch for me. I used it to feel normal in everyday situations like work or client meetings. I now realize how absurd this was. Besides marijuana, I also drank wine socially or with meals and occasionally indulged in other drinks like margaritas, whiskey, or mezcal. While these legal substances offered temporary relief, I noticed that I required increasing amounts to feel the same level of contentment. Life has its share of challenges, and seeking solace through a glass of alcohol or a puff of marijuana seemed like an easy solution to take the edge off. Like the rest of society, I'd become conditioned to seek the quick fix: take this pill, smoke this, drink this, snort this. It was 2019 when I stopped, realizing there was no fast track to getting healthy.

Eventually, I comprehended the significance of enduring hardship. It dawned on me that life isn't always meant to be perfect. How I handle highs and lows plays a crucial role in my well-being. While embracing positivity is valuable, solely focusing on "Good vibes only" can lead me to a spiritual bypass of the true essence of life.

I have successfully embraced sobriety, quitting cold turkey after a life of substance use and occasional binges of abuse. Although I was compulsive, a workaholic, I never saw myself as an addict or an alcoholic. Regardless, I am proud to say that I have no urges to partake in any of those acts again.

Rather than avoiding the wounds, I've leaned into them. If you are like me and seeking to go deeper into trauma healing, I highly recommend reading books by Gabor Maté. A renowned trauma doctor, Maté offers valuable insights, methods, and advice on achieving genuine happiness, fostering hope, and healing profound emotional wounds. Peter A. Levine and Bessel van der Kolk have also contributed significantly to our understanding of the modern relationship between physical and mental states. Studying their work has given me valuable insight into intricate relationships and interconnectedness.

I often think about the delicate balance of fortune and affection that shapes our human experience. Is it better to live humbly, surrounded by love, or to have wealth and privilege without it? The answer, I believe, lies in understanding what truly matters.

While money can provide comfort and security, it can't fulfill our deep need for connection. Love, in all its forms, gives us a sense of belonging and purpose that goes beyond material things. It's in the warmth of human connection, shared laughter, and understanding that we find true happiness.

But it's not just love that enriches our lives. It's also the way we think and learn that gives our existence meaning. From the moment we're born, our minds are constantly growing and changing. Every experience, every interaction, every challenge shapes our thoughts and makes us who we are. When I think about how my mind has developed, I'm filled with a sense of wonder. I think about all the moments that have shaped my thoughts, the words that have sparked my imagination, and the questions that have pushed me to learn more. It's in thinking about these experiences that I find real meaning.

Ultimately, it's the combination of love, wealth, and knowledge that creates a truly fulfilling life. Material things come and go, but the bonds we form with others and the power of our minds stay with us. As we navigate life's ups and downs, let's focus on cultivating both, valuing human connection and the amazing capacity of our minds.

I envision a world where mental, emotional, and physical well-being are given the same level of attention as physical injury. For example, "Hey

Rob, I'm sorry to hear about your girlfriend's betrayal; consider seeing Dr. So and So for support." A world like this would undoubtedly be a better place, and we are moving in that direction.

I have chosen to forgive my mother and father, and everyone else I encountered while a helpless child, including the two deejays who molested me. The only way forward is to let go. I don't believe anyone is born evil, which allows me to find the capacity to forgive. Generational trauma left Mom and Dad holding a bundle of the past they were not equipped to handle. Without offloading that sack of stuff, they unwittingly passed it on to me and my siblings—as many in their generation did.

Their damage, though unwitting, affected my life. My innate intelligence, imagination, hard-won skills, and sweat were, at times, held back by my anxiety, or substance use, all due to trauma. This, in turn, caused me to make bad choices, and left me unable to fully realize my potential. Nonetheless, death brings a softness to life, or to those still alive.

There was a wren that tapped on my window every morning for two weeks. She was beautiful, with a cinnamon breast. I thought of my mother as I heard the *tap, tap, tap*. It felt like a message, a gentle nudge from beyond. Maybe it was Mom's way of saying hello since I couldn't call her though I sometimes had the urge to hear her voice from a decade before. Or maybe it was just a quirky bird. But in those quiet mornings, I felt a sense of peace, a comforting presence. It was a reminder that love can transcend the boundaries of life and death. Life, of course, continued. And with it came new ventures, new distractions, and new ways to channel my energy.

Since my so-called retirement in 2019, I have focused on managing my rental properties and engaging in various entrepreneurial pursuits. I developed an art startup with a famous neighbor, Brandon Boyd of the rock band Incubus, which involved selling limited-edition signed prints by celebrity visual artists. The idea arose when a friend asked me if I knew anyone who might want to buy her online poster art business. I took this opportunity to approach Boyd, himself an artist, and we became business partners. After a year of development, we realized that the concept worked better as a boutique sideline for him rather than the colossal company I had envisioned. He bought my share of the business, and we remain friends.

While working on becoming a better me, I am constantly discovering different aspects of my artistic and creative talent, the likes of which I'd deployed with excitement when I created interactive physical and digital exhibits for corporations, drawing inspiration from, and weaving in, bands and music festivals. I'd also gained experience in remodeling homes and developing properties from scratch. Whether it was a nightclub in Mexico or a house in the mountains of Los Angeles, these endeavors gave me immense satisfaction. The artistic sensibility they require fuels my passion for these projects.

While I may not possess any official credentials or accolades, I take comfort in knowing that my work, spatial planning, and foresight have earned the admiration of numerous individuals, including myself. What truly matters to me is the recognition that these pursuits align with my authentic self, influenced by my mom's excellence in this area and the environments I encountered during my disordered upbringing.

My latest artistic/creative endeavor, of course, is this book. My goal is to shine a light on once-taboo subjects such as mental health, sexual abuse, and the resultant emotional pressure. Writing this was scary because it revealed a vast amount of my buried self. I was a complex child and experienced everything intensely—hearing, seeing, and feeling deeply. Sometimes, my emotions overwhelmed me so quickly that it made those around me uneasy. But there's no reason for me to continue to feel shame, to bury the past.

Music has been a constant light, bringing me joy and success. Each chapter title in this book represents a song or snippet that applies to the underlying story. The Talking Heads song "Once in a Lifetime," in particular, has always been one of my favorites. I admire the driving rhythm, quirky lyrics, and overall sense of recklessness. Personalizing it, from the time I entered the world, I have been swimming upstream against a strong current.

In my lifetime I've come across self-help books that were general, technical, literal, or even institutional. My overarching objective with *this* book is to entertain and remind everyone how our experiences impact our future, for better or for worse. It will be entirely worthwhile if I can help one individual through this process, besides being a healthy cathartic release for me.

Four framed portraits once hung in a formal living room, a room that was off-limits for me, echoing the loneliness I often felt as a child. Now, I have the one of myself, the pastel drawing that hung above the piano. It's a reminder of a past that feels both distant and achingly familiar, a past where a family was together, yet somehow still apart. We are scattered now, those four figures in the frames, each holding the fragments of a shared history. And sometimes, I realize our family is as broken and dysfunctional as any other, our individual paths diverging like those portraits that once hung together. The loneliness lingers, a quiet ache of those childhood days in that forbidden room.

Perhaps that sense of isolation explains some of my past behaviors. At times, I might have come across to others as careless, even belligerent. I've often been called an asshole. My unsavory actions were driven by deep-seated fear and pain. It was like I was trapped in survival mode, constantly reacting to old wounds. I hurt people, and I regret that deeply. But a powerful part of living in peace; healing is learning to forgive myself, self-love.

Where do I go from here? I want to explore aspects of life that have so far eluded me, including a lasting and meaningful romantic relationship. *Crazy to try at my stage of life?* Maybe, but I still have some hope. My great-uncle Harry didn't marry until he was sixty-five, but Great-Uncle Leo remained single his entire life. The women who've mattered most entered my life like sunlight through a window, those real-life encounters that feel increasingly rare. Now, with online connections dominating the dating scene, I, like most people, have to navigate a digital landscape that feels a bit daunting.

Other than that, who knows? I bounce around ideas about relatively different possibilities. Maybe I'll eliminate all my belongings and adopt a nomadic lifestyle. I could also stay where I am and continue riding this wave. With a determined mindset, I continue to live freely, welcoming vulnerability and authenticity while focusing on personal growth and the quest for enlightenment with the help of the universe, my higher power. To readers who have journeyed with me, I am immensely grateful. You have discovered the ups and downs of my roller-coaster life, and hopefully, you can identify with some of the things I have written, or have had moments of revelation.

While I have certainly learned a lot from the past, I am determined not to live in it. I'm also working on not thinking too much, or worrying, about the future. As the great writer F. Scott Fitzgerald once said, "We must be willing to let go of the life we have planned, so as to have the life that is waiting for us."

So, I am living in the moment, for the moment—at least, at the moment. And right now, the moment is this: Ernie lounges by the pool, paws crossed, a light breeze, soaking up the sun, chestnut eyes watching me, loving me.... My thoughts drift off for a moment as I reflect on time and all it means—and all it doesn't. While I can't reclaim lost seasons, there are still more seasons onward. And in the time I have left, I'm determined to live boldly. There's so much ahead to embrace. I choose to focus on making every moment count. I choose to make myself be seen, I choose to make myself be heard.

And, like Ernie, I choose to love—my family, my friends, and, most of all, myself.

ACKNOWLEDGMENTS

Writing this book took great determination and encouragement. Typically, authors express gratitude to their romantic partners, family members, and perhaps business associates or friends who might have helped them remember anecdotes from their lives or their careers. However, my situation is far from traditional. Unmarried and childless, I relied solely on friends and former colleagues for support.

First, I am grateful to an old journalist friend, Thomas K. Arnold, who provided valuable support early on by reading one of the chapters and recognizing my storytelling abilities while highlighting my need for organizational skills as a writer. He kindly served as a developmental editor and experienced guide throughout writing this book.

My sincere appreciation also goes to Walt Morton, that rare triple (or quadruple?) threat (artist, marketer, author, and the culprit behind this book's disruptive title). He not only urged me to spill my unfiltered thoughts onto the page but also lent his genius to crafting a title that, well, speaks for itself.

I'd also like to acknowledge my therapist at the time I embarked on this project, Dr. Mari Murao. She enlightened me on the healing power of catharsis and encouraged me to put my thoughts to paper as a means of self-recovery.

I am also deeply appreciative of anyone who took the time to read excerpts or chapters prior to the final printing. Your feedback and insights were incredibly valuable to me. To each of these individuals, I offer my sincere thanks and appreciation.

I want to express my gratitude to all the individuals I have met throughout my life who have come across this memoir. If you find yourself mentioned in these pages, I am genuinely thankful for your presence in my sometimes-tumultuous journey. Please understand that there may be some inaccuracies in my recollection of our interactions, and I apologize for any such errors. To those I have encountered but have not explicitly mentioned, I also want to extend my profound appreciation. I recognize that there were times when I was far from enlightened and perhaps challenging to bear. Your patience and endurance during those periods are greatly acknowledged, and I appreciate your support.

APPENDIX 1:

CHAPTER TITLE SONG INSPIRATIONS

Listen to the Playlist on Spotify: "A*hole Chapters"

Parts One, Two, and Three: "Us and Them" by Pink Floyd

Chapter 1: "Jumpin' Jack Flash" by The Rolling Stones

Chapter 2: "Born to Run" by Bruce Springsteen

Chapter 3: "Stay Together for the Kids" by blink-182

Chapter 4: "San Francisco (Be Sure to Wear Flowers In Your Hair)" by Scott McKenzie

Chapter 5: Vacation, Had to Get Away —"Vacation" by The Go-Go's

Chapter 6: "Ring of Fire" by Johnny Cash

Chapter 7: "Every Picture Tells a Story" by Rod Stewart

Chapter 8: "Comfortably Numb" by Pink Floyd

Chapter 9: "Living in the U.S.A." by Steve Miller Band

Chapter 10: "Family Affair" by Sly and the Family Stone

Chapter 11: Teenage Wasteland—"Baba O'Riley" by The Who

Chapter 12: "Wake Me Up When September Ends" by Green Day

Chapter 13: "Everybody Hurts" by R.E.M.

Chapter 14" "Mad World" by Tears for Fears

Chapter 15: "Give a Little Bit" by Supertramp

Chapter 16: "London Calling" by The Clash

Chapter 17: I Am a Deejay...—"D.J." by David Bowie

Chapter 18: "Sex on Fire" by Kings of Leon

Chapter 19" "Fields of Gold" by Sting

Chapter 20: "Californication" by Red Hot Chili Peppers

OTHER SONGS AND ARTISTS MENTIONED (CHRONOLOGICALLY)

Listen to these songs on the "Other Songs and Artists mentioned in A*Hole" Spotify playlist created by the author.

The Supremes, Bob Dylan, and The Beatles: These artists were mentioned to illustrate the dynamic music scene in 1962, the year I was born.

Frank Sinatra, Perry Como, and Neil Diamond: My mother loved to listen to these three. She found their music to be a form of escape.

Bing Crosby: My father loved listening to Bing Crosby's music. He found it comforting and joyful.

Santana, The Chambers Brothers, The Temptations, Van Morrison, The Doors, Curtis Mayfield, and Isaac Hayes: My siblings and I grew up listening to a variety of rock 'n' roll music, including these artists.

Lawrence Welk: My grandfather enjoyed watching the champagne music variety show, "The Lawrence Welk Show."

Neil Young: A friend and I listened to Neil Young's album *Harvest* and especially loved the song "Heart of Gold."

Johnny Cash: For my tenth birthday, I asked my dad to take me to Folsom Prison, the one Johnny Cash sings about in his song "Folsom Prison Blues." I loved the haunting sound of the train whistle in that song.

Abner Jay: I saw Abner Jay perform live at a club in Atlanta during a family road trip and was impressed by his musical talent and unique style.

Hank Williams: I was introduced to the music of Hank Williams by Jim Elder, a worker at my dad's bottling plant, who loved the song "Hey, Good Lookin'."

Electric Light Orchestra (ELO): I won a "living thing" in a radio contest, which turned out to be a houseplant, in honor of a new ELO song.

Supertramp: "Give a Little Bit" by Supertramp was playing when I was sexually abused by Richard Irwin, my boss at the radio station.

Leif Garrett: I met Leif Garrett when he performed at the California State Fair. His popular song was "I Was Made for Dancin'."

Prince: I was reminded of Prince's song "Erotic City" when remembering a sexual encounter with my brother's girlfriend's friend.

Merle Haggard and Buck Owens: These country music artists were mentioned because they were from Bakersfield, where I moved to work at a radio station.

Cheap Trick: I saw Cheap Trick in concert in Fresno.

The Rolling Stones: I saw The Rolling Stones in concert in Los Angeles.

The Go-Go's: I saw and met The Go-Go's in concert in Los Angeles.

The Police: I enjoyed listening to The Police.

The Monkees: Debra told me that she was attracted to me because I reminded her of Davy Jones from The Monkees.

"Weird Al" Yankovic: I created a radio promotion based on "Weird Al" Yankovic's parody song "Eat It."

Michael Jackson: "Weird Al" Yankovic's song "Eat It" was a parody of Michael Jackson's "Beat It."

Ray Charles: I worked with Dick Clark on a TV commercial for 69 XTRA Gold that used Ray Charles's song "What'd I Say."

The Temptations: I worked with Dick Clark on a TV commercial for 69 XTRA Gold that used The Temptations' song "My Girl."

Genesis: I created a radio promotion where the grand prize was a trip to

Australia to see and meet Genesis.

The Kingsmen: I organized a "Louie, Louie" promotion at 91X, which culminated in a live performance by The Kingsmen.

Black Flag, The Beach Boys, The Kinks, Toots and the Maytals, and Motorhead: These artists have all covered the song, "Louie, Louie."

Oingo Boingo: Oingo Boingo headlined MeXfest, a music festival I organized in Tijuana. Some of their popular songs include "Weird Science" and "Dead Man's Party."

The Fixx: The Fixx performed at MeXfest. Some of their hits include "Red Skies," "One Thing Leads to Another," "Stand or Fall," and "Saved by Zero."

Chris Isaak: Chris Isaak performed at MeXfest. He was known for his song "Blue Hotel."

The Bangles: The Bangles performed at MeXfest. They were popular for songs like "Manic Monday" and "Walk Like an Egyptian."

Hoodoo Gurus: The Hoodoo Gurus performed at MeXfest. They were known for their song "What's My Scene."

Squeeze: Squeeze performed at MeXfest. Some of their hits include "Tempted," "Black Coffee in Bed," and "Cool for Cats."

The Who: MEGA paired up The Who with Schlitz Beer for a corporate sponsorship.

The Beach Boys: MEGA paired up The Beach Boys with Sunkist for a corporate sponsorship.

Thompson Twins: MEGA paired up Thompson Twins with Swatch for a corporate sponsorship.

Led Zeppelin: Stormin' Norman had designed and crafted jackets for Led Zeppelin.

Lisa Lisa and Cult Jam: I managed the Swatch tour sponsorship for Lisa Lisa and Cult Jam, whose *Spanish Fly* album had two number-one hits.

David Lee Roth: I was tasked with finding an automaker to sponsor David Lee Roth.

David Bowie: I went on a date to see David Bowie at Giants Stadium.

Red Hot Chili Peppers: I wanted the band to play at the Swatch Impact Tour, but it was deemed too expensive.

The Who, The Police, and INXS: Fahn & Silva Presents promoted concerts for these artists.

Jason Mraz: Bill Silva managed Jason Mraz.

Eddie Vedder: While I was meeting with Robert Noble at the Whaling Bar, future Pearl Jam frontman Eddie Vedder was working at La Valencia as a security guard.

Wall of Voodoo: I named the Tijuana club Iguanas, inspired by Wall of Voodoo's song "Mexican Radio."

Jane's Addiction: Jane's Addiction headlined the opening night of Iguanas.

Jack Mack and the Heart Attack: Jack Mack and the Heart Attack performed at a pre-opening press event for Iguanas.

Samantha Fox: Samantha Fox performed at Iguanas.

Nirvana, The Fixx, Rage Against the Machine, Sonic Youth, The Ramones, Bad Religion, Pearl Jam, Public Image Ltd., Nine Inch Nails, and GWAR: These artists all performed at Iguanas.

Guns N' Roses: Pirate Radio launched with Guns N' Roses' song "Welcome to the Jungle."

Joni Mitchell and Jim Morrison: These artists were mentioned in the context of Laurel Canyon, where I lived.

Warrant: The band Warrant played at the party celebrating the new Pirate Radio studios.

Jan and Dean: Jan and Dean's song "Dead Man's Curve" was about a stretch of Sunset Boulevard.

Red Hot Chili Peppers, Ministry, Ice Cube, Soundgarden, The Jesus and Mary Chain, Pearl Jam, Lush, Rage Against the Machine, Cypress Hill, House of Pain, Stone Temple Pilots, and Temple of the Dog: These artists were mentioned in the context of Lollapalooza, a music festival I was trying to get the syndicated radio broadcast rights for.

The Doobie Brothers: I was a fan of The Doobie Brothers growing up, and I attended their reunion concert at The Greek Theatre in Los Angeles.

Linda Ronstadt: Linda Ronstadt introduced The Doobie Brothers at a concert I attended in Sacramento in 1978.

The Human League: I met Martita, my girlfriend, while she was working as a waitress in a cocktail bar, which reminded me of The Human League song "Don't You Want Me."

U2: I worked with U2's management to secure the broadcast rights for their *Zooropa* tour.

Bob Marley and Roxy Music: These artists were mentioned in the context of Chris Blackwell, who signed U2 and other famous acts.

Paul McCartney: I met Paul McCartney at a meet-and-greet before his concert in Charlotte, North Carolina.

Don Henley: I worked with Don Henley on a benefit concert for The Walden Woods Project.

Elton John, Sting, Jimmy Buffett, Aerosmith, Melissa Etheridge: These artists performed at the Concert for Walden Woods benefit.

The Rolling Stones: I saw The Rolling Stones in concert in Oakland in 1978 and again in 1994 at RFK Stadium in Washington, DC.

Buddy Holly: The Rolling Stones opened their 1994 concert with "Not Fade Away," a Buddy Holly song.

Bernard Fowler: Bernard Fowler was a backup vocalist for The Rolling Stones for over thirty-five years.

Pink Floyd: I saw a Pink Floyd concert in Toronto.

The Rolling Stones: I saw The Rolling Stones in concert in Oakland in 1978 and again in 1994 at RFK Stadium in Washington, DC. Some of the songs they played were "You Got Me Rocking," "Tumbling Dice," "Shattered," "Satisfaction," "Beast of Burden," "Wild Horses," "Street Fighting Man," "Honky Tonk Woman," "Brown Sugar," and "Jumpin' Jack Flash."

Aerosmith, Tom Petty and the Heartbreakers, Bruce Springsteen, Paul McCartney, Rod Stewart, The Doobie Brothers, U2, and the Eagles: These artists were mentioned in the context of my work at Westwood One, where I secured deals with many superstars of rock.

"Weird Al" Yankovic: The facility manager at Westwood One was the drummer for "Weird Al" Yankovic.

Beck, Cypress Hill, Robert Cray, Taj Mahal, No Doubt, Bruce Hornsby, Lou Reed, Meat Loaf, Ozzy Osbourne, Lenny Kravitz, Metallica, The Cure, Steve Earle, The Smashing Pumpkins, The Cranberries, Bad Religion, Bob Weir, Indigo Girls, Pantera, Tears for Fears, and Sting: I secured agreements with these artists for *On Tour*.

Filter: Filter opened for The Smashing Pumpkins in Dublin.

Lone Justice: Maria McKee was formerly a member of Lone Justice.

Sammy Hagar: I once worked on a Westwood One syndicated special featuring Sammy Hagar.

The Cure: Misha, my girlfriend, eloped with Roger, the keyboard player in The Cure.

The Suicidal Tendencies, Madonna, Def Leppard, Metallica, and Hole: These artists were mentioned in the context of Q Prime, a management company.

The Rolling Stones: I co-produced a Rolling Stones concert film that aired as a PBS pledge drive special.

Smashing Pumpkins and The Cranberries: I produced concert films for The Smashing Pumpkins and The Cranberries.

Michael Jackson: Michael Jackson and Pepsi had a groundbreaking relationship that lasted nearly a decade.

blink-182, Fall Out Boy, and Bad Religion: These bands were mentioned in the context of the Vans Warped Tour.

Moby: I facilitated a tour sponsorship connecting Yahoo! with Moby.

Crosby, Stills, Nash & Young: David Crosby was a member of Crosby,

Stills, Nash & Young.

Journey: Steve Perry, who worked at an ad agency, had the same name as the singer in Journey.

blink-182: The first Honda Civic Tour featured blink-182.

Christina Aguilera: Eric Conn mentioned a hair dryer in relation to Christina Aguilera when she performed at the NCAA halftime show.

Linkin Park and Fall Out Boy: These artists were mentioned in the context of the Honda Civic Tour.

Bob Geldof and Midge Ure: These artists organized Live Aid, a benefit concert to raise funds for famine relief in Ethiopia.

Band Aid: Band Aid released the charity single "Do They Know It's Christmas?"

Madonna, U2, Destiny's Child, Jay-Z, and Pink Floyd: These artists performed at Live 8, a series of benefit concerts.

Duran Duran, Frank Zappa, and Missing Persons: Warren Cuccurullo, who owned Via Veneto, was a former member of Duran Duran and had also played with Frank Zappa and co-founded Missing Persons.

Soundgarden, Green Day, and Lady Gaga: These artists performed at Lollapalooza.

Jack White, The Roots, Beck, and Childish Gambino: These artists performed at the Sasquatch! festival.

Danger Mouse and Jack White: I sat adjunct to Danger Mouse having dinner with Jack White at the Sasquatch! festival.

My Chemical Romance, Maroon 5, and Kelly Clarkson: These artists were featured on the Honda Civic Tour.

Eagles: I attended the premiere of the documentary *History of the Eagles, Part One*.

Kings of Leon: I had tentatively secured Kings of Leon for the Honda Civic Tour, but the deal fell through.

One Direction, Demi Lovato, Nick Jonas, and One Republic: These artists were featured on the Honda Civic Tour.

Incubus, Maroon 5, One Direction, Demi Lovato, Fall Out Boy, Black Eyed Peas, Paramore, OneRepublic, Panic! at the Disco, and Charlie Puth: I worked with these artists on the Honda Civic Tour.

John Legend, Steve Miller Band, The B-52's, Kenny Loggins, Train, Zac Brown Band, Ziggy Marley, Pitbull, Jewel, Paul Simon, Santana, Brian Wilson, Eagles, The Foo Fighters: I interacted with these artists through various projects at Marketing Factory.

Bob Dylan: Levi, a former employee of Marketing Factory, was recommended by Bob Dylan's manager.

Weezer: Weezer performed at the final Honda dealer meeting that I produced.

Sly and the Family Stone, The Clash, Willie Nelson, U2, The Rolling Stones, and Die Antwoord: These are some of my favorite music artists.

Billy Idol: I spilled a beer on Billy Idol's leather pants.

Lou Reed: I got bitched out by Lou Reed.

Gene Simmons: I got bitched out by Gene Simmons.

Kenny Loggins: I drove Kenny Loggins around Napa.

Don Henley and Glenn Frey: I sat between Don Henley and Glenn Frey at the Sundance Film Festival premiere of the Eagles documentary.

Guns N' Roses: I drove an almost passed-out Steven Adler, the original Guns N' Roses drummer, in the back of my SUV.

Counting Crows: I played golf with Counting Crows guitarist Dave Bryson.

U2: I went to a theatrical performance with U2's The Edge.

Van Halen: I got booted from a strip club while hanging with Eddie Van Halen.

Casey Kasem: I worked with Casey Kasem, the host of *American Top 40*.

Prince: I met Prince at a post-Grammy Awards party.

Macy Gray: Macy Gray was DJing at a party hosted by Paris Hilton.

Rage Against the Machine: I saw Rage Against the Machine in concert and met Tom Morello.

Ringo Starr and His All Starr Band: I went to see Ringo Starr and His All Starr Band at the Moody Theater in Austin.

Simon Le Bon: Andrea, my yoga instructor, would go on to teach Simon Le Bon.

Ziggy Marley: Andrea, my yoga instructor, would go on to teach Ziggy Marley.

The Talking Heads: The Talking Heads' song "Once in a Lifetime" is one of my favorites.

Incubus: I developed an art startup with Brandon Boyd of the rock band Incubus.

Learn more at RobTonkin.com

APPENDIX 3: PHOTOGRAPHS

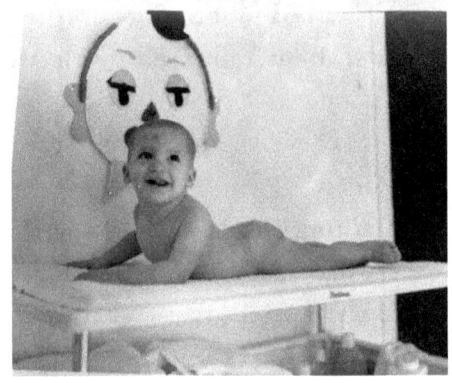

Dad pictured in 1944 during WWII. He served as a supply sergeant in Okinawa and was commissioned as a second lieutenant.

A tiny "Yours truly" during our brief time in Sacramento's Arden Park in my first year, just before William Land Park became our family's next chapter.

At my Bar Mitzvah ceremony at Temple B'Nai Israel in Sacramento, surrounded by Dad, Uncle Harry, and Rabbi Frazin, I held the sacred Torah, embracing my responsibilities as a Jewish adult within our Reform community.

Joe, my paternal grandpa. He emigrated from Odessa, Russia on the Black Sea and came to Portland in 1906. A real character.

Mom and Dad at their wedding, held at her family home, decorated with white flowers and lighted with tall white candles in January 1949.

Mom was wearing her fur coat, which made me cringe. She was picking me up, and we're pictured with The Christian's in Reno: Their dog, Beverly, me, mom, Gruff, and Maynard.

Same photo set of the cover of this book, just a sitting pose at the piano before I chickened out of being the ring bearer at a cousin's wedding.

Skylake Yosemite Camp: where memories were made and fashion rules were...optional? Last day by my tent cabin, rocking the two-shoe trend before it was cool.

More than just a plaque, this "Camper of the Week" award from Skylake Yosemite Camp, which became part of the lodge railing, represented one of the highest honors of my childhood.

Skylake vibes: Wrangler Award winner (and apparently future bicep enthusiast) showing off in my favorite horse ring.

My family, sans Mom, emotionally supporting my Dad. Brother Jim, Sister Sue, Millard, Ann and myself.

This beautiful honeymoon photo of Mom and Dad carries a bittersweet weight, knowing their love story would ultimately have a different ending.

Dad with his camera, Mom by his side, and me standing close with my eyes closed. A pre-divorce moment.

Not your typical childhood vacation: bullfighting a juvenile bull in Spain during a European adventure.

A teenaged radio deejay headshot. Ready to hit the airwaves.

The beloved maroon Dodge van, my first vehicle that helped launch my mobile deejay business, and was a source of pride and inspiration.

Mobile deejay in the early 80s. Me on the mic, soaking up the sounds and the incredibly cool vibe radiating from that Debbie Harry poster. It defined the era!

With the groundbreaking all-female band, The Go-Go's, back-stage at The Greek Theater in 1981. Also pictured are Dana Morris of A&M Records and two very happy contest winners.

Reliving 1987. Here I am with Lisa Lisa, sporting one of the Stormin' Norman jackets I created for her iconic tour.

On the air in 1983 as a radio deejay for The Mighty 690, my voice traveled from the wood-paneled isolation of a small studio near the Baja Malibu coast, south of Tijuana, Mexico, to countless listeners.

Pirate Radio billboard getting a change! Scott Shannon makes way for the station's new mascot, the party pig.

With the one and only Hunter S. Thompson in San Diego, moments before his appearance on January 30, 1988 – Super Bowl XXII weekend. This speaking event was one of the highlights of my work with Bill Silva Presents.

Me backstage at the one-off reunion performance of Spinal Tap at the Hollywood Palladium on October 6th, 1991, with the renowned guitarist Joe Satriani filling in on bass. This was a memorable event for those who were there! A visionary night for me.

Catching up with Kevin Lyman way back in the early 1990s. Little did we know the impact he'd have on the punk scene and beyond with the Vans Warped Tour. Now a respected professor at USC, he's still inspiring the next generation of musicians.

Meeting the legendary Sir Paul McCartney in Charlotte, North Carolina during the New World Tour in 1994 was a moment of pure excitement.

Me, Norm Pattiz, Paul McGuinness, Thom Ferro, Sheila Roche backstage at the final concert in Dublin, Ireland of the U2 Zooropa World Tour in 1993.

Rob, my step-dad, a hero in my life. I'll always be grateful for his love and support.

Carole and Rob, my Mom and step-dad, captured here during what looks like a glamorous evening in San Francisco or perhaps aboard a cruise. Their two-and-a-half-decade romance truly felt like a storybook.

Mom, sporting a fur coat in her single years. A fashion statement of the era, long before I was born.

Always was a learning experience to spend time with Tetsuo Iwamura, CEO of American Honda Motor, at the annual Honda dealer meeting.

My young nephew Jess meeting Paris Hilton at her Malibu beach home in the summer of 2007. Behind the camera? Yours truly.

With Casey Kasem, most famous for his trademark voice, from his countdown shows to Shaggy in Scooby Doo, to commercial voice overs, and as the voice of NBC television.

Milo, my best friend. He loved beach days, mountain hikes, swims, and endless games of fetch. An unconditional loving bond like ours is rare. I'll miss him forever.

Milo guarding the surfboards while Jay and I checked the waves in Venice, California.

Cooper the cat, and Ernest the dog, not just pets but my beloved housemates and best friends, who fill my home with joy and unconditional love.

Riding a wave backside near the Venice Fishing Pier. Early morning surf session in Venice Beach, California.

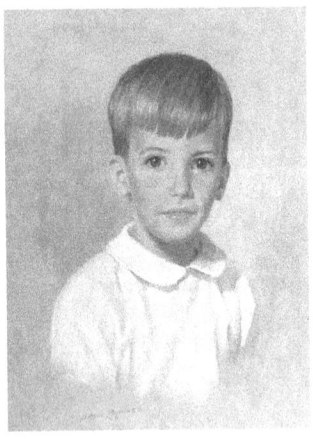

This pastel portrait, a familiar sight above the upright piano in our living room, stirs a wave of memories – a mix of feelings from the house where I grew up.

ABOUT THE AUTHOR

Rob Tonkin began his career in Sacramento radio at 14 and went on to produce the iconic Honda Civic Tour. *Asshole* tells the story of how childhood trauma fueled success—and nearly destroyed him—before leading to hard-earned redemption.

For more information or to contact the author, visit RobTonkin.com